D1383243

INDUSTRIAL RELATIONS RESEARCH
ASSOCIATION SERIES

Employment Dispute Resolution and Worker Rights in the Changing Workplace

EDITED BY

Adrienne E. Eaton and Jeffrey H. Keefe

First Edition

Library of Congress Catalog Card Number: 50-13564

ISBN 0-913447-77-3

INDUSTRIAL RELATIONS RESEARCH ASSOCIATION SERIES:
Proceedings of the Annual Meeting, Volumes 1 and 2
Annual Research Volume
Membership Directory (every fourth year)
IRRA Newsletter (published quarterly)
Perspectives on Work (published periodically)

Inquiries and other communications regarding membership, meetings, publications, and general affairs of the Association, as well as notice of address changes should be addressed to the IRRA national office.

INDUSTRIAL RELATIONS RESEARCH ASSOCIATION
University of Illinois–Champaign-Urbana
121 Labor and Industrial Relations Building
504 East Armory Avenue
Champaign, IL 61820 USA
Phone: 217/333-0072

CONTENTS

CHAPTER 1

Introduction and Overview

ADRIENNE E. EATON AND JEFFREY H. KEEFE
Rutgers University

The ongoing restructuring and reorganization of work, labor relations, and society affects virtually every aspect of workplace operations from the boardroom to the shopfloor. None of these effects is potentially more important to workers than the impact on workplace dispute resolution. This research volume is motivated by a sense of uneasiness about the state of one of the core institutions of American collective bargaining, the grievance and arbitration system. On the one hand, there are widespread criticisms among scholarly observers (see, for instance, virtually any collective bargaining textbook) that the system's much-vaunted benefits—speed, informality, flexibility, openness, low cost—have eroded over time. More disturbing perhaps is the suggestion that the system is too adversarial, increasingly sclerotic, and ineffective at resolving conflict. Critics portray the once problem-solving system as ensnared by procedures that have institutionalized hostility and failed to provide adequate solutions, remedies, or deterrence. Some propose reforms that aim at reducing costs and promoting more consensual labor relations. These include proposals for employee counseling, rather than progressive discipline for errant employees; direct employee involvement in rule making and peer discipline systems, rather than management's reserved right to make and enforce reasonable rules; interest-based mediation approaches, rather than grievance arbitration; and expedited arbitration, rather than a multistep grievance procedure capped by rights arbitration. Other reforms seek to expand civil rights by extending due process guarantees into the workplace either by importing judicial standards and procedures into the private dispute resolution systems or by creating a specialized court system to adjudicate the growing volume of litigation over workplace and employment rights.

On the other hand, even with the decline of union membership and union bargaining power, the grievance-arbitration system appears remarkably stable. In contrast to the dramatic changes in pay, benefits, job security, and work administration, union contract language governing grievance-arbitration procedures remains relatively settled. Just cause

1

rather than the at-will employment contract persists as one of the hall-mark distinctions between union and nonunion workplaces. Virtually every union grievance procedure culminates in arbitration. Widely accepted judicial and NLRB deferral to labor arbitration has enshrined the procedure with a degree of finality uncharacteristic of most other American dispute resolution procedures. Indeed, many of the proposals for dealing with the rising levels of litigation over employment disputes in the nonunion sector replicate significant aspects of the union system (see, for example, Dunlop Commission 1994).

Given the contradictory claims and evidence about the transformation of the industrial relations system, it is a good moment to focus on dispute resolution and to evaluate the research on the established system and the newly developing reforms. In particular, we are interested in identifying the degree of change and examining assertions about the transformation of industrial relations in the U.S. through a different window. Our sense is that compared with the extensive body of empirical work on the traditional system, there is a paucity of good empirical research on emerging changes in union and nonunion dispute resolution and that this ultimately hinders our ability to make an authoritative evaluation of the current landscape. Thus we hoped to begin to set a research agenda for this important area of our field.

We turn now to a more detailed look at some of the central concerns of the volume. Following that, we present brief descriptions of each chapter. We then turn to a more detailed treatment of issues that are touched upon by the chapters but that deserve further explication and raise particular questions of importance for future research and theory.

The Changing Workplace

Perhaps the most profound change for the industrial relations community as a whole has been the steady decline of unionization rates and the concomitant growth of the nonunion sector. And with the growth in that sector has come widespread experimentation with dispute resolution. We must confess that we originally agreed to include some chapters on the developments in the nonunion sector more out of a sense of obligation than of real interest. It has become clear, however, that dispute resolution in the nonunion sector is the Wild West to the union sector's settled and somewhat staid "back East." The Wild West is both more thrilling for the scholarly observer and most likely more frightening for those who "live" there. By these observations, however, we do not mean to repeat Kochan, Katz, and McKersie's (1986) claims that the nonunion sector is more innovative than the union and that it is time for the union sector to learn from it. Indeed, in the case of dispute resolution, the nonunion sector seems to be searching for the order and integrity of the union system without, of course, accepting the fundamental institutional arrangements which undergird it. Three chapters in the volume focus on this sector. Two—Katherine Stone and Arnold Zack—critique the existing legal framework surrounding mandatory arbitration in the nonunion sector. Stone does so from an historical perspective; Zack from the point of view of a practitioner who has worked assiduously within the dispute resolution community to alter practice. The third chapter, by Lisa Bingham and Denise Chachere, reviews the empirical literature on nonunion dispute resolution. All three are described in more detail below.

While all observers can agree on the importance of the growth of the nonunion sector, there is more heterogeneity of views as to what is going on in the union sector. We, for instance, share a certain level of skepticism regarding the dominant discourse within industrial relations about workplace and labor relations system "transformation." This discourse typically focuses on a particular type of transformation, now often termed "high-performance work systems." Though HR scholars have defined (or understood) the term somewhat differently, IR academics and practitioners have focused on increased direct worker and union involvement in firm and workplace decision making. These practices are "high performance" because they are believed to yield positive outcomes for all stakeholders: owners, managers, and workers. Since these changes are argued to be transforming our labor relations system, and an integral part of that system is its dispute resolution component, specifically the grievance system, it would seem likely that they would provide pressure on that system to change as well.

This concern directly motivated two chapters and is reflected in substantial ways in two others. Peter Feuille's chapter deals with grievance mediation, a direct and formal "reform" of the grievance system that often accompanies or is often championed by advocates of other types of labor relations reform. Michelle Kaminski's chapter looks at the status of the grievance procedure in workplaces with extensive worker and/or union participation in management decision making. Research on "high-performance workplaces" and their impact both on grievance handling and on our basic understanding of the union grievance procedures are among the themes discussed in David Lewin's comprehensive review of the empirical literature on the union grievance procedure and arbitration. Finally, Jill Kriesky's review of developments in the public sector, of necessity, touches repeatedly on these same themes.

Related to the developments above, primarily the decline in unionization, has been the work of some scholars to rethink basic models of union representation (Cobble 1991—occupational unionism; Heckscher 1996—associational unionism; Piore 1991—community unionism; Rogers 1994—a unionism with claims on the broad public interest and embedded in an alternate industrial relations system). While each of the models proposed has implications for workplace dispute resolution, the occupational model proposed by Cobble for service workers overlaps in substantial ways with the craft model still practiced in large part by building trades unions today. In that sense, it has the advantage of both being less utopian than the others as well as being observable in practice. Further, certain aspects of this system—union participation in skill formation, career development, and job seeking; increased peer management; and the inclusion in the bargaining unit of employees making managerial decisions—are creeping into other sectors. These practices have potentially profound implications for dispute resolution, implications with which craft unions have long familiarity. Thus we include a chapter by Heather Grob that describes in a detailed way the unique dispute resolution components of the unionized construction industry.

A final concern also relates to declining unionization but specifically concerns waning union power. This concern is rooted in the assumption that organized collective power in the form of political and social movements demanding rights is the foundation and guarantor of rights, be they in the workplace or in the society at large. In this view, particular rights in the workplace are not established and are not enforced and do not effectively exist without an organized and powerful interest group behind them.[1] Thus, with the decline of union power, we would expect to see an impact on rights and therefore workplace dispute resolution. For instance, unions might be under pressure to weaken the procedural rights concerning discipline typically embedded in the collective bargaining agreement. While the expansion of alternative dispute resolution (ADR) has wide appeal for many reasons, critics of ADR in the legal scholarly community typically argue that power is even more important in the kind of informal procedures that characterize ADR than in more formal settings (Abel 1982, Bryan 1992, Delgado et al. 1985). While none of the chapters addresses the question of power and its impact on rights and dispute resolution at length, these issues are either mentioned or are implicit in several. Both Stone and Zack in their chapters dealing with the nonunion sector point out the problems with dispute resolution procedures developed in the face of sharply unequal bargaining power between the parties. Kaminski also mentions power in her discussion of developments in workplaces with high levels of direct worker or union participation in managerial decisions.

Description of the Chapters

Below we present brief descriptions of each chapter. The ordering of the chapters takes us first through emerging practice in the nonunion sector. The chapters that focus on the union sector follow. This section begins with Lewin's overview of theory and research in the union sector. We then turn to a review of a particular reform, grievance mediation, found in small numbers throughout that sector. The remaining chapters deal with developments in particular subsectors.

Employment Arbitration under the Federal Arbitration Act—Katherine V. W. Stone

This opening chapter provides a historical foundation for the treatment of both labor and employment arbitration in federal law. As such, it makes clear that arbitration of labor-management disputes and the privilege accorded it by the Supreme Court in the famous Steelworkers "trilogy" cases were not unique in the world of arbitration. Both the wider practice and law of arbitration have a history rooted in the philosophy and practice of associationalism and self-regulating communities. Stone further argues that the extension of arbitration's privileged place into the nonunion sector appears to violate all the assumptions which earned it that place.

Agreements to Arbitrate and the Waiver of Rights under Employment Law—Arnold M. Zack

Zack covers some of the same ground as Stone but does so from a practitioner's viewpoint. He describes the pathbreaking *Gilmer* case in which the Supreme Court held that an employee could be required to arbitrate claims of a violation of statutory rights. The bulk of Zack's chapter then reviews the aftermath of *Gilmer* including the growth of *Gilmer*-sanctioned employer-crafted mandatory arbitration procedures and the backlash against such procedures, particularly in the dispute resolution community. He discusses the development of the "Due Process Protocol" intended or hoped to govern nonunion arbitration in the future and reviews the implications of these developments for the industrial relations practitioner and scholarly community.

Dispute Resolution in Employment: The Need for Research—Lisa B. Bingham and Denise R. Chachere

Bingham and Chachere provide a thorough review of the empirical research on nonunion (employment) dispute resolution procedures involving a third party. The areas of inquiry reviewed include factors affecting adoption of ADR by nonunion employers, design aspects of dispute resolution and outcomes for both organizations and individual participants related to characteristics of the procedures themselves and the settings in which they are adopted. In each case, some comparisons are made between the thin but emerging literature from the nonunion sector and the older and thicker literature on the union sector and particularly grievance arbitration. Given the relative youth of both practice and research, it is not surprising that the authors identify numerous areas for future investigation.

Theoretical and Empirical Research on the Grievance Procedure and Arbitration: A Critical Review—David Lewin

Lewin's chapter is intended to provide a conceptual and empirical foundation for our understanding of the union grievance procedure. It provides a broad grounding in both the theoretical and research literature and identifies gaps therein. In particular, Lewin concludes that much is known about factors affecting grievance initiation, processing, and settlement. He also suggests that insufficient attention has been paid to the largely reactive nature of the formal grievance procedure. Perhaps relatedly, he suggests there may be a paradox emerging from the literature on grievance procedures and organizational performance. This paradox can be summed up simply: while it appears to be a good thing for organizational performance to have a grievance procedure, the use of the procedure has a negative impact on the same kinds of outcomes. He identifies an additional troubling area of research—the consistent findings of negative outcomes for grievant system participants following the settlement of their cases.

Grievance Mediation—Peter Feuille

Most of the chapters in the volume concern developments in a single (though in the case of the nonunion chapters, very broad and large) sector. The chapter by Feuille differs in that it examines a single practice, grievance mediation, across many sectors. The review of available empirical research, of which there is not a tremendous volume, suggests that many of the benefits purported to result from grievance mediation—more rapid and less costly settlement, high rates of settlement, and generally high levels of satisfaction—are real. Despite this, grievance mediation has not experienced widespread diffusion and, Feuille argues, has not freed itself from an intimate procedural relationship with arbitration. Feuille's explanations for the failure of GM to diffuse may ultimately tell us more about the strength and resiliency of arbitration than it does about GM's weakness.

New Forms of Work Organization and Their Impact on the Grievance Procedure—Michelle Kaminski

Kaminski identifies and describes different forms of worker "voice" in the workplace. She suggests that traditional grievance systems are essentially a "reactive" form of voice. She then reviews the various forms of proactive voice that are increasingly found in U.S. workplaces today. Finally, she suggests that while, on the one hand, certain tensions may arise between the two general types of voice, workplace democracy actually requires both types of voice. Further, union leaders de-emphasize or block access to individual grievance procedures at the peril of member commitment and/or their own tenure as leaders.

Trends in Dispute Resolution in the Public Sector—Jill Kriesky

Kriesky's chapter describes emerging developments in dispute resolution in the public sector. Some of the trends closely resemble those in the private sector: widespread experimentation with new forms of dispute resolution in some jurisdictions and the growth of employee and union involvement schemes that directly impact the nature of workplace disputes and their resolution. Similarly, there are some commonalities in the sources of pressure for change, largely in the form of demands for improved services at reduced costs. What may be most unique to the public sector, however, are the inefficiencies related to a proliferation of dispute resolution fora, including union grievance procedures, litigation, and civil service procedures. Kriesky suggests that paring back the number of available fora will be difficult and should, in any case, be informed by research on the relative strengths and weaknesses of each. Relatedly, the public sector includes a tremendous range of unionized (and nonunion) occupations, including, it might be noted, managers; a "one-size-fits-all" approach, thus, may not be appropriate.

Dispute Resolution in the Building and Construction Trades—Heather Grob

Grob provides a rich description of the alternative dispute resolution system commonly practiced in the unionized construction industry. This system is embedded in the transient nature of work in that sector and in the craft model in which the union itself controls access to and maintains standards of work. The author reviews a range of dispute types and the diverse procedures for their settlement. She emphasizes the important role of internal union tribunals within this system and describes in general terms the formal procedures typical of those tribunals. Unfortunately, relatively little is known about how they work in practice. The author concludes that more research is needed, in particular to better understand diversity in actual practice within the sector.

Stability and Change in Workplace Dispute Resolution: Research Needs

In the following section we discuss some issues that are touched upon in the chapters but that we think are deserving of further exploration. In part, our goal is to evaluate the extent to which dispute resolution has actually changed in the past two decades at a time when other aspects of the industrial relations system have been described as being in transformation. Our analysis draws on the chapters but makes use of other data and our own observations. Implicit in our analysis is a framework for understanding the workplace and workplace disputes and their resolution that is highly political. Thus the section below reflects what we believe are important gaps, both conceptual and empirical, in current thinking and research about workplace dispute resolution. Ultimately, the discussion is intended, as the volume itself is, to shape the future research agenda in this area. We believe the issues raised have important empirical and theoretical implications for the study of dispute resolution and for the field more broadly.

Developments in Language and the Formal Rules of the Union System

In this volume, Feuille observes that the process of grievance arbitration is one of the most stable and enduring features of U.S. union-management relationships. David Fellner in his classic article, "A General Theory of the Collective Bargaining Agreement," provides an established framework to understand the importance of the grievance arbitration system. Fellner (1973) advances the theory that the collective agreement provides a system of law for the workplace. Under the collective agreement a system of law replaces arbitrary decisions, and reason replaces the use of force and coercion in disputes (Kuhn 1961). Specifically, if the collective agreement is to limit the arbitrary exercise of managerial power, the union must have recourse to an enforcement mechanism, which is capable of reversing management's action. According to this theory, the enforcement mechanism is the essence of the collective agreement (Fellner 1973). The primary obligation of the employer is to comply with the grievance and arbitration procedure adopted by the agreement. A worker, a work group, or the union can then file a complaint alleging that management has failed to act in a way that is consistent with the jointly agreed-upon rules. The grievance-arbitration procedure adjudicates the complaint and enforces the jointly agreed upon rules through its awards. The system of workplace common law evolves.

If the essence of the collective agreement is the adjudication and enforcement mechanism, as Fellner's theory suggests, then current practice suggests that collective bargaining is remarkably resilient and stable. According to Lewin and Peterson in their exhaustive review, there is little evidence to suggest employers or unions wish to abandon or substantially modify existing grievance and disciplinary procedures (Lewin and Peterson 1988: 209). The BNA data reported in Table 1 offer further confirmation that the parties have not sought to significantly modify grievance-arbitration procedures.

TABLE 1

BNA Sample of Collectively Bargained Provisions

	1975	1995		Percentage Change
Discipline & Discharge				
Just Cause or Cause Provision	79%	92%	°	16
Notice about Specific Grounds for Discharge	66	82	°	24
Notice to Union for Discharge	43	54	°	26
Notice to Union for Discipline	29	51	°	76
Time Limits on How Long Discipline Held in File	17	40	°	135
Progressive Discipline Specified	62	69	°	11
Grievances & Arbitration				
Grievance Procedure	98	100	°	2
Arbitration	96	99	°	3
Scope of Grievance Procedure Specified	68	97	°	43
One Step in Grievance Procedure	6	8		33
Two Steps in Grievance Procedure	18	21		17
Three Steps in Grievance Procedure	48	51		6
Four Steps in Grievance Procedure	25	19	°	-24
Five Steps in Grievance Procedure	3	1	°	-67
Formal First Step Procedures	93	98	°	5
Specific Requirements for Filing Appeals	80	87	°	9
Conciliation and Mediation Instead of Arbitration	2	0.5	°	-75
Conciliation and Mediation Prior to Arbitration	3	3		0
Expedited Arbitration	74	79		7
Pay for Union Representatives for Grievance Time	49	50		2
Job Security Provision for Union Reps	44	29	°	-34
Ad Hoc Selection Instead of Panel of Arbitrators	80	73	°	-9
Restrictions on Arbitrators' Awards	80	82		2
Specification of the Scope of Arbitration	65	98	°	51
Arbitration Expenses Shared Equally	81	91	°	12

°Significant Difference p < .01

Source: Bureau of National Affairs, *Basic Patterns of Union Contracts*, 1975, 1995.

Table 1 extends the analysis presented in Katz and Keefe (1992) by investigating the extent and nature of change of the union dispute resolution system. We compare the Bureau of National Affairs (BNA) 1975 and 1995 samples of 400 collective bargaining agreements reported in *Basic Patterns of Union Contracts* on discipline and discharge and grievance-arbitration procedures.

As Fellner's theory would predict, the BNA data reported in Table 1 reveal that grievance and arbitration process remains an essential and stable part of all collective bargaining agreements. All 400 contracts contain a formal grievance procedure, and 99.5% rely on arbitration as the final step in resolving disputes. The scope of issues that the grievance procedure (97%) and arbitration (98%) can address is increasingly formalized in the agreement.

In the area of employee discipline and discharge, for example, the parties have continued to codify the arbitral standard of "just cause" for discipline (note the 16% rise in the frequency of just cause provisions). Management also continues to expand its use of the contract to provide general notice to employees about dischargeable rule infractions (see the 24% rise in the use of specific grounds provisions). Unions more frequently have negotiated notification requirements for employee discipline (rise of 76%) and discharge (rise of 26%), which if handled properly by the union, can assist in resolving problems early and add a level of protection to both parties from duty of fair representation suits. The widely accepted standard of progressive discipline (Nolan 1998) is increasingly formalized in 69% of collective agreements. Unions have also increasingly negotiated time limit provisions where warning, reprimands, and suspensions are pulled from an employee's personnel file, which then no longer count as a step in progressive discipline.[2]

The BNA data indicate very few significant changes in grievance procedures. Although there has been a renewed interest in grievance mediation in recent years, we detect no major movement toward its adoption. Only 3% of agreements in 1995, as in 1975, include mediation as a step between the grievance procedure and arbitration. As a final step in the grievance procedure, mediation has declined from 2% of agreements to .5%. Feuille, in this volume, offers several explanations for the failure of mediation to diffuse more widely. Perhaps the most important explanation is the close linkage in practice of mediation to arbitration. In many cases, the mediator, who is often also a trained arbitrator, provides an opinion at the close of the mediation process as to the outcome if the case is arbitrated. Often it is that nonbinding opinion that encourages settlement. Feuille's analysis indicates that mediation will not displace arbitration as the preferred method of rights dispute settlement in union settings. (See also Bingham and Chachere in this volume on mediation in nonunion settings.)

Lewin and Peterson report positive outcomes from expedited grievance procedures, which speed up grievance settlement, heighten perceptions of the importance of grievance issues, and raise the sense of equity of grievance settlements (1988: 209). Although almost three-fourths of collective bargaining agreements provide for expedited arbitration, these provisions have not become significantly more widespread during the last twenty years.

Most contract language changes between 1975 and 1995 further institutionalized and codified grievance-arbitration procedures. First step grievances have become increasingly formalized (93% to 98% of agreements), and the specific requirements for the union to file appeals have been increasingly made explicit (80% to 87%). Arbitration expenses are increasingly shared on an equal basis, suggesting that calls for a loser-pays system to reduce frivolous arbitration cases have not been heeded in practice. Although ad hoc selection of arbitrators remains the dominant method of selection in 73% of contracts, arbitration panels are significantly more often relied upon by the parties than in 1975.

Apparently, the reduction of levels in the management hierarchy from recent corporate restructuring is reflected in the reduction in the number of grievance procedures with more than three steps. However, there may be some problems for the grievance procedure lurking behind the reduction in steps. One complaint is that by reducing the levels in the appeal procedure, management eliminates an independent or fresh review of the case. Some unions are concerned that their grievance procedure does not allow an appeal beyond the original decision maker. Not having a relatively disinterested representative of management involved in the grievance process undermines the procedure's legitimacy. Second, the labor relations function has increasingly lost its independent status, often being merged into human resources. Reportedly, labor relations in these reorganizations has also lost its authority to be the final decision maker in the grievance procedure prior to arbitration. Many labor relations staffs, as with human resources generally, offer only advice to operating managers. The final decision on whether to settle has been returned to operations management. Even when labor relations formally appears as the final step in the grievance hierarchy, it is increasingly unable to overrule operations management decisions. In 1975 most labor relations staffs had ultimate decision-making authority over union-management relations, particularly in grievance arbitration matters. As with most contemporary human resources activities, labor relations now serves in an advisory capacity to management. Researchers need to investigate whether there is a trend to shift grievance handling back to operations management, which prevents an independent review by management of the case, and whether this is eroding legitimacy for the grievance procedure.

In this volume, Lewin reports on some disturbing research results on post-grievance retaliation. These findings are inconsistent with Fellner's perspective that the collective agreement is a system of law, which constrains arbitrary behavior. Lewin concludes that management does appear to punish employees who file grievances and especially to punish the supervisors of those employees. This is consistent with a reprisal explanation for grievance filing and suggests that despite deepening institutionalization, there is more than adjudication and enforcement occurring in the grievance arbitration system.

The research and the BNA data, nevertheless, demonstrate the remarkable stability and further institutionalization of the grievance-arbitration process during the last twenty years. This finding reinforces the notion that the enforcement and adjudication process is the essence of the collective agreement. A conclusion of stability and institutionalization of the common law of the shop through the grievance arbitration system is substantially at odds with the transformation of industrial relations argument advanced during the last fifteen years.

However, a somewhat different view emerges if we move away from the formality of rules and rule making and onto the shopfloor. Here we begin to see that the shifts taking place are sometimes subtle though perhaps still profound. Their subtlety has made them difficult for researchers to see, especially those using survey research and quantitative methods.

The Grievance Procedure as a Form of Shopfloor Bargaining

If the rules of the workplace and work community are the focus of inquiry in industrial relations (Dunlop 1958: 281), then viewing the collective agreement as a system of law that is adjudicated and enforced by the grievance-arbitration process, captures only one aspect of the workplace rule-making procedure. Workplace rules not only include those contained in collective agreements, corporate policies, regulations, awards, or laws, but those established by custom, practice, or informal shopfloor negotiations. Often an established practice is at variance with the formal rules and regulations (Dunlop 1958: 110). Industrial conflict is frequently a surface symptom in the more fundamental process of rule making and administration (p. 281).

In practice then the grievance procedure is more than a judicial process of rule enforcement; it developed into a complicated system that extended bargaining and rule making into the workplace. Decades ago

Kuhn (1961) observed that grievances both are reactions to management policy and procedures and also actively seek to reshape workplace rules through shopfloor bargaining. Workers, work groups, and union representatives often use the grievance procedure proactively. In this view the grievance procedure is a forum for continuous shop bargaining.[3] It not only adjudicates disputes over rules or enforces the jointly agreed-upon rules, it creates and interprets a much wider range of workplace rules. Further, the formal organization collides with the system of self-governance, customs, established practices, conventions, norms, aspirations and values of work groups in the grievance procedure. According to this analysis, the concept of the grievance procedure is broader than the legal definition incorporated in the collective agreement. Grievances along with employee protests, lobbying, complaints, wildcats, slowdowns, overtime strikes, and other pressure tactics are all efforts to initiate change in the rules of the formal organization or to force management's retreat from the workplace. The workers' aim is the establishment, enforcement, and extension of work rules based on their values. Workers have always participated in defining many shop rules, regulations, and rights, a large number of which originate as customary practices within the shop (Kuhn 1961). Their grievances may seek more advantageous working conditions, freedom from supervision, or enforcement of their customary rules. In fact, it is often impossible to distinguish shopfloor bargaining from the "legitimate" grievances that charge the contract has been violated, since in it are the employees, not those above them in the hierarchy, who are originating and driving both activities (Sayles 1958).

Kuhn called this process of proactive shopfloor bargaining "fractional bargaining" since it goes on below the level of the formal agreement on behalf of a fraction of the workforce. Fractional bargaining, however, is an integral part of collective bargaining. Grievance procedures and the presence of shop stewards in the workplace favored its development. The grievance system, however, is not responsible for it but gave a new direction and added strength to the work group (Kuhn 1961). Kuhn observed that work groups display a wide range of democratic control and participation. Sayles (1958) classified work groups into four categories by their capacity and willingness to engage in shopfloor bargaining: strategic, erratic, conservative, and apathetic. Sayles (1958) believed that technology, workplace organization, and occupation shaped the capability of work groups to engage in shopfloor bargaining.

Shopfloor union representatives may simply enable this interest group behavior by finding a contractual pretext for advancing issues, or they can organize and lead or at least tacitly support group actions which they believe will secure group demands. Their legally protected status reassures the workers they will get a hearing. As long as political support is to be gained and political loss avoided by fractional bargaining, union representatives feel compelled to engage in it. On the other hand, managers and supervisors engage in these negotiations in part because they may be sympathetic to the workers' demands, because they need to get the work completed in a timely manner, or because they can gain some advantage in the system of workplace social exchange. Fractional bargaining allows supervisors an area of initiative and a measure of control that otherwise they might not have (Kuhn 1961). From this vantage point, the grievance procedure facilitates continuous shopfloor bargaining, which as Weber (1967) observes makes the basic unit in any bargaining structure the work group. Lewin believes, as we do, that one of the most fruitful areas of research is in the area of informal dispute resolution. As he points out, the vast majority of workplace conflicts are resolved informally, "backstage," out of public view.

Fairris (1997) argues that by the mid-1960s the workplace labor relations system based on shopfloor fractional bargaining was largely replaced by a bureaucratized system of shopfloor contractualism. This new system, according to Fairris, denied initiative to the shopfloor work groups, union representatives, supervisors, and managers, resulting in higher grievance rates, grievance backlogs, more strikes over work administration issues, reduced productivity, and an increase in workplace injuries. We are somewhat skeptical of this account. Shopfloor bargaining is not epochal but rather more likely cyclical, its range and scope varying with the business cycle. In periods of full employment and high demands to get the work completed, work groups gain power and management is willing to make shopfloor accommodations. In periods of high unemployment or slack work, management tightens up its procedures, rolling back some of the gains and variances that have been achieved by work groups. Its range and scope also likely vary, as Sayles' classification above suggests, according to certain characteristics of the workgroup itself.

Thus we argue that shopfloor bargaining continues today, at some times and some places more constrained than others.[4] After the mid-1970s wildcat strikes became more infrequent and this most visible public symbol of shopfloor bargaining receded. With this ebbing and with the increasing distance of industrial relations scholars from the workplace itself, shopfloor bargaining became largely invisible to the field. But an awareness of its ongoing importance suggests several important research questions for industrial relations scholars to consider which are otherwise ignored. How capable are employees organized in work groups or teams in acting collectively in the workplace (Hodson et al. 1993; Fantasia 1988), or is there a trend toward increasing individualization and social fragmentation (Castells 1995) which undermines workplace solidarity and impairs the ability of workers to act? Does the introduction of employee involvement plans and teams systems alter the ability of work groups and their shopfloor representatives to bargain? Do such programs undermine shopfloor informal understandings, often governed by a kind of "don't ask; don't tell" rule? Does the reduction in grievance rates often associated with participation plans reflect a shifting pattern or forum in employee interest group behavior and negotiations? If so, does that mean that the grievance procedure is no longer the focal point for fractional bargaining but largely the arena for adjudication and enforcement? Kaminski's essay in this volume summarizes the limited research on these topics and develops a set of hypotheses for future research. Her summary reveals that many of these questions are inadequately explored in the current research and therefore remain unanswered. We argue that one cannot understand either the formal dispute resolution system or these new forms of more direct participation without a consideration of informal work group behavior including bargaining.[5]

The political perspective on the workplace and work groups advanced by Sayles (1958) and Kuhn (1961) represents a road largely untraveled by recent industrial relations research. Nevertheless, it still holds great promise for uncovering the dynamics of workplace governance, rule making, and the articulation of the web of workplace rules. By decisively breaking with the human relations conception of workers and work groups as being governed solely by emotions and sentiments, capable only of reactive behavior to a rational management, they offer a political framework for understanding the dynamics of the workplace. In this conception, the work group is a politically engaged interest group. With varying degrees of capacity, each group advances its own interests through a variety of tactics such as threats, pressures, lobbying, bargaining, cartoons, promotion, grievances, and negotiations over the rules. Each also participates and attempts to shape the adjudication and enforcement of rules that are partly of their own making. This framework could be readily linked to a political or power view of organizations. Organizations are made up of conflicting interest groups, changing coalitions, with multiple goals, operating in a negotiated environment with variable power resources (e.g., Perrow 1986).

The Grievance Procedure and Organizing

While the phenomena of shopfloor bargaining is decades old, a change may be taking place in local union organization with potentially great ramifications for the grievance procedure. This change results directly from the current focus within the labor movement on external organizing. High percentages of union resources at both the local and national level are tied up in grievance handling, a major component along with the negotiation of new agreements of what is often called the "service" function of unions. As unions begin to shift their resources (particularly human resources) to organizing, the resources available for servicing and especially for grievance handling will shrink. Unions will have to seek new ways to service current members. There has been little public discussion of this shift by the labor movement and almost no scholarship that addresses it. Fletcher and Hurd's case studies (1998) of SEIU locals are the one exception. The locals studied include a half dozen which have deliberately diverted resources from servicing to organizing. Fletcher and Hurd present a rich description of the search for alternatives to full-time representatives focused on grievance handling. These include, somewhat ironically, the use of "temp" grievance specialists as well as pushing more responsibility onto stewards and pressuring all players on the union side of the system, including members, to reduce the number of formal grievances. The changes described in these cases have not been without consequences, particularly and not surprisingly some disgruntlement among members. Ultimately, changes of this type may have more profound implications for the grievance and arbitration system than do some of the issues discussed above and thus bear close attention from the academic community interested in dispute resolution.

Transformation and the Rise of Nonunion Employment Structures

Despite the essential stability within the union sector described above, there are "transformations" taking place in employment. The growth of nonunion employment is well-documented and its implications for dispute resolution are discussed in the volume. However, closely tied to the growth in this sector has been a shift in the occupational distribution of employment. The classical solution to a dispute in the nonunion workplace is reflected in the at-will employment contract: employees are free to quit and employers are free to terminate. As the employment system becomes more complex and regulated, some nonunion employers have adopted alternative dispute resolution systems in the nonunion workplace. Three chapters in this volume address different facets of nonunion employment dispute resolution. However, we suspect that most nonunion dispute resolution systems are aimed at the new middle class of educated employees. Indeed, we think it may be necessary to deconstruct or disaggregate the nonunion sector, especially regarding dispute resolution.

While the self-employed middle class had declined from 18% to 8% of the labor force in the post-World War II period, the growth of what has been variously characterized as the managerial class (Burnham 1941; Chandler 1977), the technocracy (Galbraith 1967), the knowledge class (Bell 1973; Berger 1979), the professional-managerial class (Ehrenreich and Ehrenreich 1978), the white collar (Mills 1951), the symbolic analysts (Reich 1992), or simply the "new class" (Gouldner 1979) has greatly transformed the landscape of American middle class employment. Managerial and supervisory employees have become the almost exclusive focus of contemporary human resources research and policies. While numerically still a minority, managerial and supervisory employees are the fastest growing group in the U.S. labor force. In the post-World War II period, managerial and supervisory employment quadrupled, growing at twice the rate of total employment by some estimates.

Applying the Supreme Court's class analysis contained in its interpretations of the Taft-Hartley amendments (such as *Bell Aerospace*, 416 US 267 [1974]) to Current Population Survey data suggests that as many as two out of every five full-time employees (some 40%) may be considered as either managerial or supervisory employees. Other data using the narrower definitions found in the National Employment Survey indicate that 31% of employees are in supervisory and managerial positions, which nonetheless represent an increase of one-third in their proportion during the last fifty years. Regardless of measurement method, this growing managerial class appears to share several characteristics. In contrast to nonmanagerial workers, managerial employees tend to have rising or stable earnings, higher levels of formal education, more firm-based formal training, more stable employment, lower levels of unemployment, and we believe a higher propensity to sue their employer.

Many of the major precedent-setting cases in the employment litigation are argued on behalf of managerial employees who file complaints against their employer alleging discrimination or wrongful discharge. We, however, do not know of a single study that systematically examines whether managerial employees are the primary moving force behind the employment litigation explosion. Bingham and Chachere review studies of the adoption of ADR by employers. The level of analysis of these studies is typically the organization; at best they may report what percentage of employees are covered by procedures. They do not tell us what occupational groups are covered.[6] If, as is widely assumed, managerial and professional employees are the principal complainants in employment litigation, it is important to know why this is so. Popular explanations have centered on their higher earnings and greater ability to retain counsel. Other explanations are possible and should be examined empirically:

Have these groups internalized norms of due process that are unmet or are they more familiar with the law?[7] If they are, in fact, the primary source of employment litigation, are the new compulsory predispute agreements aimed primarily at them? There are numerous fruitful research questions involving managerial employees, litigation, and the growth of compulsory arbitration. In contrast to the grievance-arbitration under collective bargaining, the methods for resolving disputes with managerial employees appear unstable, ad hoc, costly, and lacking in due process. The articles by Stone, Zack, and Bingham and Chachere provide considerable insight into this emerging area of nonunion employment dispute resolution system and its many shortcomings.

Under some public sector state labor laws, lower-level managerial and supervisory employees and supervisors are eligible for collective bargaining. As Kriesky's article points out, there is considerable experimentation among these employees with alternative forms of dispute resolution. Public-private research comparisons might generate some interesting research questions. For example, are union-represented public sector managerial and supervisory employees creating a more stable dispute resolution framework than their private sector counterparts? What elements of the public system might be transferable to the nonunion arbitration system?

During the last twenty-five years, nonunion working class employees have had a different experience than their managerial counterparts. In the 1970s, nonunion workers led working class employees down the real earnings escalator, as employers substituted cheaper nonunion labor for union workers. Average real weekly worker earnings declined by 14% to 19% during the last twenty-five years, depending on the data and definitions. Accompanying the decline in real earnings, there has been the de-unionization of working class employment. With the loss of union coverage, workers lose access to the grievance arbitration system and their "just cause" employment contract embedded in the collective agreement. The growing amount of employment turbulence in working class jobs reported in current research (see, for example, Davis, Haltiwanger, and Schuh 1996) suggests that exit may have largely replaced voice in working class employment. We know very little about the coverage of alternative dispute resolution procedures and their efficacy for this class of nonunion workers.

A final change deserves mention, the growth of contingent work. While the extent of the growth of contingent work has probably been overstated (Freeman and Rogers 1999: 9-11), the protection of contingent workers' rights and resolution of their work-related disputes remains highly problematic both in the U.S. legal framework as well as those of other industrial democracies. We should note that the next IRRA research volume will deal exclusively with the topic of contingent work. Nonetheless, as proposed by Cobble (1991), the craft model practiced by the building trades and described here by Grob may constitute one answer to the problem of contingent workers rights. Construction workers don't leap to mind as typical contingent workers and yet they fit the definition—their jobs are by nature temporary. Indeed, one reason we don't think of them as contingent is precisely because of the protections enjoyed by the workers in that sector who are union members.

Power and Rights in the Workplace

As discussed above, concerns and assumptions about the importance of power were motivating factors in assembling this volume. The primary assumption is that because collective power is needed to guarantee rights, declining union power will have the consequence of diminishing workplace rights for all workers. While most of the chapters don't deal directly with this issue, there is evidence both for and against this proposition.

On the one hand, the three chapters on the nonunion sector document a growth in alternative dispute resolution procedures in the nonunion sector. Stone and Zack argue persuasively that central to this growth has been the expansion of *Gilmer*-type binding arbitration procedures lacking due process and with limited appeal rights. To the extent these procedures are substituting for the right to sue, they can be viewed as diminishing rights. Within the union sector, Kaminski presents evidence that in some participative workplaces, individual rights and complaints have been traded off for collective participation in decisions.

Scholarly critiques of ADR argue that ADR, especially mediation, places less powerful parties at a disadvantage (see Bingham and Chachere in this volume as well as Abel 1982, Brunet 1987, Bryan 1992, Delgado et al. 1985). Some of the most powerful examples come from divorce mediation where women are under intense pressure to waive rights under the law in order to preserve family relationships and appear cooperative (Bryan 1992). Assuming that labor is the weaker party (either inherently or situationally) in the labor-management relationship, we might observe a similar compromising of rights in this context. On balance, Feuille's review of the experience of grievance mediation (GM) would suggest that this dynamic is not common in the union context, although the lower levels of satisfaction with the process among grievants themselves as compared to other participants might suggest otherwise. In the labor-management context, it appears that there may be more pressures on management to compromise on cases they could most likely win in other fora. Management is the more powerful party socially and economically but also legally. Thus mediation in the union-management context may encourage management to waive substantive rights.

In sum as discussed above, the union grievance procedure, at least on the surface, has been remarkably stable. If anything, the analysis of contract language presented above suggests, on balance, a strengthening of due process. Declining union power does not appear to have led, on average, to diminished rights at least as defined and enforced by the collective bargaining agreement. There are multiple possible explanations for this. The strongest probably lies in the power of institutionalization. The institutionalization of claims to rights confers a stability on those rights that may transcend fluctuations in the power of interest groups attached to those rights. In the workplace context, this was perhaps most evident during the Reagan era. Despite strong ideological opposition to government regulation, the Reagan administration was not able to completely gut the nation's labor and employment laws. They may not have been enforced well or completely and there may have been retrenchment in interpretation, but the laws were still enforced.[8] Further, it is clear throughout this volume that employers themselves see some benefits to the institutionalization of conflict and its resolution. Alternatively, union employers may have found it palatable to institutionalize procedural rights in an era of union concessions on the substantive terms and conditions of employment.

The situation in the nonunion sector is even more challenging theoretically. Stone argues that to receive legal deference, arbitration should be embedded in a self-regulating normative community in which members participate in creating norms and standards. This view is consistent or similar to the view that the existence of the collective underpins rights.[9] Nonunion arbitration almost by definition cannot meet Stone's standard. At the same time, it appears the dispute resolution community has in some sense "stood in" for the shared community through the creation and diffusion of the Due Process Protocol (DPP). The Zack and Bingham and Chachere chapters both suggest that the DPP may be having a real impact on nonunion practice. In this case, it appears that the power of the dispute resolution community to control access to legitimate ADR processes may ultimately guarantee a level of procedural fairness. Relatedly, Feuille argues that the DR professionals have the strongest incentives, as providers, for advocating the expansion of grievance mediation. Thus dispute resolution in the workplace may have spawned an interest group outside of the traditional duality of employer and employees (with their representatives) with a commitment to rights and fairness and the power to enforce that commitment.[10]

One other point is worth making in regard to the current state of rights in the workplace. Industrial relations and perhaps to a greater degree human resource management as academic fields are increasingly focused on firm performance outcomes (see Goddard and Delaney). While firm performance is clearly an outcome of great importance to workers and other actors in the economy, it is not clear it is the right benchmark for evaluating dispute resolution. If dispute resolution fundamentally concerns the enforcement of rights in the workplace, then efficiency cannot be the only criteria on which to evaluate it (see Brunet [1987] for a discussion of efficiency versus "quality of justice" in ADR generally). At the same time, as Kriesky's chapter on the public sector makes clear, efficiency cannot be ignored. While the goal of universal due process in the workplace is a worthy one, the costs cannot be exorbitant.

Conclusion: A Research Strategy

We believe that any analysis of the workplace and workplace dispute resolution requires a framework that addresses the politics of work and the problems of governance. There are important conceptual and empirical gaps in current theory and research about workplace dispute resolution. This volume, we hope, will help shape the future research agenda in this area. We believe the issues raised in each chapter have important implications for the study of dispute resolution and provide insight into major theoretical and empirical issues for the field more broadly. Each chapter identifies research questions generated by the research literature reviewed and evaluated. However, if the research agenda outline in this volume is to advance, it requires a multimethod and multidisciplinary approach.

A considerable amount of dispute resolution activity goes on behind the scenes. For example, much of the back-stage negotiations that lead to grievance resolutions are often publicly denied by the participants, particularly managers, who engage in these negotiations, or they may hold the view that their discussions are not negotiations. It is unlikely then that a survey of managers, for example, could identify or capture these negotiating behaviors, even when they may be the critical behaviors for dispute resolution. Instead, what is needed are qualitative research methods such as ethnography, case study, clinical research, ethnomethodology, or grounded theory methods to identify the range of practices of the participants and their respective understandings of what they are engaged in when they resolve disputes. Content analysis methods may also be particularly informative, when applied to the notes that are generated by the parties to the same dispute in understanding. Such analysis could help us understand, for example, how the "facts" evolve and get reinterpreted or understood to support settlements. Or as can be seen in Stone's chapter in this volume, historical methods can expose flaws in the developmental logic of an important practice. In her analysis, she demonstrates the illogic of the extension of an associational model of dispute resolution to individualized compulsory arbitration in the nonunion workplace. Or game theoretic or social psychological experiments or simulations could yield useful insights into the range of plausible strategic behaviors in dispute resolution.

Although qualitative research methods, experiments, and simulations can assist us in understanding the complexity and reflexivity of behaviors and interpretations in the process of employee dispute resolution, what they are unable to explain is whether these behaviors, practices, or understandings are widespread or idiosyncratic. To that end we need survey research, which is better informed by the categories of understanding developed in qualitative research. Once we can identify the range of critical behind-the-scenes behaviors and informal understandings, for example, we can develop questions that either can pinpoint practices or develop indicators of those practices. While survey research can begin to identify the extent of the practice, our current research sampling practice does not allow us to generalize to any known population. For example, in the analysis above, we relied on the BNA contract sample of 400 contracts; however, we do not know what relationship these 400 contracts have to the population of the 150,000 union contracts in the United States. In our own survey research, we often do not really know what the relationship is between the sample of respondents to the larger population; we do know they are somewhat unique, since they responded to our mail or telephone survey. Furthermore, the field often relies on surveys of managers, because they are more readily accessible. But in the case of dispute resolution, managers are more likely to have a distinctly different view of the process, its efficacy, and even its existence, than employees, employee representatives, or dispute resolution professionals. We clearly need more representative samples. Nevertheless, even if we had more representative samples, the measurement problems identified by Gordon and Miller (1984)—the lack of common standards across studies in measuring grievances, grievance rates, grievance volume, types of grievances and the identification of factors affecting grievance activity—still plague the research literature.

The rules of the workplace and the work community are the general focus of inquiry to be explained by theoretical analysis in industrial relations (Dunlop 1958: 281). Dispute resolution provides a unique portal into the process of rule making and enforcement. In our brief review we have identified several dispute resolution practices that are inconsistent with the dominant transformation perspective of industrial relations. We believe research into dispute resolution could propel industrial relations theory to grapple with the continuing problems of workplace governance in the union and nonunion settings and their interactions.

Endnotes

[1] Kaminsky in this volume makes this argument explicitly. This view is also implicit in many discussions of rights generally and of workplace regulation specifically. For an example of the latter, see Levitan, Carlson, and Shapiro (1986). For an example of the former, see Barber (1992). Barber argues that "without democracy, rights are empty words that depend for their realization on the goodwill of despots." Further, "The political context . . . gives rights meaning and force" (p. 27). Critical Legal Studies scholars also argue that rights have a social and political context but view this as a fundamental drawback. Tushnet (1984), for instance, argues that because rights have a social context they are fundamentally indeterminate and therefore not useful or can actually be harmful.

[2] Developments in federal labor law during this period have also strengthened employee rights to union representation in discipline and discharge cases. In 1975 the United States Supreme Court in *NLRB v. J. Weingarten, Inc.* ruled that employees have a right to assistance from union representatives during an investigatory interview. An investigatory interview occurs when management questions an employee to obtain information and when the employee has a reasonable belief that discipline may result from what he or she says. In an investigatory interview the employee has a protected right to request union representation, and if representation is not allowed, the employee has the protected right not to participate in the interview. Weingarten rights, as they are commonly referred to, allow the union to become involved in the disciplinary process before disciplinary action is taken. While not as stringent as Miranda rights, Weingarten rights provide union-represented employees some basic protections (even though they cannot exercise the equivalent of a Fifth Amendment right to not self-incriminate). Another legal development which has further strengthened the grievance process was the Supreme Court's ruling in *NLRB v. Acme Industrial Company* (1967), which requires an employer to furnish a union with information relevant to contract enforcement and process grievances. The right to information has afforded union representatives a weak form of discovery before proceeding with a grievance. Both of these legal developments further reinforce Fellner's notion that the collective agreement provides a system of law.

[3] This view of the grievance procedure is somewhat at odds with the perspectives about reactive and proactive voice advanced in this volume by both Lewin and Kaminski.

[4] We have seen vibrant shopfloor bargaining closely resembling that described by Kuhn in our own experiences and observations of various workplaces.

[5] Although the focus of our discussion above is on the union workplace, the fundamental observation regarding informal organization extends to the nonunion sector as well.

[6] In this they closely resemble virtually all of the work on the adoption or implementation of high-performance work systems. One exception is the author's unpublished study of the implementation of workplace innovations among private sector employers in New Jersey (Eaton and Keefe 1996). Interestingly, there were significant, systematic differences among occupational groups in the implementation of both on and off line forms of participation.

[7] Of Freeman and Rogers workforce survey sample (1999), 10% indicate that they failed to take a complaint against their employer to court because they couldn't find or afford a lawyer; 20% failed to do so because of fear of reprisal. Unfortunately, Freeman and Rogers do not present breakdowns on these questions by occupational groups.

[8] We don't mean to defend the Reagan administration's record—just to say that their intentions relative to labor and employment law were even worse than the actual outcomes.

[9] In Stone's argument the collective provides legitimacy. In ours, it provides power.

[10] This interest group still does not meet Stone's standard of worker participation in the construction of norms and standards. Arguably, from this point of view the DPP is a form of paternalism.

References

Abel, Richard L. 1982. "The Contradictions of Informal Justice." In Richard L. Abel, ed., *The Politics of Informal Justice, Volume 1: The American Experience*. New York: Academic Press.

Barber, Benjamin R. 1992. "Constitutional Rights—Democratic Instrument or Democratic Obstacle?" In Robert A. Licht, ed., *The Framers and Fundamental Rights*. Washington, DC: AEI Press.

Bell, Daniel. 1973. *The Coming of Post-Industrial Society*. New York: Basic Books.

Berger, Peter. 1979. "The Worldview of the New Class: Secularity and Its Discontents." In Barry Bruce-Briggs, ed., *The New Class?* New Brunswick, NJ: Transaction Books.

Brody, David. 1980. *Workers in Industrial America*. New York: Oxford University Press.

Brunet, Edward. 1987. "Questioning the Quality of Alternative Dispute Resolution." *Tulane Law Review*, Vol. 62, no. 1 (November), pp. 1-56.

Bryan, Penelope E. 1992. "Killing Us Softly: Divorce Mediation and the Politics of Power." *Buffalo Law Review*, Vol. 40, pp. 441-523.

Bureau of National Affairs. 1975, 1995. *Basic Patterns of Union Contracts*. Washington, DC: BNA.

Burnham, James. 1941. *The Managerial Revolution*. New York: John Day.

Castells, xx. 1995.

Chandler, Alfred. 1977. *The Visible Hand: The Managerial Revolution in American Business*. Cambridge, MA: Harvard University Press.

Cobble, Dorothy Sue. 1991. "Organizing the Postindustrial Work Force: Lessons from the History of Waitress Unionism." *Industrial and Labor Relations Review*, Vol. 44 (April), pp. 419-36.

Current Population Survey: www.bls.gov/cpshome.htm

Davis, Steven J., John C. Haltiwanger, and Scott Schuh. 1996. *Job Creation and Destruction*. Cambridge, MA: MIT Press.

Delgado, Richard, Chris Dunn, Pamela Brown, Helena Lee, and David Hubbert. 1985. "Fairness and Formality: Minimizing The Risk of Prejudice in Alternative Dispute Resolution." *Wisconsin Law Review*, Vol. 6, pp. 1359-1404.

Dunlop, John. 1993. Industrial Relations Systems. Rev. ed. Cambridge, MA: Harvard Business School Press.

Dunlop Commission. 1994. *Fact Finding Report: Commission on the Future of Worker-Management Relations*. Washington, DC: U.S. Department of Labor and U.S. Department of Commerce.

Eaton, Adrienne E., and Jeffrey Keefe. 1996. "The Incidence of Participative Programs in the Private Sector in New Jersey." Unpublished paper presented at Industrial Relations Research Association 48th Annual Meeting, San Francisco, January.

Ehrenreich, Barbara, and John Ehrenreich. 1978. "The Professional-Managerial Class." In Pat Walker, ed., *Between Labor and Capital: The Professional-Managerial Class*. Boston, MA: South End Press.

Fairris, David. 1997. *Shopfloor Matters: Labor-Management Relations in Twentieth-Century American Management*. New York: Routledge.

Fantasia, Rick. 1988. *Cultures of Solidarity*. Berkeley, CA: University of California Press.

Fellner, David. 1973. "A General Theory of the Collective Bargaining Agreement." *California Law Review*, Vol. 61, p. 663.

Fletcher, Bill, Jr., and Richard W. Hurd. 1998. "Beyond the Organizing Model: The Transformation Process in Local Unions." In K. Bronfenbrenner, S. Friedman, R. W. Hurd, R. A. Oswald, R. L. Seeber, eds., *Organizing to Win: New Research on Union Strategies*. Ithaca, NY: Cornell University Press.

Freeman, Richard B., and Joel Rogers. 1999. *What Workers Want*. Ithaca, NY: Cornell University Press.

Galbraith, John Kenneth. 1967. *The New Industrial State*. Boston, MA: Houghton Mifflin.

Gordon, Michael, and Sandra Miller. 1984. "Grievances: A Review of the Research and Practice." *Personnel Psychology*, Vol. 37, no. 2 (Spring), pp. 117-46.

Gouldner, Alvin. 1979. *The Future of Intellectuals and the Rise of the New Class*. (NY: Seabury Press).

Heckscher, Charles. 1996. *The New Unionism*. Ithaca, NY: Cornell University Press.

Hodson, Randy, Sandy Welsh, Sabine Rieble, Cheryl Sorenson Jamison, and Sean Creighton. 1993. "Is Worker Solidarity Undermined by Autonomy and Participation? Patterns from the Ethnographic Literature." *American Sociological Review*, Vol. 58 (June), pp. 398-416.

Katz, Harry, and Jeffrey Keefe. 1992. "Collective Bargaining and Industrial Relations Outcomes: The Causes and Consequences of Diversity." In David Lewin, Olivia Mitchell, and Peter Sherer, eds., *Research Frontiers in Industrial Relations and Human Resources*. Madison, WI: Industrial Relations Research Association.

Kochan, Thomas A., Harry C. Katz, and Robert B. McKersie. 1986. *The Transformation of American Industrial Relations*. New York: Basic Books.

Kuhn, James W. 1961. *Bargaining in Grievance Settlement: The Power of Industrial Work Groups*. New York: Columbia University Press.

Levitan, Sar A., Peter E. Carlson, and Isaac Shapiro. 1986. *Protecting American Workers*. Washington, DC: BNA.

Lewin, David, and Richard Peterson. 1988. *The Modern Grievance Procedure in the United States*. New York: Quorum Books.

Mills, C. Wright. 1951. *The White Collar*. New York: Oxford University Press.

National Employment Survey: www.bls.gov/ceshome.htm

Nolan, Dennis R. 1998. "The Standards." In Theodore St. Antoine, ed., *The Common Law of the Workplace*. Washington, DC: BNA.

Perrow, Charles. 1986. *Complex Organizations: A Critical Essay*. 3rd ed. New York: Random House.

Piore, Michael. 1991. "The Future of Unions." In G. Strauss, D. G. Gallagher, and J. Fiorito, eds., *The State of the Unions*. Madison, WI: Industrial Relations Research Association, pp. 387-410.

Reich, Robert. 1992. *The Work of Nations*. New York: Vintage.

Rogers, Joel. 1994. "Reforming U.S. Labor Relations." In S. Friedman, R. W. Hurd, R. A. Oswald, R. L. Seeber, eds., *Restoring the Promise of American Labor Law*, Ithaca, NY: Cornell ILR Press.

Sayles, Leonard. 1958. *Behavior of Industrial Work Groups*. New York: John Wiley.

Slichter, Sumner, James Healy, and E. Robert Livernash. 1960. *The Impact of Collective Bargaining on Management*. Washington, DC: The Brookings Institution.

Tushnet, Mark. 1984. "An Essay on Rights." *Texas Law Review*, Vol. 62, no. 8 (May), pp. 1363-1403.

Weber, Arnold. 1967. "Stability and Change in the Structure of Collective Bargaining." *Challenges to Collective Bargaining*. Englewood Cliffs, NJ: Prentice-Hall.

Chapter 2

Employment Arbitration under the Federal Arbitration Act

Katherine V. W. Stone
Cornell University

Nonunion arbitration is quickly becoming the primary source of workplace justice in America. At present, almost as many employees are covered by nonunion arbitration systems as are represented by unions.[1] More significantly, the use of nonunion arbitration is growing while collective bargaining and union representation are declining. If current trends continue, soon more workers will have their workplace rights determined by employer-created arbitration systems than by collective bargaining agreements.

During the course of the 1990s, nonunion arbitration procedures have become a widespread phenomenon. Prior to 1991, the use of arbitration as the final stage in nonunion dispute resolution procedures was exceedingly rare.[2] In contrast, by 1995 the General Accounting Office found that of 1448 respondent establishments surveyed, 9.9% used nonunion arbitration to resolve discrimination complaints and a further 8.4% of establishments were considering instituting arbitration procedures for discrimination complaints.[3] Although this survey may somewhat overstate the incidence of arbitration procedures,[4] two other surveys during the same period using smaller samples also found that approximately 8% to 10% of establishments had nonunion arbitration procedures.[5] The vast majority of nonunion arbitration procedures are very recent in origin, introduced in the 1990s.[6] Although nonunion arbitration continues to be a practice in a minority of workplaces, its recent growth is remarkable.

Some commentators interpret the spread of nonunion arbitration an aspect of a more general trend in human resource management policy to use a variety of dispute resolution techniques such as open-door policies, management appeal boards, peer review panels, and ombudsmen to improve morale and enhance productivity.[7] However the evidence suggests that nonunion arbitration has a different genesis than the other forms of alternative dispute resolution in use in the nonunion sector. While these other forms of workplace ADR were developed to further employers' conflict resolution and employee morale building goals, there is convincing data to show that employers instituted nonunion arbitration for other reasons. Specifically, the data suggest that employers instituted arbitration programs in the 1990s in order to limit liability for employment discrimination lawsuits, unjust dismissal lawsuits, and other suits involving individual employment rights. Many labor relations scholars have criticized the use of mandatory nonunion arbitration on precisely these grounds, claiming that it operates to deprive employees of their rights under employment discrimination laws and other statutes designed to provide employee protections.[8]

This chapter examines the Supreme Court's treatment of employment arbitration. It presents a critique of the Supreme Court's interpretation of the Federal Arbitration Act in the case of *Gilmer v. Johnson/ Interstate Lane*, in which the Court upheld an employer's use of mandatory arbitration to determine employees' statutory rights. The first section describes changes in the employment law landscape of the 1980s and early 1990s that lead employers to adopt mandatory arbitration systems. The second section traces the history of the Federal Arbitration Act—the statute that was at issue in the *Gilmer* case. The third section traces the application of the Federal Arbitration Act and the use of arbitration in the securities and collective bargaining contexts. It demonstrates that the statute was intended to permit arbitration in relationships between members of a shared normative community, not to compel arbitration between insiders to a community and others who remain outside. The last section suggests an alternative interpretation of the Federal Arbitration Act, one more consistent with the statute's history, that would permit courts to reevaluate its current hands-off posture toward arbitration in the nonunion workplace.

The Employment Law Landscape in the Early 1990s

Two changes in the legal landscape of the late 1980s and early 1990s account for the rise of nonunion arbitration: employers' exploding employment discrimination liability and the courts' newfound willingness to compel arbitration of statutory claims as a result of the *Gilmer* decision. Together these two factors provide a powerful argument that nonunion arbitration is an employer strategy for liability avoidance, not a method of improving morale, introducing justice into the workplace, or avoiding unions.

In the late 1980s, corporate mergers, buyouts, and other transformations generated large-scale corporate restructuring which often resulted in massive layoffs at all levels of the employment spectrum.[9] Corporate executives, middle-level managers, skilled workers, and unskilled workers were all affected. These layoffs, in turn, generated lawsuits. Displaced workers turned to employment discrimination theories and (in those states which permitted it) unjust dismissal theories to provide a basis for a legal claim. One sees this trend reflected in the data on job-related civil rights cases filed in the federal courts in the 1980s and 1990s. As shown in Figure 1, the number of employment discrimination cases brought in federal courts was essentially flat from 1986 through 1990 and then took off.[10] In 1991 there were 35% more cases than in 1990, and the trend was upward from there. By 1996 there were more than double the number filed in 1990.

Not only were there more lawsuits filed, but in the period 1989-90, plaintiffs began to win large judgments. As seen in Figure 2A and Figure 2B, the amount awarded to plaintiffs in employment litigation in the federal courts hit an all-time high in 1990. That year, plaintiffs who prevailed won an astounding *average* recovery of $1,989,300. Of the 254 cases that went to juries, plaintiffs prevailed 38% of the time and recovered an *average* judgment of $2,652,270.[11]

We see the same pattern, though somewhat less dramatically, in the median recoveries. As shown in Figure 2B, median awards also peaked in 1990, although they were much lower than the averages. Thus 1991 was a big year for plaintiffs in employment litigation.

To add to employers' mounting exposure, Title VII was amended in 1991 to provide for punitive damages in employment discrimination cases. The amended statute also permitted prevailing parties to collect attorney fees, which are often big-ticket items in employment discrimination litigation. Thus by 1991, discrimination litigation had become a high-stakes game for employers.

A similar story could be told about unjust dismissal litigation in the state courts. In the 1980s, state court decisions on dismissal claims began to yield high verdicts, often in the six figures and sometimes in the seven.[12] A study by the Rand Institute for Civil Justice found that the average award for prevailing plaintiffs in California unjust dismissal litigation between 1980 and 1986 was $640,000.[13] By the early 1990s there were highly publicized verdicts with even bigger numbers.

In the face of such unpredictable mega-judgments in employment-related lawsuits in the 1990s, employers sought other means to resolve

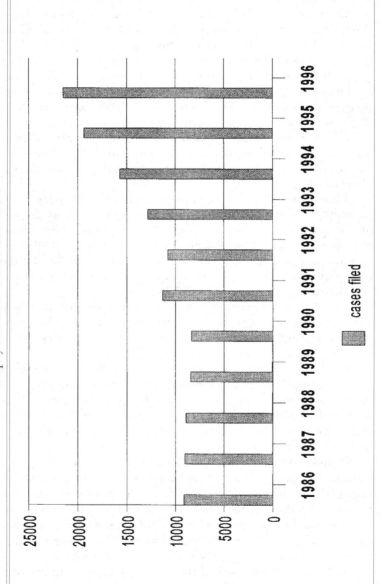

FIGURE 1
Employment Cases Filed in Federal Courts

FIGURE 2A

Mean Awards in Employment Discrimination Cases

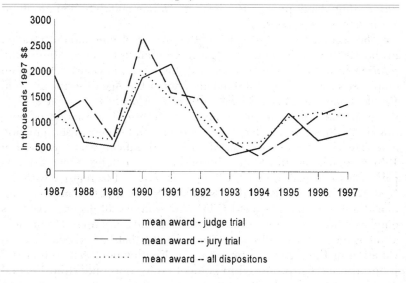

FIGURE 2B

Median Awards in Employment Discrimination Cases

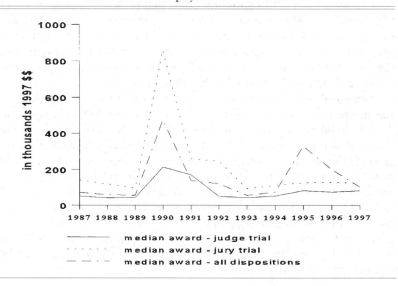

employment disputes. They tried to devise nonjudicial methods of both avoiding and resolving work-related complaints and of limiting their exposure should a dispute go to a hearing. Nonunion arbitration promised to meet these objectives.

The second factor that spurred the growth of nonunion arbitration in the 1990s was the Supreme Court decision in *Gilmer v. Interstate/ Johnson Lane Co.*[14] In the *Gilmer* case, the Supreme Court held that an employee's claim of age discrimination under the Age Discrimination in Employment Act (ADEA)[15] was subject to a promise to arbitrate. By doing so, the Court gave its approval to the use of arbitration by nonunion employers to resolve disputes over employment discrimination complaints. The case was brought by Robert Gilmer, who was hired in 1981 by defendant Interstate/Johnson Lane, a stock brokerage firm. As part of his job qualifications, Gilmer was required to register with the New York Stock Exchange. The standard NYSE registration form contained a clause that obligated Gilmer to arbitrate all disputes with his employer. Six years later, at the age of 62, Gilmer was fired. He brought a suit against Interstate/Johnson Lane alleging that he had been fired in violation of the Age Discrimination in Employment Act. Interstate/ Johnson Lane Corp. moved to compel arbitration under the Federal Arbitration Act[16] on the basis of the arbitration provision in the 1981 registration form.

Gilmer argued to the Supreme Court that he should not be required to arbitrate his ADEA claim because the arbitration clause he signed did not apply to statutory claims. The Court disagreed, stating that its previous decisions in a series of nonlabor cases in the 1980s established that statutory claims may be the subject of an arbitration agreement, enforceable under the Federal Arbitration Act."[17]

Gilmer also argued that requiring him to arbitrate an ADEA claim was inconsistent with the statutory framework of the ADEA because the ADEA embodied important social policies which should not be determined in a private tribunal. The Court rejected this argument on the grounds that it had recently held that claims arising under the Antitrust Act, the Securities Act, and the Racketeer Influenced and Corrupt Organizations Act (RICO)—statutes which also embody important social policies—are amenable to arbitration under the FAA.[18] The Court quoted from its *Mitsubishi* opinion that "so long as the prospective litigant effectively may vindicate [his or her] statutory cause of action in the arbitral forum, the statute will continue to serve both its remedial and deterrent function."[19]

The *Gilmer* Court also rejected the plaintiff's arguments that the stock exchange arbitration procedures were inherently inadequate to protect statutory rights. Rather, the Court discussed with approval the particular arbitration rules of the New York Stock Exchange (NYSE) that required arbitration panel members to disclose their employment histories and permitted parties to make further inquiries into backgrounds of potential arbitrators to discern bias. The NYSE Rules also give parties one preemptory challenge and unlimited challenges for cause. The Court further noted that the NYSE Rules permit limited discovery, including document production and depositions. And the rules require that arbitral awards be in writing, specifying the names of the parties, a summary of the issues, and a description of the award. These features of the NYSE arbitration led the Court to conclude that the arbitration procedures were adequate to safeguard Gilmer's substantive rights.[20]

Justice Stevens, in dissent, raised what was the most troublesome aspect of the *Gilmer* case from a legal point of view. Section 1 of the FAA states that the FAA does not apply to "contracts of employment of seamen, railroad employees, or *any other class of workers engaged in foreign or interstate commerce.*"[21] Stevens argued that the brokerage agreement Gilmer signed was part of a contract of employment, so that the FAA's exclusion for contracts of employment should apply. Justice Stevens explained that Congress had excluded employment contracts from the FAA out of its concern that arbitration promises contained in employment contracts were not always voluntary but might result from the coercive exercise of an employer's superior bargaining power. These concerns, he argued, should be implemented by giving an expansive interpretation to the "contract of employment" exclusion and by refusing to apply the FAA to compel arbitration of ADEA or other employment-related statutory claims.[22]

The majority opinion chose to duck Justice Stevens' argument. It said that the arbitration clause at issue originated in a contract between the plaintiff and the stock exchange and not in a contract between the plaintiff and his immediate employer, so that it was not a "contract of employment" for purposes of the FAA exclusion. In addition, the Court said that because the question of the application of the Section 1 exclusion had not been raised by the parties below, it would leave that issue for another day.[23]

Since 1991 almost all the Courts of Appeal have been expansive in their treatment of nonunion employment arbitration and narrow in their interpretation of the FAA's Section 1 exclusion. Thus even though *Gilmer* did not involve a direct employment relationship, courts have applied the holding to cases that did. They have done so by reading the FAA's exclusion for "contracts of employment" to apply only to workers who are engaged in the interstate movement of goods.[24] Furthermore, courts have not limited *Gilmer* to cases involving the Age Discrimination in Employment Act, but have expanded it to require arbitration of claims alleging violations of Title VII, ADA, ERISA, the Polygraph Protection Act and so forth.[25] In addition, most courts have ignored the language in *Gilmer* about the importance of minimal due process protections and have compelled arbitration when those minimal safeguards were not present.[26]

Thus the growth of nonunion arbitration in the 1990s can be explained by two factors: employers' increased risk of escalating and unpredictable damage judgments in discrimination and unjust dismissal lawsuits in the late 1980s, and the Supreme Court's 1991 decision in *Gilmer*. Once the Supreme Court gave its approval to the use of arbitration for discrimination claims, employers saw the possibility of using final, binding, predispute arbitration to address their problems of unbounded liability.

How does arbitration protect employers from liability? First, at arbitration employees are less likely to win their cases. Many employment arbitration systems fall far short of the due process protections that one would expect from a court. For example, employer-crafted arbitration systems often contain features such as raising the employees' burdens of proof, restricting her ability to call witnesses, and eliminating the possibility of discovery.[27] Second, most arbitration systems limit the amounts that employees can recover. Many specify that arbitrators cannot award punitive or compensatory damages, or even interest on back-pay awards. Thus by requiring employees to accept an arbitration system as a precondition for employment, employers reduce their exposure by requiring employees to waive important employment rights. Also, courts have ordered arbitration in cases in which employees not only failed to agree to arbitrate future employment disputes but were not personally notified that the employer had such a policy.[28] For these reasons, the use of compulsory predispute arbitration by employers has become the "yellow dog contract of the 1990s."[29]

The History of Arbitration under the Federal Arbitration Act

The *Gilmer* decision and the increased use of arbitration in employment have roots that long predate the 1990s. To understand the emerging and contested role of arbitration in employment and to develop an effective critique, it is necessary to examine the history of the FAA.

The *Gilmer* decision was one of several Supreme Court opinions reinterpreting the FAA in the 1980s. In the 1980s the Court transformed the Federal Arbitration Act from a little-used procedural defense that applied only to a small number of cases brought in federal courts to a central aspect of most consumer and employment litigation. First, in 1984 the Court held that the FAA has a broad preemptive scope, so that it applies in state court as well as federal court and overrides any state law that conflicts with its purposes.[30] Thus the FAA displaces any state law that seeks to restrict the use of arbitration and/or protect consumers against unfair or abusive arbitration clauses.[31] Second, the Court adopted a presumption of arbitrability, holding that when it is doubtful whether an arbitration clause applies to a particular dispute, doubts should be resolved in favor of requiring arbitration.[32] And finally, the Court determined that a wide range of statutory disputes are amenable to arbitration, including disputes concerning violations of the antitrust laws, the RICO Act, and the securities laws.[33] Once the Court reached these conclusions in nonemployment cases, its decision in *Gilmer* was almost a foregone conclusion.[34]

The reinterpretations of the FAA not only disenfranchise workers, they also threaten to privatize the entire civil justice system.[35] These doctrinal shifts were the result of importing into the FAA the regulatory philosophy of Herbert Hoover from the 1920s. Below I argue that the decision in *Gilmer* has distorted the FAA's intent and betrayed its rationale. An examination of the history of the FAA reveals how far these decisions depart from its initial rationale and from the legitimate uses of private arbitration.

Arbitration and the Rise of Trade Associations

Private dispute resolution dates back hundreds of years in the Western world. Private arbitration was a feature of the merchant and craft guilds in the early modern period in Europe. Nation-states delegated authority to the guilds to set standards for labor productivity, work quality, and norms of conduct for members of their crafts. The national legal systems also delegated to them the authority to resolve disputes regarding enforcement of contracts and norms between members of the community and to apply sanctions such as fines and exclusion from the trade. These early forms of arbitration were procedures that blended allegations of contractual breaches with allegations of breaches of customary practices of the trade. In arbitration, respected elders in the craft resolved disputes by drawing on the formal and informal norms of the community.[36]

The use of private arbitration in the United States has a similar history to that in Europe. In the colonial period, arbitration was used within a common industry in a particular locality to settle internal disputes.[37] For example, the New York Chamber of Commerce set up an arbitration system in 1768 in order to "settl[e] business disputes according to trade practice rather than legal principles."[38] It is considered the oldest surviving arbitration committee in the United States.[39]

In the late nineteenth and early twentieth century, arbitration in the United States expanded along with the growth of trade associations. Trade associations had been a feature of American life since the colonial era, but in the late nineteenth and early twentieth century new trade associations formed at unprecedented rates. Bankers, hardware dealers, lumbermen, textile manufacturers, canners, tobacco manufacturers, and the like came together to form local, regional, and national associations. The National Industrial Conference Board issued a report on trade associations in 1925 that found there were between 800 and 1,000 national trade organizations in the United States, most of which had been formed since the 1890s. When local and state trade associations were included, the Department of Commerce estimated that there were some 2,000 state and 7,700 local associations.[40] The trade associations themselves combined to form state associations and state chambers of commerce, and in 1914 they formed the United States Chamber of Commerce.[41]

Trade associations set industry standards for production and devised form contracts to standardize terms of dealings between members of a trade. Such standardized practices were a way to minimize commercial disputes and achieve certainty and order in the anarchic world of competitive trade. For the same reasons, trade associations established their own internal arbitration systems to resolve disputes between association members over contract interpretation and industry standards.[42] They were means to achieve uniformity, articulate ethics, and police malfeasance among trading partners. One advocate noted that arbitration was integral to the mission of trade associations because it facilitated uniform enforcement of industry standards and at the same time dispersed knowledge of trade standards and evolving trade customs to members of the trade.[43] Arbitration was also touted for its ability to resolve disputes between trade association members in a manner that preserved the cohesiveness of the organization. Arbitration, it was said, could restore confidence, promote trust, and keep business running smoothly. It created goodwill between members in an association and between the industry and the rest of society.[44] Trade association arbitrations were proceedings with fewer technicalities, "much more with an aim to homespun justice, than . . . actions in the courts."[45] For these reasons, some contemporaries claimed that the availability of arbitration was the most valuable feature of trade association membership.[46]

By the 1920s there were over 1,000 trade associations that had systems of arbitration for their members.[47] Most of the arbitration systems utilized a panel of arbitrators drawn from the trade association's membership and counseled the arbitrators to apply their knowledge of the trade to bring about an equitable resolution to the dispute.[48]

Early twentieth century trade associations urged and sometimes required their members to include arbitration in their standard form contracts.[49] In these standard clauses, parties agreed to use an industry-specific arbitration system to adjudicate all disputes.[50] The characteristic trade association arbitration was an informal proceeding headed by a respected member of the trade group in which the elder would resolve disputes between group members on the basis of the norms, customary practices, and unstated understandings of the community.[51]

Arbitration under the Common Law

Despite the proliferation of arbitration in commercial communities in the United States in the late nineteenth and early twentieth century, arbitration remained outside of and in tension with the legal system. Common-law courts would not issue an order to compel parties to perform agreements to arbitrate. Rather, courts considered agreements to arbitrate to be revocable by either party until an arbitral award was rendered. In practice, the "revocability doctrine" meant that if one party to an arbitration agreement refused to arbitrate, the other party was powerless to compel arbitration or to obtain a stay of litigation if the other side brought suit in court. In most states, the party seeking arbitration could go to court for damages for breach of the promise to arbitrate, but the courts awarded only nominal amounts—at most the cost of preparing for the arbitration that never occurred. Thus a party seeking to arbitrate had no effective remedy against a party who refused to abide by an arbitration agreement.[52]

Commercial lawyers saw arbitration as essential to enable the business community to resolve disputes quickly, and so they wanted the courts to facilitate rather than thwart its use. Businessmen wanted their disputes to be resolved by insiders to the trade, by experts well-versed in the facts of the dispute. As the trade association movement picked up momentum in the early years of the twentieth century, business leaders and their lawyers mounted a campaign to eliminate the revocability doctrine and make agreements to arbitrate enforceable by specific performance. The New York Chamber of Commerce was a central player in the movement to reverse the revocability doctrine. It commissioned a well-known commercial lawyer, Julius Henry Cohen, to represent the chamber as amicus curiae in a pending litigation in which the plaintiff was challenging the revocability doctrine and seeking to enforce an arbitration agreement.[53] Cohen expanded his 1916 brief into a book-length treatise called *Commercial Arbitration and the Law*, that advocated the repeal of the revocability doctrine.[54]

Cohen's book became the manifesto of the commercial community in its battle to reverse the revocability doctrine. It was followed by an avalanche of writings by the commercial law community urging courts and legislatures to change the law of arbitration. In the following years, the New York Chamber of Commerce joined with the New York Bar Association to propose a statute to the New York legislature to change the common-law rule. The statute, which Cohen drafted, was patterned on the English arbitration law of 1889, with one significant difference: the proposed New York law, unlike its English counterpart, did not contain a provision for de novo judicial review of questions of law. This difference reflected the fact that the New York Chamber of Commerce vehemently opposed any judicial review of arbitral awards.[55]

In 1920, Cohen's bill passed the New York legislature and became the New York Arbitration Act.[56] The New York statute made arbitration agreements "valid, irrevocable, and enforceable save on such grounds as exist at Law or in Equity for the revocation of any contract."[57] The New York statute served as a template for the Federal Arbitration Act, enacted five years later.

From the New York Statute to the Federal Arbitration Act

The passage of the New York statute sparked an intense debate about the proper role of arbitration within the legal order. Within three years, New Jersey and Massachusetts adopted almost identical statutes. Proponents of the New York approach included the American Bar Association (ABA) and trade associations. Some states, however, resisted the New York approach on the ground that to enforce predispute arbitration agreements would permit stronger parties to coerce weaker ones. These states were also critical of the New York approach for its failure to provide judicial review on matters of law. Illinois rejected the New York approach and enacted an arbitration law that adopted the English rule of providing judicial review of arbitral awards on matters of law. The Uniform Conference on State Laws endorsed the Illinois approach.[58]

After the enactment of the New York arbitration statute, the business community embraced arbitration with zeal.[59] The Arbitration Society of America was formed to promote the use of arbitration in industry and it quickly attracted over 1,000 leading businesses and over 65 trade groups as members.[60] The Arbitration Society, which later became the American Arbitration Association (AAA), advocated that parties include predispute promises to arbitrate as standardized terms in their business dealings. This simple device, they claimed, would "compel the parties to arbitrate."[61] The Arbitration Society also drafted a model arbitration act, the "Draft Act," which like the New York statute, made agreements to arbitrate irrevocable and specifically enforceable with no substantive judicial review. By 1933, twelve states had enacted the Draft Act.[62]

In 1922 a committee of the ABA drafted a federal statute, the Commercial Arbitration Act, based on the New York statute to submit to Congress. Julius H. Cohen served on the ABA drafting committee and was the major drafter of both pieces of legislation.[63] In 1923 Congress held hearings on the proposed Federal Arbitration Act, and in 1925, five years after the enactment of the New York statute, the United States Arbitration Act (later renamed the Federal Arbitration Act) passed both Houses of Congress unanimously.[64]

The United States Arbitration Act contained all the essential features and most of the wording of the New York Arbitration Act. Like the New York statute, the federal statute made agreements to arbitrate present or future disputes "valid, irrevocable, and enforceable." It also provided that when there is a contract containing an arbitration clause, a court must stay litigation and grant specific performance of the promise to arbitrate. And it set forth only four grounds for which a court could vacate an arbitral award: "(1) where the award was procured by corruption, fraud, or undue means; (2) where there was evident partiality or corruption in the arbitrators, or either of them; (3) where the arbitrators were guilty of misconduct in refusing to postpone the hearing, upon sufficient cause shown, or in refusing to hear evidence pertinent and material to the controversy, or of any other misbehavior by which the rights of any party have been prejudiced; or (4) where the arbitrators exceeded their powers, or so imperfectly executed them that a mutual, final, and definite award upon the subject matter was not made." None of these permitted a court to vacate an award on the basis of an error of fact or law. Thus the statute contained no grounds for substantive review of an arbitral award.

The FAA and the Regulatory Philosophy of Herbert Hoover

The Federal Arbitration Act of 1925 was part of a larger movement of associationalism, voluntarism, and self-regulation in American political thought. It was a movement of the 1920s, most prominently associated with Herbert Hoover.[65] This new social philosophy had its origins in the trade association movement of the early twentieth century and picked up momentum during World War I.[66] The FAA was an important part of Hoover's associationalist program: Hoover promoted it on the grounds that it would enable commercial groups and trade associations to escape progressive-era-style state regulation and engage in self-regulation instead.

Associationalism grew out of the wartime experience in which private associations were given unprecedented governmental powers and authority.[67] The government turned to private sector associations, such as the Chamber of Commerce and the American Federation of Labor, to staff the war agencies and advisory boards.[68] The war required continuous contact between the private sector and government to meet wartime production demands. The government in turn found it easier to deal with organized entities than with individual producers, so it encouraged the organization of trade associations and helped to reorganize whole industries into centralized entities.[69] The experience of "war guildism" gave rise to a new regulatory philosophy, known as associationalism or the "new capitalism."[70]

Herbert Hoover was one of the architects of associationalism. He served as the Director of the Food Administration during World War I. One of his primary initiatives was to reduce waste in industry.[71] From his experience in the wartime agency, he concluded that efficiency and productivity in industry could best be attained and waste could best be eliminated by voluntary associations of businessmen that could share expertise, engage in joint research, set uniform product standards, and promulgate codes of conduct for the trade.[72] Thus he became a champion of trade associations.

On the basis of his wartime experience, Hoover developed a sophisticated philosophy about the relative roles of government and industry in achieving efficiency in economic life. He advocated government facilitation of business cooperation, and he believed that regulatory power should be delegated to strong autonomous trade associations. He envisioned a government that operated not through direct regulation but through promotional conferences, expert inquiries, and other forms of public-private cooperation.[73] According to Robert Rabin, "A strong case can be made that Hoover espoused the single most influential and coherent regulatory philosophy between the Progressive Era and the New Deal."[74]

Hoover became Secretary of Commerce in 1922, and in that capacity, he promoted collaboration between industry and government in order to eliminate waste in industry, foster efficiency, and enhance productivity. He worked closely with the trade associations throughout his tenure at the Commerce Department, sponsoring over 3,000 conferences with trade groups to discuss the elimination of waste and the furtherance of efficiency.[75] He directed Commerce Department officials to work with the trade associations to create codes of ethics—business practices which were then promulgated by the department as standards of fair practices.[76] He also requested that the ABA committee draft the federal legislation that became the FAA.[77]

Described as "the St. Paul of the A Movement,"[78] Hoover crusaded for his vision of associationalism amongst other agencies and departments of government. Hoover's model of regulation was neocorporatist; it advocated that public powers be delegated to private agents to engage in self-regulation.[79] Hoover's associationalism was a rejection of progressive models of government intervention in the economy in favor of self-regulation of business through trade associations.

A cornerstone of Hoover's self-regulatory vision was the expansive use of commercial arbitration. Hoover established an information bureau within the Commerce Department to promote and monitor the progress of commercial arbitration, and he advocated national and state legislation to facilitate and legalize arbitration. He worked closely with the ABA and the Chambers of Commerce on the enactment of the New Jersey, Massachusetts, and Oregon arbitration statutes. He was a principal advocate of the FAA, introducing bills on the subject in Congress in 1923, 1924, and 1925. In a report to Congress in 1926, Hoover claimed credit for these legislative victories, bragging that the Commerce Department had made substantial progress in promoting the use of commercial arbitration within industry. He stated that commercial arbitration "eliminates waste by removing ill will, by saving costs of litigation, by preventing undue delays . . . and by strengthening contractual relations."[80] Hoover served as honorary president of the AAA from its inception in 1926.

The Problem of Insiders and Outsiders in the 1920s

In the 1920s most supporters of the FAA and the state arbitration laws intended the new statutes to apply to disputes between members of the same trade association or between participants in a common line of business.[81] Even Julius Cohen, the champion of arbitration within trade associations and drafter of the Federal Arbitration Act of 1925, cautioned about the limits of arbitration in other contexts. In 1926 he wrote:

> Not all questions arising out of contracts ought to be arbitrated. It is a remedy peculiarly suited to the disposition of the ordinary disputes between merchants as to questions of fact— quantity, quality, time of delivery, compliance with terms of payment, excuses for non-performance, and the like. It has a place also in the determination of the simpler questions of law—the questions of law which arise out of these daily relations between merchants as to the passage of title, the existence of warranties, or the questions of law which are complementary to the questions of fact which we have just mentioned.[82]

The National Industrial Conference Board (NICB) was similarly concerned about the issues arising from the imposition of arbitration for disputes among persons who were not engaged in a common trade or members of a common trade association. The NICB, in a 1925 volume on trade associations, distinguished two types of associations for purposes of designing arbitration systems. When a trade association contains persons or enterprises active in successive stages in the process of fabricating and distributing a single product or product group, it said it is a "relatively simple matter" to establish and operate an arbitration system because "the members of these associations . . . habitually deal with one another, and the disagreements and disputes which arise are confined, in large measure, to parties within the immediate and direct jurisdiction of the trade association."[83] But for trade associations representing just one stage in the production or marketing process, such as one representing only buyers or only sellers, the NICB said that arbitration is more complicated. Members of these single-stage trade associations, which comprise the vast majority of trade associations, do not normally deal with each other in the course of commerce. Rather, "[t]he commercial controversies of the members of these associations are generally with outsiders, . . . and the problem arises of inducing parties beyond the direct jurisdiction of the association to submit their claims to the judgment of a tribunal which functions under the auspices of the organization representing their opponents in interest."[84]

To solve this problem, the NICB recommended that trade associations of the latter type join with their counterparts in related trades to establish joint arbitration boards. Thus the NICB's solution to the insider-outsider problem in arbitration was to expand the definition of insiders from the boundaries of the trade association proper to members of related industries who engage in regularized and repeat transactions with one another. Arbitration before a joint board is nonetheless between members of a shared commercial community, a community defined functionally by repeat business interactions in the normal course of commerce. The joint board arbitration, while technically between insiders and outsiders to a specific trade association, would resolve disputes between entities in a shared normative community that occupied relatively comparable positions within it. The NICB's proposal further assumed that the joint board's arbitration rules would be fashioned from the joint participation of the organizations of each party to the dispute—organizations in which each party has an opportunity to help frame policies and principles.

The NICB's treatment of the problem of outsiders reveals how pervasive and powerful was the assumption that arbitration only occurred between parties that were insiders engaged in a shared business community. It did not contemplate the more serious problem that would be posed if arbitration agreements were made binding upon persons who were not engaged in a common trade.[85]

Modern Arbitration Practice and the Evolution of the FAA

The FAA was enacted in order to further a vision of voluntarism, delegation, and self-regulation within discrete business and commercial communities. Arbitration under the FAA was conceived as an institution that reflected and defined membership in a shared normative community. In the early years, it was applied to commercial arbitrations, but only in a limited set of cases. Due to the then-current interpretation of the act's jurisdictional basis, it only applied to cases involving commerce that were brought in a federal court.[86] At the same time, however, the institution of arbitration evolved, primarily in the areas of securities regulation and collective bargaining. The securities industry and collective bargaining have both been contexts in which jurists and participants have expressly embraced the concept of self-regulation as a central regulatory ideal.

Self-Regulation and Arbitration in the Securities Industry

Self-regulation has a long history in the securities industry. Since the nineteenth century, the major stock exchanges have tenaciously asserted and jealously guarded their self-regulating autonomy. In the early decades of the twentieth century, the New York and Chicago Stock Exchanges refused to incorporate on the ground that as voluntary associations they were not creatures of the state. Rather, they claimed that they were like private clubs, entitled to set their own rules of conduct and to select and discipline their own members.[87]

After the stock market crash of 1929, state legislatures imposed more regulations on the industry. However, President Hoover retained his philosophical commitment to associationalism, minimal governmental intervention, and trade association voluntarism. He rejected proposals for federal legislation to regulate the stock market and instead urged the business community to maintain wages and employment levels voluntarily.[88]

In the early 1930s, as the stock market continued its downward slide, Democrats in Congress pressed for federal regulation of the securities markets. Joint efforts with progressive Republicans ultimately resulted in the Securities and Banking Acts of 1933,[89] the Securities Exchange Act of 1934,[90] and the creation of the Securities and Exchange Commission (SEC).

In the early years, the SEC's leaders were faced with the job of regulating a skeptical, if not hostile, industry. Thus the SEC relied on self-regulation and voluntarism to implement its goals.[91] William O. Douglas, chairman of the SEC from 1937 to 1939, articulated and implemented a coherent framework for the interpretation of the new and as yet unformed law. Douglas believed that the SEC should affirm the processes of self-regulation of the industry and impose minimal external regulation. In 1936, Douglas told a congressional committee:

> My philosophy was and is that the national securities exchanges should be so organized as to be able to take on the job of policing their members so that it would be unnecessary for the Government to interfere with that business. Government should keep the shotgun, so to speak, behind the door, loaded, well-oiled, cleaned and ready for use but with a hope it would never have to be used.[92]

Douglas's leadership of the SEC followed from these principles. He established a pattern of securities regulation whereby the SEC relied on self-regulation of the industry. The agency encouraged participants to form organizations and delegated the organized exchanges a significant role in standard setting, oversight, policing, and disciplining violators. His successors have followed that pattern.

An important feature of self-regulation in the securities industry is delegation of governmental authority both to the exchanges' own rule-making capacity and to their internal dispute-resolution processes. The securities industry has one of the oldest arbitration systems in the country, long predating the 1934 Securities and Exchange Act or the FAA. The New York Stock Exchange (NYSE) has provided a mechanism for voluntary arbitration to resolve disputes between stock exchange members since at least 1845. The NYSE Constitution of 1869 expanded the voluntary arbitration system to permit nonmembers to use the arbitration mechanism in disputes with members so long as the nonmembers agreed to abide by the NYSE arbitration rules.[93]

The National Association of Securities Dealers (NASD) established a system of arbitration in 1968 that permitted nonmembers to arbitrate disputes with members so long as all parties agreed. By 1972 both the NASD and the NYSE required members to arbitrate disputes with customers if the customer so requested, but the customer had the choice of arbitrating or litigating her dispute in court. In the next decade, arbitration for customers ceased to be optional. In the early 1980s some large securities firms began to require that all customers agree to arbitrate all disputes.[94] Soon thereafter, the practice became the industry standard, making the securities industry the first to include mandatory arbitration clauses in the printed forms they gave to customers.[95]

Courts seized upon the history of self-regulation of the stock exchanges as justification for granting broad deference and minimal oversight to the industry's own internal rules and disciplinary proceedings of the securities industry. For example, in 1963 in *Silver v. New York Stock Exchange*, the Supreme Court stated that the 1934 act created a "federally mandated duty of self-policing by exchanges."[96] One component of this duty was "the obligation to formulate rules governing the conduct of exchange members." Lower federal courts also used the self-regulatory ideal as their rationale to defer to the industry's own arbitration tribunals. For example, in 1972 Judge Weinfeld of the Southern District explained why courts grant broad discretion to securities industry arbitration proceedings:

> The Exchange, in its self-regulatory role, has a legitimate interest in deciding how disputes between its members and their employees are to be resolved; it has a legitimate interest in fostering harmonious relations among the varied groups whose daily activities play a role in the complex operations of the Exchange. Considering that interest, it is not unreasonable to

require those engaged in such operations to resolve their disputes, which ofttimes may center about practices peculiar to the Exchange, through prompt and economic arbitration rather than by drawn out litigation before judges of fact who may be without experience in the trade practices and customs.[97]

Self-Regulation under Collective Bargaining

The securities industry experience with self-regulation legitimated the practice of private arbitration and therefore helped to set the stage for the *Gilmer* decision. The other precursor to *Gilmer* was the law of arbitration that developed in the collective bargaining context. Labor cases are cited extensively in FAA cases as precedent for delegating enforcement of legal rights to arbitration and restricting the scope of judicial review. Indeed, many of the cases interpreting the FAA in the 1980s and 1990s relied on cases interpreting the National Labor Relations Act[98] (NLRA) in the 1960s.[99]

Grievance arbitration was introduced into U.S. collective bargaining practices in the early decades of the 20th century in a few selected industries, but it only became widespread during World War II. The War Labor Board (WLB), intent on maintaining labor peace to ensure stable wartime production, saw arbitration as a method of resolving disputes without strikes and thus made arbitration the preferred method for resolving workplace disputes. The WLB encouraged parties to include arbitration clauses in their collective bargaining agreements and accorded arbitration awards substantial deference. After the war, many of the same officials who had staffed the WLB became professional labor arbitrators. They encouraged widespread use of arbitration as the natural outgrowth of a collective bargaining relationship.[100]

In 1947 Congress enacted Section 301 of the Labor Management Relations Act (LMRA), which stated: "Suits for violation of contracts between an employer and a labor organization . . . may be brought in any district court of the United States having jurisdiction of the parties, without respect to the amount in controversy or without regard to the citizenship of the parties."[101] On its face, this provision gave federal courts jurisdiction to hear and decide disputes arising under collective bargaining agreements. Thus it could have undercut the evolving practice of autonomous arbitrators standing as the ultimate interpreter of collective agreements. However, in 1957 in *Textile Workers Union v. Lincoln Mills*,[102] the Supreme Court interpreted Section 301 as a directive to the federal courts to develop a federal common law of collective bargaining that was supportive of and deferential to private arbitration.[103] He declared that there was a national labor policy to promote the use of private arbitration to resolve disputes arising under collective bargaining agreements. Since *Lincoln Mills*, courts have made private arbitration the central feature of our collective bargaining system.[104]

In 1960 in a group of cases known as the *Steelworkers' Trilogy*, the Supreme Court adopted several legal doctrines that have created a privileged role for arbitration within our collective bargaining system. First, in *United Steelworkers of America v. American Manufacturing Co.*,[105] the Court held that courts should grant specific enforcement of promises to arbitrate without regard to the merits of the underlying dispute. Thus it ruled that parties who agree to arbitration provisions can be required to arbitrate meritless, even frivolous, claims. Second, in *United Steelworkers v. Warrior & Gulf Navigation Co.*,[106] the Court held created a presumption of arbitrability, such that arbitration agreements should be interpreted expansively to cover any dispute to which it arguably applies. And finally, in *United Steelworkers v. Enterprise Wheel & Car Corp.*,[107] the Court held that courts should enforce arbitral awards without reviewing the merits of the award. It stated that an arbitral award should be enforced so long as "it draws its essence from the collective bargaining agreement." Furthermore, the Court stated that arbitrators have no obligation to write opinions or to give reasons for their awards. Therefore, if an award could plausibly have drawn its essence from the agreement, it must be enforced. The *Enterprise* Court's formulation of the arbitrator's obligations creates what might be termed a "presumption of arbitrator regularity"—a presumption that the arbitrator acted within the scope of his authority and that the award drew its essence from the collective agreement. The de facto presumption of arbitrator regularity combined with the presumption of arbitrability make labor arbitration almost impossible to avoid and render arbitral awards practically immune from attack.[108]

Lincoln Mills and the *Steelworkers' Trilogy* decisions created an unprecedented degree of deference by courts to private arbitration. All these opinions were written by Justice William O. Douglas. As if restating his views of the role of self-regulation in the securities exchanges that he implemented when he was chairman of the SEC in the 1930s, Justice Douglas justified the deference to labor arbitration on the ground that the unionized workplace was self-regulating. He described labor-management relations in the workplace as a microcosmic democracy and collective bargaining as an exercise in "industrial self-government."[109] As he noted: "The collective bargaining agreement . . . is more than a contract;

it is a generalized code to govern a myriad of cases which the draftsmen cannot wholly anticipate."[110] He continued, "The collective agreement covers the whole employment relationship. It calls into being a new common law—the common law of a particular industry or of a particular plant. . . . A collective bargaining agreement is an effort to erect a system of industrial self-government."[111]

Douglas concluded that in the unionized workplace, as in the securities exchanges, courts should support the self-regulatory aspects of the community and permit its internal arbitration system to adjudicate disputes. As he commented: "[T]he grievance machinery under a collective bargaining agreement is at the very heart of the system of industrial self-government. Arbitration is the means of solving the unforeseeable by molding a system of private law for all the problems which may arise."[112]

In the cross-fertilization and leap-frogging method of legal change, Douglas's opinions in the labor cases interpreting the Labor Management Relations Act have been used extensively as authority for expanding the reach of arbitration under the FAA. For example, in 1983 the Supreme Court borrowed the presumption of arbitrability from the *Warrior and Gulf* opinion and applied it in a construction dispute under the FAA in *Moses Cone Memorial Hospital v. Mercury Construction Co.*[113] Similarly, courts have plucked other arbitration doctrines from the labor context and applied them to arbitration under the FAA. For example, *Nolde Bros. v. Local No. 358, Bakery Workers*,[114] a labor law case in which the Court applied an arbitration clause to a dispute that arose after the collective bargaining agreement containing the arbitration clause had expired, has been used as authority to extend arbitration clauses beyond their expiration dates in nonlabor settings.[115]

In sum, in both the securities industry and collective bargaining, self-regulation has been a central theme in the interpretation and implementation of the statutory schemes. In both areas, courts have relied on the capability of the regulated entity to self-regulate to justify granting considerable autonomy to private arbitration. Further, both the NLRA and the Securities Exchange Act were enacted in the 1930s, both rely on governmental agencies for their implementation, and in each case the agency delegated its regulatory authority to preexisting private organizations that have long had internal governance structures that included private dispute resolution mechanisms.

In the 1980s the Supreme Court's FAA decisions transposed the rationale for arbitration developed in those two areas to a variety of settings where there is no similar infrastructure to justify a self-regulatory regime. Thus the *Gilmer* decision was the result of applying the law developed for self-regulatory institutions in contexts where there is no comparable institutional foundation.

The Road to Gilmer

Just as judicial decisions about arbitration under collective bargaining were used to redefine the law of arbitration in commercial and securities industry contexts, so too, precedents in commercial arbitration have redefined arbitration law in the employment area. The courts first confronted the question of mandatory arbitration of statutory rights in the commercial and securities fields. Until the 1980s the Supreme Court did not apply the FAA to require parties to arbitrate claims of violation of statutory rights. The 1953 case, *Wilko v. Swan*,[116] stood for the proposition that statutory rights were not appropriately adjudicated in a private tribunal. In that case the Supreme Court refused to compel arbitration of claims arising under the 1933 Securities Act. For many years *Wilko* was read expansively to bar the application of the FAA to compel arbitration of statutory rights. But the Court's position on this issue changed in the 1980s, and ultimately *Wilko* was reversed.

The first Supreme Court case to hold that arbitration was appropriate for statutory claims was *Mitsubishi Motors v. Soler Chrysler-Plymouth, Inc.*,[117] decided in 1985. There the Supreme Court applied the FAA to claims arising under the Sherman Antitrust Act. The underlying dispute in *Mitsubishi* arose from a three-party franchise transaction between Chrysler International (a Swiss subsidiary of the Chrysler Corporation), Mitsubishi Motors (a Japanese automobile manufacturer), and Soler Chrysler-Plymouth, an automobile sales franchisee in Puerto Rico. The Sales Contract by which Chrysler and Mitsubishi agreed to provide Soler with vehicles contained a clause calling for arbitration of certain disputes between Mitsubishi and Soler. After the franchise was in effect for about two years, Soler failed to meet its sales quotas and Mitsubishi sought to arbitrate under the clause. Soler counterclaimed against both Mitsubishi and Chrysler, raising numerous contract breaches and statutory claims, including a claim that Mitsubishi and Chrysler had conspired in violation of the Sherman Act to divide markets in restraint of trade. The arbitration clause did not specifically commit the parties to arbitrate statutory claims, nor did it expressly apply to disputes between Soler and Chrysler. Nonetheless, the Court held that in the face of the broad language of the arbitration clause, it would presume that this particular dispute was within the promise to arbitrate. It stated, "There is no reason to depart from [the presumption of arbitrability] where a party bound by an arbitration agreement raises claims founded on statutory rights."[118] The Court conceded that not all statutory rights are appropriate for arbitration, but it said that in each case it would look to the particular text and history of the statute involved to see if Congress intended to preclude enforcement of the statutory scheme in arbitration. It placed the burden on the party opposing arbitration to demonstrate an intent to preclude. In the instant case, the Court concluded that there was no congressional intent to preclude arbitration of claims arising under the antitrust acts.

Mitsubishi was an international case involving parties of three different nationalities and a transaction that spanned several continents. The Court's decision in part reflected its views of the unique values of arbitration in the international commercial context. One could thus read the decision as limited to international transactions. However, since the *Mitsubishi* decision, the Supreme Court has applied its reasoning to wholly domestic disputes.

The first Supreme Court case to hold that statutory rights are amenable to arbitration in a purely domestic context was *Shearson/American Express v. McMahon*, decided in 1987.[119] This case involved a claim by a customer against a brokerage house alleging various state law fraud claims, violations of the 1934 Securities and Exchange Act and violations of the civil provisions of RICO, the federal antiracketeering act.[120] When they opened their accounts, the customers had signed an agreement that contained a clause stating:

> Unless unenforceable due to federal or state law, any controversy arising out of or relating to my accounts . . . shall be settled by arbitration in accordance with the rules, then in effect, of the National Association of Securities Dealers.[121]

The Supreme Court invoked the history of self-regulation in the securities industry and concluded that all claims, including the Securities Act and RICO claims, were amenable to arbitration. Two years later, in another case between a customer and a brokerage house, *Rodriguez De Quijaas v. Shearson/American Express*,[122] the Supreme Court took the highly unusual step of overturning an earlier precedent. It overturned *Wilko v. Swan* and ordered arbitration in the dispute concerning the 1933 Securities Act.

Thus in 1991 when the Supreme Court decided the *Gilmer* case, most of the important questions concerning arbitration of statutory claims had already been decided. The proposition that parties could be compelled to arbitrate statutory rights, even important statutory rights such as those in the nondiscrimination laws, was well-established. The possibility that an arbitral procedure might differ from a court in important ways or that arbitration may offer different remedies than the statute provided had already been considered and dismissed. And the Court had already decided that once parties had an agreement to arbitrate, a party resisting arbitration had a very high burden to show that Congress did not intend the particular statutory rights in dispute to be decided in arbitration. Thus the *Gilmer* decision was unremarkable from the point of view of the Federal Arbitration Act.[123]

Assessing the Courts' Approach to Self-Regulation

Once we understand the post-*Gilmer* courts' expansive interpretation of the FAA as a form of delegation of judicial and legislative authority to self-regulating communities, we can critically assess the virtues and limitations of such an approach. It is clear that arbitration has a different valence depending upon whether it used to resolve disputes between two members of a shared normative community, such as a trade association or a stock exchange, or whether it is used in disputes between insiders to the community and others who remain outside. Within such a community, arbitration can both express and define the shared norms which give the community cohesion. However, when used between insiders and outsiders, arbitration can become a vehicle for disenfranchisement and oppression.

The use of arbitration in disputes between insiders and outsiders raises problems not merely of overt arbitrator bias; it also poses problems of more subtle bias that exists when the arbitrator has fundamentally different perspectives than one of the parties. Outsiders are disadvantaged in such settings because insiders know the norms, share the norms with the arbitrators, and expect the norms to govern resolution of their disputes. Moreover, the fact that most arbitration procedures are informal often works to the disadvantage of the outsider. Outsiders do not have ready access to relevant information, knowledge of the historical background and precedents, or ability to garner potentially helpful witnesses, making it ever more difficult to prove their case.[124]

In the area of nonunion employment arbitration, there are many instances of arbitration systems forced on nonsuspecting employees, who later find that they have lost all meaningful recourse when faced with discriminatory or other unlawful treatment. To give but one example, the case of *Lang v. Burlington Northern Railroad Co.*[125] demonstrates the fictitious nature of contractual consent in many employment arbitration cases. In that case an employer unilaterally adopted an arbitration policy in 1991 and notified incumbent employees of its existence by mail. When the plaintiff, who never received the notice, attempted to bring a suit for wrongful dismissal, the employer moved to dismiss on the grounds that the dispute must be arbitrated under the company's arbitration policy. The Court agreed with the employer, holding that by sending the employees the policy, the employer had created a binding unilateral contract.

Further, many nonunion arbitration procedures fall short of due process. For example, some provide that the employer can select the arbitrator unilaterally, some do not permit employees to be represented by counsel, some impose onerous burdens of proof on the complainant-employee, some require complainants to pay large fees just to have their case heard, and some impose severe restrictions on the remedies that a prevailing party can recover.[126] There is also wide variation in provisions for discovery and the requirement of written opinions by arbitrators.[127] When challenged in court, these provisions are usually upheld. For example, in *Pony Express v. Morris*,[128] an applicant for employment was given an arbitration agreement to sign that provided that all claims relating to her employment shall be arbitrated without discovery and that any award shall be limited to actual lost wages or six months wages, whichever is less. The agreement also said that "you will not be offered employment until it [the arbitration agreement] is signed without modification." The Texas appeals court upheld this agreement against a challenge that it was unconscionable.

We can assume that employees do not fare as well as they would in litigation because firms are establishing arbitration systems in order to limit their liability in employment litigation. They would not be doing so if the outcomes were favorable to employers. The existing evidence of outcomes of employment arbitration confirms that the results are generally favorable to employers. One study that examined the outcomes of nonunion arbitrations conducted under the auspices of the American Arbitration Association found evidence of a "repeat-player" effect, in which employers who participated in multiple arbitrations had an advantage over employees who were almost invariably one-time participants in arbitration.[129] The author found that when the employer was a repeat player in arbitration, employees were less likely to win at arbitration and received lower damages when successful.

In addition, we can observe a *"Gilmer* effect" in the aggregate data on employment litigation in the federal courts. As Figure 3 indicates, the number of federal employment cases that went to judgment between 1987 and 1997 more than doubled, from 2,592 to 5,199. During that same period, the plaintiff win rate declined from 22% of cases going to judgment to 12%. The sharp decline in the plaintiff's win rate can be accounted for by the large increase in cases decided at the pretrial stage. In 1987, 28% of all cases that went to judgment were decided on pretrial motion and the plaintiffs won those motions 11.31% of the time. In contrast, in 1997, 50% of the cases were decided on pretrial motion—double the rate of 1987. Of those decided at the pretrial stage, plaintiffs only won 3.19% of those motions—one quarter as often as 1987. Indeed, Figure 3 also shows that while plaintiff win rates at trial in the same period are rising, the overall decline in plaintiff win rates is a function of the decline in win rates on pretrial motions, combined with the big rise in the percent of cases decided at that stage.[130] It is likely that a substantial portion of pretrial motions in which cases were being decided and in which plaintiffs were losing were what can be called *Gilmer* motions—motions to dismiss because the claim was subject to an arbitration procedure.

FIGURE 3

Trends in Employment Discrimination Litigation

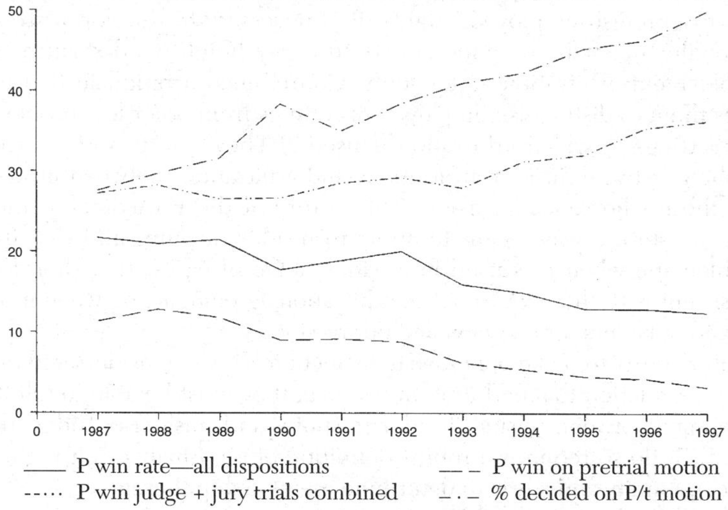

——— P win rate—all dispositions   — — P win on pretrial motion
····· P win judge + jury trials combined   _ . _ % decided on P/t motion

Some courts are beginning to police arbitration between employers and nonunion workers to prevent gross unfairness. For example, in 1997 a California appellate court held that an arbitration agreement that significantly limited employees' remedies, shortened statute of limitations and eliminated employees rights to recover for many statutory and common law actions, and that did not similarly apply to the employer was so one-sided as to be unconscionable.[131] Similarly, in *Cole v. Burns*, the Court of Appeals for the District of Columbia stated that minimal due process protections must be present to avoid such arbitrations struck down as unconscionable. It further stated that any arbitration agreement which required an employee to pay a portion of the cost of adjudicating her statutory rights would be void as unconscionable.[132]

While some courts are utilizing tools like the unconscionability doctrine and heightened scrutiny of consent to protect employees from oppressive uses of arbitration, the trend is by no means universal. Most courts continue to rubber stamp employer petitions to compel employees to arbitrate. The result, as shown in Figure 3, has been a significant decline in plaintiff win rates in employment discrimination litigation and a significant rise in the number of cases in which plaintiffs lose at the pretrial stage.

Proposals for Change

To reverse the trend toward increased use of employment arbitration to diminish employees' rights, it is necessary to develop a strong rationale that will convince courts to apply heightened scrutiny to employment arbitration agreements. Courts need a rationale that enables them to distinguish employment settings from other less problematic settings in which arbitration is used.[133] They can do so by distinguishing between insider arbitrations and arbitrations between insiders and those who remain outside. The history of the FAA demonstrates that the statute was meant to apply to insider disputes and that it is problematic when it is used in a wider range of cases. It is therefore consistent with the FAA to police arbitration agreements between insiders and outsiders for coercion and oppression.

For courts to make operative a distinction between insiders and outsiders in relation to an arbitration tribunal, they must be able to tell the difference between "insider-insider" disputes and "insider-outsider" disputes. To do so requires a robust definition of a normative self-regulating community and a way to determine membership therein.

Membership in a normative community must involve, at the very least, a set of common experiences. However, while common experiences provide the necessary basis for a normative community, they are not sufficient. If they were, employees and employers would share a community because they share in the common experiences of the workplace. However, membership also requires an opportunity to participate in framing the shared institutions, values, and rules that grow out of that common experience.[134]

The role of participation becomes clear when we consider two settings where arbitration is frequently utilized and much criticized—franchise relationships and employment relationships. The most controversial cases decided under the FAA involve franchise and employment situations. In the typical franchise case, a franchiser gives a franchisee an arbitration agreement at the outset of the relationship, and when the franchisee later attempts to assert legal rights against the franchiser, the latter successfully raises the arbitration clause as a bar to the action.[135] In employment cases the employer typically gives the employee an arbitration agreement at the outset of the relationship and as a condition of entry. When the employee subsequently attempts to bring a legal claim against the employer, the latter raises the arbitration clause as a bar.

Franchise and employment cases look like insider-insider cases because in both situations, the parties to the dispute—franchisee and franchiser, or employee and employer—share an economic interest in the well-being of the firm. In both settings the disputants are likely to wear the same company insignia and attend the same company picnics. However, the franchise and employment relationships are different from stock exchange or trade association cases in one important respect: Arbitration does not emerge from participation in a shared normative community in which both parties participate. Rather, in the franchise and employment cases, the arbitration agreement was the ticket of entrance into the community. The party seeking to avoid arbitration—the franchisee or employee—did not play a role in framing the rules, norms, and customs of the community. The arbitration clause is typically contained in the franchise agreement or the employer handbook, and the applicant franchisee/employee is told they cannot enter the "community" if they decline it. At the moment that the arbitration procedure is presented, the individual employee or franchisee is an outsider who has played no role in shaping the procedures or the norms which it embodies. Therefore, the use of arbitration in franchisee-franchiser and employee-employer relationships does not reflect the existence of a shared community nor embody its norms. While both relationships involve economic interdependency, there is no shared participation in defining the norms of the community.

The recent employment arbitration cases demonstrate that without a mechanism to ensure employee participation, employment arbitration systems will tend to be one-sided and oppressive. Thus the courts should refuse to enforce nonunion arbitration systems unless there has been employee participation in the framing of them. That participation could take the form of a labor union, a works council, or some other independent employee representation device.

Thus we arrive at a paradox: The growth of nonunion arbitration systems crafted by employers unilaterally in the absence of unions—and in part to substitute for unions—provide a powerful argument for government regulation to ensure employee participation in the workplace. This, in turn, requires more government protection for employees' right to organize.

Summary and Conclusion

To summarize and conclude, the Supreme Court's decision in *Gilmer* has facilitated a major shift in corporate human resource policies and employment practices. Employers now frequently require employees to utilize arbitration systems crafted by the employer to enforce their employment rights. The decision was based on an erroneous interpretation of the Federal Arbitration Act, a 1925 statute that was virtually rewritten by the Supreme Court in the 1980s. In large part, the expansion of the scope of the FAA and its application to employment is the result of insufficient attention to the statute's history and intent. The Supreme Court in *Gilmer* applied experiences with and doctrines about arbitration that developed in the securities industry and the collective bargaining framework to the individual employment setting. While arbitration undoubtedly has value in an institutional setting in which parties are of relatively equal power engaged in repeated interactions within a structure that the parties collectively designed, its use in one-shot relations between parties of vastly unequal bargaining power is fraught with dangers. The only meaningful corrective is to ensure that such systems are crafted with the participation of all concerned. In the employment setting, this means participation by an organization that speaks for and represents the employees, be it a union, a works council, or some other independent representation device.

Acknowledgment

The author would like to thank Alex Colvin, Ted Eisenberg, and Harry Katz for helpful comments and suggestions and Robert Fisher for excellent research assistance. This chapter was the Anne Eastabrook Distinguished Lecture in Dispute Resolution, Cornell University, April, 1999.

Endnotes

[1] In 1997 unions represented 10.8% of the private nonagricultural workforce: see, Bureau of Labor Statistics, *Union Membership (Annual)*, DEVELOPMENTS IN LABOR-MANAGEMENT RELATIONS (1998), available at http://www.bls.gov/news.release/union2.toc.htm.

[2] A survey of alumni of a masters program in human resources/industrial relations management in late 1991 found that out of 195 respondents only four (2.1%) indicated that their organization used arbitration as part of its nonunion grievance procedure. Denise R. Chachere and Peter Feuille, *Looking Fair or Being Fair: Remedial Voice Procedures in Nonunion Workplaces* 21 JOURNAL OF MANAGEMENT 27 (1995). However, this survey population was highly skewed towards large organizations with relatively sophisticated human resource management practices, so the results may overestimate the incidence of nonunion arbitration procedures in use at that time.

[3] General Accounting Office, EMPLOYMENT DISCRIMINATION: MOST PRIVATE-SECTOR EMPLOYERS USE ALTERNATIVE DISPUTE RESOLUTION, GAO/HEHS-95-150 Employment Discrimination (1995).

[4] Establishments subject to EEOC reporting requirements may tend to be larger and have more formal human resource management practices than those in the general population. In addition, follow-up contacts made by the GAO with respondents who indicated that they had nonunion arbitration procedures revealed that some of the respondents mistakenly reported using nonunion arbitration when in fact they only had union arbitration procedures.

[5] In a nonrandom September 1993 survey of employment dispute resolution practices, McDermott found that of 92 responding organizations, nonunion arbitration was used in 10 (10.9%) and under consideration in a further 13 (14.1%): E. Patrick McDermott, *Survey of 92 Key Companies Using ADR to Settle Employment Disputes* 50(1) DISPUTE RESOLUTION JOURNAL 8 (1995). A September 1994 survey of human resource professionals by the Society of Human Resource Management found that just under 8% of firms used nonunion arbitration: William M. Howard, *Arbitrating Claims of Employment Discrimination: What Really Does Happen? What Really Should Happen?* 50(4) DISPUTE RESOLUTION JOURNAL 40 (1995).

[6] A recent survey of 80 nonunion arbitration procedures found that 85% of them were introduced in the last five years, since the Supreme Court's *Gilmer* decision, and 20% were introduced after 1995. Mei L. Bickner, Christine Ver Ploeg, and Charles Feigenbaum, *Developments in Employment Arbitration* 52(1) DISPUTE RESOLUTION JOURNAL 8 (1997).

[7] *See, e.g.*, Richard A. Bales, COMPULSORY ARBITRATION: THE GRAND EXPERIMENT IN EMPLOYMENT at 102-114 (1997); Lamont E. Stallworth, *Government Regulation of Workplace Disputes and Alternative Dispute Resolution*, in Bruce E. Kaufman, Ed., GOVERNMENT REGULATION OF THE EMPLOYMENT RELATIONSHIP, 369, 369-401 (1997).

[8] *See, e.g.*, Katherine Van Wezel Stone, *Mandatory Arbitration of Individual Employment Rights: The Yellow Dog Contract of the 1990s*, 73 Denver L. Rev. 1017, 1034 (1996); David S. Schwartz, *Enforcing Small Print to Protect Big Business: Employee and Consumer Rights Claims in an Age of Compelled Arbitration*, 1997

Wis. L. Rev. 33 (1997); Joseph R. Grodin, *Arbitration of Employment Discrimination Claims: Doctrine and Policy in the Wake of Gilmer*, 14 Hofstra Labor Law J. 1 (1996).

[9] Katherine Van Wezel Stone, *Policing Contracts within the Nexus-of-Contracts Firm*, 43 U. OF TORONTO LAW J. 353, 353-5 (1993).

[10] The data presented are derived from the Eisenberg-Clermont database, found at teddy.law.cornell.edu:8090/cgi-bin/betaall8797. The Eisenberg-Clermont database contains all employment discrimination claims in the federal courts. These are cases alleging claims of discrimination on the basis of race, gender, disability, age, national origin, pregnancy, and so forth—most of which arose as challenges to dismissals and layoffs. The database reports on cases completed in each year. For the relevant years, it shows that the average duration of each case was approximately one year. Hence it is estimated that the number of cases completed in 1991 is a reasonable approximation of the number of cases that were filed in 1990, the number completed in 1990 reflects the number filed in 1989, and so forth.

[11] *See* Eisenberg-Clermont data base, *supra.*

[12] *See* Katherine Van Wezel Stone, *Legacy of Industrial Pluralism: The Tension between Individual Employment Rights and the New Deal Collective Bargaining System*, 59 CHI. L. REV. 575, 630 & n. 225 (1992).

[13] James Dertouzos, Elaine Holland, and Patricia Ebener, THE LEGAL CONSEQUENCES OF WRONGFUL TERMINATION vii (1988). This Rand Institute study also found that the median award for prevailing plaintiffs was $177,000. *Id.* The fact that the mean was so much higher than the median indicates that there were some extremely high awards. Arguably, the fear of an occasional mega-verdict may motivate potential defendants to alter their behavior as much or more than any considerations of average verdict levels.

[14] 500 U.S. 20 (1991).

[15] 29 U.S.C. Sec. 621 *et seq.*

[16] 9 U.S.C. Sec. 1 *et seq.*

[17] *Gilmer,* 500 U.S. at 26 (citing *Mitsubishi Motors Corp. v. Soler Chrysler-Plymouth, Inc,* 473 U.S. 614 (1985), and *Shearson/American Express, Inc. v. McMahon,* 482 U.S. 220 (1987)).

[18] In *Mitsubishi Motors* and *Shearson/American Express,* the Court had found that claims arising under the Sherman Antitrust Act, the 1934 Securities and Exchange Act, and the RICO Act were amenable to arbitration under the FAA.

[19] *Gilmer,* 500 U.S. at 28 (quoting *Mitsubishi Motors,* 473 U.S. at 637 (1985)).

[20] *Id.* at 30-32.

[21] 9 U.S.C. § 1 (emphasis added).

[22] *Gilmer,* 500 U.S. at 36-40 (Stevens, J., dissenting).

[23] *Id.* at 51-52.

[24] *See* Tenney Engineering, Inc. v. United Electrical Radio & Machine Workers, 207 F.2d 450 (3d Cir. 1953); Pryner v. Tractor Supply Co., 103 F.3d 354 (7th Cir. 1997); Schulte v. Prudential Ins. Co., 133 F.3d 225 (3d Cir. 1998).

[25] *See, e.g.,* Maye v. Smith, Barney, Inc., 897 F. Supp. 100 (S.D.N.Y. 1995 (race discrimination); Scott v. Farm Family Life Ins. Co., 827 F. Supp. 76 (D. Mass. 1993 (pregnancy discrimination); Pritzker v. Merrill Lynch, Pierce, Fenner & Smith, Inc., 7 Fed. 3d 1110 (3d Cir. 1993) (ERISA); Saari v. Smith, Barney, Inc., 789 F. Supp. 155 (D.N.J. 1992) (Polygraph Protection Act).

[26] *See* Stone, *Mandatory Arbitration, supra* n. 8 at 034 & 1039-40.

[27] *Id.* at 1040-41.

[28] *See, e.g.,* Lang v. Burlington Northern RR Co., 835 F. Supp. 1104 (D. Minn. 1993) (enforcing arbitration policy that employer adopted unilaterally and notified employees by mail).

[29] Stone, *Mandatory Arbitration, supra* n. 8 at 1037.

[30] Southland Corp. v. Keating, 465 U.S. 1 (1984).

[31] The Court affirmed the extremely broad reach of FAA preemption in Perry v. Thomas, 482 U.S. 483 (1987); Allied-Bruce Terminex Cos. v. Dobson, 513 U.S. 265 (1995) and Doctor's Association v. Casarotto, 517 U.S. 681 (1996).

[32] Moses H. Cone Memorial Hospital v. Mercury Construction Corp., 460 U.S. 1 (1983).

[33] Mitsubishi Motors Corp, 473 U.S. 614 (1985) (antitrust laws); Shearson/American Express v. McMahon, 482 U.S. 220 (1987) (RICO and 1933 Securities Acts).

[34] The most significant new issue posed by *Gilmer* concerned the interpretation of the exclusion in the FAA for contracts of employment, discussed above. While the *Gilmer* court ducked the issue, since 1991, all but one of the courts of appeals that have considered the issue have read the FAA's exclusion for "contracts of employment" to apply only to workers who are engaged in the interstate movement of goods, thereby applying *Gilmer* to a full range of employment contracts.

[35] *See* Katherine Van Wezel Stone, *Rustic Justice: Community and Coercion under the Federal Arbitration Act,* 77 N. CAROLINA L. REV. 931, 955-56 (1999).

[36] *Id.* at 969-973.

[37] *See* Norman S. Poser, *When ADR Eclipses Litigation: The Brave New World of Securities Arbitration,* 59 BROOK. L. REV. 1095, 1095 (1993).

[38] Linda R. Singer, SETTLING DISPUTES: CONFLICT RESOLUTION IN BUSINESS FAMILIES, AND THE LEGAL SYSTEM 5 (1990).

[39] *See* Nathan Isaacs, *Two Views of Commercial Arbitration,* 40 HARV. L. REV. 929, 934-35 (1927); *see also* NATIONAL INDUSTRIAL CONFERENCE BOARD, TRADE ASSOCIATIONS: THEIR ECONOMIC SIGNIFICANCE AND LEGAL STATUS 278 (1925) (describing the influence of the New York Chamber of Commerce in encouraging the use of arbitration procedures).

[40] *See* NATIONAL INDUSTRIAL CONFERENCE BOARD, *id.* at 11-13 & at App. at 325-326. The NICB warns that its data on numbers of trade associations involve imprecise estimates due to problems of definition and double-counting. *See id.* App. at 319-26.

[41] *See* ROBERT H. WIEBE, BUSINESSMEN AND REFORM: A STUDY OF THE PROGRESSIVE MOVEMENT 18-25 (1962).

[42] *See* Soia Mentschikoff, *Commercial Arbitration,* 61 COLUMBIA L. REV. 846, 852-53 (1961).

[43] *See* Franklin D. Jones, TRADE ASSOCIATION ACTIVITIES AND THE LAW 196 (1922).

[44] *See* Frances Kellor, ARBITRATION IN THE NEW INDUSTRIAL SOCIETY 14 (1934). *See also* Jones, *id.* at 197 (stating that "arbitration [is] a conserver of good will and preserver of prosperity").

[45] Julius Henry Cohen & Kenneth Dayton, *The New Federal Arbitration Law,* 12 VIRGINIA L. REV. 265, 279-80 (1926).

[46] *See* Jones, *supra* note 43 at 197.

[47] *Id.*

[48] For example, the *Arbitration Rules of the National Dried Fruit Association* state: "Arbitrators should proceed on the one great principle of exact equity as between the parties. Technical breaches of the letter of an agreement where its spirit has been observed and no resulting damage is shown, should be disregarded." SELECTED ARTICLES ON COMMERCIAL ARBITRATION, *id.* at 120.

[49] *See* Harlan F. Stone, *The Scope and Limitation of Commercial Arbitration,* PROC. ACAD. POL. SCI. CITY N.Y., July 1923, at 195, 195-96.

[50] *See* Mentschikoff, *supra* note 42 at 849; Philip G. Phillips, *Commercial Arbitration under the N.R.A.,* 1 CHI. L. REV. 424, 426-27 (1933).

[51] *See, e.g., Arbitration Plan of the Food Trade,* in Daniel Bloomfield, ed., SELECTED ARTICLES ON COMMERCIAL ARBITRATION 115, 116 (1927) (directing that the arbitration panel is to be two wholesale grocers and one broker or two brokers and one wholesale grocer); *National-American Wholesale Lumber Association Inc.,* in SELECTED ARTICLES ON COMMERCIAL ARBITRATION, *id.* at 123, 126 (directing that arbitration panels consist of three people selected from a list of six that contains at least three members of the trade association).

[52] The American doctrine of revocability had its origins in English arbitration law. Gradually, beginning at the end of the eighteenth century and continuing throughout the nineteenth century, the English Parliament abandoned the revocability doctrine. In America, by contrast, the revocability doctrine held firm throughout the nineteenth century. See Julius Henry Cohen, COMMERCIAL ARBITRATION AND THE LAW, 53-55 (1918).

[53] *See* Charles L. Bernheimer, *Introduction,* in COHEN, COMMERCIAL ARBITRATION AND THE LAW, *id.* at xi. Cohen's first-hand knowledge of arbitration dated back to 1910, when he helped frame the Protocols of Peace for the New York City ladies' garment industry that settled the 1910 citywide strike.

[54] *See* COHEN, *supra* note 52 at xiii-xv.

[55] *See* Isaacs, *supra* note 39 at 934-35.

[56] 1920 N.Y. Laws ch. 275, § 2 (current version at N.Y. C.P.L.R. 7501-7514 [McKinney 1998 & Supp. 1999]).

[57] N.Y. Civil Practice Act § 1448 (1920).

[58] *See* National Conference on Uniform State Laws PROCEEDINGS 69-70 (1924).

[59] Harlan F. Stone, PROCEEDINGS, Academy of Political Science 195-96 (1923).

[60] *See* Joseph Wheless, *Arbitration as a Judicial Process of Law*, a 30 W. VA. L. Q. 209, 228-30 (1924).

[61] *Id.* at 231. The AAA standard arbitration clause was exceedingly broad, reading: "'Any controversy or claim arising out of or relating to this contract or the breach thereof, shall be settled by arbitration, in accordance with the rules then obtaining, of the American Arbitration Association. . . .'" Philip G. Phillips, *The Paradox in Arbitration Law: Compulsion as Applied to a Voluntary Proceedings*, 46 HARV. L. REV. 1258, 1277 n. 87 (quoting CODE OF ARBITRATION: PRACTICE AND PROCEDURE OF THE AMERICAN ARBITRATION TRIBUNAL 205 (Frances Keller, ed., 1931)).

[62] Phillips, *id.* at 1262-65.

[63] *See, Report of the Committee on Commerce, Trade and Commercial Law*, 47 Rep. A.B.A. 288, 289, 289, 295 & 315-18 (1922).

[64] *See* United States Arbitration Act of 1925, ch. 213, 43 Stat. 883 (codified as amended at 9 U.S.C. §§ 1-307 (1994)); Moses H. Grossman, *Trade Security Under Arbitration Laws*, 35 YALE L. J. 308, 312-13 n. 9 (1925).

[65] *See, e.g.*, Ellis Hawley, *Herbert Hoover, the Commerce Secretariat, and the Vision of an "Associative State," 1921-1928*, 61 J. AM. HIST. 116, 118 (1974) (describing the trend towards associationalism and away from the old industrialism).

[66] *See* RUDOLPH J. R. PERITZ, COMPETITION POLICY IN AMERICA, 1888-1992: HISTORY, RHETORIC, LAW 78 (1996); Ellis Hawley, *Three Facets of Hooverian Associationalism: Lumber, Aviation, and Movies, 1921-1930, in* REGULATION IN PERSPECTIVE 95, 97 (Thomas K. McGraw, ed., 1981); *see also* Allen R. Kamp, *Between-the-Wars Social Thought: Karl Llewellyn, Legal Realism, and the Uniform Commercial Code in Context*, 59 ALB. L. REV. 325, 373-75 (1995) (describing the growth of trade associations from the 19th century to the 1920s).

[67] *See, e.g.*, VALERIE JEAN CONNER, THE NATIONAL WAR LABOR BOARD 18 (1983).

[68] *See id.* at 21, 28; *See also*, Jones, *supra.* note 43 at 249-50; *The United States Arbitration Act and its Applications*, 11 A.B.A. REP. 153, 153 (1925).

[69] JOSEPH HENRY FOTH, TRADE ASSOCIATIONS: THEIR SERVICES TO INDUSTRY 21-22 (1930); *see also* NATIONAL INDUSTRIAL CONFERENCE BOARD, *supra.* note 39 at 25-27 (discussing how the exigencies of World War I led the government to work with and rely upon trade associations).

[70] *See* ROBERT F. BURK, THE CORPORATE STATE AND THE BROKER STATE: THE DUPONTS AND AMERICAN NATIONAL POLITICS 1925-1940, at 16-17 (1990).

[71] *See* generally HERBERT HOOVER, THE MEMOIRS OF HERBERT HOOVER: YEARS OF ADVENTURE, 1874-1920, at 239-80 (1951) (discussing Hoover's time at the Food Administration).

[72] *See* BENJAMIN S. KIRSH, TRADE ASSOCIATIONS: THE LEGAL ASPECTS 14 (1928) (quoting Herbert Hoover from 1922 SECRETARY OF COM. ANN. REP. 30). *See* generally Hawley, *supra* note 65 at 117-19 (describing Hoover's support of a synthesis between the old and new systems).

[73] *See* Hawley, *Three Facets of Hooverian Associationalism, supra* note 66 at 99.

[74] Robert L. Rabin, *Federal Regulation in Historical Perspective*, 38 STAN. L. REV. 1189, 1237 (1986).

[75] *See* HERBERT HOOVER, THE MEMOIRS OF HERBERT HOOVER: THE CABINET AND THE PRESIDENCY, 1920-1933, at 62 (1951).

[76] *Id.* at 172-73; *see also* PERITZ, *supra* note 66 at 86-87 (describing standard setting in the lumber industry).

[77] *See Report of the Committee on Commerce, Trade and Commercial Law*, *supra* note 66 at 293-94.

[78] LOUIS GALAMBOS, COMPETITION AND COOPERATION: THE EMERGENCE OF A NATIONAL TRADE ASSOCIATION 74 (1968).

[79] *See* Gerald P. Berk, *Approaches to the History of Regulation*, in REGULATION IN PERSPECTIVE 187, 197 (Thomas K. McGraw, Ed. 1981).

[80] *See* HOOVER, MEMOIRS, *supra* note 75 at 68-69.

[81] *See, e.g.*, Comment, *Arbitration and Award: Commercial Arbitration in California*, 17 CAL. L. REV. 643, 664 (1929) ("[A]rbitration may be successful only where both parties are willing to arbitrate, or where the parties are members of trade or industrial organizations in which there are common interests, conducive to co-operation.").

[82] Cohen & Dayton, *supra* note 45, at 281.

[83] National Industrial Conference Board, TRADE ASSOCIATIONS: THEIR ECONOMIC SIGNIFICANCE AND LEGAL STATUS 280 (1925).

[84] *Id.*

[85] There was a paradox, however: It should not have been necessary to have laws to compel arbitration in disputes between trade association members because membership in a common organization created not only a spirit of cooperation but also the availability of "extrajudicial methods" for enforcing arbitration agreements. As one lawyer noted at the time, the bylaws of many trade associations provided that members who refused to arbitrate disputes would be expelled. Others authorized lesser penalties, such as publishing in the industry trade journal the name of any member who refused to arbitrate a dispute with another member. For their part, the courts upheld such measures when they were challenged. Thus one is left to wonder why the commercial community made legal enforceability of arbitration agreements such a high priority. See Philip G. Phillips, *Commercial Arbitration under the N.R.A.*, 1 CHI. L. REV. 424, 426-28 (1933).

[86] Bernhardt v. Polygraph Co., 350 U.S. 198 (1956). See generally, Stone, *Rustic Justice*, *supra* n. 35, at 944-45.

[87] *See* Richard W. Jennings, *Self-Regulation in the Securities Industry: The Role of the Securities and Exchange Commission*, 29 LAW & CONTEMP. PROBS. 663, 663 n. 2 (1964).

[88] *See* JOEL SELIGMAN, THE TRANSFORMATION OF WALL STREET: A HISTORY OF THE SECURITIES AND EXCHANGE COMMISSION AND MODERN CORPORATE FINANCE 5-6 (rev. Ed. 1995).

[89] *See* Securities Act of 1933, ch. 38, 48 Stat. 74 (current version at 15 U.S.C. §§ 77a-77aa (1994)); Banking Act of 1933, ch. 89, § 32, 48 Stat. 194 (current version at 12 U.S.C. § 78 (1994)).

[90] Act of June 6, 1934, ch. 404, 48 Stat. 881 (current version at 15 U.S.C. §§ 78a-78ll (1994)).

[91] *See* MICHAEL E. PARRISH, SECURITIES REGULATION AND THE NEW DEAL 181, 209; Jennings, *supra* note 87, at 677.

[92] *Reprinted in* WILLIAM O. DOUGLAS, DEMOCRACY AND FINANCE 82 (1940).

[93] *See* Norman S. Poser, *Making Securities Arbitration Work*, 50 SMU L. REV. 277, 280 (1996).

[94] *See, e.g.*, Dean Witter Reynolds, Inc. v. Byrd, 470 U.S. 213, 215 (1985) (describing the arbitration clause in the Customer's Agreement that the plaintiff signed when he first invested his funds with Dean Witter in 1981).

[95] *See* Poser, *supra* note 37, at 1097.

[96] 373 U.S. 341 (1963).

[97] *Id.* at 718.

[98] 29 U.S.C.A. §§ 151-169 (1998).

[99] *See, e.g.*, Mitsubishi Motors Corp. v. Soler Chrysler-Plymouth, Inc., 473 U.S. 614, 626 (1985) (referring to the presumption of arbitrability in *Steelworkers v. Warrior & Gulf Navigation Co.*, 363 U.S. 574 (1960)). *See* generally, Stone, *Rustic Justice, supra* n. 35 at 1014.

[100] JAMES B. ATLESON, LABOR AND THE WARTIME STATE: LABOR RELATIONS AND LAW DURING WORLD WAR II 60-65 (1998).

[101] § 301(a), 61 Stat. at 156 (codified at 29 U.S.C. § 185(a) (1994)).

[102] 353 U.S. 448 (1957).

[103] *Id.* at 451. At that time, a number of labor law scholars urged the court to interpret Section 301 in a way that respected the emerging role of arbitration in labor-management relations. See, e.g., Archibald Cox, *Reflections upon Labor Arbitration*, 72 HARV. L. REV. 1482, 1512 (1959); Harry Shulman, *Reason, Contract, and Law in Labor Relations*, 68 HARV. L. REV. 999, 1023-24 (1955). See generally, Katherine Van Wezel Stone, *The Postwar Paradigm in American Labor Law*, 90 YALE L. J. 1509 (1981).

[104] *See, e.g.*, United Paperworkers Int'l Union v. Misco, Inc., 484 U.S. 29, 36-37 (1987) (noting the preference for private arbitration in labor disputes); Boys Mkts., Inc. v. Retail Clerks Union, Local 770, 398 U.S. 235, 252 (1970) (noting the integral role arbitration plays in collective bargaining).

[105] 363 U.S. 564 (1960).

[106] 363 U.S. 574 (1960).

[107] 363 U.S. 593 (1960).

[108] *See* United Steel Workers v. Warrior & Gulf Navigation Co., 363 U.S. 574, 582-83 (1960).

[109] United Steelworkers v. Warrior & Gulf Navigation Co., 363 U.S. 574, 581 (1960).

[110] *Id.* at 578.

[111] 363 U.S. at 581. Douglas' description of collective bargaining has been termed "industrial pluralism." Stone, The *Post-War Paradigm, supra* n. 103 at 1511. In this view, management and labor are like political parties in a representative democracy—each represents its own constituency and, as in a legislature, engages in debate and compromise. Thus management and labor together determine wages and working conditions through a legislative-type process. These rules are embodied in the collective bargaining agreement, which the industrial pluralist metaphor calls a statute or a constitution. *See* generally, Stone, *id.* at 1514-1515 (summarizing the industrial pluralist view).

[112] 363 U.S. at 581. Douglas was not alone in characterizing the unionized workplace as industrial self-government. *See* Archibald Cox, *Some Aspects of the Labor Management Relations Act, 1947*, 61 HARV. L. REV. 1, 1 (1947); Harry Shulman, *Reason, Contract, and Law in Labor Relations*, 68 HARV. L. REV. 999, 1002-03 (1955). A central aspect of the self-regulatory ideal, and the mini-democracy metaphor they employed, was the role of arbitration. *See* generally Stone, *The Post-War Paradigm, id.* at 1515.

[113] 460 U.S. 1 (1983). *Compare* Moses Cone Mem'l Hosp., 460 U.S. at 24-25 (holding that "any doubts concerning the scope of arbitrable issues [under collective bargaining agreements] should be resolved in favor of arbitration") with Warrior & Gulf Navigation Co., 363 U.S. at 582-83 ("An order to arbitrate . . . should not be denied unless it may be said with positive assurance that the arbitration clause is not susceptible of an interpretation that covers the asserted dispute. *Doubts should be resolved in favor of coverage*" (emphasis added)). *See generally*, Jonathan R. Nelson, *Judge-Made Law and the Presumption of Arbitrability:* David L. Threlkeld & Co. v. Metallgesellschaft Ltd., 58 BROOK. L. REV. 279, 303 (1992) (noting that the Court transplanted the presumption of arbitrability from *Warrior & Gulf* to *Moses H. Cone* and arguing that there was neither federal labor policy nor international commercial considerations to justify such a fundamental transformation in arbitration jurisprudence).

[114] 430 U.S. 243 (1977).

[115] *See, e.g.*, Sweet Dreams Unlimited, Inc. v. Dial-A-Mattress Int'l, Ltd., 1 F.3d 639, 643 (7th Cir. 1993) (applying reasoning of *Nolde Bros.*, a Section 301 case concerning the applicability of arbitration after a collective agreement has expired, to an FAA case). See also, First Options of Chicago, Inc. v. Kaplan, 514 U.S. 938, 942-44 (1995) (conflating Section 301 cases and FAA cases concerning arbitration); *accord*, Mastrobuono v. Shearson Lehman Hutton, Inc., 514 U.S. 52, 56-58 (1995).

[116] 346 U.S. 427 (1953).

[117] 473 U.S. 614 (1985).

[118] *Id.* at 626.

[119] 482 U.S. 220 (1987).

[120] 18 U.S.C. Sec. 1862(c).

[121] *Id.* at 223.

[122] 490 U.S. 499 (1989).

[123] The major new issue posed in *Gilmer* was the interpretation of the contracts of employment exclusion in Section 1 of the FAA. As discussed above, the Supreme Court declined to decide that issue.

[124] From a practical perspective, information an outsider requires to meet its burden of proof is often in the insiders' possession. *See, e.g.,* David S. Schwartz, *Enforcing Small Print to Protect Big Business, supra* n. 8 at 46-49 (discussing cases in which lack of discovery hindered plaintiff in employment discrimination arbitration).

[125] 835 F. Supp. 1104 (D. Minn. 1993).

[126] *See* generally, Stone, *Mandatory Arbitration, supra* n. 8 at 1036-1041.

[127] GAO Study, *supra* n. 3, at 12-14; Bickner et al., *supra* n. 6, at 80-81. In the GAO survey only 3 of 26 arbitration policies contained discovery procedures. Arbitrator costs were either split evenly (9 policies), included a limited employee contribution (6 policies), paid entirely by the employer (4 policies), or not discussed at all (7 policies). Sixteen of 26 policies provided for a written decision, although some only required summary conclusions: GAO, *id.* at 13-15. In the Bickner et al. survey, about two-thirds of plans provided for discovery, though usually with limitations, half required the employee to share all or part of the arbitrator's costs, while half did not require an employee contribution, and only some of the plans required findings of fact and conclusions. Some also allowed oral decisions: Bickner et al., *id.* at 80-81.

[128] 921 S.W.2d 817 (Tex. Ct. App. 1996).

[129] Lisa B. Bingham, *Employment Arbitration: The Repeat Player Effect,* 1 EMPLOYEE RIGHTS AND EMPLOYMENT POLICY JOURNAL 189 (1997).

[130] Calculated from Eisenberg-Clermont database, *infra* n. 10.

[131] Stirlen v. Supercuts, 60 Ca. Rptr. 2d 138, 158-59 (Ct. App. 1997).

[132] 105 F.3d 1465, 1479-83 (D.C. Cir. 1997).

[133] The argument that courts should create a special law for employment arbitration because of the unique nature of the employment relationship has been rejected. Rather, all the Courts of Appeals except the Ninth Circuit have refused to apply the FAA's statutory exclusion for contracts of employment to ordinary employment arbitrations.

[134] Cf. Gregory S. Alexander, *Dilemmas of Group Autonomy: Residential Associations and Community,* 75 CORNELL LAW REV. 1, 44-47 (1989) (arguing that homeowner associations lack genuine participatory self-governance and thus do not foster civic participation or small-scale democracy).

[135] *Southland* involved a dispute between a franchisee and a franchiser about alleged acts of fraud and breach of contract. *Mitsubishi* involved a franchise relationship between Chrysler and Soler in which the franchisee accused the franchiser of violations of the Sherman Antitrust Act. *Doctors Associates v. Casaretto* involved an attempt by a franchisee to arbitrate fraud and breach of good faith claims.

CHAPTER 3

Agreements to Arbitrate and the Waiver of Rights under Employment Law

ARNOLD M. ZACK
Arbitrator

Among the core issues for those of us involved in collective bargaining has always been the development of a system of procedural and substantive rights to provide a standard of fairness and a level playing field in resolving workplace disputes. For half a century unions and management have fine-tuned those standards by negotiation, sometimes with the help of mediators and occasionally with some prodding by arbitrators, to achieve a credible forum for resolving workplace disputes. But though we may flatter ourselves to believe that we provide a societal panacea, our universe of concern has been in the small portion of the workforce that is unionized.

In the last decade an arbitration structure quite foreign to our experience has arisen in the much larger nonunionized workforce. It is foreign because it has not evolved from joint negotiation of its terms by the parties of relatively equal power willing to be bound by such agreement. Rather, it has evolved because one side, the employer, crafts the arbitration system and requires job applicants to sign the agreement to gain employment or for existing employees to continue their employment. This new arbitration structure imposes on employees a commitment to waive procedural, substantive, and, indeed, statutory rights at the time of signing, well before they could be aware of any potential statutory violations or their rights under the law. This form of arbitration with restrictions on the employee's choice of arbitrator, on their right to representation, and even without an obligation to issue a written opinion following the law was endorsed by the United States Supreme Court in its 1991 *Gilmer* decision (*Gilmer v. Interstate Johnson Lane Corporation*, 500 U. S. 29). The rush of employers to craft such arbitration agreements for their employees to sign on hire has placed under a cloud the heralded fairness that the public has for half a century ascribed to "our" labor-management arbitration. The deprivation of rights under such procedures has not gone unnoticed by the press, Congress, the labor-management community, civil rights groups, designating agencies, the lower courts, and even the very security industry that spawned the *Gilmer* case.

There is increasing reason to hope that even if *Gilmer* remains the law of the land, it will be possible to provide employees in the nonunionized sector the same elements of fairness long accepted as reasonable in the unionized sector in labor-management arbitration. But whether fairness and equity are attained in these new procedures or the inequities of "cram down" employer-imposed arbitration are perpetuated, spreading adoption of nonnegotiated arbitration structures raise serious problems for our labor-management community. These include the following:

- Will individual employees in employer-crafted systems have adequate access to representation to provide assistance in pursuing their statutory and equity claims? Is this a potential role for trade unions?

- Will the Supreme Court endorsement of employer-crafted arbitration systems accelerate the move toward a uniform termination-at-will statute and the governmentally provided arbitration that such a path contemplates? What impact might that have on collective bargaining relationships?

- What will be the impact of these new arbitration systems on the effectiveness of trade unions organizing in the nonunionized sector?

- Should unions seek the integration of such statutory arbitration procedures into their collective bargaining agreements to co-opt the resolution of statutory employment issues into the collective bargaining dispute settlement structure?

This chapter examines some though not all of the issues listed above. More specifically, it explores the evolution of the basic problem, its current dimensions, and the prospects for overcoming the deprivation of procedural and substantive rights which plague those covered under these new employment arbitration disputes settlement structures.

The Labor Management Model of Arbitration

Those of us who have grown up and indeed grown old in the field of labor-management arbitration have a rather myopic view of what is now called "employment arbitration." We point with pride to the success of the process in maintaining industrial stability and tranquillity in the American workforce for more than half a century. However, in our pride we seem to ignore the fact that negotiated labor-management arbitration protects less than 16% of the workforce if we count those covered by collective bargaining agreements. Although labor-management arbitration is virtually universal in the organized sector, more than 84% of the 126 million person workforce have no such negotiated protection.

In addition, we cite with approval the role of the Supreme Court in endorsing and encouraging the final and binding nature of labor-management arbitration awards and the parties' right to establish their own internal judicial system for monitoring their agreements. We often scoff at the inadequacies of the labor-management partners in other countries in failing to match our achievement in developing such a sophisticated system of private self-regulation and governance. We hail the self-defined fairness of the process, which has evolved over years of collective bargaining negotiation between each union and management, with negotiated procedures for the appeal of cases, and the selection of the arbitrator, and the rules and authority under which the arbitrator operates. These standards are frequently amended in negotiation and tempered and monitored by the rulings of the parties' chosen arbitrators to ensure that the rights of the covered employees are adequately protected. Over the decades the procedures have evolved in similar fashion throughout industry and government creating a relatively uniform system of workplace justice and extending its benefits and protections to virtually all organized employees.

The pride we take in our sophisticated system of labor-management dispute settlement is indeed justified. The universality of grievance and arbitration systems throughout the organized sector has in fact virtually eliminated wildcat strikes, while strikes over interest disputes are at a continuing low. The conventional wisdom has been that the rest of the workforce has the right to join labor unions, that the union movement has the will and skill to organize, and that the labor-management model of arbitration to protect workplace rights will spread. But we seem to block out the reality that the more than 100 million workers who make up the rest of the workforce have long remained unorganized, with no collective bargaining and certainly without grievance and arbitration procedures to protect them and ensure their workplace rights. And the data suggest no immediate solution to their longstanding dilemma of denied rights. At its apex, the unionized sector embraced only a third of the workforce.

Since 1960 we in the labor-management arbitration field have been reassured by the endorsement of the fairness of our arbitration procedures by the decisions of the United States Supreme Court in the Steelworkers

Trilogy (*United States of America v. American Mfg. Co.*, 363 U.S. 564, 1960; *United Steelworkers of America v. Warrior and Gulf Navigation Co.*, 363 U.S. 574, 1960; *United Steelworkers of America v. Enterprise Wheel and Car Corp.*, 363 U.S. 593, 1960). At that time the Court went so far as to say that except for the judiciary's role in determining whether in fact the parties had agreed to grant authority to the arbitrator (substantive arbitrability disputes), the arbitrator would be the judge of procedural and substantive disputes between the parties. In *United Steelworkers v. Warrior and Gulf Navigation* the Court explicitly stated:

> In the commercial case, arbitration is a substitute for litigation. Here arbitration is a substitute for industrial strife.
>
> Arbitration is the means of solving the unforeseeable by molding a system of private law for all the problems which may arise and to provide for their solution in a way which will generally accord with the variant needs and desires of the parties.
>
> The ablest judge cannot be expected to bring the same experience and competence to bear on the termination of a grievance, because he cannot be similarly informed. (363 U.S. at 578-79)

This endorsement and encouragement followed the Court's examination of the process, the role of the grievance and arbitration system, the parties' role in selecting their choice of arbitrator, and their deferral to the arbitrator on all matters feeding into the process. In announcing their hands-off attitude toward labor arbitration in cases where the parties have empowered the arbitrator, the Court noted in *United Steelworkers v. American Manufacturing Co.*:

> The function of the court is very limited when the parties have agreed to submit all questions of contract interpretation to the arbitrator. It is confined to ascertaining whether the party seeking arbitration is making a claim which on its face is governed by the contract. Whether the moving party is right or wrong is a question of contract interpretation for the arbitrator. In these circumstances the moving party should not be deprived of the arbitrator's judgment when it is his judgment and all that it connotes that was bargained for. (363 U.S. at 567-68)

In short, the Court recognized the arbitrator and not the courts as the protector and enforcer of the rights that employees were provided under the parties' grievance and arbitration structure.

Court Restrictions on Arbitrators Deciding Statutory Issues

It was with great disappointment among the arbitrators, therefore, when fourteen years later in 1974, the Court in the case of *Alexander v. Gardner-Denver* stepped back from full endorsement of the arbitrator as the parties' final and only dispute settler (415 U.S. 36, 1974). Many arbitrators were crushed by the audacity of the Court in holding that our decisions on issues under the contract were not indeed final and binding when appealed to court. The Court held that even though the arbitrator had the contractual right to resolve workplace disputes, that authority did not bar the employee's right to appeal to administrative agencies and courts to enforce individual statutory rights, which existed outside the contract. The arbitrator who upheld Harrell Alexander's discharge for poor workmanship did not address his claim of racial discrimination. The Court held that the right to invoke the discrimination issue in court was exclusive to the employee and was not surrendered when he appealed a claim of unjust dismissal through to arbitration under the collective agreement. The Court held that Alexander had the right to pursue a statutory claim on discrimination grounds even though he had already lost his claim for reinstatement before the arbitrator. In footnote 19 the Court pointed out that because appeal to arbitration under the collective bargaining agreement was the exclusive prerogative of the union, it raised the specter of possible collusion between the employer and the union to discriminate against a worker of a different race. By declining to appeal an employee's case to arbitration the union could collude with the employer to block employee access to appeal to that step. So if the arbitrator's authority under the agreement extended to enforcement of statutory rights, it would leave the employee without any appeal to have his legal claim heard. Thus after *Alexander v. Gardner-Denver,* the employee's right to raise individual legal claims to administrative agencies and to the courts continued in both unionized and nonunion employment. Arbitration continued to resolve contractual claims in the union labor-management sector.

The Federal Arbitration Act

Outside the labor-management field, arbitration has long been invoked for a wide range of individual management agreements, commercial, construction, international, and other matters. In 1924 Congress enacted the Federal Arbitration Act, a statute recognizing the right of contracting parties to agree to employ an arbitrator of their mutual choice to resolve any disputes which might arise between them over implementation of their negotiated contract. Thus if a merchant in Chicago purchased a product from a vendor in New York, an arbitrator would be agreed upon to resolve any dispute that might arise over whether the shipped product fulfilled their contractual commitment. The language of the act specified that it was not to apply to contracts of employment in interstate commerce.

With the Federal Arbitration Act applying to disputes other than those arising from employment relationships, the only employment arbitration occurring outside collective bargaining was an occasional executive employment contract negotiated between an employer and a prospective managerial employee. These employees presumably had enough knowledge and clout to negotiate the terms and procedures under which any arbitration of disputes between them would take place. Such agreements were entered into voluntarily with both parties having relatively equal bargaining power in agreeing to the terms and conditions of the contract and the arbitration provision for resolving disputes thereunder. Thus prior to 1991 the Federal Arbitration Act was not viewed as applying to contracts of employment involving an employer and its employees, let alone requiring arbitration of statutory issues that had theretofore been resolved only through litigation in administrative agencies and/or the courts.

The Court Empowers Arbitrators to Decide Statutory Issues

That all changed in 1991 when the Supreme Court issued its decision in *Gilmer v. Interstate Johnson Lane Corporation* (500 U.S. 24). That case involved Robert Gilmer, a 62-year-old securities representative employed by the New York Stock Exchange under a National Association of Securities Dealers (NASD) Form U-4 Registration arrangement which mandated arbitration of "any dispute claim or controversy" arising with his employer. When he was terminated and replaced by a 28-year-old as senior vice president, he sought to file an age discrimination in employment claim with the EEOC. His employer sought to block the ADEA claim asserting that Gilmer was committed to arbitrate the dispute under the terms of the arbitration agreement he signed when hired.

The case was appealed to the U.S. Supreme Court. In its decision the Court held that the Federal Arbitration Act "manifests a liberal federal policy favoring arbitration," that the act applied to contracts of employment outside actual interstate transportation, and that the arbitration agreement Gilmer signed was undertaken both knowingly and voluntarily (500 U.S. 29, 1991). It took the position that the existence of unequal bargaining power between the employer and the job applicant did not bar enforcement of the commitment to arbitrate since the "FAA's purpose was to place arbitration agreements on the same footing as other contracts" (500 U.S. 33, 1991). The decision restricted the definition of interstate commerce to that in use at the time of the passage of the statute. It went further to require Gilmer to exhaust the procedures he had agreed to under the arbitration agreement which he signed as a condition of accepting his employment. That in turn meant that the statutory claim would be resolved in arbitration, depriving him of any right to invoke litigation to enforce his claimed violation of the Age Discrimination in Employment Act.

The *Gilmer* decision is noteworthy because for the first time it applied the Federal Arbitration Act, which had been enacted to resolve commercial disputes, to the arbitration of a statutory issue, saying that there was nothing in the ADEA or its legislative history precluding arbitration of such disputes. It dismissed the notion that arbitration panels appointed by the industry would be biased in favor of the employer, as well as the idea that discovery would be narrower than in the federal courts. It noted that "by agreeing to arbitrate a statutory claim, a party does not forgo the substantive rights afforded by the statute; it only submits their resolution in an arbitral rather than a judicial forum" (citing *Mitsubishi Motors Corp. v. Soler Chrysler-Plymouth, Inc.* 473 U.S. 624 at 628 [1985]).

In short, the Supreme Court held that a securities broker who, on hire, had signed a Securities Registration Agreement calling for arbitration of disputes concerning claims and fees arising in his work in the securities industry was mandated to arbitrate a claim of age discrimination which otherwise could be pursued through the EEOC and the courts. That is so even though the statutory issue in dispute was not listed in the initial arbitration coverage since the arbitration "agreement" ceded to the employer the right to change the terms of the agreement after the applicant's signature was affixed.

How does the employee's mandated commitment to arbitrate stack up against the collective bargaining agreement or the commercial agreement to arbitrate or even the agreement crafted by an employer and a managerial executive to arbitrate employment issues? In those agreements there is relative parity of negotiating power, and the parties agree at signing to the coverage of the agreement. Although it could be argued that the unionized employee coming to work in the enterprise is, like Gilmer, bound by a preexisting agreement to arbitrate, that collective agreement is the product of years of negotiations on the employees' behalf by the union. The employer in that negotiating history has in fact recognized the union as the representative for its present and future employees.

Although the Court found that Gilmer had voluntarily agreed to arbitration under the NASD rules, it is difficult to agree that there was indeed voluntarism. Gilmer was a stockbroker seeking employment in an industry that embraced the NASD arbitration rules. If one were to ascribe common meaning to the term "voluntary," it would suggest that he undertook the arbitration forum rather than some other venue to resolve a pending dispute. But Gilmer's "choice" was made prior to any dispute arising when he signed the agreement to arbitrate at the time of hire. That, the Court asserts, was a voluntary signing because Gilmer could have opted to go work for some other employer which did not require such commitment to arbitrate. But the reality was that Gilmer had no alternative for practicing his craft with any other employer inasmuch as all securities firms subscribed to the same industrial structure. Thus his voluntary choice was to sign the agreement or seek work in some other profession or industry other than where he had previously earned his living.

It might have been just as reasonable for the Court to have taken the alternative position, i.e., that requiring the agreement to arbitrate was an unenforceable contract of adhesion, a contract which the employee had no practical alternative but to accept. In that light the grievant was forced to waive his right of free choice as to where to work. But that is not the only waiver of rights that Gilmer underwent in seeking to retain employment in the securities industry. The terms of the arbitration agreement bound Gilmer to further waiver of procedural rights that would protect him in court and even under a collective bargaining agreement.

For example, the panel of arbitrators was selected exclusively by the industry, and the employee had but one peremptory challenge of a name from that list before having an arbitrator assigned by the industry to decide his claim. The employer paid the arbitrator's fee rather than splitting it as is traditional in labor-management arbitration, placing the arbitrator in the awkward position of recognizing that selection in future cases is up to only one of the parties—the employer who pays the bill. Although the Court had asserted in the Mitsubishi case that arbitration was merely a substitute forum for the courts, the NASD arbitration structure had no requirement that the arbitrator be an attorney or be familiar with the statutes involved, or indeed even cite the law. In fact, the decision need not even be accompanied by a written opinion, precluding inquiry of whether the law had in fact been taken into consideration, let alone followed.

The deprivation of rights was made more appalling by the fact that the statutory issue at stake in that case, i.e., whether there had been a violation of the Age Discrimination in Employment Act, was not covered by the agreement when Gilmer signed it. The agreement he signed reserved to the employer the right to revise the arbitration procedure and the coverage thereof. It was in furtherance of that employer-retained right that the agreement was revised after the date of signing but before Gilmer's claim to extend to statutory issues such as the Age Discrimination in Employment Act.

Gilmer could have been decided narrowly. The Court could have avoided application of the Federal Arbitration Act on the grounds that Gilmer was an executive and beyond the ken of the employment contract standard of the Federal Arbitration Act. It could have followed the more contemporary standard of interstate commerce as being much broader than actual movement between states in defining the contract of employment. It could have established standards on which it or lower courts would review the fairness of employer procedures to make sure the standards, goals, and remedies of the statutes were met. It could have prescribed standards for establishing a fair arbitration panel or procedures for equality in selecting the arbitrator or requirements for the form of the award and remedy. It could have said the decision applied only to those statutes where there was no assurance of a right to a jury. But the Court's decision did none of these things.

Although the Court did not reverse *Alexander v. Gardner-Denver*, it created an anomaly. On the one hand, an employee in a unionized plant with a negotiated arbitration system and the right of representation continued to have individual access to the courts to assert statutory rights. On the other hand, an employee in a nonunion setting who signed an employer-promulgated arbitration agreement had waived any right to go to court, being bound instead to arbitrate under whatever conditions the employer had created, including presumably an arbitrator untutored in the law.

Burgeoning Employer-crafted Arbitration Schemes

There has been abundant speculation as to why the Court decided *Gilmer* as it did. Most observers claim it was an effort at achieving docket control for a federal court system which had seen case filings quadruple in the preceding two decades. (See, for example, U.S. Commission on the Future of Worker-Management Relations [Dunlop Commission] 1994: 124.) Whatever the motivation, the impact was clear. The Court gave a green light to thousands of employers to unilaterally develop arbitration procedures that waived the employees' traditional right to go to an administrative agency or court. Certainly the employee was free to go to work elsewhere, but if the job was needed, the employee was essentially required to sign. Even more insidiously, for employees already at work when the employer created the structure, the requirement was sign or lose your job. Many in the field continue to consider these as contracts of adhesion. That was not so for executives who could negotiate the terms of the arbitration agreement, but it was certainly so for those without such leverage.

In the years following the 1991 decision, employer-created systems multiplied with scant regard to due process and substantive law protections. In virtually all cases the employer paid the arbitrator's full fee and in many cases established the panel from which the employee may or may not have had a right of selection. The employee would have had no way of ascertaining the experience of the arbitrator in prior cases, while the employer certainly would have such records. Many systems proclaiming the procedure was to be kept "within the family" denied employees the right to legal representation and sometimes restricted the options for representation at all. Most restricted or prohibited discovery or depositions. Few, if any, mandated the arbitrator follow the law, and many required a decision without a written opinion. Virtually all prohibited the arbitrator from awarding punitive damages or attorneys' fees or even interest, confining the arbitrator to awarding only compensatory damages and often with a cap thereon. These arbitration schemes did spread, frequently enlisting the services of presumably neutral agencies such as the American Arbitration Association, Jams/Endispute, and CPR (Center for Professional Responsibility). These groups fulfilled the administrative roles relegated to them by the employer-promulgated systems such as providing facilities or arranging for hearings. But in doing so they followed the lead of the Supreme Court that such agreements were indeed knowing and voluntary and deserving of implementation.

Since the *Gilmer* decision most of the circuit courts have followed the lead of the Supreme Court in giving it broader application than the facts of the case warrant. Rather than confining the viability of the employer programs to the ADEA, they have approved the extension of *Gilmer* to other statutes and even into arbitration agreements negotiated between unions and management. All of the circuit courts except the ninth have extended the application of *Gilmer* to Title VII. On the other hand, all of the circuits except the fourth have taken the position that *Gilmer* does not apply in cases where there is a negotiated collective bargaining agreement.

The Turn from *Gilmer* to Fairness

The impact of the 1991 *Gilmer* decision endorsing "cram-down" mandatory arbitration and the deprivation of legal rights which employers were thereby able to impose on employees has begun to meet increasing resistance since that time. The negative reaction to the waiver of rights was registered by a number of forces concerned with the deprivation of statutory rights that it imposed.

Some of the negative reaction came from the press. The *Wall Street Journal* wrote an article pointing out the frustrations of an employee awarded $300 after seeking redress under an employer-promulgated system (Jacobs 1994). The male supervisor accused of sexually harassing a female employee pointed out that he had served as an arbitrator in such cases in the past, considered the NASD arbitration as rigged, and noted that there was no need to adhere to statutory standards in arbitrating such issues. Other articles highlighting the unfairness of statutory deprivations in arbitration followed (*Business Week* 1997).

The Commission on the Future of Worker Management Relations, chaired by Harvard Professor John T. Dunlop, was another source of negative reaction. Part of the commission's mission was to explore what could be done to help parties resolve workplace disputes without resort to the courts and government regulatory agencies. In its Fact Finding Report, the commission emphasized the deprivation of protection to the nonunionized workforce, the high cost and unavailability of legal representation or access to the courts for low-wage earners, and the need to provide workplace protection akin to that provided to the unionized sector through collective bargaining (Dunlop Commission 1994). The report noted the four-fold increase in federal court employment litigation from 1971 to 1991, restricting of enforcement agency funding with continuing decline in staff numbers, and a resulting increase in the EEOC backlog to 100,000 cases by 1995. It cited the need for protection for low-wage workers lacking representation and the deprivations of fairness and due process standards under employer-promulgated arbitration schemes. Chairman Dunlop asked this author to attempt to adapt the labor-management arbitration structure to this emerging problem.

Out of that came a significant challenge to *Gilmer*, the Due Process Protocol (reprinted in the Appendix). In August 1994, during a speech to the Council of the Labor and Employment Law Section of the American Bar Association, I pointed out the threat that talk of rigged arbitration posed to the credibility and integrity of "our" labor-management arbitration. That led the section to call for the establishment of a Due Process Task Force to fashion a set of standards to provide fairness and statutory compliance for workers forced to arbitration under employer-promulgated systems. The task force was composed of designees from the American Arbitration Association, the American Bar Association, the American Civil Liberties Union, the Federal Mediation and Conciliation Service, the National Academy of Arbitrators, the National Employment Lawyers Association, and the Society of Professionals in Dispute Resolution. It met from September 1994 until May 1995 to hammer out the Protocol. That document enumerated the following rights to which employees, unionized and unorganized, should be entitled in mediating and/or arbitrating employment disputes. Those rights included (1) a neutral administering agency to develop a demographically diverse roster of neutrals; (2) neutrals to be trained in the statutes in dispute; (3) the right of joint selection of the neutral from the panel; (4) access of the parties to the names of the parties who had most recently presented cases to the neutrals under consideration; (5) procedures for assuring discovery and a reasonable number of depositions; (6) the right of representation by a representative of the employee's own choosing; (7) a requirement that the opinion and decision of the arbitrator be in writing and consistent with the law; (8) the expectation that the arbitrator fashion a remedy consistent with that afforded by the statute under consideration; and (9) a right of limited judicial review.

Despite its unanimity on the foregoing elements of due process, the task force was unable to reach agreement on what should be the triggering event for introducing the Protocol. Some participants took the position that since the Court had found such agreements to arbitrate to be voluntary, the Protocol should apply to mandatory arbitration agreed to as a condition of hire or continued employment. The remainder took the view that despite the Court's ruling, such contracts to arbitrate, when crafted by the employer and imposed as a condition of hire or continued employment, were inherently unfair. A real voluntary agreement could only occur when there was a choice of forum once a dispute arose. Under that reasoning the triggering event for invocation of the Protocol should be a justiciable incident. Only then could there be a free and voluntary choice to use arbitration in lieu of the courts.

The impact of the Due Process Protocol spread. It was adopted by the Massachusetts Commission against Discrimination for cases under its jurisdiction (Dunlop and Zack 1997: 179-92). It was also promulgated in the Federal Register by the Department of Labor for cases involving claims under the Family and Medical Leave Act, several federal Whistleblower Statutes, and for monitoring compliance with OSHA and Title VII Settlement Agreements (*Federal Register* 1997). The House of Delegates of the American Bar Association adopted the Protocol at its winter meeting in 1997.

The EEOC and the NLRB have also both proclaimed their opposition to imposed arbitration. The EEOC stated its position in securing a permanent injunction on April 19, 1995, against an employer who required employees to sign arbitration agreements after 21 employees had filed EEOC complaints (*EEOC v. River Oaks Imaging and Diagnostic*, No. H-95-755, 1995 WL 264003, SD Texas). In its Motions on Alternative Dispute Resolution adopted one week later on April 25, 1995, it proclaimed its "opposition to agreements as a condition of initial or continued employment that mandate binding arbitration of employment discrimination disputes." It committed itself to continue receiving and processing discrimination charges without regard to the existence of a claimed obligation to arbitrate under an employer-created scheme. A similar position was taken by the National Labor Relations Board which held that terminating an employee through the use of an employer-promulgated arbitration structure that denied recourse to the board for enforcement of the act would be an unfair labor practice (*Great Western Bank*, Case No. 12-CA-16886 and *Bentley's Luggage Corp.*, Case No. 12-CA-16658, 1995).

One important result of the Protocol has been a change in attitude by the neutral designating agencies. The AAA as well as JAMS/Endispute adopted the Protocol and announced that they would only administer cases under a new set of employment rules that replicated Protocol standards. These neutral agencies and the CPR shifted from implementing any employer-promulgated system in which they were named designating agency to setting standards consistent with the Protocol under which they would administer disputes. The fact that the three major designating agencies have refused to be used to implement unfair procedures has put great pressure on the employers seeking to deprive their employees of basic due process. They have in effect told the employers with unfair systems that they can no longer gain the appearance of credibility by invoking the name of a prestigious neutral agency. In its September 15, 1997, *Guidelines to Employers*, the AAA noted:

The Association's experience and belief is that any ADR method used in the employment context is most effective when the parties knowingly and voluntarily agree on the process and have confidence in the neutrality of the mediator or arbitrator and the procedures and the institution under which the case is being administered. (*Currents* 1997)

The National Academy of Arbitrators, which had been the initiating force behind the Protocol, went further, proclaiming its commitment only to post-dispute agreements to arbitrate, recognizing that the current state of the law was otherwise. On May 21, 1997, the NAA adopted the following position,

We oppose mandatory employment arbitration as a condition of employment when it requires waiver of direct access to either a judicial or administrative forum for the pursuit of statutory rights. We recognize that given the current case law, NAA members may serve as arbitrators in these cases. (*Daily Labor Report* 1997)

The NAA also provided its members with a list of guidelines to encourage their working within the Due Process Protocol when doing such cases.

The challenge to *Gilmer* has also occurred on the political front with a number of bills introduced in Congress to bar such preemployment requirements to arbitrate, although none to date has resulted in congressional hearings or bills being passed. The several bills reflect a growing political concern over employees being dragooned into such procedures often in communities where there is no other employment alternative.

While bound by the precedent of the Supreme Court, some of the circuit courts have resisted extending the umbrella as widely as expected by *Gilmer* or as widely as employers empowered by *Gilmer* tried to extend their schemes. In *Duffield v. Robertson, Stephens and Co.* the 9th Circuit took the view that the Civil Rights Act of 1991 with its congressional "directive to read Title VII broadly so as to best effectuate its remedial purposes" would "preclude the enforceability of arbitration agreements imposed as a condition of employment" (1998 U.S. App. Lexis 9284 at 50). The Supreme Court on November 9, 1998, denied certiorari in *Duffield*, apparently respecting the 9th Circuit's view that the employees right to invoke Title VII in a lawsuit is not precluded by the employees having signed a commitment to arbitrate at the time of hire. Thus the 9th Circuit is the only or perhaps the first circuit in which employees who have been forced to sign such agreements now have the right to go to court on Title VII issues.

Much as the courts seek to embrace arbitration as a forum of preference, there are still several other areas in which the court may begin to restrict the impact of *Gilmer*. The first arose as a result of the *Wright v. Universal Maritime Services Corporation*, where the Supreme Court held that for any collective bargaining agreement to require arbitration of a statutory right, the submission of the statutory issue "must be particularly clear" (No. 96-2850, 1997 WL 422869, 4th Circuit July 29, 1997; Certiorari Granted 118 S. Ct. 1162, 1998). Justice Scalia, writing for the majority, distinguished the situation in *Wright* from that of *Gilmer* by emphasizing the need for an explicit inclusion of statutory issues and, therefore, the waiver of the right to go to court when the arbitration alternative was part of a collective rather than individual bargain. The decision overturned a 4th Circuit ruling similar to that in *Austin v. Owens Brockway Glass Container, Inc.* (78 F3rd 875, 4th Circuit, 1996). In that case, the 4th Circuit held that although the union rather than the individual is party to the arbitration agreement and the parties may not have negotiated to incorporate statutory coverage in their agreement to arbitrate, the claimant was still bound to that forum in lieu of the courts. A quite different standard for the unionized sector is that enunciated by the 11th Circuit in *Brisentine v. Stone and Webster Engineering Company* (117 F3rd 519, 1997). *Brisentine* held that statutory arbitration in the unionized context was acceptable if the agreement contained language embracing coverage of the specific statute, if it empowered the arbitrator to interpret and apply those statutes, and if the employee rather than the union had control over the right to appeal the case to arbitration.

Future questions for the courts may arise over mandatory arbitration where the statutes (particularly those postdating *Gilmer*) specify a claimant's right to a trial by jury, where the arbitrator has not conformed to the standards or tenets of the statute, or where the arbitrator's decision is at variance with the damage and remedy requirements of the statute. Although the courts are unlikely to take appeals on the merits of the dispute that had been arbitrated, they may be prone to take procedural challenges to the arbitration proceeding if it deprives employees of vital statutory rights. Perhaps the Supreme Court will even throw out employer procedures which it finds to be in violation of the standards provided by the Due Process Protocol. Among these, of course, would be insufficient discovery or depositions, the denial of a right of representation, or unfairness in the selection of the arbitrator. The *Gilmer* ruling itself concerned a rather narrow set of issues. While most of the circuit courts to date have not seen fit to confine their rulings to its narrow dictate, that trend may not continue indefinitely.

Finally, perhaps the most ironic post-*Gilmer* change has been the abandonment by the NASD itself of the industrywide requirement of mandatory arbitration. In July 1997, the NASD proposed that its rules be changed to abandon the requirement that all licensed brokerage employees must arbitrate discrimination disputes under the industry system (*Wall Street Journal* 1997). These were the same procedures that were the subject of the *Gilmer* endorsement. In the summer of 1998 the NASD left to the individual firms the choice of system they would adopt for resolving such disputes, and in October 1998 it went so far as to assert adoption of the Due Process Protocol (Feinberg interview 1998). On May 7, 1999, the Federal Register set forth the new NASD Rules expressly citing the Protocol as its standard (SR-NASD-99-08, May 7, 1999). The New York Stock Exchange and Merrill Lynch Investment Company have both taken the position that they would not compel arbitration as a condition of employment. The NYSE position was taken out of respect of the EEOC policy opposing predispute commitments to arbitrate and to avoid facilitating a practice that EEOC asserts undermines its efforts. Whether NASD will replicate those moves remains to be seen.

The Lessons of *Gilmer*

The foregoing history shows a number of things. For one, the labor-management system of arbitration which evolved through collective bargaining as the preferred procedure of unions and management for the resolution of their workplace disputes has achieved a standing and credibility which led employers empowered by the *Gilmer* decision to cash in on its reputation. As a consequence, there was a widespread undertaking to fabricate "look-alike" arbitration structures which in reality deprived employees of substantive and procedural rights. That movement has thwarted the commonly understood term "voluntary" in relation to arbitration: a choice of forums when seeking to resolve an immediate issue. Rather, "voluntary" has been expanded or misused to include the "choice" one makes to take or keep a job when the employer says, "Sign here for arbitration of whatever dispute you may have over employment during your future decades of work here, or go work elsewhere."

Second, our myopic view that we were the only game in town to resolve workplace disputes has ignored the fact that our system was contract-based, often requiring even unionized employees to pursue any individual statutory claims of workplace discrimination outside the traditional labor-management channel. The explosion in protective legislation in the past years may be evidence that workplace protection is better achieved through legislation than through the collective bargaining route which affects less than 16% of the workforce. But it is also an alert that the 84%-85% of workers in the unorganized sector need greater protection than is currently afforded by the courts and their employers to achieve workplace justice.

Still, despite the endorsement of restrictive employer-promulgated arbitration by the conservative docket controlling the Supreme Court, there has been a widespread effort to stake out protection of both procedural and substantive rights for employees. The initiative has come from the Congress, which after *Gilmer* sought stronger substantive protection for covered employees in several statutes. It has come from the Due Process Protocol and the recognition by designating agencies that their credibility as neutral agencies would be sacrificed by unprotesting participation in whatever system the employer left on their desks. And most importantly, it has come from several of the U.S. district and circuit courts which have sought to interpret *Gilmer* in a manner that can most practicably reconcile the holding of the Supreme Court with the goals of the disputed legislation to provide workplace protection against employers discrimination.

We in the labor-management community should recognize how we now fit into the broader picture of providing workplace equity. There are now more than 126 million people in the workforce. Most have the right to workplace protection afforded by statutes such as the wage and hour laws, Labor Management Relations Act, OSHA, Title VII, Americans with Disabilities Act, Age Discrimination in Employment Act, Family and Medical Leave Act, and whistleblower statutes. Employees seeking to exercise the rights provided by these statutes are usually on their own to initiate their claims to an administrative agency or the courts. When statutory issues overlap with contractual ones, trade unions will help employees enforce their contractual rights through the grievance procedure and traditional labor-management arbitration.

It is estimated that some 8 to 12 million employees work under *Gilmer*-type employer-promulgated systems of arbitration. At the same time, some 17.9 million employees work under collective bargaining agreements. Thus almost as many employees are covered by employer schemes providing for arbitration of statutory issues as are covered by unionized agreements calling for arbitration of contractual issues. And the nonunion schemes are clearer and consistent in their coverage of statutory issues, while the law is somewhat confused and practice varied in the union sector. Given this consistency, the nonunion system of statutory arbitration, *if done fairly*, could provide more employees with greater *statutory* protection than they may achieve through collective bargaining.[1] Such procedures would be faster, cheaper, and forgo the appeals to the court system on substantive issues while permitting shared selection of the decision maker.

Fortunately, the accelerating chorus of institutions troubled with the deprivation of workplace rights for such a significant portion of our workforce has brought into focus the need and opportunity provided by the current state of the law. The public is now focusing more on providing equitable procedures for resolving statutory issues for covered employees. It is in the interest of all that we encourage such equitable processes. It is of particular importance to those of us who come from the collective bargaining sector and wish to preserve the credibility of arbitration to make sure that those procedures do provide the protections they advertise to their employees.

What Can We Do?

While recognizing the suzerainty of the courts and hoping for a turn toward more liberal holdings which would minimize deprivations of procedural and substantive rights, we in the labor-management community must recognize our inability to alter the national landscape created as a consequence of the *Gilmer* decision. But with our experience and the continuing need to protect the integrity of our own arbitration we must do our share to bring about greater workplace equity in the nonunionized sector. Unions have done that for generations, lobbying for legislation that helps the unorganized as well as the unionized worker. The Adamson Eight-Hour-Day law in 1908 and most of the more recent civil rights statutes which *Gilmer* beneficiary companies have sought to override are excellent examples of that tradition. In order to achieve that goal there are several courses of action that could be explored.

First, can we help to make the *Gilmer*-type procedures more equitable and more just? Such procedures if administered fairly and consistently with the law could indeed provide a substitute forum for time-consuming and costly litigation that is too often subjected to endless costly appeals. Protocol-based procedures have the potential for bringing greater justice to more employees than if such employer-promulgated systems did not exist. Despite its mandatory nature, arbitration consistent with the Due Process Protocol provides a faster process than litigation, precludes endless and costly appeals, and in most cases is funded by the employer compared with the requirement of having to hire a lawyer to go to an administrative agency or to litigation. The most pressing issue has been to make sure that the procedures are fair. Except for the mandatory, cram-down nature of the *Gilmer*-type structures, most such procedures have been brought in line with the requirements of the Due Process Protocol. At least that is true of cases being administered by the neutral designating agencies such as AAA, JAMS/Endispute, and CPR. The NASD structure is currently undergoing change, abandoning the industrywide system that spawned *Gilmer* and working to develop structures consistent with the Protocol within the individual brokerage firms.

Beyond achieving compliance with the Protocol, there is still much that can be done to make these structures more conforming to statute and more accessible to employees. The litany of litigation goes on, and one area yet unexplored is whether the arbitration decision is in substantial conformity to what would have occurred in litigation. The mantra that arbitration is merely a substitute forum needs further verification. We in our various roles should support litigation which seeks to protect the rights of workers by assuring procedural due process protections as well as substantive law allegiance and conformity to statutory remedy provisions.

Second, can we help to level the playing field by ensuring employees representation in such nonunion proceedings? Most of these cases lack the glamour, big salaries, and high fees which characterize many of the employment law cases. An effort should be mounted by worker and protective organizations such as the ACLU, NELA, Working Today, the union movement, and the labor bar to provide representation to employees asserting their rights under such structures. The element of the Protocol which guarantees employees the right of representation accomplishes little if there is no resource to provide such representation when cases arise. The rules of the AAA do provide that the AAA office will help to secure such assistance. Unfortunately, there is seldom a local agency equipped to provide that assistance with substantive knowledge in the discrimination or employment law field. But the worker-oriented organizations should take the initiative to provide a national cadre of worker representatives, attorneys or not, who are conversant with the statutes involved to make the right of representation truly meaningful.

Third, we should begin to accelerate efforts to achieve the adoption of the termination-at-will legislation which has been reported by the

Commissioners of Uniform State Laws. Although Montana is the sole state which does currently provide an arbitration structure for resolving termination cases consistent with the standards of just cause, the need is much more widespread to provide standards of just cause and fairness for employees who lose their jobs throughout the unorganized sector. The great majority of industrialized nations and even many developing nations of the world have labor courts to protect employees against employer violation of protective legislation usually providing the employees with free access to such tribunals. In the United States, however, there is no such governmental safety net for our 126 million workers. In the nonunion sector there is no equity standard to invoke on termination and no forum where workers can invoke it. Employees are on their own to utilize the administrative and court system to enforce whatever statutory rights they might claim violated. And unionized employees are not exempt from the financial burden of resort to the courts. But for the rare *Brisentine*-type conjecturers, our collective bargaining arbitration system focuses on the interpretation of collective agreements rather than on enforcement of external statutory law against discrimination, unfair dismissal, excessive hours, subminimum wages and the like. While contractual and statutory issues may overlap, there are still ample occasions where union members must pursue their statutory rights through the courts at their own expense.

While one objection to legislation providing a labor court or arbitration under the Uniform Act might be that it would undercut the role of union organizing as the preferred means of securing such arbitration rights, the reality is different. Union membership remains relatively stagnant as more and more jobs are created, and an enormous underclass of unorganized workers still has no protection against unfair dismissal. The rate of unionization is in fact greater in many countries such as Germany or Scandinavian countries which have long had such labor courts. Certainly the unionized sector and even the *Gilmerized* sector could be argued as having such protections. But the reality is that there are over 100 million workers who have no such protection and who, when they are terminated for a reason other than a claimed statutory violation, have little recourse and few rights. The model statute and even comparable federal legislation could and should be enacted to ensure that employees who are terminated for reasons other than statutory violation still have a forum where they can be protected against the arbitrary and capricious wrongdoing of their employers.

Fourth, unions themselves should consider the organizing potential of seeking out enterprises where employer-promulgated systems are in place and make available to employees representation in their appeals to arbitration. If the AFL-CIO has been able to offer direct union membership and credit card services to employees in unorganized enterprises, it should be able to provide some form of low-cost legal service insurance or representation to employees who may represent a viable organizing potential for the future. Considering that such enterprises are usually large with many employees becoming the victims of termination, involvement with these employee claims may provide information valuable to organizing (knowing the extent of the employers dismissal activity and the reasons therefore) as well as grateful new members.

Fifth, unions might consider the introduction of Gilmer-type systems into their own collective bargaining structures. While the 4th Circuit in the *Owens Brockway* and *Wright* cases held that union-management arbitration agreements obligated unions to process such cases under their collective bargaining agreements, the prevailing view has become that represented by the *Brisentine* case cited above. With the advent of significant discrimination legislation in the past few years and with the focus of those disputes being in the administrative agencies and the courts, it may be time for the unions to reassess their contract language. There is a significant representation role to be played in this field. Restructuring the parties' collective agreements to provide that arbitrators have the right to issue decisions on statutory issues that are consistent with the law and to give the employee the right to appeal such a dispute to the arbitration step might reveal significant areas where the employer has deprived employees of their rights, might give the unions a more forceful representation role, and might permit the parties to steer such disputes to professional arbitrators of their own choice.

Sixth, there should be reconsideration by the labor-management arbitrators of whether they should be doing such cases where the employer pays the full or predominant fee and where the employer rather than the union is more likely to reuse arbitrator's services. In the labor-management field we arbitrators are accustomed to our names being known by a small circle of partisans and to our fees being evenly shared between the parties. The nonunionized sector is different. And while the *Gilmer* decision certainly legitimizes the role of arbitrators handling such employer-paid cases, they may raise perceptions of bias on the part of unionized employees sensitive to neutrals' dependence on employers for increasing volumes of work. Such practices certainly skew the traditional wisdom that arbitrators are neutral because both parties share equally in paying their bills. The issue is not that doing such cases is unethical, nor is the issue the fact that working in the unorganized sector makes one complicit with management in attempting to evolve and implement a union avoidance strategy. Rather, the issue is simply one of perception and disclosure. Employees in the labor-management world are entitled to full disclosure of cases where the arbitrator has received compensation from one party. Serving as a consultant to an advocate may be considered a breach of the Code of Professional Responsibility. Is the situation any different if the employer is a nonunionized plant which pays the arbitrator's full fee? The issue need not constitute a violation of the code, if disclosed. The issue then becomes one of whether the arbitrator routinely fully discloses such employer payments, and for how long after such payments must disclosure be made? And if disclosed, is there a quantum of expected employer-paid work which would adversely impact on the arbitrator's neutrality or the parties' perception thereof? As this work becomes a bigger portion of the practice of labor management, it raises more and more issues of arbitrator neutrality or perceptions thereof.

Seventh, the murky area of statutory dispute settlement would greatly profit by extensive research into its breadth, depth, and potential. The New York State School of Industrial and Labor Relations at Cornell is now doing a survey among established neutrals to determine how much of their case load involves mediation and arbitration of noncollective bargaining issues and, in particular, to determine the amount of statutory arbitration that is being done. That may give us some guidance as to the number of cases which are coming to mediation and arbitration, but it does not tell us how widespread the use of employer-promulgated systems has become. The American Arbitration Association, Jams/Endispute, CPR, the United States Mediation and Arbitration, Inc., and other designating agencies all have clients who make these systems available. But there has been little research done as to whether these are pre- or post-dispute systems and little research done to determine whether their structures are in fact fair or in conformity to the Due Process Protocol. Nor indeed has there been any investigation as to the percentage of disputes administered by the bodies which involve statutes rather than collective bargaining look-alike termination cases. And within the statutory area, there is desperate need to determine which statutes the claimants are invoking. Beyond the private sector there are cases where government agencies are in the position to defer cases to ADR. The U.S. Department of Labor Federal Register listing promises to encourage employers to use mediation and arbitration for Family and Medical

Leave claims, whistleblower disputes, and enforcement of agreements resolving Title Seven and OSHA disputes. There is need for research as to the volume of such cases in the past and their potential for the future. Similar enforcement procedures run through legislation covering other aspects of employment as administered by a diverse number of federal agencies. These should be examined and categorized to determine the full range of the market for ADR. That problem is exacerbated when one thinks of the employment laws and regulations in the fifty states. They too should be explored to gain a reasonable estimate of the universe for application of ADR in the employment field.

Conclusion

The landscape of employment arbitration has changed. Many of the organizations and institutions in the country have concluded that the Supreme Court overreached in its *Gilmer* decision. Our concern should not be over the Gilmers of the workforce. They are educated and sophisticated and may indeed have the leverage to negotiate arbitration agreements with a realistic anticipation of what they are getting into. Our real concern should be for the tens of millions who are forced into signing such agreements under threat of not securing or retaining employment. They are powerless to avoid mandatory arbitration and should be assured legal protection. Ironically, however, with a fair system they may be better off than those who are free to fend through the courts. Our society is rich enough to be able to provide a fair and inexpensive system for resolving their workplace disputes, now perhaps through postdispute employer-promulgated arbitration systems consistent with the Protocol and perhaps in the near future through adoption of state-sponsored arbitral forums to which employees may bring their cases for rapid, inexpensive resolution before qualified neutrals. The development of arbitration in the nonunion sector has created a new process with its own problems for the parties and the arbitrators. The system is here to stay. It has the potential for providing more equity to more employees. The question is how to harness this new monster in our midst to meet those same goals of employee fairness that spawned the labor-management model of dispute resolution.

APPENDIX

A Due Process Protocol for Mediation and Arbitration of Statutory Disputes Arising out of the Employment Relationship

The following Protocol is offered by the undersigned individuals, members of the Task Force on Alternative Dispute Resolution in Employment, as a means of providing due process in the resolution by mediation and binding arbitration of employment disputes involving statutory rights. The signatories were designated by their respective organizations, but the Protocol reflects their personal views and should not be construed as representing the policy of the designating organizations.

Genesis

This task force was created by individuals from diverse organizations involved in labor and employment law to examine questions of due process arising out of the use of mediation and arbitration for resolving employment disputes. In this Protocol we confine ourselves to statutory disputes.

The members of the task force felt that mediation and arbitration of statutory disputes conducted under proper due process safeguards should be encouraged in order to provide expeditious, accessible, inexpensive and fair private enforcement of statutory employment disputes for the 100,000,000 members of the workforce who might not otherwise have ready, effective access to administrative or judicial relief. They also hope that such a system will serve to reduce the delays which now arise out of the huge backlog of cases pending before administrative agencies and courts and that it will help forestall an even greater number of such cases.

Pre- or Post-Dispute Arbitration

The task force recognizes the dilemma inherent in the timing of an agreement to mediate and/or arbitrate statutory disputes. It did not achieve consensus on this difficult issue. The views in this spectrum are set forth randomly as follows:

- Employers should be able to create mediation and/or arbitration systems to resolve statutory claims, but any agreement to mediate and/or arbitrate disputes should be informed, voluntary, and not a condition of initial or continued employment.
- Employers should have the right to insist on an agreement to mediate and/or arbitrate statutory disputes as a condition of initial or continued employment. Postponing such an agreement until a dispute actually arises when there will likely exist a stronger redisposition to litigate will result in very few agreements to mediate and/or arbitrate, thus negating the likelihood of effectively utilizing alternative dispute resolution and overcoming the problems of administrative and judicial delays which now plague the system.
- Employees should not be permitted to waive their right to judicial relief of statutory claims arising out of the employment relationship for any reason.
- Employers should be able to create mediation and/or arbitration systems to resolve statutory claims, but the decision to mediate and/or arbitrate individual cases should not be made until after the dispute arises.

The task force takes no position on the timing of agreements to mediate and/or arbitrate statutory employment disputes, though it agrees that such agreements be knowingly made. The focus of this Protocol is on standards of exemplary due process.

Right of Representation

Choice of Representative. Employees considering the use of or, in fact, utilizing mediation and/or arbitration procedures should have the right to be represented by a spokesperson of their own choosing. The mediation and arbitration procedure should so specify and should include reference to institutions which might offer assistance, such as bar associations, legal service associations, civil rights organizations, trade unions, etc.

Fees for Representation. The amount and method of payment for representation should be determined between the claimant and the representative. We recommend, however, a number of existing systems which provide employer reimbursement of at least a portion of the employee's attorney fees, especially for lower paid employees. The arbitrator should have the authority to provide for fee reimbursement, in whole or in part, as part of the remedy in accordance with applicable law or in the interests of justice.

Access to Information. One of the advantages of arbitration is that there is usually less time and money spent in pretrial discovery. Adequate but limited pretrial discovery is to be encouraged and employees should have access to all information reasonably relevant to mediation and/or arbitration of their claims. The employees' representative should also have reasonable prehearing and hearing access to all such information and documentation.

Necessary prehearing depositions consistent with the expedited nature of arbitration should be available. We also recommend that prior to selection of an arbitrator, each side should be provided with the names, addresses, and phone numbers of the representatives of the parties in that arbitrator's six most recent cases to aid them in selection.

Mediator and Arbitrator Qualification

Roster Membership. Mediators and arbitrators selected for such cases should have skill in the conduct of hearings, knowledge of the statutory issues at stake in the dispute, and familiarity with the workplace and employment environment. The roster of available mediators and arbitrators should be established on a nondiscriminatory basis, diverse by gender, ethnicity, background, experience, etc., to satisfy the parties that their interest and objectives will be respected and fully considered.

Our recommendation is for selection of impartial arbitrators and mediators. We recognize the right of employers and employees to jointly select as mediator and/or arbitrator one in whom both parties have requisite trust even though not possessing the qualifications here recommended as most promising to bring finality and to withstand judicial scrutiny. The existing cadre of labor and employment mediators and arbitrators, some lawyers, some not, although skilled in conducting hearings and familiar with the employment milieu is unlikely, without special training, to consistently possess knowledge of the statutory environment in which these disputes arise and of the characteristics of the nonunion workplace.

There is a manifest need for mediators and arbitrators with expertise in statutory requirements in the employment field who may without special training lack experience in the employment area and in the conduct of arbitration hearings and mediation sessions. Reexamination of rostering eligibility by designating agencies, such as the American Arbitration Association, may permit the expedited inclusion in the pool of this most valuable source of expertise.

The roster of arbitrators and mediators should contain representatives with all such skills in order to meet the diverse needs of this caseload.

Regardless of their prior experience, mediators and arbitrators on the roster must be independent of bias toward either party. They should reject cases if they believe the procedure lacks requisite due process.

Training. The creation of a roster containing the foregoing qualifications dictates the development of a training program to educate existing and potential labor and employment mediators and arbitrators as to the statutes, including substantive, procedural and remedial issues to be confronted and to train experts in the statutes as to employer procedures governing the employment relationship as well as due process and fairness in the conduct and control of arbitration hearings and mediation sessions.

Training in the statutory issues should be provided by the government agencies, bar associations, academic institutions, etc., administered perhaps by the designating agency, such as the AAA, at various locations throughout the country. Such training should be updated periodically and be required of all mediators and arbitrators. Training in the conduct of mediation and arbitration could be provided by a mentoring program with experienced panelists.

Successful completion of such training would be reflected in the resumé or panel cards of the arbitrators supplied to the parties for their selection process.

Panel Selection. Upon request of the parties, the designating agency should utilize a list procedure such as that of the AAA or select a panel composed of an odd number of mediators and arbitrators from its roster or pool. The panel cards for such individuals should be submitted to the parties for their perusal prior to alternate striking of the names on the list, resulting in the designation of the remaining mediator and/or arbitrator.

The selection process could empower the designating agency to appoint a mediator and/or arbitrator if the striking procedure is unacceptable or unsuccessful. As noted above, subject to the consent of the parties, the designating agency should provide the names of the parties and their representatives in recent cases decided by the listed arbitrators.

Conflicts of Interest. The mediator and arbitrator for a case has a duty to disclose any relationship which might reasonably constitute or be perceived as a conflict of interest. The designated mediator and/or arbitrator should be required to sign an oath provided by the designating agency, if any, affirming the absence of such present or preexisting ties.

Authority of the Arbitrator. The arbitrator should be bound by applicable agreements, statutes, regulations and rules of procedure of the designating agency, including the authority to determine the time and place of the hearing, permit reasonable discovery, issue subpoenas, decide arbitrability issues, preserve order and privacy in the hearings, rule on evidentiary matters, determine the close of the hearing and procedures for posthearing submissions, and issue an award resolving the submitted dispute.

The arbitrator should be empowered to award whatever relief would be available in court under the law. The arbitrator should issue an opinion and award setting forth a summary of the issues, including the type(s) of dispute(s), the damages and/or other relief requested and awarded, a statement of any other issues resolved, and a statement regarding the disposition of any statutory claim(s).

Compensation of the Mediator and Arbitrator. Impartiality is best assured by the parties sharing the fees and expenses of the mediator and arbitrator. In cases where the economic condition of a party does not permit equal sharing, the parties should make mutually acceptable arrangements to achieve that goal if at all possible. In the absence of such agreement, the arbitrator should determine allocation of fees. The designating agency, by negotiating the parties' share of costs and collecting such fees, might be able to reduce the bias potential of disparate contributions by forwarding payment to the mediator and/or arbitrator without disclosing the parties' share therein.

Scope of Review

The arbitrator's award should be final and binding, and the scope of review should be limited.

Dated: May 9, 1995

Christopher A. Barreca, Co-Chair
Partner
Paul, Hastings, Janofsky & Walker
Rep., Council of Labor & Employment Section, American Bar Association

Max Zimny, Co-Chair
General Counsel, International
Ladies' Garment Workers' Union Association
Rep., Council of Labor and Employment Section, American Bar Association

Arnold Zack, Co-Chair
President, National Academy of Arbitrators

Carl E. VerBeek
Management Co-Chair Union Co-Chair
Partner
Varnum Riddering Schmidt & Howlett
Arbitration Committee of Labor and Employment Section, ABA

Robert D. Manning
Angoff, Goldman, Manning, Pyle, Wanger & Hiatt, P.C.
Union Co-Chair
Arbitration Committee of Labor and Employment Section, ABA

Charles F. Ipavec, Arbitrator
Neutral Co-Chair
Arbitration Committee of Labor and Employment Section, ABA

George H. Friedman
Senior Vice President
American Arbitration Association

Michael F. Hoellering
General Counsel
American Arbitration Association

W. Bruce Newman
Rep., Society of Professionals in Dispute Resolution

Wilma Liebman
Special Assistant to the Director Federal Mediation and Conciliation

Joseph Garrison, President
National Employment Lawyers Association

Lewis Maltby
Director, Workplace Rights Project, American Civil Liberties Union

Endnote

[1] It should be noted that where statutory and contractual claims overlap, and in the absence of explicit incorporation of the statute in the collective bargaining agreement, labor-management arbitration may still in effect adequately protect the statutory rights, although it is the contractual claims upon which the arbitration will focus.

References

"AAA Clarifies Employment Policy." 1997. *Currents* (Summer), p. 4.

Daily Labor Report. 1997. Washington, DC: Bureau of National Affairs, pp. E-1-2.

Dunlop, John T., and Arnold M. Zack. 1997. *The Mediation and Arbitration of Employment Disputes.* San Francisco: Jossey-Bass.

Federal Register. 1997. February 12, pp. 11734-48.

Feinberg, Linda, Vice President, National Association of Securities Dealers, Regulation. 1998. Telephone interview by author, October 25.

Jacobs, Margaret. 1994. "Men's Club: Riding Crop and Slurs: How Wall Street Dealt with a Sex Bias Case," *Wall Street Journal*, June 9, p. B1.

U.S. Commission on the Future of Worker-Management Relations (Dunlop Commission). 1994. Report and Recommendations. Washington, DC: U.S. Dept. of Labor and U.S. Dept. of Commerce.

"Wall Street's Forced Arbitration of Bias Claims Set Back by EEOC." 1997. *Wall Street Journal*, September 12, p. B24.

"When It's Time to Do Battle with Your Company." 1997. *Business Week*, February 10, pp. 130-31.

CHAPTER 4

Dispute Resolution in Employment: The Need for Research

LISA B. BINGHAM
Indiana University

DENISE R. CHACHERE
Saint Louis University

Employment dispute resolution (i.e., the use of a third-party ombuds program, mediation, or arbitration to resolve employment disputes outside a collectively bargained grievance procedure) is a relatively new subject for researchers in industrial relations and human resource management. Still, its literature is diverse and dispersed. It has intellectual antecedents in the extensive literature on voice and grievance systems (Bies 1987; Folger 1977; Greenberg 1996; Lewicki, Weiss, and Lewin 1992; Lewin 1987; Sheppard, Lewicki, and Minton 1992; Sitkin and Bies 1993), on grievance mediation and arbitration in collective bargaining (Dunlop and Zack 1997; Fleming 1967; Zack 1999; Feuille 1995, 1999; Ury, Brett, and Goldberg 1989), and on negotiation and dispute resolution (Arrow et al. 1995; Carnevale and Pruitt 1992; Kressel, Pruitt and Associates 1989; Lind and Tyler 1988; Wall and Lynn 1993).

In addition, employment dispute resolution occurs in the shadow of the law. While labor dispute resolution is an organic part of a negotiated, ongoing, and dynamic relationship, employment dispute resolution is generally a substitute for legal remedies available through administrative agencies and the courts (Dunlop and Zack 1997). For that reason, there is also a growing body of literature on alternative dispute resolution (ADR) coming from law as an academic discipline (Bingham 1998a; Moberly 1998). Lastly, employment dispute resolution is closely linked to the new field of practice and scholarly inquiry known as dispute system design (Costantino and Merchant 1996; Ury, Brett, and Goldberg 1989). This field examines how to structure an organization's dispute, complaint, and/or grievance processes to best serve the organization and its internal and external stakeholders.

The practitioner journals seem to recognize that conflict is inherent in the workplace (at times making clear that conflict is not always negative because conflict can lead to change by fostering innovation and creativity and to collaboration and unity through increased communication) and that employers should proactively address this aspect of the employment relationship. This difference in understanding and treatment of conflict has been one of the great dividing lines between industrial relations (IR) and human resources management (HRM). That is, IR tends to take the perspective that conflict is continuous and unavoidable and thus requires processes and institutions to reconcile the competing interests. In contrast, HR has its roots in planning, organizing, leading, monitoring, and controlling rather than in problem solving and mediation. Could it be that this dividing line is breaking down as the use of ADR grows?

This chapter provides an overview of recent empirical research on the adoption of, setting for, design characteristics of, and organizational outcomes attributable to ombuds, mediation, and arbitration processes for nonunion employment disputes. Because of the limited nature of the literature, each section begins with a brief summary of the equivalent literature from the labor/management and collective bargaining context. We believe this provides a useful starting point for researchers to identify what we do and do not know about employment dispute resolution. The chapter focuses on third-party neutrals (here defined as ombuds persons, mediators, or arbitrators) operating either in the context of an employer-sponsored plan or a program annexed to an administrative agency with jurisdiction over that category of employment dispute. Thus in-house, final-step dispute resolution procedures, such as an open-door policy or peer review panel or any dispute resolution plan steps prior to mediation or arbitration, are outside the scope of this chapter (see Lewin [1998] for a review of this literature). In addition, the chapter focuses on empirical literature. It provides examples of relevant recent law review and descriptive literature only where that literature raises questions capable of empirical investigation or provides an essential context.

First, the chapter addresses the limitations on research stemming from the confidential nature of employment dispute resolution. Second, it examines literature on the adoption and use of these programs. Third, it examines the setting of employment dispute resolution programs in the public and private sector. Fourth, it considers the literature concerning the design of the dispute resolution intervention including various structural elements. Lastly, the chapter examines the limited research on organizational outcomes attributable to employment dispute resolution programs.

It will come as no surprise to the reader that we conclude this is a fertile field for future research. There are too many unanswered questions to conclude otherwise.

Researching Confidential Processes

Much of the literature on employment dispute resolution is descriptive, anecdotal, proscriptive, and normative. Relatively little literature examines ombuds programs, employment mediation, or arbitration empirically. There are obstacles to rigorous empirical research—specifically, a tradition of confidentiality—and the consequent lack of access to data. Most employment mediation occurs in the context of an agreement under which all parties agree to maintain confidentiality within the process and often not to disclose its outcome (Marksteiner 1998). Mediated settlements and employment arbitration awards are unpublished and confidential. In order to obtain access to data, researchers must demonstrate a willingness to respect that confidentiality and must develop data collection plans in collaboration with the source. Mediators are even more reluctant than arbitrators to introduce an observer into the delicate interpersonal dynamics of an employment dispute.[1]

Common methods researchers have used to overcome this problem include mail and telephone surveys to organizations or the neutral mediators or arbitrators involved regarding employment dispute resolution plans; mail and telephone surveys with participants in the processes; experimental research in which neutrals provide data regarding a hypothetical case; and less commonly, examination of archival case files where available. Survey methods often present problems due to low response rate or sample selection bias. For example, selection bias may occur when employees have a choice of employment dispute resolution process, as in the case of a discrimination complaint. Often, it is not feasible to afford mediation to employees by random assignment; it would not be perceived as fair. Therefore, a researcher may have samples of employees who use mediation and employees who choose not to, but these categories are not random. It is rarely possible to use a pilot site/control site method to structure a study, although this approach is certainly desirable in larger organizations. In order to use a comprehensive before-and-after design, the researcher must become involved with an organization early in its development of an employment dispute resolution program and collect data over a prolonged period of time.

Moreover, researchers may be unable to independently confirm managers' or employees' self-reports about ADR. In a survey research project where data were collected from union and management representatives from the same workplace, Eaton (1994) found systematic differences in the answers given by labor and management about the existence of employee involvement programs as well as details about how those programs operated. The results suggest respondent bias (or ignorant bias) may be a problem with research that relies on managerial response alone. These problems of sample selection bias and response bias often undermine the best conceived research strategies. They may even be amplified for ADR research because secrecy is one of its primary benefits.

Todor and Owen (1991) advocate a macrojustice assessment as an approach to research in this field. They define a macrojustice assessment as looking at the pattern of outcomes produced by different dispute resolution systems. However, possibly most harmful to any effort in understanding ADR fully is the fact that many organizations do not collect and/or release objective data on the results of ADR beyond resolution statistics (U.S. GAO 1997). In addition, there is no systematic collection or reporting of these data; thus each researcher is responsible for designing and collecting his or her own data. There is a lack of collaboration or sharing of data, perhaps understandable when data are obtained under a confidentiality agreement; however, this leads to duplication of effort because collecting data for each individual project increases the cost of conducting this research. Indeed, all of the research to date has had to confront these difficulties. Together, they operate to limit what researchers have learned about employment dispute resolution. Prospective researchers need to understand the limitations on conclusions drawn from this prior research and the research dilemma they face in future efforts.

The Adoption and Use of Employment Dispute Resolution

Beginning in the 1980s, articles began to appear among managerial practitioner journals to encourage the use of ADR (specifically, nonunion grievance procedures) to avoid union organizing attempts. These articles continued to appear through the 1990s using more "acceptable" reasons. The most commonly stated reasons given by organizations to explain the adoption of ADR are the increased volume of employment claims; lower cost in time, risk, and money relative to more formal dispute resolution processes (i.e., lawsuits and EEOC action); the speed with which ADR can resolve them; changes in the regulatory environment which encouraged (directly and indirectly) workplace ADR; a focus on disputants' underlying interests rather than on the validity of their positions; an effort to maintain and/or enhance productivity (through enhanced long-term working relationships via reduced absenteeism and turnover and increased morale and organizational loyalty); greater degree of confidentiality available from ADR; the expertise of the neutrals superior to that of a jury; and union avoidance (Briggs and Gundry 1994; Egler 1995; Ettingoff and Powell 1996; Evans 1994; Flores 1993; U.S. GAO 1997; Goldstein and Payson 1995; Lipsky and Seeber 1998b; Mayer and Ghais 1997; McDermott 1995; Miller 1994; Pell 1993).

Businesses have also more recently sought out ADR because of their declining faith in the civil justice system. A survey of business lawyers and executives (Lande 1998) found that a majority of executives felt the court system was not working well, they were not satisfied with either the process or results of litigation, and most of these lawsuits were frivolous. A continuing legal studies outline, for instance, reported that if a company fires a 42-year-old minority woman shop steward with a bad back and 4 years 11 months seniority, the company could face at least 36 different litigation claims (Panken, Babson, and Webb 1997). This perception has given rise to a number of articles by consultants recommending ADR to address a company's litigation woes (e.g., Hubert 1998).

A major theme from the practitioner and legal journals seems to be that employers adopt these procedures as a litigation risk and cost reduction strategy. ADR is not a panacea, however. These same authors also summarized criticisms of ADR in employment, particularly using arbitration for discrimination claims (Ganzel 1997). Problems include the difficulty in overturning an arbitrator's award, the expense of an adversarial arbitration hearing, the tendency of arbitrators to try to grant broader equitable relief, and the likelihood that the neutrals will be biased.

In spite of these criticisms, there is ample evidence from the descriptive, legal, and empirical literature to suggest that the adoption of ADR is rapidly increasing. Indeed, a limited but growing body of research on the implementation of ADR procedures for nonunion employees supports the conclusion that about half of "large" private employers have established some sort of formal dispute resolution procedure for their nonunion employees. For example, Delaney, Lewin, and Ichniowski (1989) found these procedures existed in half of their sample of almost 500 large employers; Edelman (1990) found that 65% of 52 organizations had established at least one nonunion grievance procedure; and Feuille and Chachere (1995) reported the existence in 57% of 111 large manufacturing firms. A broad government study of ADR among private organizations and federal agencies also found that the use of ADR had increased during the 1990s and further concluded that 52% of large private companies had some form of ADR for nonunion employees (U.S. GAO 1995). Chachere (1997) reported that these procedures existed in 376 hospitals in a nationwide study of nonunion voice procedures.

A few studies also support the conclusion that the implementation of these procedures will continue to grow. For example, in a study of 92 Fortune 500 organizations about their ADR plans, 90% indicated that ADR was an attractive organizational policy (McDermott 1995). In its 1997 Employment Litigation Survey, the Society for Human Resource Management found that while only 14% of the 616 respondents (representing various firm sizes and industries) include an ADR clause in their employment agreements, there is still widespread belief that it will solve cases quicker and the adoption rate will increase as companies conclude that ADR is less costly than litigation (SHRM 1997).

Research comparing adopters to nonadopters has indicated certain organizational factors associated with adoption. First, there is a positive relationship between size and organizational formality (Child 1973; Oldham and Hackman 1981): larger organizations appear more likely to implement formal ADR policies. The second factor concerns the role of human resource management within an organization. Organizational subunits engage in self-interest behavior to enhance their positions (Pfeffer 1981). If it is in the interest of HR managers to support the adoption of ADR, then organizations that place a higher value on the human resource function and organizations that have more progressive human resource policies in general are more likely to also adopt ADR. Studies of ADR implementation by Delaney and Feuille (1992), Edelman (1990), and Feuille and Chachere (1995) supported all of these hypotheses.

The presence of a union covering some employees in the organization has been found to be negatively associated with ADR policies (Delaney and Feuille 1992; Feuille and Chachere 1995) which suggested a decreased interest in or need for these policies for nonunion employees when the organization also handles union employee grievances. This is an area that could use more investigation. Why would employers with experience in union grievance handling be less willing to handle nonunion employee complaints in a similar manner? Although Edelman (1990) found that the presence of a union elsewhere in the organization had no influence on the adoption of ADR, perhaps more interestingly, she found that proximity to the public legal environment made an employer more vulnerable to normative pressure to adopt ADR in its quest for legitimacy. That is, over time, exposure to increasing legal regulation of the employment relationship has encouraged employers to adopt ADR.

Adoption of ADR in the public sector is somewhat different from the private sector. In the federal sector, Congress enacted the Administrative Dispute Resolution Act (ADRA) in 1990 to spur agencies to consider using ADR (Dunlop and Zack 1997; Evans 1998). In a 1994 study (U.S. G.A.O.1995), 31% of federal agencies had some form of ADR in place for employee complaints. By 1996 the federal agency rate had increased to 49% (U.S. GAO 1997).

At the state and local government level, there is wide variation nationally. There are state offices of dispute resolution in many states, located in the executive and judicial branches of state government (Dillon 1994). Some states have legislation similar to the federal ADRA (i.e., Texas), but most do not. Although there is a significant body of research on mediation and arbitration in public sector labor relations (Kochan 1981), we have found no literature examining state or local government use of employment dispute resolution. Much dispute resolution at the local level occurs in the context of community mediation centers, which are not limited in focus to employment disputes. Moreover, the lack of literature may in part be a function of higher rates of union organizing in the public sector. On the other hand, the existence of such research in federal agencies which also have high rates of unionism (e.g., United States Postal Service) suggests that state and local government use of ADR warrants further investigation. Indeed, very little is known about employment relations in the public sector, in general, and dispute resolution, in particular, in the still sizable portion of the public sector that is nonunion. This remains a wide-open field ready for investigation.

The Setting for Employment Dispute Resolution: Private or Public Sector

Context can shape dispute resolution procedures and their results (Kolb 1989, Kolb and Associates 1994). Thus employment dispute resolution system design is affected by its setting, that is, whether it is operating in the private or public sector. For example, the use of arbitration as a part of these procedures is growing quickly in the private sector relative to the public sector. While an earlier study found only four of 111 private employers used outside arbitration in 1991 (Feuille and Chachere 1995), by 1995 the GAO found that 10% of all employers with 100 or more employees used binding arbitration for employment disputes, and as many as half of these may have imposed mandatory arbitration as a condition of employment (U.S. GAO 1995).

As discussed above, there is relatively little work on dispute resolution in the public sector outside of the field of labor relations, and that work does not address employment so much as the field of public policy (Mills 1991). There has been a systematic comparison of labor arbitration outcomes in the public and private sectors (Mesch 1995a) but no similar comparison as to employment arbitration. In the area of non-union employment dispute resolution, the GAO compared ADR techniques used by five private sector companies and five federal agencies (U.S. GAO 1997). It found that the private companies more frequently used arbitration, while federal agencies more frequently used mediation as a technique for employment disputes. Private companies had more variation in processes and made wider use of ADR. The settlement rate for mediation was comparable in the private and federal sectors. Furthermore, in spite of federal legislation to guide these practices in the public sector, there is still a concern for the lack of quality standards found in public sector ADR policies (Dibble 1997).

Five years after the ADRA, a survey showed that the vast majority of cabinet and non-cabinet-level federal agencies were experimenting with the use of mediation in personnel and employment disputes (Bingham and Wise 1996). Cabinet-level agencies made use of a wider variety of processes in a wider variety of cases than did non-cabinet-level agencies. However, only a small minority of agencies made even limited use of arbitration, largely because of concerns over loss of control and delegation of governmental authority to a private decision maker. The original version of the ADRA allowed agencies to reject and vacate an arbitration award within 30 days after receiving it; the amended ADRA of 1996, a permanent addition to the federal Administrative Procedure Act, has eliminated that option so that federal agencies are also bound by the award (Evans 1998). Thus one open research question is whether this statutory change will affect federal agency use of arbitration.[2]

Robinson (1992) examined grievance mediation of state employee grievances under a collective bargaining agreement and found that structural variables such as the organization of state government and the union, the availability of funds, and political pressure from membership were important to determine the social relationship of labor and management within which grievance mediation occurred. Clearly, the culture of a workplace would be an important determinant of success for any dispute resolution intervention.

All of these aspects of a dispute resolution system's setting in turn affect its design and structural elements.

Design of an Employment Dispute Resolution Intervention

An employer's choices regarding dispute system design determine many aspects of a nonunion dispute resolution program and its outcomes (Ury, Brett, and Goldberg 1989; Costantino and Merchant 1997). This section attempts to identify important design elements and review the literature with a bearing on the outcomes associated with these elements. These include the nature of the intervention, due process safeguards, the timing of the intervention in the life of a dispute, who selects and/or pays for the third-party neutral, the role and characteristics of the neutrals, what if any decision standard the neutral uses, and characteristics of the disputants.

Nature of the Intervention: Comparative Research on Ombuds, Mediation, and Arbitration Programs

The choice of whether to have an ombuds, mediation, or arbitration program, or some combination of the three is a critical element of dispute system design. Using a procedural justice framework (Lind and Tyler 1988; Lind et al. 1993), researchers have conducted comparisons of third-party neutral interventions in the field of labor relations (Shapiro and Brett [1993], finding higher satisfaction with mediation than arbitration), in the study of court-annexed dispute resolution programs (Lind, MacCoun et al. [1990], finding higher satisfaction with arbitration than judicial settlement conferences), and in experimental research on complainant-respondent differences using a landlord tenant hypothetical (Peirce, Pruitt, and Czaja 1993).

The only comparative work on employment dispute resolution is as part of broader studies of ADR processes in general. Lipsky and Seeber (1998a) conducted a survey of executives and lawyers in private companies, and their reasons for choosing mediation compared with arbitration for disputes including employment. The survey addressed choices to use dispute resolution both within and outside established company programs. They found that survey respondents used mediation because it allowed the parties to resolve the dispute themselves, gave them greater control, was a more satisfactory process, and preserved good relationships. However, respondents said they used arbitration because it is required by contract and better than litigation. Brett, Barsness, and Goldberg (1996) compared mediation and arbitration outcomes based on a sample of 449 cases administered by four different major ADR providers and found that mediation was less expensive and more satisfactory to the parties than arbitration; it also settled about 78% of the cases, whether mediation was mandatory or voluntary. This study included a sample of contract cases that would cover employment. Nevertheless, we have found no systematic comparisons of how these types of employment dispute resolution differ in their effect upon an organization or upon the participants.

Ombuds programs. Commentators emphasize the potential for non-adjudicative processes, such as those available through an ombuds office, to improve relationships at the workplace (Gadlin 1991; Hayes 1998; Kolb and Silbey 1990; Rowe 1981, 1990a, 1990b). A workplace ombuds is a neutral operating inside and on the payroll of an organization to assist other employees in resolving disputes informally through confidential, informal means. The ombuds serves as an information resource, channel of communications, complaint handler and dispute resolver (Robbins and Deane 1986). Using qualitative interviews of key agency stakeholders, Meltzer (1998) found that a federal workplace ombuds office is likely to be most effective when the Equal Employment Opportunity (EEO) office has too many non-EEO complaints; the employee assistance plan is receiving workplace complaints outside its mandate; personnel-related offices are not working together; employee morale is low; there is poor employee-management communication; significant workplace issues emerge and surprise management; there are poor labor-management relations; and there are frequent employee claims of retaliation.

There is a professional association and code of ethics for ombuds persons requiring strict confidentiality (see Ombudsman Association 1997). There are also a number of interesting practitioner reports from the ombuds' perspective within a university conflict management system (see generally the electronic journal *UCI Ombudsman: The Journal*). Warters (1995) suggested that ombuds can perform a valuable role researching the campus conflict management culture.

However, there is also the risk that employers may distort the ombuds title in unilaterally adopted nonunion arbitration programs. For example, one employer had its ombuds represent employees as their advocate in arbitration and select the arbitrator on behalf of both parties; this resulted in repeated selection of the same arbitrator, who always ruled for management (Bingham 1996). This structure, where the ombuds departs from a neutral role, gives at least the appearance of a conflict of interest.

Because an ombuds office is small, and the ombuds is often a single person, these programs are particularly difficult to evaluate empirically. The confidential nature of the work, combined with the ease of tracking down a given case to the individual parties, often make ombuds persons reluctant to cooperate with research or evaluation. Moreover, one of the advantages of an ombuds office is the flexibility to design it as best fits the organization (Kolb 1987); this means there is considerable variability from one office to the next.

Nevertheless, one author conducted interview case studies of five federal agency workplace ombuds programs (Meltzer [1998], which also contains a useful history of ombuds programs and review of the literature). She found that the offices have not conducted formal evaluations of their effectiveness but enjoyed institutional and management support. Where ombuds offices maintained statistical information, they were able to report that the sample of employees seeking assistance from their office mirrored workplace demographics as a whole. All offices reported anecdotally a low rate of reprisal against employees for resorting to their services. Qualitative data from interviews with key agency stakeholders yielded perceptions that the ombuds office was effective, but occasionally there were careful and politically sensitive interactions between the ombuds office and union representatives in meshing the role of the traditional collectively bargained grievance procedure with that of the ombuds.

Another method used for research on ombuds offices is that of reflective practice, where the neutral examines experiences with a series of cases on the same subject and draws out general principles for use in future practice. This method has been used to examine an ombudsman's mediation of sexual harassment cases in a public university setting (Gadlin 1991) to examine the parties' shared and differing interests. The author concluded that it was desirable and feasible to mediate these claims.

Unanswered research questions include the extent to which ombuds programs have been adopted, how they interact with other dispute resolution interventions such as the use of an outside neutral mediator, and the extent to which such programs have any measurable impact on organizational level outcomes.

Mediation programs. Mediation is the use of a third party who is impartial and neutral to assist the disputants in reaching a voluntary, mutually agreed upon resolution to their dispute through confidential communications with each other and through the neutral (Moore 1996). There is a substantial body of research on grievance mediation in the labor-management context that may help guide future research on nonunion employment mediation. While many commentators endorse mediation as a superior method for resolving employment disputes (i.e., Bedman 1995; Bowers, Seeber, and Stallworth 1982; Conti 1985; McDermott 1995; Sherman 1995; Singletary, Shearer, and Kuligofski 1995), researchers are only now beginning to examine its function in a nonunion context.

In the labor-management context, researchers have extensively examined mediation as an alternative to a more adjudicative process such as traditional grievance arbitration in the context of a collectively bargained grievance procedure (Block, Beck, and Olson 1996; Brett and Goldberg 1983; House 1992; LaMothe 1994; McPherson 1956; Penna 1993; Roberts, Wolters, Holley, and Feild 1990; Robinson 1992; Silberman 1989; Skratek 1987a, 1987b, 1990; Ury, Brett, and Goldberg 1989; for a more comprehensive review of this literature, see Feuille 1992, 1999; and Feuille and Kolb 1994). Authors ascribe certain benefits to using grievance mediation: parties perceived it as less costly and time consuming relative to arbitration; it facilitated interest-based rather than rights-based bargaining; neither party relinquished decision control; procedurally it was less formal and structured than arbitration; the mediator acted as a facilitator to reach agreement; and it provided an educational role to each party about the other. Brett and Goldberg (1983) and Ury, Brett, and Goldberg (1989) found in participant surveys that the parties were highly satisfied with the grievance mediation process and that labor and management were equally satisfied with the process, although labor was slightly less satisfied than management with the outcome. Using qualitative and quantitative data from 22 mediated cases, Block, Beck, and Olson (1996) found that grievance mediation did not result in outcomes more favorable to one party than the other. Some commentators report anecdotal accounts that the participants acquired improved conflict resolution skills after grievance mediation in a labor-management setting (House 1992; Quinn, Rosenbaum, and McPherson 1990). Others caution that an important factor is the specific labor-management relationship within its social context (Robinson 1992).

Some organizations have adopted mediation programs for workplace disputes arising outside the collective bargaining agreement (i.e., Bedman 1995; Bingham 1997b; Clarke 1997; Youngblood, Trevino, and Favia 1992). These programs may exist in a nonunion workplace, or they may coexist with a union grievance procedure. Employers with well-established collective bargaining relationships are experimenting with alternatives to the administrative agency complaint processes under a variety of employment laws including those prohibiting discrimination.[3] In some cases, an administrative agency outside the employer-employee relationship may also offer mediation or other forms of dispute resolution. The EEOC and the Department of Labor have conducted successful pilot programs providing a mediation option for disputes these agencies would otherwise adjudicate or litigate on behalf of an employee or group of employees (see McEwen 1997; Schulyer 1993).

Using a procedural justice framework (Lind and Tyler 1988; Tyler 1988), Bingham (1997b) found that supervisors and employees were equally satisfied with the outside neutral mediator and the process of mediation of federal employee discrimination complaints at the United States Postal Service and that there was the same pattern with respect to satisfaction with outcome that other researchers had found in labor grievance mediation. Specifically, complainant employees were slightly less satisfied with the outcome of mediation than respondent supervisors.

Youngblood, Trevino, and Favia (1992) examined the operation of a South Carolina conciliation office for employees not covered by a union, civil service protection, or other legislation. The office was created under a statute that gave the commissioner of labor broad powers to deal with industrial disputes between employers and employees and the power to investigate, ascertain cause, try to remove misunderstanding, and to induce voluntary settlements in these cases. The researchers conducted a field study examining archival records and interviewing a sample of the participants in the program to determine why at-will employees viewed their dismissal as unjust and how they viewed third-party dispute resolution. The study found that participants generally felt both the process and outcome of conciliation was unfair or unjust. From a distributive justice standpoint, only 6% of the employees were reemployed as a result of conciliation; 81% felt the outcome of conciliation was unfair. From a procedural justice standpoint, employees complained that the conciliation process was unfair. The process generally did not result in face-to-face meetings or a hearing, and 75% of the interviewees were dissatisfied with the process. Both distributive and procedural justice contributed to the low employee satisfaction.

Clarke (1997) examined a North Carolina mediation program for workers' compensation cases. The evaluation used a random assignment method to allocate cases either to a mediation group or a control group.

Under this program, a state mediator would review the file, refer it to mediation if appropriate, and forward a list of mediators to the parties. Parties were required to attend, and mediation generally took from two to six hours. Mediation settled 26.1% of the total cases in the mediation group. In addition, a number of the mediation group cases settled outside of mediation, bringing the total settlements in the mediation group to 60.8%. The total settlements in the control group were 47.6%. In other words, mediation diverted some parties from bilateral settlement, but it also diverted some parties from a hearing. The program reduced median time to disposition by 60 days, from 372 days in the control to 312 days in the mediation group. While legal counsel was present in many cases, not all parties had legal counsel in all cases. Legal counsel and mediators surveyed generally responded favorably about the program.

Scholars who have reviewed the empirical literature on mediation observed that there has been relatively little work done on one particular category of outcomes for the participants: the effect of mediation on their relationship and perceptions of each other. Wall and Lynn (1993: 176-77) observed that some evidence from community justice centers, divorce mediation, and international conflict suggested that mediation seldom alters the long-run climate for conflict, but they cited no evidence in the employment arena. Instead, they felt the link between mediation outcomes and the postdispute climate or working relationship was an open issue warranting further research (see also Lewicki, Weiss, and Lewin 1992: 241; Carnevale and Pruitt 1992: 569-70). Bush and Folger (1994) suggested that mediation can transform the relationship between the parties by affording the parties opportunities for empowerment and recognition of each others' perspectives. Anderson and Bingham (1997) found that both employees and supervisors at the United States Postal Service reported that supervisors were improving their listening skills through participation in the mediation program for discrimination complaints. However, the potential of a nonadversarial process to improve workplace relationships and climate remains a fertile area for research.

Another area largely unexplored is the impact of different models of mediation on participant and organizational outcomes. Mediation can be a process in which the mediator gives the parties an expert opinion on the merits of the dispute; this form of mediation is sometimes characterized as evaluative (Waldman 1998). It represents one end of a continuum of mediator directiveness. Less directive is the traditional labor mediator, who will actively test the parties' best alternative to a negotiated agreement and provide information about reasonable comparable settlements in the industry. Sometimes referred to as a problem-solving or "facilitative" model is one in which the mediator attempts to help the parties identify and dovetail their interests (Fisher, Ury, and Patton 1991; Waldman 1997, 1998). Still less directive is the model of mediation that comes out of a family and community mediation tradition. Sometimes referred to as "transformative" mediation (Bush and Folger 1994; Folger and Bush 1996), this model focuses on empowering the parties in the sense that they control all aspects of the mediation and are not pressured to accept any particular proposal or settlement but are rather encouraged to clarify their own interests, goals, and choices. In addition, the mediator attempts to foster moments of recognition, in which each party reaches a better understanding of the other's perspective and acknowledges the other's perspective. The choice of a mediation model may influence participant and organizational outcomes.

An area of debate among policymakers concerns the relative balance of power in mediation. Stallworth has used the example of a 17-year-old sexual harassment claimant who is illiterate, speaks limited English as a second language, and is a single parent.[4] What happens when this claimant enters mediation without the benefit of legal counsel and the restaurant chain against whom she filed her complaint brings in its labor and employment counsel and HR director? Can mediation possibly achieve a fair result under these circumstances? Others respond that the alternative is for this claimant to enter an administrative adjudication or courtroom without counsel, and mediation is likely to be at least as fair a process as the alternative.

This issue of power in mediation leads to still more difficult research questions; for example, how should one measure success in mediation? Some would argue that mediation should produce the same range of settlements as the traditional process for resolving similar disputes. This approach would compare mediation with litigation or administrative adjudication and expect to find similar outcomes. However, proponents tout mediation because it can produce superior outcomes, such as an apology, that one could not achieve in court. This would suggest systematic differences between mediation outcomes and those produced by other traditional processes. This too is an important and largely unexplored area of research and one amenable to the macrojustice assessment approach proposed by Todor and Owen (1991).

Arbitration. Arbitration is a quasi-judicial process in which the disputants hire a third-party decision maker to adjudicate their dispute.

Generally, arbitration takes the form of an informal adversarial hearing, allowing for broad admissibility of evidence and argument and resulting in a written award (Dunlop and Zack 1997; Zack 1999).

The legal context for employment arbitration differs significantly from that of mediation or ombuds programs. These two latter third-party dispute resolution processes are generally voluntary and result in a voluntary settlement as their outcome. This mutual agreement usually takes the form of an enforceable contract. In contrast, arbitration may result in a binding award, with substantial finality (Bethel 1993). A strong national policy of deferral to labor arbitration awards (for a review of the Steelworkers Trilogy and related law see Cole [1997], Corrada [1998], Estreicher [1990], Feller [1998]) has given rise to an equally strong federal policy of enforcing nonunion employment arbitration clauses and the term "mandatory arbitration" (Bales 1994, 1997; Bingham 1998a; Buse 1995; Cole 1996; Dean 1998; Gershenfeld 1996; Lynd 1998; Marler 1996; Ray 1998; Rowe 1996; Yatsco 1998; Zick 1998). This term refers to the ability of an employer to force an employee to accept arbitration of all disputes as a condition of employment, including binding arbitration for statutory claims (Estreicher 1997; Feller 1997; Manuszak 1997). Commentators have discussed adhesive arbitration agreements in the securities industry (Davis 1998; Frankhauser 1995; Press 1997) for franchise terminations (Emerson 1998), for employment discrimination claims (Silberman et al. 1994), and for director and officer indemnification disputes (Wells 1997). Some have criticized the development of mandatory arbitration, pointing out the unequal bargaining power in the relationship between the unrepresented employee and an employer (Maltby 1994; McGowan 1998). Others have argued that mandatory arbitration clauses themselves represent a form of prohibited discrimination under Title VII (Cherry 1998). Meanwhile, case backlogs in courts and administrative agencies may render arbitration the only real "day in court" an employee receives (Baxter and Hunt 1989; Gould 1987; Heflin 1997; Kaufman and Chanin 1994; St. Antoine 1998).

This development has led to calls for fairness in employment arbitration (Bingham 1996, 1997a, 1998a; Carrington 1998; Commission on the Future of Worker-Management Relations 1994; Dunlop and Zack 1997; EEOC 1997; Haagen 1998; Hayford and Peeples 1995; Motley 1998; Ponte 1997; Speidel 1998; Zack 1997, 1999). Leading representatives of the dispute resolution field from groups including the American Arbitration Association, the National Academy of Arbitrators (1997), the American Bar Association, the American Civil Liberties Union, and the

National Employment Lawyers Association together developed self-regulatory standards in the form of the Due Process Protocol for Mediation and Arbitration of Statutory Employment Disputes (Dunlop and Zack [1997], see appendix and included in this volume as an appendix to the chapter by Zack). The American Arbitration Association (Wilson 1998) and JAMS-Endispute (Young 1998) have adopted the standards in the protocol and guarantee employees the right to counsel, reasonable discovery, participation in selecting the arbitrator, a reasoned award, and allocation of the costs of arbitration.

There is a rapidly evolving body of cases regarding the grounds upon which a court may overturn an employment arbitration award (Jacob 1997). These include unconscionability (Jacob 1997); manifest disregard of the law (Davis 1997; Poser 1998); and the lack of meaningful, knowing or voluntary consent in certain very limited circumstances (Axenson 1998; Levin 1997; Ware 1996). For a further discussion on the limited nature of judicial review, see Stone (1999).

There has been substantial research regarding what predicts outcomes in labor arbitration cases, where employees are represented by a union and the arbitrator interprets a collective bargaining agreement. In an illustrative but not exhaustive review of this literature, one finds that researchers have examined the impact of arbitrator characteristics such as gender (e.g., Bemmels 1988a,b,c), age (e.g., Nelson and Curry 1981), and arbitrator experience (e.g., Thornton and Zirkel 1990; Zirkel and Breslin 1995); the impact of grievant characteristics such as job category, gender (e.g., Bemmels 1988a), and party resources and representation by counsel (i.e., Block and Stieber 1987; Mesch and Dalton 1991, 1992), and the impact of case factors such as antiunion animus or work history (e.g., McCammon and Cotton 1990; Simpson and Martocchio 1995), statutory criteria (e.g., Bazerman 1985; Dell'Omo 1989), and normative criteria on arbitrator decision making (e.g., Hilgert 1995). For reviews of the literature in labor arbitration, see Thornton and Zirkel (1990) on labor arbitrator predictability, Luthar and Bonnici (1998) on discrimination complaint arbitration cases, Leap and Stahl (1985) on medically based grievances, and Allen and Lucero (1998) on arbitration cases concerning assaults by employees on their supervisors.

The literature on employment arbitration is less well-developed. Theorists have suggested that mandatory arbitration of employment discrimination claims may have adverse effects on perceptions of both procedural and distributive justice (Cohen and Domagalski 1998). On the question of distributive justice, Bingham (1995) examined arbitration outcomes in actual employment arbitration cases decided under the AAA Commercial Rules in 1992. She considered the factors of whether the employer or employee was claimant and whether the arbitrator was paid or worked pro bono and found that recoveries were lower in cases where the arbitrator was paid a fee, but there was no evidence of overall proemployer bias. Bingham (1996) also examined the arbitration rules under which the claim was filed in actual employment arbitration cases decided in 1993 under the AAA Commercial and Employment Rules and found evidence of due process problems in the early years of employment arbitration.

The ability of an employer to structure employment arbitration unilaterally and the weaker bargaining power of the individual employee were examined in a series of studies on the employer as a repeat user of arbitration (Bingham 1997a, 1998a). Again looking at a sample of actual arbitration awards decided under AAA rules, Bingham (1997a, 1998a) found that employers who make repeated use of arbitration have superior outcomes and are more likely to be arbitrating pursuant to a unilaterally imposed personnel manual. In addition, the relative bargaining power of the employee, operationalized as white-, blue-, or pink-collar employment category, was also relevant to success in arbitration. White-collar employees did better (Bingham 1997a). Employees arbitrating pursuant to a unilaterally imposed personnel manual did worse (Bingham 1998a). Bingham and Chachere (1998) found that a repeat player employer's success was related to the underlying factors of the personnel manual arbitration clause and repeat use of a single arbitrator. All of these studies were conducted on arbitration cases decided before the advent of the Due Process Protocol; thus future research could produce different results. (For additional studies on arbitration, see discussion below regarding decision standard.)

Howard (1995) examined mean damage awards in discrimination cases, comparing litigated and arbitrated outcomes. Arguing in favor of employment arbitration, Howard observed that plaintiffs' lawyers will take only one in twenty cases, and then only when the employee is capable of advancing a retainer and has high provable damages; thus a quick, economical, and final process could level the playing field. Comparing samples of cases litigated in federal court (21,518 cases) with arbitration awards issued under American Arbitration Association rules (510 cases) and arbitration awards issues in the securities industry where discrimination was alleged (61 awards), Howard found that in litigation, employees recovered something in 71% of the cases pre- and post-trial but only recovered something in 28% of the cases that proceeded to trial. They did better in jury trials (38% recovery rate) than nonjury trials (19% recovery rate). In AAA arbitration, by contrast, employees recovered something in 68% of the cases and in 48% of the cases of securities arbitration. Howard also conducted a survey of employment lawyers and found that although 79% to 84% of litigated cases settled prior to litigation, only 31% to 44% arbitrated cases settled. Defense counsel estimated attorneys' fees at $96,000 to defend an employment discrimination case in court but only $20,000 to defend in arbitration.

There is indication that employers are more willing now than in the past to consider employment arbitration. In addition to reports of increasing usage, 78% of 92 Fortune 500 organizations indicated that they would allow arbitration (McDermott 1995). Bickner, Ver Ploeg, and Feigenbaum (1997) surveyed employers to identify arbitration components of their dispute resolution plans. They found that about 25% of employers limit their use of arbitration to dismissal cases and that most employers adopted their plans with little or no employee input but rather out of a concern over perceived runaway jury damage awards. Edelman and her colleagues (1993) studied perceptions about the risk of wrongful discharge litigation and found these to be exaggerated, often the product of consultants eager to assist the employer in reforming human resource management practices.

There are a number of dispute system design issues that call out for empirical research in the field of employment arbitration. These include the source of the neutral (in-house peer panel or umpire, an outside permanent umpire or panel, an ad hoc arbitrator identified through a third-party administrator, or a court-appointed master or factfinder); the nature of the process (early neutral evaluation, factfinding, nonbinding arbitration or binding arbitration, interest or rights arbitration); and as discussed next, the procedural rules (discovery, evidence, burden of proof, a written decision, due process, voluntary self-regulation or protocol), among others.

Due Process Safeguards

In all occupational fields, one finds normative advice on how to establish "model" procedures for effective and efficient nonunion ADR in the workplace. For example, Pell (1993) wrote that after a clear line of communication is established in an organization, the next step is to establish a formal procedure for employees to correct their problems. He recognized that workplace conflicts are "natural" and that something is wrong with an organization that boasts of having few employee complaints. The model procedure he described is along the lines of most prescriptions seen in the practitioner journals aimed at providing some formal system of dealing with the complaints that arise naturally from the employment relationship.

An important area for research is the relation of procedural protections to the function of employment dispute resolution. Procedural protections are often referred to as "due process," a term of art from the Constitution defined by the courts to include notice, reasonable discovery of relevant evidence, an opportunity to be heard, to confront and cross examine witnesses, the right to counsel or a representative, an impartial hearing officer, a record of the proceedings, and a reasoned decision explaining what evidence persuaded the decision maker. How many of these procedural safeguards must be present to satisfy the requisites of due process under the Constitution will vary with the nature of the protected interest at stake, the risk of error, and the nature of the public interest. Technically, due process under the Constitution applies only where there is government action and hence does not govern the private sector. However, most of these safeguards are available during the typical labor arbitration. Particularly in dispute resolution processes that result in a binding outcome, the availability of procedural safeguards may make a difference; this is the whole point of the Due Process Protocol (Dunlop and Zack 1997; Zack 1999).

Not surprisingly, however, there are very few studies that examine the characteristics of procedural due process contained within these nonunion complaint procedures. One study that made an explicit comparison to an objective standard of due process found that employers tend to include characteristics in their ADR policies that go beyond simply writing down a policy that says an employee has the right to grieve (Feuille and Chachere 1995). Among the 111 reported procedures, most were accessible to all employees for a wide range of subjects and average 3.4 steps for review. The study concluded that there were limits, however, on how far employers were willing to go in providing employees with procedural protections. For example, only 55 of 110 employers allowed employees to be accompanied by a representative, and only 11 of 107 employers allowed the final decisions on grievances to be made by decision makers who are arguably independent from management.

In another study, Chachere (1997) reported similar results in a sample of 393 hospital ADR procedures. That is, 93% of the respondents indicated that all employees were eligible to use the procedure, and

80% indicated that employees could grieve all work-related issues. As far as due process protections, however, very few of the respondents (18%) used a standard of proof for evidence, although as many as 52% gave the employee the right to call witnesses. Further, only 224 of 393 hospitals allowed employee representation, and only 54 (13%) allowed for independent decision making. These two systematic studies of procedural due process indicated that although employers provide numerous procedural due process characteristics for their nonunion employees who have workplace related complaints, most employers strongly preferred to keep the processing and resolution within their control. Research conducted since the adoption of the Due Process Protocol may, however, indicate a change. For example, of 87 organizations of various types but all reporting use of ADR, 46% used arbitration and 44% used mediation (SHRM 1997).

Another area ready for investigation is one that examines the impact of the lack of due process found in these procedures on both employees and employers. Data are more readily available from the union sector through a variety of sources such as government, union, and employer organizations. Using these data, some studies of union dispute resolution results may give us insight into what may be occurring in the nonunion sector. In one such study, Ponak and his colleagues (1996) applied event history analysis to a sample of 600 grievance arbitration awards filed during the period of 1985-88 in the province of Alberta to examine the factors that contribute to delay in the process. They concluded that the most consistent predictor of delay is the nature of the case-discharge cases which were handled more quickly than other complaints—suggesting that mutual interest plays a role in process delay. Interestingly, the presence of legal counsel reduced delay, a finding that was contradictory to the study's research hypotheses, previous research, and anecdotal evidence. The findings of this study suggested that nonunion ADR processes that limit the role of outside legal counsel may work against the organization in its desire to obtain an efficient outcome relative to formal litigation.

Timing of the Intervention

The timing of the intervention may affect program level outcomes. For example, where does the intervention fall in relation to the four classic litigator points of settlement (before a written complaint, immediately after a written complaint, after discovery is completed, or on the eve of trial)? Does timing the intervention relatively late in the life of the dispute divert cases from voluntary settlement by encouraging them to wait for the mediator? Is there a narcotic effect like that reported regarding dispute resolution for collective bargaining negotiations in the public sector? Does providing early mediation reduce the caseload for more adjudicatory processes? Brett and Goldberg (1983) studied interventions occurring within a day of the labor grievance and observed that early intervention was an important design factor. Moreover, an intervention may affect all the steps of a process which precede it. Effects from anticipating later steps in a collectively bargained grievance procedure have been observed in the early steps (Fortado 1998). Practitioners have also observed an interaction between mediation and arbitration steps of a single process (Hoellering 1997). However, the optimal sequence and timing of these steps is an open research issue in the area of nonunion dispute resolution.

Who Selects and/or Pays for the Third-Party Neutral

Studies have examined the selection of arbitrators in labor relations (Bloom and Cavanagh 1986; Briggs and Anderson 1980). However, there is a major difference between dispute resolution in labor relations and employment; in labor relations both parties are institutional repeat players, but in employment dispute resolution, only the employer is a repeat player (Bingham 1995, 1996, 1997a, 1998a). As an institutional repeat player, the employer has superior resources in terms of information regarding selection of a neutral, ability to pay a neutral, institutional memory, ability to provide future business to a neutral, long-term relationships with dispute resolution institutions and organizations, the ability to play for precedent, and take more risks (Galanter 1974; see also Denenberg and Denenberg 1994; Edwards 1993). Although Bingham (1995) found no proemployer bias in cases where the arbitrator earned a fee (regardless of how allocated between employer and employee) compared to cases where the arbitrator served pro bono, overall outcomes (defined as the proportion of the original claim awarded in damages) were lower in fee-paying cases than in pro bono cases. However, this was probably attributable to the nature of the cases, because the arbitrators served pro bono for cases requiring only one hearing day but earned a fee if the hearing required more than one day. The multiday cases were probably more hotly contested. Although repeat player employers enjoy greater success in employment arbitration than one-shot employers (Bingham 1997a, 1998a), there is no reported finding of a relationship between the employer's payment of the arbitrator's fee and the outcome of a case. This open question becomes even more interesting from a policy standpoint as courts require that employers assume the full cost of the arbitrator's fee (*Cole v. Burns International*, D.C. Circuit Court of Appeals 1997), while the Due Process Protocol recommends sharing payment for the neutral.

The Nature of the Cases for Which Dispute Resolution Is Available

Continuing a labor relations tradition (e.g., Bemmels [1991a] and Bohlander [1994] on discipline; Clay and Stephens [1994] on absenteeism; Karim [1993] on discharge; Leap and Stahl [1985] on medical cases; Ponak [1987] on discharge; Scott and Taylor [1983] on absenteeism), most studies currently examine employment dispute resolution in the context of a common case subject matter (e.g., Bingham [1997b] and Anderson and Bingham [1997] examining discrimination claims; Clarke [1997] using workers compensation claims; Howard [1995] examining discrimination claims; McEwen [1997] using discrimination claims filed with the EEOC; Schuyler [1993] using wage and hour claims filed with the U.S. Department of Labor; Youngblood, Trevino, and Favia [1992] examining a pool of state wrongful dismissal claims), or they use a pool of cases but do not compare outcomes based on the subject matter of the underlying complaint (e.g., Bingham [1995, 1996, 1997a] examining a pool of employment arbitration awards on different types of claims). Bingham (1998a) compared employment arbitration outcomes of cases based on adhesive personnel manual arbitration clauses with individually negotiated arbitration clauses and found that employers had greater success in arbitration under the former than the latter (see also Bingham and Chachere 1998). It is also an open question whether there are entire categories of cases for which employment dispute resolution is inappropriate (contrast Daus [1995] regarding mediation for discrimination claims and Gadlin [1991] advocating dispute resolution in sexual harassment cases with Nigro and Waugh [1998], examining local government responses to workplace violence, including zero tolerance policies that would appear to preclude use of dispute resolution). However, the work on the nature of cases is limited.

Role and Characteristics of the Neutrals

There have been studies on the demographic characteristics of arbitrators in labor relations (Bemmels 1990a,b; Crow and Logan 1994; on arbitrator background, Heneman and Sandver 1983; age, Nelson and Curry 1981; and arbitrator experience, Oswald 1991; Oswald and Caudill 1991; Thornton and Zirkel 1990; Zirkel and Breslin 1995). Until recently, there were so few female or minority arbitrators that it was difficult to study the gender or race of the arbitrator as a factor in outcomes. However, that may be changing as a result of efforts to diversify the composition of employment mediator and arbitrator panels. Bingham (1998b) found significantly more female arbitrators in employment arbitration cases decided after the AAA implemented the Due Process Protocol and new Employment Dispute Resolution Panel in June 1996 than before. Commentators debate whether it is desirable to match the gender or ethnicity of the neutral with that of the grievant or claimant (Winograd 1995). Bennett and Hermann (1996:115-16) report that minority small claims court litigants do better in mediation with minority mediators. Litigants challenging arbitration in the securities industry have argued that the skewed demographic composition of the arbitrator panels (most frequently older white males with experience working in the securities industry) resulted in structural bias against women and minorities (Sternlight 1996). However, it is interesting that the alternative to arbitration is adjudication before judges who are also most frequently older white males. It is also interesting that this lively debate is occurring in the absence of systematic empirical research on these issues.

Bingham and Mesch (1999 forthcoming) conducted an experimental study using four versions of a hypothetical arbitration case involving dismissal of an employee. These were mailed to random samples from four groups of arbitrators: AAA labor arbitrators, National Academy of Arbitrators members, or commercial employment arbitrators on the former AAA Commercial panel for employment disputes, and graduate students. They examined the factors of arbitrator type and decision standard. For decision standard, the hypothetical case used either just cause or good cause under the Model Employment Termination Act. They found that employment arbitrators reinstate employees less frequently than labor arbitrators, NAA members, or students. However, when they controlled for arbitrator characteristics such as education and experience, this difference was no longer significant. The result suggested that there were systematic differences in the composition of the arbitrator panels. It should be noted that the employment arbitrator panel was not the new AAA Employment Dispute Resolution Panel but its predecessor, a subgroup of Commercial Panel arbitrators.

What makes for a better quality neutral or dispute resolution panel is an open area of research. Commentators have suggested that while there may be core common skills for high quality mediators (including substantive knowledge, experience, facilitation skills, breadth of approach, communication and problem-solving skills), the skills necessary may vary depending upon case context (Mareschal 1998). Not surprisingly, as the adoption of ADR processes evolves, the role of the workplace dispute resolution professional also evolves. Demographic changes in the workforce and the movement toward employee participation in decision making will present still further opportunities for ADR professionals. In a review of the pattern of workplace dispute resolution over the last century, Denenberg and Denenberg (1994) noted that ADR could become a mechanism for social cohesion among a more variegated workforce that naturally results from integration, immigration, and assimilation.

Another issue concerning the role of the neutral is that of professional ethics. Mediator and arbitrator professional associations such as the Society for Professionals in Dispute Resolution and the National Academy of Arbitrators have taken the lead in developing professional codes in response to the challenges of employment dispute resolution. The Due Process Protocol (Zack 1999 this volume) is a significant step forward for employees not represented by a union and who are not able to conduct meaningful negotiations with employers over the content of a dispute resolution procedure.

All of these areas concerning the characteristics and role of the neutral are ripe for theoretical and empirical investigation.

Decision Standard in Adjudicatory Processes

Scholars have also examined statutory standards in labor arbitrator decision making in interest arbitration (e.g., Bazerman 1985; Dell'Omo 1989, 1990) and normative criteria on arbitrator decision making (e.g., Hilgert 1995). However, there is very little research on these factors in employment dispute resolution. Bingham (1996) found some evidence that employment arbitrators were defining just cause differently from the way that term has been used in labor arbitration. In labor arbitration, the term has been given meaning over time through a case-by-case decision process analogous to the common law and generally requires that the employer assume the burden of proving by a preponderance of the evidence that the employee engaged in conduct warranting dismissal (Elkouri and Elkouri 1991). Many labor arbitrators use the Daugherty seven tests for just cause, which include reasonable performance standards, whether the employee was on notice that the conduct would result in discipline, the employee's work record, etc. However, in employment arbitration cases involving employee dismissal, the burden of proof is generally on the employee to show dismissal violated a statute or an express contract; this is generally where the burden of proof would lie in litigation. Because these cases are not published, there is no dialogue going on among the professional arbitrator community as to how these cases should be decided. Employment arbitrators are more commonly lawyers and may take a narrower view of their remedial powers than labor arbitrators acting under the charter of a collective bargaining agreement.

In the Bingham and Mesch (forthcoming 1999) experimental study discussed above, different types of arbitrators made decisions concerning a hypothetical employee dismissal. The subjects used either just cause or good cause under the Model Employment Termination Act (for a review of the META, see Fox and Hindman 1993; Seidman and Aalberts 1993). All of the arbitrator groups reinstated employees less frequently under the statutory good cause META standard than under the just cause standard.

Characteristics of the Disputants

There is substantial research examining the impact of variables including grievant gender on labor arbitrator decision making (e.g., Bemmels 1988a, 1988b, 1988c, 1991b; Dalton et al. 1987; Dalton et al. 1995; Dalton and Todor 1985a, 1985b; Mesch 1995b; Scott and Shadoan 1989). Bingham and Mesch (1999 forthcoming) examined grievant gender as a factor in employment and labor arbitrators' decisions on a hypothetical employment arbitration case and found marginally significant but inconclusive results tending to show that female grievants were reinstated more frequently than male grievants. Other demographic variables—such as race, ethnicity, age, or education—may affect how parties experience employment dispute resolution and their perceptions of its outcome.

Workforce diversity is an important issue in employment dispute resolution and one that is underresearched (Stallworth and Malin 1994). Some commentators have suggested that minority grievants have objectively weaker outcomes in mediation. Bennett and Hermann (1996) describe a small claims court study in which minority claimants did worse in mediation than white claimants or than minority claimants in court; however, the disparity disappeared when the mediators were also minorities.

Other disputant characteristics, such as relative power in an organization, likely would affect dispute resolution outcomes. For example, it is important to explore differences between supervisor and subordinate employee outcomes, particularly because processes structured unilaterally by an employer without a negotiator or union to represent employees may contain structural bias. Bingham (1997b) compared employee and supervisor perceptions of procedural justice in employment mediation and found that while both groups were generally satisfied with the process and mediators, supervisors were slightly more satisfied with outcome than employees. This result was comparable to work examining union and management perceptions of grievance mediation (Brett and Goldberg 1983) and plaintiff and defendant perceptions of court-annexed dispute resolution (Lind et al. 1990) and thus tended to point to reasons other than structural bias to explain the outcomes such as disparities in parties' expectations going into the process. Bingham (1997a) compared employment arbitration success for white-collar, blue-collar and pink-collar workers and found that white-collar workers had superior success. It is likely that white-collar, more highly compensated employees had greater access to legal counsel who negotiated arms-length employment contracts. This would tend to balance the table in negotiating the design of an employment dispute resolution process.

Outcomes of ADR for Organizations

Despite the data limitations and the cost to collect primary data in the nonunion sector, a variety of outcomes have been examined empirically from both the employee and employer perspectives. For example, researchers using the organizational justice literature have long established that perceptions of fairness are an important factor in assessing the effectiveness of ADR systems for employees (see Boroff 1991; Blancero 1995; and Phillips 1996 for reviews). To assess organizational results, one would like to see objective data to make conclusions along two organizational dimensions: goal attainment (effectiveness) and utility (efficiency). Numerous possibilities exist for examination (see the goals listed earlier in the paper); however, limited data availability and lack of organizational cooperation with researchers to collect the data have contributed to a lack of research in this area.

There are a few studies that investigate ADR as a proactive human resource policy. For example, Chachere (1997) used primary data from the hospital industry to assess the relationship between both the existence of ADR and its procedural characteristics with the rate of turnover of registered nurses. The data did not support the hypotheses for a negative relationship; however, the results did support the conclusion that ADR as a component of a system of human resource policies was associated with lower levels of employee turnover. This result was consistent with other research that positive organizational outcomes are associated with the use of methods to voice dissatisfaction within a system of human resource practices in nonunion organizations (Spencer 1986; Huselid 1995; Kaufman 1993).

There are anecdotal reports of organizational success with company employment dispute resolution programs. A program widely recognized as well-designed and fair is that of Brown and Root; its legal counsel reports that the overwhelming majority of employment disputes are resolved at mediation, and very few proceed to the binding arbitration step of the procedure (Bedman 1995). However, given that most organizations do not collect the necessary data to properly evaluate "success," it is surprising that managers still firmly believe (perhaps incorrectly) that ADR saves their organizations time and money by avoiding formal litigation through the courts and/or the EEOC. For example, a 1997 SHRM survey asked human resource professionals about the effect of ADR on the number of employee lawsuits. Even though 25% responded that the number had decreased and 2% indicated an increase, 55% reported that there was no effect and 18% did not know or had no answer. Systematic research that investigates these issues is obviously necessary.

Conclusion

The field of employment dispute resolution is young, and its literature is still growing. There is much we do not know about why organizations adopt these programs or how third-party processes will function in a nonunion context. The structural characteristics of employment dispute resolution systems vary widely and warrant further research, particularly on how these design features affect participant outcomes. We also need to examine whether there is an empirical basis for the claims that employment dispute resolution programs will have some positive impact on organizational outcomes such as effectiveness of dispute resolution programs and organizational efficiency. Because these are confidential processes, it will not be easy to do this research. However, it is work that needs to be done.

Endnotes

[1] The mediator may already be concerned about an imbalance of power between the employee and supervisor and unwilling to bring another person who is a stranger into the caucus with either party.

[2] The 1996 ADRA also sought to address concerns over the confidentiality of communications during federal agency mediations by broadening protection; however, it is uncertain how that new guarantee will interact with federal labor relations laws giving unions a right to be present during discussions between a third party acting at the behest of an employer and the employee (Marksteiner 1998).

[3] Workers' compensation or minimum wage and overtime claims are subject to state or federal law, depending on the nature of the employer. These claims are often outside the scope of a collective bargaining agreement.

[4] This is an example Professor Lamont Stallworth has used in sessions at the annual meeting of the Society for Professionals in Dispute Resolution.

References

Allen, Robert E., and Margaret A. Lucero. 1998. "Subordinate Aggression against Managers: Empirical Analyses of Published Arbitration Decisions." *International Journal of Conflict Management*, Vol. 9, no. 3, pp. 234-57.

Anderson, J. F., and L. B. Bingham. 1997. "Upstream Effects from Mediation of Workplace Disputes: Some Preliminary Evidence from the USPS." *Labor Law Journal*, Vol. 48, pp. 601-15.

Arrow, Kenneth, Robert H. Mnookin, Lee Ross, Amos Tversky, and Robert Wilson. 1995. *Barriers to Conflict Resolution*. New York, NY: W. W. Norton & Co.

Axenson, Tanya J. 1998. "Mandatory Arbitration Clauses and Statutory Rights: The Legal Landscape after Nelson." *Harvard Negotiation Law Review*, Vol. 3 (Spring), pp. 271-84.

Bales, Richard A. 1994. "Compulsory Arbitration of Individual Employment Rights." *Houston Law Review,* Vol. 30, no. 5 (Spring), pp. 1863-913.

_____. 1997. "The Discord between Collective Bargaining and Individual Employment Rights: Theoretical Origins and a Proposed Reconciliation." *Boston University Law Review,* Vol. 77, no. 4 (October), pp. 687-760.

Baxter, R. H., Jr., and E. M. Hunt. 1989. "Alternative Dispute Resolution: Arbitration of Employment Claims." *Employee Relations Law Journal,* Vol. 15, pp. 187-207.

Bazerman, M. H. 1985. "Norms of Distributive Justice in Interest Arbitration." *Industrial and Labor Relations Review*, Vol. 38, pp. 558-70.

Bedman, W. L. 1995. "From Litigation to ADR: Brown and Root's Experience." *Dispute Resolution Journal,* Vol. 50, no. 4, pp. 8-14.

Bemmels, B. 1988a. "The Effect of Grievants' Gender on Arbitrators' Decisions." *Industrial and Labor Relations Review,* Vol. 41, pp. 251-62.

_____. 1988b. "Gender Effects in Discipline Arbitration: Evidence from British Columbia." *Academy of Management Journal*, Vol. 31, pp. 699-706.

_____. 1988c. "Gender Effects in Discharge Arbitration." *Industrial and Labor Relations Review*, Vol. 42, pp. 63-76.

_____. 1990a. "The Effects of Grievants' Gender and Arbitrator Characteristics on Arbitration Decisions." *Labor Studies Journal*, Vol. 15, pp. 48-61.

_____. 1990b. "Arbitrator Characteristics and Arbitrator Decisions." *Journal of Labor Research*, Vol. 11, pp. 181-92.

_____. 1991a. "Attribution Theory and Discipline Arbitration." *Industrial and Labor Relations Review*, Vol. 44, pp. 548-62.

_____. 1991b. "Gender Effects in Grievance Arbitration." *Industrial Relations*, Vol. 30, pp. 150-62.

Bennett, Mark D., and Michele S. G. Hermann. 1996. *The Art of Mediation*. Notre Dame, IN: The National Institute for Trial Advocacy.

Bethel, Terry A. 1993. "Wrongful Discharge: Litigation or Arbitration?" *Journal of Dispute Resolution*, Vol. 1993, no. 2, pp. 289-304.

Bickner, Mei L., Christine Ver Ploeg, and Charles Feigenbaum. 1997. "Developments in Employment Arbitration: Analysis of a New Survey of Employment Arbitration Programs." *Dispute Resolution Journal*, Vol. 52, no. 1, pp. 8-15, 78-84.

Bies, R. J. 1987. "The Predicament of Injustice: The Management of Moral Outrage." In L. L. Cummings and B. M. Staw, eds., *Research in Organizational Behavior*, Vol. 9. Greenwich, CT: JAI Press, pp. 289-319.

Bingham, Lisa B. 1995. "Is There a Bias in Arbitration of Nonunion Employment Disputes? An Analysis of Actual Cases and Outcomes." *International Journal of Conflict Management*, Vol. 6, no. 4, pp. 369-86.

_____. 1996. "Emerging Due Process Concerns in Employment Arbitration." *Labor Law Journal*, Vol. 47, no. 2, pp. 108-26.

_____. 1997a. "Employment Arbitration: The Repeat Player Effect." *Employee Rights and Employment Policy Journal*, Vol. 1, no. 1, pp. 189-220.

_____. 1997b. "Mediating Employment Disputes: Perceptions of Redress at the United States Postal Service." *Review of Public Personnel Administration*, Vol. 17, no. 2, pp. 20-30.

_____. 1998a. "On Repeat Players, Adhesive Contracts, and the Use of Statistics in Judicial Review of Arbitration Awards." *McGeorge Law Review*, Vol. 29, no. 2, pp. 223-60.

_____. 1998b. "Employment Arbitration and the Due Process Protocol: Preliminary Evidence That Self-Regulation Makes a Difference." Invited Paper presented at Arbitration in the 21st Century, a conference cosponsored by the American Bar Association Dispute Resolution Section and the Association of the Bar of the City of New York, September 25, 1998, New York.

Bingham, Lisa B., and Charles R. Wise. 1996. "The Administrative Dispute Resolution Act of 1990: How Do We Evaluate Its Success?" *Journal of Public Administration, Research and Theory*, Vol. 6, no. 3, pp. 383-414.

Bingham, Lisa B., and Denise R. Chachere. 1998. "Repeat Use of Arbitrators and the Repeat Player Effect in Employment Arbitration." Presented at the Workplace Conflict and Cooperation in a New Century: Prospects for Employee Representation Conference (University of Illinois Institute of Labor and Industrial Relations, May 2).

Bingham, Lisa B., and Debra J. Mesch. Forthcoming. "Decision Making in Employment and Labor Arbitration." *Industrial Relations*.

Blancero, D. 1995. "Nonunion Grievance Systems: Systems Characteristics and Fairness Perceptions." *Academy of Management Best Papers Proceedings*, Vol. 1995, pp. 84-8.

Block, Richard N., J. Beck, and A. R. Olson. 1996. "A Look at Grievance Mediation." *Dispute Resolution Journal*, Vol. 51, no. 4, pp. 54-61.

Block, Richard N., and Jack Stieber. 1987. "The Impact of Attorneys and Arbitrators on Arbitration Awards." *Industrial and Labor Relations Review*, Vol. 40, no. 4 (July), pp. 543-55.

Bloom, D. E., and C. L. Cavanagh. 1986. "An Analysis of the Selection of Arbitrators." *American Economic Review*, Vol. 76, no. 3, pp. 408-22.

Bohlander, G. W. 1994. "Why Arbitrators Overturn Managers in Employee Suspension and Discharge Cases." *Journal of Collective Negotiations*, Vol. 23, no. 1, pp. 73-89.

Boroff, Karen E. 1991. "Measuring the Perception of the Effectiveness of a Workplace Complaint System." In D. Sockell, D. Lewin, and D. Lipsky, eds., *Advances in Industrial Relations*, Vol. 5. Greenwich, CT: JAI Press, pp. 207-33.

Bowers, M., R. L. Seeber, and L. E. Stallworth. 1982. "Grievance Mediation: A Route to Resolution for the Cost-Conscious 1980s." *Labor Law Journal*, Vol. 33, pp. 459-64.

Brett, Jeanne M., Zoe I. Barsness, and Stephen B. Goldberg. 1996. "The Effectiveness of Mediation: An Independent Analysis of Cases Handled by Four Major Service Providers." *Negotiation Journal*, Vol. 12, no. 3 (July), pp. 259-69.

Brett, Jeanne M., and Stephen B. Goldberg. 1983. "Grievance Mediation in the Coal Industry: A Field Experiment." *Industrial and Labor Relations Review*, Vol. 37, no. 1, pp. 49-67.

Briggs, S., and L. Gundry. 1994. "The Human Dimensions of Grievance Peer Review." *Journal of Collective Negotiations in the Public Sector*, Vol. 23, no. 2, pp. 97-113.

Briggs, S. S., and J. C. Anderson. 1980. "An Empirical Investigation of Arbitrator Acceptability." *Industrial Relations*, Vol. 19, no. 2, pp. 163-74.

Buse, Michele M. 1995. "Contracting Employment Disputes Out of the Jury System: An Analysis of the Implementation of Binding Arbitration in the Nonunion Workplace and Proposals to Reduce the Harsh Effects of a Nonappealable Award." *Pepperdine Law Review*, Vol. 22, no. 4, pp. 1485-540.

Bush, R. A. B., and J. Folger. 1994. *The Promise of Mediation: Responding to Conflict through Empowerment and Recognition*. San Francisco: Jossey-Bass Publishers.

Carnevale, P. J., and D. G. Pruitt. 1992. "Negotiation and Mediation." *Annual Review of Psychology*, Vol. 43, pp. 521-82.

Carrington, Paul D. 1998. "Statute: Regulating Dispute Resolution Provisions in Adhesion Contracts." *Harvard Journal on Legislation*, Vol. 35, pp. 225-32.

Chachere, Denise R. 1997. "Does Employee Voice Reduce Turnover? Some Evidence from Nonunion Grievance Procedures." Presented at the Industrial Relations Research Association Annual Meeting (New Orleans, January 5).

Cherry, Miriam A. 1998. "Not-So-Arbitrary Arbitration: Using Title VII Disparate Impact Analysis to Invalidate Employment Contracts That Discriminate." *Harvard Women's Law Journal*, Vol. 21, pp. 267-307.

Child, J. 1973. "Predicting and Understanding Organizational Structure." *Administrative Science Quarterly*, Vol. 18, pp. 168-85.

Clarke, Stevens H. 1997. "Mandatory Mediation in On-the-Job Injury Cases." *Popular Government*, Vol. 1997 (Fall), pp. 19-26.

Clay, J. M., and E. C. Stephens. 1994. "An Analysis of Absenteeism Arbitration Cases: Factors Used by Arbitrators in Making Decisions." *International Journal of Conflict Management*, Vol. 5, no. 2, pp. 130-42.

Cohen, Cynthia F., and Theresa Domagalski. 1998. "The Effects of Mandatory Arbitration of Employment Discrimination Claims: Perceptions of Justice and Suggestions for Change." *Employee Responsibilities and Rights Journal*, Vol. 11, no. 1, pp. 27-40.

Cole, Sarah R. 1996. "Incentives and Arbitration: The Case against Enforcement of Executory Arbitration Agreements between Employers and Employee." *University of Missouri at Kansas City Law Review*, Vol. 64, pp. 449-82.

_____. 1997. "A Funny Thing Happened on the Way to the (Alternative) Forum: Reexamining *Alexander v. Gardner-Denver* in the Wake of *Gilmer v. Interstate/Johnson Lane Corp.*" *Brigham Young University Law Review*, Vol. 1997, no. 3, pp. 591-629.

Commission on the Future of Worker-Management Relations. 1994. *Report and Recommendations, GPO-CTLG, L1.2-F 98/2* (AKA: The Dunlop Report). Washington, DC: U.S. Department of Labor and U.S. Department of Commerce.

Conti, A. J. 1985. "Mediation of Workplace Disputes: A Prescription for Organizational Health." *Employee Relations Law Journal*, Vol. 11, pp. 291-310.

Corrada, Roberto L. 1998. "The Arbitral Imperative in Labor and Employment Law." *Catholic University Law Review*, Vol. 47, no. 3 (Spring), pp. 919-40.

Costantino, C. A., and C. S. Merchant. 1996. *Designing Conflict Management Systems: A Guide to Creating Productive and Healthy Organizations*. San Francisco, CA: Jossey-Bass Publishers, Inc.

Crow, S. M., and J. W. Logan. 1994. "Arbitrators' Characteristics and Decision-Making Records, Gender of Arbitrators and Grievants, and the Presence of Legal Counsel as Predictors of Arbitral Outcomes." *Employee Responsibilities and Rights Journal*, Vol. 7, no. 2, pp. 169-85.

_____. 1995. "A Tentative Decision-Making Model of the Strong and Weak Forces at Labor Arbitration." *Journal of Collective Negotiations*, Vol. 24, no. 2, pp. 111-20.

Dalton, D. R., W. D. Todor, and C. L. Owen. 1987. "Sex Effects in Workplace Justice Outcomes: A Field Assessment." *Journal of Applied Psychology*, Vol. 72, pp. 156-59.

Dalton, D. R., and W. D. Todor. 1985a. "Gender and Workplace Justice: A Field Assessment." *Personnel Psychology*, Vol. 38, no. 1 (Spring), pp. 133-51.

_____. 1985b. "Composition or Dyads as a Factor in the Outcomes of Workplace Justice." *Academy of Management Journal*, Vol. 28, no. 3 (September), pp. 704-12.

Dalton, D. R., D. J. Mesch, C. L. Owen, and W. D. Todor. 1995. "The 'Iron Law of Paternalism' in Organizational Justice Outcomes? Two Field Assessments." *Labor Law Journal*, Vol. 46, no. 11 (November), pp. 669-77.

Daus, M. W. 1995. "Mediating Claims of Discrimination." *Dispute Resolution Journal*, Vol. 50, no. 4, pp. 51-4.

Davis, Kenneth R. 1997. "When Ignorance of the Law Is Not Excuse: Judicial Review of Arbitration Awards." *Buffalo Law Review*, Vol. 45, no. 1 (Winter), pp. 49-139.

_____. 1998. "The Arbitration Claws: Unconscionability in the Securities Industry." *Boston University Law Review*, Vol. 78, no. 2, pp. 255-327.

Dean, Justin M. 1998. "Going, Going, Almost Gone: The Loss of Employees' Rights to Bring Statutory Discrimination Claims in Court." *Missouri Law Review*, Vol. 63, no. 4 (Fall), pp. 801-20.

Delaney, John T., and Peter Feuille. 1992. "The Determinants of Nonunion Grievance and Arbitration Procedures." In John F. Burton, Jr., ed., *Proceedings of The Forty-Fifth Annual Meeting*: January 1992, New Orleans. Madison, WI: Industrial Relations Research Association, pp. 529-38.

Delaney, J. T., D. Lewin, and C. Ichniowski. 1989. *Human Resource Policies and Practices in American Firms*. BLMR 137. Washington, DC: U.S. Department of Labor, Bureau of Labor-Management Relations and Cooperative Programs.

Dell'Omo, G. G. 1989. "Wage Disputes in Interest Arbitration: Arbitrators Weigh the Criteria." *The Arbitration Journal*, Vol. 44, pp. 4-13.

_____. 1990. "Capturing Arbitrator Decision Policies under a Public Sector Interest Arbitration Statute." *Review of Public Personnel Administration*, Vol. 10, pp. 19-38.

Denenberg, Tia S., and Richard V. Denenberg. 1994. "The Future of the Workplace Dispute Resolver." *Dispute Resolution Journal*, Vol. 49, no. 2, pp. 48-58.

Dibble, R. E. 1997. "Alternative Dispute Resolution of Employment Conflicts: The Search for Standards." *Journal of Collective Negotiations in the Public Sector*, Vol. 26, no. 1, pp. 73-84.

Dillon, Kristen L. 1994. *Statewide Offices of Dispute Resolution: Initiating Collaborative Approaches to Dispute Resolution in State Government*. Washington, DC: The National Institute for Dispute Resolution.

Dunlop, John T., and Arnold M. Zack. 1997. *The Mediation and Arbitration of Employment Disputes*. San Francisco: Jossey-Bass Publishers.

Eaton, Adrienne. 1994. "Factors Contributing to the Survival of Participative Programs in Unionized Settings." *Industrial and Labor Relations Review*, Vol. 47, no. 3 (April).

Edelman, Lauren B. 1990. "Legal Environments and Organizational Governance: The Expansion of Due Process in the American Workplace." *American Journal of Sociology*, Vol. 95, no. 6 (May), pp. 1401-40.

Edelman, Lauren B., Howard S. Erlanger, and John Lande. 1993. "Internal Dispute Resolution: The Transformation of Civil Rights in the Workplace." *Law and Society Review*, Vol. 27, no. 3, pp. 497-534.

Edwards, R. 1993. *Rights at Work: Employment Relations in the Post-Union Era*. Washington, DC: The Brookings Institution.

Egler, T. D. 1995. "The Benefits and Burdens of Arbitration." *HR Magazine*, Vol. 40, no. 7, pp. 27-30.

Elkouri, F., and E. Elkouri. 1991. *How Arbitration Works*. 4th ed. Washington, DC: Bureau of National Affairs, Inc.

Emerson, Robert W. 1998. "Franchise Terminations: Legal Rights and Practical Effects When Franchisees Claim the Franchise or Discriminates." *American Business Law Journal*, Vol. 35, no. 4 (Summer), pp. 559-645.

Estreicher, Samuel. 1990. "Arbitration of Employment Disputes without Unions." *Chicago-Kent Law Review*, Vol. 66, no. 3, pp. 753-97.

_____. 1997. "Predispute Agreements to Arbitrate Statutory Employment Claims." *New York University Law Review*, Vol. 72, no. 6 (December), pp. 1344-74.

Ettingoff, Cindy Cole, and Gregory Powell. 1996. "Use of Alternative Dispute Resolution in Employment-related Disputes." *University of Memphis Law Review*, Vol. 26, no. 3, pp. 1131-67.

Evans, Robin J. 1998. "Notes and Comments: The Administrative Dispute Resolution Act of 1996: Improving Federal Agency Use of Alternative Dispute Resolution Processes." *Administrative Law Review*, Vol. 50, no. 1, pp. 217-33.

Evans, S. 1994. "Doing Mediation to Avoid Litigation." *HR Magazine*, Vol. 39, no. 3, pp. 48-51.

Feller, David E. 1997. "Fender Bender or Train Wreck? The Collision between Statutory Protection of Individual Employee Rights and the Judicial Revision of the Federal Arbitration Act." *St. Louis University Law Journal*, Vol. 41, no. 2 (Spring), pp. 561-74.

_____. 1998. "Taft and Hartley Vindicated: The Curious History of Review of Labor Arbitration Awards." *Berkeley Journal of Employment and Labor Law,* Vol. 19, no. 2, pp. 296-306.

Feuille, Peter. 1992. "Why Does Grievance Mediation Resolve Grievances?" *Negotiation Journal,* Vol. 8, no. 2, pp. 131-45.

_____. 1995. "Dispute Resolution Frontiers in the Unionized Workplace." In Sandra E. Gleason, ed., *Workplace Dispute Resolution: Directions for the Twenty-First Century.* East Lansing, MI: State University Press, pp. 17-55.

_____. 1999. "Grievance Mediation." In Adrienne E. Eaton and Jeffrey H. Keefe, eds., *Employment Dispute Resolution and Worker Rights in the Changing Workplace.* Madison, WI: Industrial Relations Research Association.

Feuille, Peter, and Denise R. Chachere. 1995. "Looking Fair or Being Fair: Remedial Voice Procedures in Nonunion Workplaces." *Journal of Management,* Vol. 21, no. 1, pp. 27-42.

Feuille, P., and D. M. Kolb. 1994. "Waiting in the Wings: Mediation's Role in Grievance Resolution." *Negotiation Journal,* Vol. 10, no. 3, pp. 249-64.

Fisher, R., W. Ury, and B. Patton. 1991. *Getting to Yes.* 2d ed. New York: Penguin Books.

Fleming, R. W. 1967. *The Labor Arbitration Process.* Urbana, IL: University of Illinois Press.

Flores, G. M. 1993. "Handling Employee Issues through Alternative Dispute Resolution." *Bankers Magazine,* Vol. 176, no. 4, pp. 47-50.

Folger, Joseph P., and Robert A. Baruch Bush. 1996. "Transformative Mediation and Third-Party Intervention: Ten Hallmarks of a Transformative Approach to Practice." *Mediation Quarterly,* Vol. 13, no. 4, pp. 263-78.

Folger, R. 1977. "Distributive and Procedural Justice: Combined Impact of 'Voice' and Improvement on Experience Inequity." *Journal of Personality and Social Psychology,* Vol. 35, pp. 108-19.

Fortado, Bruce. 1998. "Managerial Justice: A Field Study of the Initial Steps of Appeal." *Employee Responsibilities and Rights Journal,* Vol. 11, no. 3, pp. 215-36.

Fox, J. B., and H. D. Hindman. 1993. "The Model Employment Termination Act: Provisions and Discussion." *Employee Responsibilities and Rights Journal,* Vol. 6, no. 1, pp. 33-44.

Frankhauser, M. M. 1995. "Arbitration: The Alternative to Securities and Employment Litigation." *The Business Lawyer,* Vol. 50, no. 4, pp. 1333-79.

Gadlin, H. 1991. "Careful Maneuvers: Mediating Sexual Harassment." *Negotiation Journal,* Vol. 7, pp. 139-54.

Galanter, Marc. 1974. "Why the 'Haves' Come Out Ahead: Speculations on the Limits of Legal Change." *Law and Society Review,* Vol. 9, pp. 95-105.

Ganzel, R. 1997. "Second-Class Justice?" *Training,* Vol. 34, no. 10, pp. 84-95.

Gershenfeld, Walter J. 1996. "Preemployment Dispute Arbitration Agreements: Yes, No, and Maybe." *Hofstra Labor Law Journal,* Vol. 14, pp. 245-63.

Goldstein, J. I., and M. F. Payson. 1995. "Alternative Dispute Resolution of Employment Matters in the Public Sector." *Spectrum: The Journal of State Government,* Vol. 68, no. 4, pp. 36-42.

Gould, W. B., IV. 1987. "Stemming the Wrongful Discharge Tide: A Case for Arbitration." *Employee Relations Law Journal,* Vol. 13, pp. 404-25.

Greenberg, Jerald. 1996. *The Quest for Justice on the Job: Essays and Experiments.* Thousand Oaks, CA: Sage Publications.

Haagen, Paul H. 1998. "New Wineskins for New Wine: The Need to Encourage Fairness in Mandatory Arbitration." *Arizona Law Review*, Vol. 40, no. 3 (Fall), pp. 1039-68.

Hayes, Kristine L. 1998. "Prepostal Prevention of Workplace Violence: Establishing an Ombuds Program as One Possible Solution." *Ohio State Journal on Dispute Resolution*, Vol. 14, no. 1, pp. 215-33.

Hayford, Stephen, and Ralph Peeples. 1995. "Commercial Arbitration in Evolution: An Assessment and Call for Dialogue." *Ohio State Journal on Dispute Resolution*, Vol. 10, pp. 343-416.

Heflin, H. 1997. "Alternative Dispute Resolution: A Guarantee Our Justice System Works." *Vital Speeches of the Day*, Vol. 63, no. 23, pp. 709-12.

Heneman, H. G., III, and M. H. Sandver. 1983. "Arbitrators' Backgrounds and Behavior." *Journal of Labor Research*, Vol. 4, no. 2, pp. 115-24.

Hilgert, R. L. 1995. "An Arbitrator Looks at Grievance Arbitration." *Employee Responsibilities and Rights Journal*, Vol. 8, no. 1, pp. 67-73.

Hoellering, Michael F. 1997. "Mediation and Arbitration: A Growing Interaction." *Dispute Resolution Journal*, Vol. 52 (Spring), pp. 23-25.

House, N. C. 1992. "Grievance Mediation: AT&T's Experience." *Labor Law Journal*, Vol. 43, pp. 491-95.

Howard, William M. 1995. "Arbitrating Claims of Employment Discrimination: What Really Does Happen? What Really Should Happen?" *Dispute Resolution Journal*, Vol. 50, no. 4, pp. 40-50.

Hubert, Denise V. M. 1998. "Exactly What Is Employment ADR?" *Human Resource Professional*, Vol. 1998 (July/August), pp. 23-27.

Huselid, Mark A. 1995. "The Impact of Human Resource Management Practices on Turnover and Productivity." *Academy of Management Journal*, Vol. 38, no. 3 (June), pp. 635-72.

Jacob, Anthony J. 1997. "Expanding Judicial Review to Encourage Employers and Employees to Enter the Arbitration Arena." *John Marshall Law Review*, Vol. 30, no. 4 (Summer), pp. 1099-125.

Karim, A. R. 1993. "Arbitrator Considerations in Modifying Discharge Decisions in the Public Sector." *Journal of Collective Negotiations*, Vol. 22, no. 3, pp. 245-51.

Kaufman, Bruce E. 1993. *The Origins and Evolution of the Field of Industrial Relations in the United States*. Ithaca, NY: ILR Press.

Kaufmann, S. M., and J. A. Chanin. 1994. "Directing the Flood: The Arbitration of Employment Claims." *Labor Lawyer*, Vol. 10, pp. 217-38.

Kochan, Thomas A. 1981. "Empirical Research on Labor Law: Lessons from Dispute Resolution in the Public Sector." *University of Illinois Law Review*, Vol. 1981, no. 1, pp. 161-80.

Kolb, Deborah M. 1987. "Corporate Ombudsman and Organization Conflict Resolution." *Journal of Conflict Resolution*, Vol. 31, no. 4 (December), pp. 673-91.
_____. 1989. "How Existing Procedures Shape Alternatives: The Case of Grievance Mediation." *Journal of Dispute Resolution*, Vol. 1989, pp. 59-87.

Kolb, D. M., and S. S. Silbey. 1990. "Enhancing the Capacity of Organizations to Deal with Disputes." *Negotiation Journal*, Vol. 6, pp. 297-304.

Kolb, Deborah M., and Associates. 1994. *When Talk Works: Profiles of Mediators*. San Francisco, CA: Jossey-Bass Publishers, Inc.

Kressel, Kenneth, and Dean G. Pruitt and Associates. 1989. *Mediation Research.* San Francisco, CA: Jossey-Bass Publishers, Inc.

LaMothe, L. A. 1994. "Thinking about Mediation." *Litigation,* Vol. 19, no. 4, pp. 1-4.

Lande, John. 1998. "Failing Faith in Litigation? A Survey of Business Lawyers' and Executives' Opinions." *Harvard Negotiation Law Review,* Vol. 3, no. 1, pp. 1-70.

Leap, T. L., and M. J. Stahl. 1985. "Modeling Labor Arbitration Decisions: Factors Used in Medically Based Grievances." *Psychological Reports,* Vol. 56, pp. 559-66.

Levin, Murray S. 1997. "The Role of Substantive Law in Business Arbitration and the Importance of Volition." *American Business Law Journal,* Vol. 35, no. 1 (Fall), pp. 105-80.

Lewicki, R. J., S. E. Weiss, and D. Lewin. 1992. "Models of Conflict, Negotiation, and Third-Party Intervention: A Review and Synthesis." *Journal of Organizational Behavior,* Vol. 13, pp. 209-52.

Lewin, David. 1987. "Dispute Resolution in the Nonunion Firm: A Theoretical and Empirical Analysis." *Journal of Conflict Resolution,* Vol. 31, no. 3, pp. 465-502.

_____. 1998. "Nonunion Employment Dispute Resolution." Presented at the Workplace Conflict and Cooperation in a New Century: Prospects for Employee Representation Conference (University of Illinois Institute of Labor and Industrial Relations, May 2).

Lind, E. A., C. T. Kulik, M. Ambrose, and M. V. de Vera Park. 1993. "Individual and Corporate Dispute Resolution: Using Procedural Fairness as a Decision Heuristic." *Administrative Science Quarterly,* Vol. 38, pp. 224-51.

Lind, E. A., R. J. Maccoun, P. A. Ebener, W. L. F. Felstiner, D. R. Hensler, J. Resnick, and T. R. Tyler. 1990. "In the Eye of the Beholder: Tort Litigants' Evaluations of Their Experiences in the Civil Justice System." *Law & Society Review,* Vol. 24, no. 4, pp. 953-96.

Lind, E. A., and T. R. Tyler. 1988. *The Social Psychology of Procedural Justice.* New York: Plenum Press.

Lipsky, David B., and Ronald L. Seeber. 1998a. "In Search of Control: The Corporate Embrace of ADR." *University of Pennsylvania Journal of Labor and Employment Law,* Vol. 1, no. 1, pp. 133-57.

_____. 1998b. *The Appropriate Resolution of Corporate Disputes: A Report on the Growing Use of ADR by U.S. Corporations.* Ithaca, NY: Cornell/PERC Institute on Conflict Resolution, Cornell University.

Luthar, Harsh K., and Joseph Bonnici. 1998. "The Arbitration of Discrimination Complaints: A New Look at the Issues." *Employee Responsibilities and Rights Journal,* Vol. 11, no. 3, pp. 159-70.

Lynd, Patrick A. 1998. "Recent Developments Regarding Mandatory Arbitration of Statutory Employment Disputes." *Oregon Law Review,* Vol. 77, no. 1 (Spring), pp. 287-307.

Maltby, Lewis. 1994. "Paradise Lost—How the Gilmer Court Lost the Opportunity for Alternative Dispute Resolution to Improve Civil Rights." *New York Law School Journal of Human Rights,* Vol. 12, pp. 1-20.

Manuszak, Jennifer N. 1997. "Predispute Civil Rights Arbitration in the Nonunion Sector: The Need for a Tandem Reform Effort at the Contracting, Procedural, and Judicial Review Stages." *Ohio State Journal on Dispute Resolution,* Vol. 12, no. 2, pp. 387-432.

Mareschal, Patrice M. 1998. "Providing High Quality Mediation: Insights from the Federal Mediation and Conciliation Service." *Review of Public Personnel Administration,* Vol. 18, no. 4, pp. 55-67.

Marksteiner, Peter. 1998. "How Confidential are Federal Sector Employment-related Dispute Mediations?" *Ohio State Journal on Dispute Resolution,* Vol. 14, no. 1, pp. 89-155.

Marler, Jennifer A. 1996. "Arbitrating Employment Discrimination Claims: The Lower Courts Extend *Gilmer v. Interstate/Johnson Lane Corp.* to Include Individual Employment Contracts." *Washington University Law Quarterly,* Vol. 74, no. 2 (Spring), pp. 443-79.

Mayer, B. S., and S. Ghais. 1997. "Principles of Designing Employee Grievance Procedures." *Human Resources Professional,* Vol. 10, no. 5, pp. 16-19.

McCammon, M., and J. L. Cotton. 1990. "Arbitration Decisions in Subcontracting Disputes." *Industrial Relations,* Vol. 29, pp. 135-44.

McDermott, E. P. 1995. "Survey of 92 Key Companies: Using ADR to Settle Employment Disputes." *Dispute Resolution Journal,* Vol. 50, 1, pp. 8-13.

McEwen, Craig A. 1997. *An Evaluation of the Equal Employment Opportunity Commission's Pilot Mediation Program.* Washington, DC: Equal Employment Opportunity Commission.

McGowan, Kathleen C. 1998. "Unequal Opportunity in At-Will Employment: The Search for a Remedy." *Saint John's Law Review,* Vol. 72, no. 1 (Winter), pp. 141-83.

McPherson, W. H. 1956. "Grievance Mediation under Collective Bargaining." *Industrial and Labor Relations Review,* Vol. 9, pp. 200-12.

Meltzer, D. Leah. 1998. "The Federal Workplace Ombuds." *Ohio State Journal on Dispute Resolution,* Vol. 13, pp. 549-609.

Mesch, Debra J. 1995a. "Grievance Arbitration in the Public Sector: A Conceptual Framework and Empirical Analysis of Public and Private Sector Arbitration Cases." *Review of Public Personnel Administration,* Vol. 15, no. 4, pp. 22-36.

_____. 1995b. "Arbitration and Gender: An Analysis of Cases Taken to Arbitration in the Public Sector." *Journal of Collective Negotiations in the Public Sector,* Vol. 24, no. 3, pp. 207-18.

Mesch, D. J., and D. R. Dalton. 1991. "Workplace Justice Outcomes 'In the Name of the Union': A Field Assessment." *The International Journal of Conflict Management,* Vol. 2, pp. 45-54.

_____. 1992. "Workplace Justice Outcomes: Arbitration 'In the Name of the Union'." *The International Journal of Conflict Management,* Vol. 3, pp. 31-43.

Miller, S. W. 1994. "Mediation—An Alternative Dispute Resolution Methodology Whose Time Has Come." *The CPA Journal,* Vol. 64, no. 7, pp. 54-55.

Mills, Miriam K., ed. 1991. *Alternative Dispute Resolution in the Public Sector.* Chicago, IL: Nelson Hall Publishers.

Moberly, Robert B. 1998. "Introduction: Dispute Resolution in the Law School Curriculum: Opportunities and Challenges." *Florida Law Review,* Vol. 50, no. 4 (September), pp. 583-89.

Moore, Christopher. 1996. *The Mediation Process.* 2d ed. San Francisco, CA: Jossey-Bass Publishers, Inc.

Motley, John-Paul. 1998. "Compulsory Arbitration Agreements in Employment Contracts from Gardner-Denver to Austin: The Legal Uncertainty and Why

Employers Should Choose Not to Use Preemployment Arbitration Agreements." *Vanderbilt Law Review,* Vol. 51, no. 3 (April), pp. 687-720.

National Academy of Arbitrators. 1997. *Policy Guideline on the Arbitration of Employment Disputes.* Washington, DC: NAA.

Nelson, N. E., and E. M. Curry. 1981. "Arbitrator Characteristics and Arbitral Decisions." *Industrial Relations,* Vol. 20, pp. 312-17.

Nigro, Lloyd G., and William L. Waugh, Jr. 1998. "Local Government Responses to Workplace Violence: A Status Report." *Review of Public Personnel Administration,* Vol. 18, no. 4, pp. 5-17.

Oldham, G. R., and J. R. Hackman. 1981. "Relationships between Organizational Structure and Employee Reactions: Comparing Alternative Frameworks." *Administrative Science Quarterly,* Vol. 26, pp. 66-83.

Ombudsman Association. 1997. "Code of Ethics." Accessed 4/22/99. www.naples.cc.sunysb.edu/Pres/ombuds.nsf/pages/ethics.

Oswald, S. L. 1991. "Students as Arbitrators: An Empirical Investigation." *Industrial Relations,* Vol. 30, pp. 286-93.

Oswald, S. L., and S. B. Caudill. 1991. "Experimental Evidence of Gender Effects in Arbitration Decisions." *Employee Responsibilities and Rights Journal,* Vol. 4, no. 4, pp. 271-81.

Panken, Peter M., Stacey B. Babson, and Robert Webb. 1997. "Avoiding Employment Litigation: Alternative Dispute Resolution of Employment Disputes in the '90s." *American Law Institute–American Bar Association Continuing Legal Education,* Vol. SB36, pp. 1151-69.

Peirce, Robert S., Dean G. Pruitt, and Sally J. Czaja. 1993. "Complainant-Respondent Differences in Procedural Choice." *International Journal of Conflict Management,* Vol. 4, no. 3, pp. 199-222.

Pell, A. R. 1993. "What—No Grievances?" *Manager's Magazine,* Vol. 68, no. 10, pp. 29-30.

Penna, C. M. 1993. "Mediation: In the Mainstream." *New York Law Journal,* pp. 32-37.

Pfeffer, Jeffrey. 1981. *Power in Organizations.* Marshfield, MA: Pitman.

Phillips, V. 1996. "Mediation: The Influence of Style and Gender on Disputants' Perception of Justice." *New Zealand Journal of Industrial Relations,* Vol. 21, no. 3, pp. 297-311.

Ponak, A. 1987. "Discharge Arbitration and Reinstatement in the Province of Alberta." *Arbitration Journal,* Vol. 42, pp. 47-67.

Ponak, A., W. Zerbe, S. Rose, and C. Olson. 1996. "Using Event History Analysis to Model Delay in Grievance Arbitration." *Industrial and Labor Relations Review,* Vol. 50, no. 1, pp. 105-21.

Ponte, Lucille M. 1997. "In the Shadow of Gilmer: How Post-*Gilmer* Legal Challenges to Predispute Arbitration Agreements Point the Way towards Greater Fairness in Employment Arbitration." *Ohio State Journal on Dispute Resolution,* Vol. 12, no. 2, pp. 359-86.

Poser, Norman S. 1998. "Judicial Review of Arbitration Awards: Manifest Disregard of the Law." *Brooklyn Law Review,* Vol. 64, no. 2 (Summer), pp. 471-518.

Press, Matthew J. 1997. "Arbitration of Claims under the Securities Exchange Act of 1934: Exclusive Jurisdiction Still Justified?" *Boston University Law Review,* Vol. 77, no. 3, pp. 629-54.

Quinn, T. J., M. Rosenbaum, and D. S. McPherson. 1990. "Grievance Mediation and Grievance Negotiation Skills: Building Collaborative Relationships." *Labor Law Journal,* Vol. 41, pp. 762-72.

Ray, Amy L. 1998. "When Employers Litigate to Arbitrate: New Standards of Enforcement for Employer-mandated Arbitration Agreements." *SMU Law Review,* Vol. 51, no. 2 (Jan-Feb), pp. 441-68.

Robbins, Lee P., and William Deane. 1986. "The Corporate Ombuds: A New Approach to Conflict Management." *Negotiation Journal,* Vol. 2, no. 2, pp. 195-205.

Roberts, M. T., R. S. Wolters, W. H. Holley, Jr., and H. S. Feild. 1990. "Grievance Mediation: A Management Perspective." *Arbitration Journal,* Vol. 45, no. 3, pp. 15-23.

Robinson, Betty D. 1992. "Considering Grievance Mediation." *Employee Responsibilities and Rights Journal,* Vol. 5, no. 2, pp. 143-53.

Rowe, Beth A. 1996. "Binding Arbitration of Employment Disputes: Opposing Predispute Agreements." *University of Toledo Law Review,* Vol. 27, no. 4 (Summer), pp. 921-50.

Rowe, M. P. 1981. "Dealing with Sexual Harassment." *Harvard Business Review,* Vol. 59, no. 3, pp. 42-47.

_____. 1990a. "People Who Feel Harassed Need a Complaint System with Both Formal and Informal Options." *Negotiation Journal,* Vol. 6, no. 2, pp. 161-72.

_____. 1990b. "Helping People Help Themselves: An ADR Option for Interpersonal Conflict." *Negotiation Journal,* Vol. 6, no. 3, pp. 239-48.

Schuyler, Marilynn L. 1993. *A Cost Analysis of the Department of Labor's Philadelphia ADR Pilot Project.* Washington, DC: U.S. Department of Labor.

Scott, C., and E. Shadoan. 1989. "The Effect of Gender on Arbitration Decisions." *Journal of Labor Research,* Vol. 10, no. 4, pp. 429-36.

Scott, K. D., and G. S. Taylor. 1983. "An Analysis of Absenteeism Cases Taken to Arbitration: 1975-1981." *Arbitration Journal,* Vol. 38, pp. 61-70.

Seidman, L., and R. J. Aalberts. 1993. "Managing Employer-Employee Conflict: A Case for Arbitration and the Model Employment Termination Act." *The International Journal of Conflict Management,* Vol. 4, pp. 263-75.

Shapiro, Debra L.,and Jeanne M. Brett. 1993. "Comparing Three Processes Underlying Judgments of Procedural Justice: A Field Study of Mediation and Arbitration." *Journal of Personality and Social Psychology,* Vol. 65, no. 6, pp. 1167-77.

Sheppard, B. H., R. J. Lewicki, and J. W. Minton. 1992. *Organizational Justice: The Search for Fairness in the Workplace.* New York: Lexington Books.

Sherman, M. R. 1995. "Is There a Mediator in the House?" *Dispute Resolution Journal,* Vol. 50, no. 2, pp. 48-54.

Silberman, A. D. 1989. "Breaking the Mold of Grievance Resolution: A Pilot Program in Mediation." *Arbitration Journal,* Vol. 44, no. 4, pp. 40-45.

Silberman, R. G., S. E. Murphy, and S. P. Adams. 1994. "Alternative Dispute Resolution of Employment Discrimination Claims." *Louisiana Law Review,* Vol. 54, pp. 1533-58.

Simpson, P., and J. Martocchio. 1995. "The Past as Present: The Influence of Work History Factors on Arbitral Decision Making." Paper presented at the 1995 Academy of Management Meeting in Vancouver, BC.

Singletary, C. R., R. A. Shearer, and E. M. Kuligofski. 1995. "Securing a Durable Mediation Agreement to Settle Complex Employment Disputes." *Labor Law Journal,* Vol. 46, pp. 223-27.

Sitkin, S. B., and R. J. Bies. 1993. "Social Accounts in Conflict Situations: Using Explanations to Manage Conflict." *Human Relations*, Vol. 46, no. 3, pp. 349-70.

Skratek, S. 1987a. "Grievance Mediation of Contractual Disputes in Washington State Public Education." *Labor Law Journal*, Vol. 38, pp. 370-76.

_____. 1987b. "Grievance Mediation of Contractual Disputes in Public Education." *Journal of Dispute Resolution*, Vol. 1987, pp. 43-75.

_____. 1990. "Grievance Mediation: Does It Really Work?" *Negotiation Journal*, Vol. 6, no. 3, pp. 269-80.

Society for Human Resource Management. 1997. "Legal News Briefs: ADR Still the Exception." *HR Focus*, Vol. 74, no. 12 (December), p. S5.

Speidel, Richard E. 1998. "Consumer Arbitration of Statutory Claims: Has Predispute Mandatory Arbitration Outlived Its Welcome?" *Arizona Law Review*, Vol. 40, no. 3 (Fall), pp. 1069-94.

Spencer, Daniel G. 1986. "Employee Voice and Employee Retention." *Academy of Management Journal*, Vol. 29, no. 3 (September), pp. 488-502.

St. Antoine, Theodore J. 1998. "Mandatory Arbitration of Employee Discrimination Claims: Unmitigated Evil or Blessing in Disguise?" *Thomas M. Cooley Law Review*, Vol. 15, no. 1, pp. 1-9.

Stallworth, Lamont E., and Martin H. Malin. 1994. "Workforce Diversity: A Continuing Challenge for ADR." *Dispute Resolution Journal*, Vol. 49, no. 2, pp. 27-41.

Sternlight, Jean R. 1996. "Panacea or Corporate Tool? Debunking The Supreme Court's Preference for Binding Arbitration." *Washington University Law Quarterly*, Vol. 74, no. 3, pp. 637-712.

Stone, Katherine. 1999. "Employment Arbitration under the Federal Arbitration Act." In Adrienne E. Eaton and Jeffrey H. Keefe, eds., *Employment Dispute Resolution and Worker Rights in the Changing Workplace*. Madison, WI: Industrial Relations Research Association.

Thornton, Robert J., and Perry A Zirkel. 1990. "The Consistency and Predictability of Grievance Arbitration Awards." *Industrial and Labor Relations Review*, Vol. 43, pp. 294-307.

Todor, William D., and C. L. Owen. 1991. "Deriving Benefits from Conflict Resolution: A Macrojustice Assessment." *Employee Responsibilities and Rights Journal*, Vol. 4, no. 1, 37-49.

Tyler, Thomas. 1988. "What Is Procedural Justice? Criteria Used by Citizens to Assess the Fairness of Legal Procedures." *Law & Society Review*, Vol. 22, no. 1, pp. 103-35.

UCI Ombudsman: The Journal. www.ombuds.UCI.edu/JOURNALS/

U. S. General Accounting Office. 1995. *Employment Discrimination: Most Private-Sector Employers Use Alternative Dispute Resolution*. GAO/HEHS-95-150. Washington, DC: United States General Accounting Office.

_____. 1997. *Alternative Dispute Resolution: Employers' Experiences with ADR in the Workplace*. GAO/GGD-97-157. Washington, DC: United States General Accounting Office.

Ury, William, Jeanne Brett, and Stephen Goldberg. 1989. *Getting Disputes Resolved: Designing Systems to Cut the Cost of Conflict*. San Francisco: Jossey-Bass Publishers.

Vargyas, Ellen J. 1997. "EEOC Rejects Mandatory Binding Employment Arbitration." *Dispute Resolution Journal*, Vol. 52, no. 4 (Fall), pp. 8-14.

Waldman, Ellen A. 1997. "Identifying the Role of Social Norms in Mediation: A Multiple Model Approach." *Hastings Law Journal*, Vol. 48, no. 4 (April), pp. 703-69.

Waldman, Ellen A. 1998. "The Evaluative-Facilitative Debate in Mediation: Applying the Lens of Therapeutic Jurisprudence." *Marquette Law Review*, Vol. 82, no. 1 (Fall), pp. 155-70.

Wall, James A., and A. Lynn. 1993. "Mediation: A Current Review." *Journal of Conflict Resolution*, Vol. 37, no. 1, pp. 160-94.

Ware, Stephen J. 1996. "Employment Arbitration and Voluntary Consent." *Hofstra Law Review*, Vol. 25, pp. 83-160.

Warters, Bill. 1995. "Researching Campus Conflict Management Culture(s): A Role for Ombuds?" *UCI Ombudsman: The Journal 1995*, an electronic journal published by the California Caucus of College and University Ombudsmen, http://www.ombuds.UCI.edu/JOURNALS/1995/. Accessed 4/22/99.

Wells, Robert A. 1997. "The Use of Arbitration in Director and Officer Indemnification Disputes." *Ohio State Journal on Dispute Resolution*, Vol. 13, no. 1, pp. 199-220.

Wilson, Agnes. 1998. "Resolving Employment Disputes: A Practical Guide." *Practicing Law Institute-Commercial Law and Practice Course Handbook Series*, Vol. 770, pp. 119-43.

Winograd, Barry. 1995. "Men as Mediators in Cases of Sexual Harassment." *Dispute Resolution Journal*, Vol. 50, no. 2, pp. 40-43.

Yatsco, Tanya A. 1998. "How About a Real Answer? Mandatory Arbitration as a Condition of Employment and the National Labor Relations Board's Stance." *Albany Law Review*, Vol. 62, no. 1, pp. 257-91.

Young, Michael D. 1998. "Selected J.A.M.S./Endispute Materials." *American Law Institute-American Bar Association Continuing Legal Education*, Vol. SC59, pp. 911-82.

Youngblood, Stuart A., Linda Klebe Trevino, and Monica Favia. 1992. "Reactions to Unjust Dismissal and Third-Party Dispute Resolution: A Justice Framework." *Employee Responsibilities and Rights Journal*, Vol. 5, no. 4, pp. 283-307.

Zack, Arnold M. 1997. "Can Alternative Dispute Resolution Help Resolve Employment Disputes?" *International Labor Review*, Vol. 136, no. 1, pp. 95-108.

_____. 1999. "Agreements to Arbitrate and the Waiver of Rights under Employment Law." In Adrienne Eaton and Jeffrey Keefe, eds., *Employment Dispute Resolution and Worker Rights in the Changing Workplace*. Madison, WI: Industrial Relations Research Association.

Zick, Vicki. 1998. "Reshaping the Constitution to Meet the Practical Needs of the Day: The Judicial Preference for Binding Arbitration." *Marquette Law Review*, Vol. 82, no. 1 (Fall), pp. 247-80.

Zirkel, Perry A., and P. H. Breslin. 1995. "Correlates of Grievance Arbitration Awards." *Journal of Collective Negotiations*, Vol. 24, no. 1, pp. 45-54.

Chapter 5

Theoretical and Empirical Research on the Grievance Procedure and Arbitration: A Critical Review

David Lewin
University of California–Los Angeles

The grievance procedure is widely regarded by scholars and practitioners as the centerpiece of union-management relations. From an "output" perspective, it is also often judged to be the leading accomplishment of collective bargaining between the parties in that it provides an orderly, workable, and acceptable process for resolving employment disputes during the life of a collective bargaining agreement (Peterson 1992; Staudohar 1977; Thomson and Murray 1976; Peach and Livernash 1974; Chamberlain and Kuhn 1965; Slichter, Healy and Livernash 1960). But from a research perspective, one may ask, What do we know about the grievance procedure? An answer to this question depends largely on what aspect or dimension of the grievance procedure one has in mind. This review will show that if one is interested in the determinants of grievance initiation or in the settlement of grievances, especially through arbitration, then it can be said that we know quite a lot about the grievance procedure. But it will also show that if one is interested in the viability of the employment relationship after grievances have been settled, then we know relatively little about the grievance procedure.

This critical review of recent grievance procedure research is organized as follows.[1] I begin by considering several theoretical perspectives on the grievance procedure, especially what may be termed "the grievance procedure as reactive conflict resolution." Then I examine empirical research on grievance initiation, focusing on the determinants of such initiation. Next, research on selected aspects of grievance processing, settlement, and effectiveness, including arbitration, is reviewed. This is followed by an examination of perhaps the two leading areas of

137

recent grievance procedure research. One of these is the postgrievance settlement behavior and experiences of the parties to grievances; the other is grievance procedures and organizational performance. I conclude by offering an overall assessment of recent grievance procedure research and an agenda for future research.

Theoretical Perspectives

The purpose of this section is to review and summarize leading theoretical perspectives on the unionized grievance procedure that characterize the recent literature on this subject. To assist the reader in this regard, Table 1 provides a summary of these theories together with their core predictions/relationships, key hypotheses, and main empirical findings. Some of these theories are discussed in this section, others in later sections of the chapter.

Until recently, grievance procedure research was often decried for being "largely descriptive and atheoretical" (Bemmels and Foley 1996: 360). Efforts to model the grievance process as a system of workplace dispute resolution, however, have recently been made by Lewin and Peterson (1988), Knight (1986), Lewin (1983, 1984) and Peterson and Lewin (1982). The systems models presented in these works emphasize interrelationships among variables representing determinants, dynamics, and outcomes of the grievance procedure and, in the case of Knight (1986), feedback from the outcomes of grievance settlements to the parties' subsequent behavior. These systems or "big picture" models of the grievance procedure have been criticized for not being able to take account of the many individuals involved in grievance processing and of the likelihood that key research issues and questions will vary across multiple steps of the grievance process. Further, such models are perhaps more descriptive than predictive in that they do not readily lead to testable hypotheses. Indeed, some critics even claim that "further attempts to develop such a [systems] 'theory' may be misguided" (Bemmels and Foley 1996: 361).

What is largely missing from recent theoretical treatments of the grievance procedure, however, is explicit recognition that the grievance procedure may represent a form of reactive conflict resolution and that alternative, preventive forms and mechanisms of workplace conflict resolution may exist and be used by labor and management.[2] This is surprising, especially in light of Hirschman's (1970) exit-voice-loyalty theory which has often been used by labor economists to model and study union-management relations and union impacts on management (Bemmels

TABLE 1

A Summary of Leading Theories of the Unionized Grievance Procedure

Theory and Researchers	Core Prediction/ Relationship	Key Hypotheses	Main Findings
Systems Theory: Lewin & Peterson (1988, 1999), Chayowski, Stotsve & Butler (1992), Knight (1986), Lewin (1983, 1984), Lewin & Peterson (1982)	G.P. system characteristics affect grievance processing, dynamics, outcomes, and feedback/learning by labor and management	G.P. system characteristics affect grievance filing, processing, settlement and post-settlement outcomes; parties learn from prior grievance cases	Management, union, and labor relations characteristics systematically related to grievance filing, processing, settlement and postsettlement outcomes; feedback from prior grievance cases positively related to subsequent grievance settlement
Exit-Voice-Loyalty Theory: Boroff & Lewin (1997), Bemmels (1997), Lewin & Boroff (1996), Rees (1991)	Employee voice and loyalty negatively related to employee exit	Grievance filing and employee loyalty negatively related to voluntary employer turnover	Employee loyalty negatively related to grievance filing and intent to exit; grievance filing positively related to intent to exit; employees fear reprisal for filing grievances
Procedural-Distributive Justice Theory: Olson-Buchanan (1996), Fryxell & Gordon (1989), Gordon & Bowlby (1988), Lewin & Peterson (1988), Gordon (1988)	Perceptions of procedural fairness influence employee attitudes toward G.P.	Perceived procedural fairness of the G.P. positively related to satisfaction with the G.P.; access to a G.P. negatively related to job performance and intent to exit	Perceived fairness of the G.P. positively related to employee satisfaction with the G.P., management, and union; perceived fairness of grievance handling has stronger effects on employee satisfaction than perceived fairness of G.P. outcomes; access to G.P. negatively related to job performance and intent to exit
Compensating Wage-Efficiency Theory: Cappelli & Chauvin (1991), Klaas (1989), Ichniowski & Lewin (1987)	Employees compare cost and effectiveness of filing grievances with other responses to unfair treatment	Local area wage premium and unemployment rate positively related to grievance filing	Local area wage premium positively related to grievance filing; local area unemployment rate positively related to grievance filing

TABLE 1 (*Continued*)

A Summary of Leading Theories of the Unionized Grievance Procedure

Theory and Researchers	Core Prediction/ Relationship	Key Hypotheses	Main Findings
Industrial Relations- Due Process Theory: Lewin & Mitchell (1995), Peterson (1994), Meyer & Cooke (1992), Meyer & Cooke (1988), Staudohar (1977), Thomson & Murray (1976), Peach & Livernash (1974), Chamberlain & Kuhn (1965), Kuhn (1961)	G.P. provides for the settlement of industrial disputes and is part of the bargaining process between labor and management	Labor and management bargain over grievance settlement, factors other than merit affect grievance settlement	Labor and management engage in fractional bargaining over grievances; economic, political and organizational factors affect grievance processing and settlement; non-meritorious grievances filed to influence bargaining power
Organizational Punishment-Industrial Discipline Theory: Lewin & Peterson (1988, 1999), Lewin (1997), Olson-Buchanan (1996), Barnacle (1991), Klass, Heneman & Olson (1991), Klass & Denisi (1989), Knight (1987), Arvey & Jones (1985), Labig, Helburn, & Rodgers (1985), Shantz & Rogow (1984), Malinowski (1981), Adams (1979)	G.P. involvement leads to negative postgrievance settlement outcomes	G.P. involvement negatively related to postsettlement job performance and promotions; positively related to post-settlement absenteeism and turnover, reinstatement following dismissal positively related to turnover	G.P. involvement negatively related to post-grievance settlement job performance and promotion of grievants and supervisors of grievants, positively related to absenteeism and turnover of grievants and supervisors of grievants, reinstatement of dismissed employees positively related to turnover following reinstatement

TABLE 1 (*Continued*)
A Summary of Leading Theories of the Unionized Grievance Procedure

Theory and Researchers	Core Prediction/ Relationship	Key Hypotheses	Main Findings
Displacement Theory: Kleiner, Nickelsburg & Pilarski (1995), Ichniowski (1986, 1992), Katz, Kochan & Weber (1985), Katz, Kochan & Gobeille (1983)	Grievance activity displaces productive work time	Grievance activity negatively related to plant productivity, product quality positively related to labor costs	Grievance activity negatively related to manufacturing productivity and product quality, grievance activity curvelinearly related to labor costs; labor-management cooperation initiatives negatively associated with grievance rates
Human Resource Management Theory: Ichniowski, Shaw & Prennushi (1997), MacDuffie (1995), Huselid (1995), Arthur (1994), Mitchell, Lewin & Lawler (1990)	High-involvement human resource practices/bundles, including a G.P., have positive effects on organizational performance	High-involvement human resource practices negatively related to turnover, positively related to productivity, product quality, and return on capital	High-involvement work practices, including a G.P., negatively related to employee turnover, positively related to productivity, product quality, return on assets, and return on investment

1997; Rees 1991; Freeman and Medoff 1984). This theory, which was developed in a product market rather than a labor market setting, addresses the question of why some customers who are dissatisfied with the price or other attribute of a firm's product will not, as economic theory predicts, switch to the product of another firm but will instead complain to the original firm with the intent of having the problem addressed and thus their dissatisfaction redressed. In this theory, switching to another firm constitutes exit behavior, while complaining to the original firm constitutes the exercise of voice.[3] But perhaps the key condition or proposition of this model is that the customer who brings a complaint to the firm does so only after having experienced a "deteriorated state" in terms of his relationship with the firm.

In applying this theory to the labor market, unionization has been modeled as the voice mechanism that is specifically manifested through collective bargaining and the grievance procedure. Those workers who are dissatisfied with one or another aspect of their employment relationship can bring such dissatisfaction to the attention of management. They do so periodically through the collective bargaining process but, more to the point and more frequently, perhaps even continuously, through the grievance procedure. Absent unionism, according to this research, workers are significantly more likely to exit the firm than to exercise voice in the firm (Bemmels 1997; Freeman and Medoff 1984). But, as with the case of a customer, a worker who files a grievance does so only after having experienced the aforementioned "deteriorated state" of his relationship with the firm. Hence it may be said that this theory is, in effect, a theory of reactive conflict resolution with respect to the employment relationship generally and the grievance procedure in particular. This is not to say that in theory or practice, all or even most grievances can be attributed to the deteriorated state of workers' relationships with their firms (employers). A broader perspective on this issue suggests that workers file grievances because they want to be involved in important workplace decisions and/or exert influence over management policies and practices so as to improve their relative position in the workplace. But it is to say that despite considerable application of exit-voice-loyalty theory to unionism and collective bargaining, contemporary grievance procedure research has largely failed explicitly to develop or test a theory of the grievance procedure as a reactive conflict resolution mechanism in which grievance filing stems primarily from the deteriorated state of the worker's relationship with the firm.

Another theoretical framework that has been applied to workplace dispute resolution is that of procedural and distributive justice (Sheppard, Lewicki and Minton 1992). This framework, too, was not initially applied to the labor market. Rather, it was first used in courtroom settings to advance understanding of how juries perceived the processes and outcomes of trials (Greenberg 1990; Lind and Tyler 1988). From this research developed the proposition that perceptions of fairness, justness, or equity of trial proceedings are relatively more important to jurors than perceptions of justness, fairness, or equity of trial outcomes. That is, jurors' overall assessments of trials—specifically their assessments of trial effectiveness and satisfaction with their trial experiences (as jurors)—are more heavily influenced by their perceived fairness of trial processes than by their perceived fairness of trial outcomes.

This framework has also been used in research on unionized grievance procedures. In a study of steel workers, retail clerks, nurses, and public school teachers, Lewin and Peterson (1988) found evidence to support the proposition that workers' assessments of the effectiveness of grievance procedures are more significantly influenced by their perceptions of grievance procedure fairness than by their perceptions of grievance procedure outcomes. Similarly, Gordon (1988) found that the perceived fairness of grievance handling processes outweighed the perceived fairness of grievance procedure outcomes in unionized workers' overall assessments of grievance procedures. In a related study, Fryxell and Gordon (1989) found that unionized workers' perceptions of procedural justice in grievance handling (together with their job satisfaction) was a significant predictor of these workers' satisfaction with their union and with management. Despite this evidence and the important theoretical perspective it provides, however, grievance procedure research based on procedural-distributive justice theory does not explicitly consider whether workers have experienced deterioration of their relationships with employers and, thus, that the grievance procedure is largely a reactive form of workplace conflict resolution.

If the grievance procedure is in fact a reactive form of conflict resolution, what might constitute more preventive forms of workplace conflict resolution? There are several possibilities in this regard, but one that has received much attention (though for the most part not in the grievance procedure literature) is worker participation in decision making. Here, emphasis is placed on worker involvement in areas traditionally reserved to supervision and management, for example, deciding what work to do, how to do it and, perhaps most of all, working in teams rather than individually to diagnose and solve workplace problems (Pil and MacDuffie 1996; Lawler 1986; Kaminski 1999). In such "high-involvement" workplaces, workers are said to be empowered, work is said to be performed flexibly rather than rigidly, high commitment is said to prevail over high control, and labor-management cooperation is said to prevail over labor-management adversarialism (Walton 1985). Indeed, some scholars view employee participation in decision making as a core competence of the firm that, together with other "innovative" human resource management practices, can provide the firm with sustainable competitive advantage (Pfeffer 1994).

The grievance procedure, by contrast, is rarely included in scholars' lists of human resource management practices that can provide sustained competitive advantage to the firm (but see Pil and MacDuffie 1996; Huselid 1995). Yet, in the rush to embrace worker participation and high-involvement work practices, both in theory and practice, it is easy to lose sight of the fact that unionization, collective bargaining, and of central interest to this chapter, the grievance procedure, are also mechanisms for employee participation in decision making. But these participative mechanisms can fundamentally be viewed as reactive forms of workplace conflict resolution, as emphasized by Kaminski (1999) elsewhere in this volume. Is it nevertheless possible for the grievance procedure to be regarded from and modeled as a preventive conflict resolution device?

Perhaps so, if we consider what industrial relations scholars have long known, namely, that most "grievances," that is, work-related issues that workers raise with management, are settled in informal discussions between workers and supervisors. While many scholars (e.g., Kuhn 1961; Chamberlain and Kuhn 1965) consider such informal discussion to be the first step of the grievance procedure, it may be argued that informal discussion of a work-related issue between worker and supervisor is a form of consultation qualitatively *different* from the decision and action of a worker to file a formal grievance or of management to respond to and rule on the grievance. From this perspective on informal grievance discussions, a perspective previously advanced by Kuhn (1961) in his analysis of grievance resolution as "fractional bargaining," workers consult with supervisors to gain advice and guidance about how to deal with and resolve workplace problems—much as management may consult with employees about dealing with and resolving workplace problems. Thus informal discussions of grievances may be said to have an integrative (problem-solving) quality or potential that bespeaks preventive conflict resolution, in contrast to distributive, issue- (rather than problem-) oriented formal grievance filing, processing, and settlement that bespeak reactive conflict resolution. In this regard, one may observe that unionized Japanese enterprises eschew formal grievance procedures in favor of informal, consensus-based discussion of workplace problems between labor and management (Morishima 1996). More fundamentally, the main point of emphasis here is that received theories of the grievance procedure are apparently predicated on (even though they do not explicitly acknowledge) the deteriorated state of the grievant's relationship with his employer. As such, these theories focus exclusively on a reactive form of workplace conflict resolution to the exclusion of alternative and putatively more preventive forms of workplace conflict resolution.

But for whatever advantages accrue to workers and employers from high-involvement or other preventive forms of workplace conflict resolution, these mechanisms and practices generally do not provide protections for or enforcement of employee rights. Rather, it is the traditional reactive grievance procedure that appears to offer protections for and enforcement of such rights. Consequently, a key issue that emerges from this analysis of theoretical perspectives on the grievance procedure is the extent to which high-involvement, consultative human resource management practices featuring teams and worker-management problem solving can be combined with grievance procedures which preserve and protect employee rights that attach to the employment relationship. Unfortunately, very little theory and empirical research has examined this issue (but see Kaminski 1999; Levine 1997).

As to grievance procedure research that has been conducted in recent years and that is summarized in Table 1, it can be concluded that there has been a shift away from an emphasis on the grievance procedure as the locus for continuation of collective bargaining and primary attention to labor-management relations, industrial work groups, and industrial governance toward an emphasis on the grievance procedure as a mechanism for effective conflict resolution and primary attention to individual orientation, behavior, and attitudes as they bear upon the grievance procedure.

Grievance Initiation

To assist the reader in sorting out and interpreting empirical research on the grievance procedure reviewed in this and the next section, Table 2 presents a summary of the leading dimensions, hypotheses, measures, and main findings contained in this research.

TABLE 2

A Summary of Empirical Research on Dimensions of the Grievance Procedure

Dimension and Researchers	Key Hypotheses	Empirical Measures	Main Findings
Grievance Initiation: Lewin & Peterson (1988, 1999), Boroff & Lewin (1997), Lewin & Boroff (1996), Kleiner, Nickelsburg & Pilarski (1995), Bemmels (1994), Bemmels, Reshef & Stratton-Devine (1991), Cappelli & Chauvin (1991), Duane (1991), Dastmalchian & Ng (1990), Gordon & Bowlby (1989), Meyer & Cooke (1988), Labig & Greer (1988), Labig & Helburn (1986), Allen & Keaveny (1985)	Grievance filing related to environmental, management, union, union–management relationship and employee characteristics, employee attitudes, grievable events, industry, sector, technology	Pay premiums, area unemployment rates, perceived unfair treatment, management monitoring, management's performance, disciplinary standards and management grievance processing practices, supervisory structure and consideration, union grievance processing practices, shop steward behavior and perceptions, quality of labor-management relationship, bargaining unit size and skill mix, work group size, employee age, sex, race, occupation, length of service, loyalty, fear of reprisal	Grievance filing significantly positively related to perceived unfair treatment, pay premiums, area unemployment rates, management's performance and disciplinary standards, management practice of taking grievances as far as possible through the procedure, supervisory structure, union practice of taking grievances as far as possible through the procedure, shop steward effort to convince employees to file grievances, private sector employment, employment in transportation and heavy manufacturing, discipline issues, skilled, male, minority employee status; grievance filing significantly negatively related to employee loyalty, fear of reprisal, informal discussions between shop stewards and employees
Speed/Level of Settlement: Ponak & Olson (1992), Davy, Stewart & Anderson (1992), Stewart & Davy (1992), Bollander (1992), Mesch & Dalton (1992), Dastmalchian & Ng (1990), Ng & Dastmalchian (1989), Lewin & Peterson (1988)	Speed/level of settlement related to industrial relations climate, requirement that grievances be written, number of G.P. steps, grievance issue, provision for expedited processing, industry, union-management cooperation program	Time (in days) to settlement, level of settlement, grievance issue, policy of requiring written grievances at first step, number of steps in the G.P., perceived industrial relations climate, expedited grievance processing, union-management cooperation program, industry	Most grievances settled at lowest steps; speed of (time to) settlement significantly positively related to grievances over discipline, management and union policies to take grievances as far as possible through the procedure, investigative requirements, number of steps, employment in heavy manufacturing, significantly negatively related to expedited processing, written rather than oral first step (positive) industrial relations climate, union-management cooperation program; level of settlement significantly positively related to grievances

TABLE 2 (Continued)

A Summary of Empirical Research on Dimensions of the Grievance Procedure

Dimension and Researchers	Key Hypotheses	Empirical Measures	Main Findings
Perceived Grievance Procedure Effectiveness: Bemmels (1995), Fryxell (1992), Eaton, Gordon & Keefe (1992), Clark, Gallagher & Pavlak (1990), Fryxell & Gordon (1989), Gordon & Bowlby (1988), Clark & Gallagher (1988), Lewin & Peterson (1988)	Perceived G.P. effectiveness related to perceived fairness of processing and outcomes, perceived effect of G.P. on workplace equity, extent to which the G.P. represents worker interests, perceived importance of grievance issues, satisfaction with the union, commitment to employer, union and union-employer, belief in a just workplace	Perceived G.P. effectiveness, perceived fairness of grievance processing and outcomes, perceived effect of G.P. on workplace equity, perceived extent to which G.P. represents worker interests, perceived importance of grievance issues, satisfaction with the union, belief in a just workplace, commitment to union, commitment to employer, dual commitment (to union and employer)	over discipline, management and union practice to take grievances as far as possible; significantly negatively related to (favorable) industrial relations climate, union-management cooperation program Perceived G.P. effectiveness significantly positively related to perceived fairness of grievance processing, perceived effect of G.P. on workplace equity, perceived extent to which G.P. represents worker interests, perceived importance of grievance issues, perceived fairness of grievance outcomes, satisfaction with the union, commitment to the union, commitment to the employer, dual commitment; perceived G.P. effectiveness unrelated to speed and level of grievance settlement
Grievance Decisions/Outcomes: Meyer (1994), Gordon & Fryxell (1993), Bemmels (1991), Klaas (1989), Meyer & Cooke (1987), Dalton & Tudor (1987), Knight (1987), Kuhn (1961)	Grievance outcomes (wins-losses for employee or employer) related to employee personal characteristics, arbitrator personal characteristics, employee prior work history, economic and political factors, attempt to gain bargaining power	Grievance outcomes (wins-losses for employee and employer), employee age, sex, race and occupation, arbitrator age and sex, employee's length of employment, disciplinary record, job performance and prior grievance activity, union-management political factors, union-management bargaining power	Grievance outcomes significantly positively related to employee gender and arbitrator gender, employee's disciplinary record, job performance and prior grievance activity, introduction of political factors into grievance processing, use of grievance processing to influence union-management bargaining power

Having broached the matter of informal discussion of grievances between workers and supervisors, we may ask, How widespread is informal grievance discussion and settlement? Because these are non-recorded, nonobservable events, one can only broadly estimate the incidence of informal grievance handling. Writing in 1988 and using a ratio of ten informal unwritten grievances for every one formal written grievance, Lewin and Peterson estimated that perhaps twelve million informal grievance discussions take place annually in the unionized sector of the United States economy.[4]

When it comes to formal written grievances, a substantial amount of research has recently been done on grievance initiation. In reviewing and assessing these studies, however, consider that the filing of a grievance begins with a "grievable event." In unionized enterprises, a grievable event presumably involves an alleged violation of the collective bargaining agreement between labor and management. Absent such specific violation, there is no grievable event or, therefore, grievance. In reality, that is, in real world workplaces, various issues and complaints may be taken through the grievance procedure whether or not they meet the strict test of violating a contractual provision. Yet, in research on this topic, which typically begins with grievance rates in an organization or sample of employees, grievable events have rarely been modeled or controlled. The analytical issue here is that in the absence of controls for grievable events, every worker is assumed to be equally likely (or unlikely) to file a grievance, all events are assumed to be of equal importance and frequency, and all organizations selected for study are assumed to experience comparable rates of grievance events (as presumably reflected in grievance rates). As a consequence, most empirical studies of grievance initiation (and other dimensions of the grievance process) are likely to contain biased estimates of the determinants of such initiation. Based on a careful review of the relevant literature, it appears that only Boroff and Lewin (1997) and Lewin and Boroff (1996) have directly controlled for grievable events in research on grievance initiation. They did so by surveying a random sample of employees in a large, unionized, global telecommunications company and then censoring the data to include in their analysis only those employees who perceived themselves to have experienced unfair workplace treatment.

What does extant research tell us about the determinants of grievance initiation? In individual-level studies, which typically compare grievance filers with nonfilers within or across organizational units, the following may be noted. Allen and Keaveny (1985) found that grievants had significantly lower job satisfaction, more negative attitudes toward their supervisors, greater perceived pay inequity, stronger preferences for worker participation in decision making, and lower satisfaction with their unions than nongrievants. Interestingly, and perhaps notable in this study, grievants were more active in their unions than nongrievants. Important for assessing Allen and Keaveny's findings is the fact that theirs was an ex post facto study, meaning that attitudinal data were obtained (only) after employee-grievants filed their grievances.

In a series of studies, Lewin and Peterson (1988, 1999) found significant differences between grievants and nongrievants in four organizations over two different time periods. Grievants were younger and less educated than nongrievants, and minority workers were significantly more likely to file grievances than majority (Caucasian) workers. In three of the four organizations, men were significantly more likely than women to file grievances. Labig and Greer (1988) found that grievants were younger, held more skilled jobs, and had higher absenteeism rates, dispensary visits, and insurance claim filings than nongrievants. Gordon and Bowlby (1989) conducted one of the few experimental studies of grievance initiation, grounding their work in attribution and reactance theory. They found that perceived threats to workers' freedom and actions attributed to organizational sources and personal disposition were more strongly associated with intention to file a grievance than threats attributed to environmental sources. Restricting their analysis to a sample of unionized employees who perceived that they had experienced unfair workplace treatment, Boroff and Lewin (1997) and Lewin and Boroff (1996) found that employee loyalty was significantly inversely related to the likelihood of filing a grievance (that is, more loyal employees were less likely to file a grievance than less loyal employees). Not only was this finding contrary to the prediction drawn from Hirschman's exit-voice-loyalty model, it led the researchers to conclude that highly loyal employees are more likely (than employees with low loyalty) to "suffer in silence" rather than file a grievance.

Turning to organizational-level studies of grievance initiation, Cappelli and Chauvin (1991) developed and tested an efficiency model of grievance activity which posits that employees who feel unfairly treated will compare the cost and effectiveness of filing a grievance with other responses, such as exit and silence. In this model, which is similar to the compensating differentials model of the grievance procedure developed by Ichniowski and Lewin (1987), the cost of exit depends on labor market conditions. One of these conditions is the wage premium in a plant compared to local labor market wages. The greater this premium, the greater the cost of exit, and consequently, the higher the incidence of grievances (that is, grievance filing). Another labor market condition is the area unemployment rate, which reflects the availability of alternative employment opportunities. The higher the area unemployment rate, the greater the cost of exit, and hence the higher the grievance rate. Cappelli and Chauvin's analysis of data from 86 plants in one manufacturing enterprise found support for both of these hypotheses. Moreover, the findings from this study tend to confirm Klaas' (1989) research, grounded in expectancy theory and procedural-distributive justice theory, which concluded that employees do indeed evaluate the relative costs and benefits of grievance filing compared to other options in deciding whether or not to file grievances.

Several early studies of grievance procedures (for example, Sayles 1958; Kuhn 1961; Peach and Livernash 1974; Nelson 1979) concluded that certain aspects of technology were positively related to grievance filing. More recent studies (Bemmels 1994; Bemmels, Reshef, and Stratton-Devine 1991), however, which operationalized multiple measures of technology, found virtually no support for the proposition that differences in technology explain interorganizational variation in grievance filing rates. However, neither older nor more contemporary studies provide theoretical frameworks for deriving hypotheses about relationships between technology (or technological change) and grievance filing rates.

Certain management factors have been found by researchers to influence grievance initiation. For example, Labig and Helburn (1986) found the strictness of management's performance and disciplinary standards to be significantly positively related to grievance rates. Lewin and Peterson (1988) found a management policy of committing grievances to writing to be significantly positively related to grievance rates in all four of the organizations they studied, but a management policy of taking certain grievances fully through the grievance procedure to be significantly positively related to grievance rates in only one of the four organizations. Following on earlier work by Fleishman (1957), Bemmels (1994), and Bemmels, Reshef, and Stratton-Devine (1991) found supervisory consideration—the supervisor's consideration of employees in a work group—to be significantly inversely related to grievance filing rates. Bemmels (1994), but not Bemmels, Reshef, and Stratton-Devine (1991), found supervisory structure—the supervisor's emphasis on production and achievement of organizational goal—to be significantly positively related to grievance filing rates.

Bemmels (1994) and Bemmels, Reshef, and Stratton-Devine (1991) also developed measures of shop stewards' assessments of how frequently employees approach them with complaints, proposing that such complaints are a precursor to grievance filing. Both studies found that work groups with employees who more frequently complained to supervisors had higher grievance filing rates than work groups with employees who infrequently complained to supervisors. In addition, the researchers found that shop stewards' assessments of the supervisor's knowledge of the collective bargaining agreement was negatively related to grievance filing rates. A study by Kleiner, Nickelsburg, and Pilarski (1995) found, as expected, that management monitoring of employees was significantly positively associated with grievance filing rates and, unexpectedly, that management's planned production rate was significantly negatively associated with grievance filing rates. However, these authors provide no theoretical justification for their specification of managerial monitoring of employees, and it is arguable whether their empirical work actually operationalizes and tests for this variable.

Studies of union factors in grievance initiation focus on union policies regarding the grievance procedure and the behavior of union officials concerning grievance filing. Using a five-item survey measure of union encouragement of grievances, Labig and Helburn (1986) found that the extent to which union officials screen grievances, seek out contract violations, and encourage union members to file grievances were significantly positively associated with grievance filing. Similarly, Lewin and Peterson (1988) found that union policies of committing grievances to writing and taking certain grievances fully through the grievance procedure were significantly positively associated with grievance filing rates. Following research by Dalton and Tudor (1982), Bemmels, Reshef, and Stratton-Devine (1991) found that grievance filing rates were positively related to shop steward efforts to convince employees to file grievances and negatively related to shop steward attempts to resolve workplace disputes informally. Duane (1991) also found grievance filing rates to be inversely associated with the extent of informal discussion of workplace disputes between employees and shop stewards. In addition, he found that shop steward perception of the extent to which employees prefer more competitive interaction between shop stewards and management was positively associated with grievance filing rates.

Concerning the union-management relationship, several studies have examined characteristics of this relationship in terms of their influence on grievance initiation. For example, size of work group, size of bargaining unit, and skill mix/occupational diversity of the bargaining unit were variously included in grievance procedure studies by Stewart and Davey (1992); Bemmels (1994); Bemmels, Reshef, and Stratton-Devine (1991); Cappelli and Chauvin (1991); and Lewin and Peterson (1988). Empirically, however, these union-management relationship characteristics were generally not significantly associated with grievance filing rates. Several grievance procedure studies have also included perceptual measures of the quality of the union-management relationship, the most common of which is perceived conflict in the collective bargaining relationship. This variable has usually been found to be significantly positively associated with grievance filing rates (Dastmalchian and Ng 1990; Meyer and Cooke 1988). But as Labig and Greer (1988) observe, this association is difficult to interpret and may reflect an underlying tautology. That is, the grievance rate itself appears to be a behavioral (rather than attitudinal) measure of conflict in the relationship between union and management and, thus, should be highly correlated with perceived union-management conflict; in effect, one variable serves as a proxy for the other. Therefore, it is questionable whether perceptual measures of the quality of or conflict in the union-management relationship add to our understanding of the determinants of grievance initiation. More fundamentally, there is little theoretical motivation for the inclusion of union-management characteristics variables in studies of the grievance procedure, as is reflected in the treatment of such characteristics primarily as control variables in these studies.

Attention has also been paid by researchers to the relationship between grievance filing and the collective bargaining cycle. Using a fractional bargaining construct, Kuhn (1961) found that grievance filing rates increased as the time to renegotiate collective bargaining agreements drew nearer. Chamberlain and Kuhn (1965) suggested that this empirical finding could be generalized to collective bargaining relationships more broadly. More recently, in their four-organization study and controlling for other variables, Lewin and Peterson (1988) found that grievance filing rates were lowest at the midpoint of collective bargaining cycles and highest during the period just prior to the expiration of collective bargaining agreements. On the whole, this research indicates that workplace conflict, as reflected in grievance filing rates, is systematically related to collective bargaining cycles and that the grievance procedure is itself a form of bargaining.

Recent grievance procedure research finds significant differences in grievance filing rates among sectors and industries. In these and related studies, the grievance filing rate is typically measured by the number of written grievances filed during a specific time period (such as one year) by every 100 workers. For example, Stewart and Davey (1992) found significantly higher grievance filing rates in private sector than in public sector organizations in the United States. Using Canadian data, Bemmels (1994) examined sector/industry variation in grievance filing rates and found rates ranging from a high of 48.2 in railway transportation to a low of 0.6 in education. Using United States data, Lewin and Peterson (1988) found annual grievance rates of 16.3 in steel manufacturing firms, 10.3 in nonprofit hospitals, 7.8 in retail department stores, and 7.7 in local public schools. Though little attention has been devoted to explaining intersector and interindustry variation in grievance filing rates, Bemmels (1994) and Cappelli and Chauvin (1991) found that industry average grievance rates were significantly related to industry labor market conditions but not to industry technology.

Recent grievance procedure research also finds that grievance rates vary by grievance issues. For example, in Lewin and Peterson's (1988) research, grievances involving discipline represented 10.4% of all grievances compared to 6.6% involving work assignments and 1.9% involving paid leave time. Bemmels (1994) also found that grievances involving discipline accounted for about 10% of all grievances, while Bemmels, Reshef, and Stratton-Devine (1991) reported a higher rate, namely, 17.7%. Lewin and Peterson's (1988) study is one of the very few to have examined grievance issues by level of grievance settlement. They found, for example, that grievances over discipline represented 26.3% of all grievances settled through arbitration in the organizations they studied. Analyzing Lewin-Peterson's as well as their own data, Bemmels and Foley (1996) concluded that union officials are more likely to push grievances over discipline to arbitration than any other grievance issues. These researchers also concluded, however, that grievance procedure research has given little theoretical or empirical attention to variation in grievance initiation and settlement by grievance issue.

In summary, it can be concluded that grievance initiation is significantly influenced by (1) certain environmental factors, such as area pay and unemployment rates; (2) management policies and practices, such as strict performance standards, requiring grievances to be put in writing, and monitoring of grievances; (3) supervisor behavior, such as consideration and initiating structure; (4) shop steward behavior, such as seeking out contract violations and assessment of supervisors' knowledge of the collective bargaining agreement; and (5) employee behavior and attitudes, such as bringing complaints to shop stewards, assessment of the relative costs and benefits of grievance filing, preference for participation in decision making, and satisfaction with work, pay, supervision and the union. In addition, grievance initiation has been shown to vary significantly by industry and sector, employee characteristics (demography), work-related issue, and stage of the collective bargaining cycle. In general, union-management relationship characteristics and technology are not significantly related to grievance initiation. Surprisingly, very few grievance initiation studies control for (worker perceptions of) grievable events, and no study, save perhaps for Lewin and Peterson (forthcoming), has incorporated all or even most of these variables into a comprehensive model of grievance initiation.

Grievance Processing, Settlement, and Effectiveness

Numerous and varied studies of grievance processing, dynamics, and settlement in unionized settings have been conducted. The dependent variables in this research include overall grievance settlement rates, settlement rates at steps of the grievance procedure, the win-lose rate for each party at each step of the procedure, arbitration rates, time to settlement, perceived importance of grievance issues, perceived equity of grievance settlement, and feedback about grievance processing and settlement. Sometimes combinations of some of these measures have been used to assess overall grievance procedure effectiveness. Nevertheless, the relevant literature shows that there is a lack of consensus among researchers about what exactly constitutes grievance procedure effectiveness.

Perhaps the most widely used measure of grievance procedure effectiveness is time to or speed of settlement. Swifter settlements are preferred to slower settlements, and a substantial body of work has focused on delay in grievance settlement (Ponak and Olson 1992; Lewin and Peterson 1988). Writing in 1992, Ponak and Olson studied the time to grievance settlement as reported in studies over a twenty-year period and concluded that the average time to settlement was increasing. For grievances that eventually were settled at the final step of the grievance procedure, that is, arbitration, these authors report average time to settlement of approximately one year and suggested that this delay had increased significantly over time. Relatively few grievances are settled at the arbitration step, however. For example, Lewin and Peterson (1988) found that only about 2% of all grievances were settled at the arbitration step of the grievance procedure, with the rate being highest in steel manufacturing (2.7%) and lowest in retail department stores (1%). These researchers also found that most grievances were settled at the lowest (that is, first two) steps of the grievance procedure and that the average time to grievance settlement (inclusive of all steps) ranged between 37 and 33 days depending on grievance issue. In a more recent study, Lewin and Peterson (1999) reported that the average days to grievance settlement in four large unionized organizations declined from 69 days in the early 1980s to 52 days in the early 1990s.

Concerning the factors influencing time to grievance settlement, Davy, Stewart, and Anderson (1992) found that a requirement that grievances be put in writing at the first step of the procedure, as opposed to being presented orally, was significantly positively associated with first step settlements. They interpret this finding to mean that putting a grievance in writing helps to clarify grievance issues, thereby leading to swift settlement. However, Stewart and Davy (1992) found that the greater the number of steps in the grievance procedure the lower the settlement rate at the lower steps of the procedure.

Lewin and Peterson (1988) found that provisions for expedited grievance handling were significantly related to higher step grievance settlements, especially arbitration, but also to speedier settlements. According to this research, and if one regards speed of settlement as the leading measure of grievance procedure effectiveness, then provisions for expedited grievance processing seem to be serving their intended purpose. But Lewin and Peterson (1988) also found that union policies requiring employee-members to put grievances in writing and union and management policies of taking certain grievances (for example, over discipline) fully through the grievance procedure were significantly associated with lengthier settlements and higher-step settlements, notably higher arbitration rates. In a survey-based study of public sector organizations, Bohlander (1992) found that scheduling conflicts and investigative requirements were considered by employers to be the leading factors lengthening the time to grievance settlement. Dastmalchian and Ng (1990) and Ng and Dastmalchian (1989) found that managers' perception of a favorable industrial relations climate was significantly associated with higher grievance settlement rates and settlements at lower steps of the grievance procedure. In a study of grievance processing in a large utility company, Mesch and Dalton (1992) found that the effects of a new union-management cooperation program to introduce fact finding into the grievance procedure included more frequent settlements at lower steps of the procedure and more frequent compromise settlements.

There is reason to doubt that speed of settlement is a leading or even valid measure of grievance procedure effectiveness, however. In a study of grievants' perceptions and evaluations of the grievance procedure, Gordon and Bowlby (1988) found that perceived fairness of grievance processing and of grievance decisions were significantly more important than speed of settlement to grievants' overall evaluation of the grievance procedure. Clark and Gallagher (1988) surveyed union members concerning their attitudes toward the grievance procedure. They found that perceived effect of the procedure on workplace equity, perceived fairness of grievance processing, the extent to which the procedure represents worker interests, and the importance of having a grievance procedure were significantly positively associated with overall attitudes toward the grievance procedure. Taken alone, speed of grievance settlement was unrelated to these workers' attitudes toward the grievance procedure.

Lewin and Peterson (1988) included measures of union and management officials' perceptions of the importance of grievance issues and equity of grievance settlements in their multidimensional measure of grievance procedure effectiveness. They found that a management policy of taking certain grievances as fully through the procedure as possible and the length of the bargaining relationship between the parties were significantly associated with higher perceived importance of grievance issues and higher perceived equity of grievance settlement. Fryxell and Gordon (1989) and Eaton, Gordon, and Keefe (1992) found that union members' perceptions of grievance procedure effectiveness were significantly positively related to their overall satisfaction with the union. Fryxell (1992) concluded that workers' perceptions of grievance procedure effectiveness were shaped by and subsidiary to their broader perceptions of and belief in a just workplace. Further, several researchers (for example, Clark, Gallagher, and Pavlak 1990; Bemmels 1995) have found that union members attitudes toward and assessments of the effectiveness of the grievance procedure are strongly influenced by their commitment to the union, commitment to the employer, and dual commitment to the union and employer.

The uses of grievance processing and settlement information by union and management officials may also be considered dimensions of grievance procedure effectiveness. For example, Knight (1986) found that frequency of use of feedback from prior grievance settlements was significantly positively related to subsequent grievance settlement rates. He also found significant variation in union and management officials' assessments of their use of feedback from prior grievance settlements and arbitration decisions in subsequent grievance processing. Nevertheless, Knight's research suggests that union and management officials' learning from prior grievance settlements be included in measures of overall grievance procedure effectiveness. In a related study, Chayowski, Stotsve, and Butler (1992) analyzed the impact of prior grievance settlements involving a particular issue on the likelihood of resolving subsequent grievances on the same issue. They found a lower likelihood of first-step settlement on issues that had previously been grieved and settled at the first step, but a higher likelihood of second-step settlement on issues that had previously been grieved and settled at the second step. This research also can be interpreted to suggest that the parties' learning from prior grievance settlements be included in measures of overall grievance procedure effectiveness. Several studies show that factors other than the merit of a grievance influence grievance settlements (Gordon and Fryxell 1993). Dalton, Tudor, and Owen (1987) found that the gender of a grievant and the gender of a grievance decision maker, such as an arbitrator, are significantly related to grievance outcomes. Bemmels (1991) also found that an arbitrator's gender was significantly related to the outcomes of arbitrated grievances. Klaas (1989) has shown that grievants' job performance, length of employment, disciplinary record, and prior grievance activity are related to the outcomes of grievance decisions, including cases where such data and characteristics apparently are unrelated to the merits of the grievance at hand. Meyer (1994) and Meyer and Cooke (1988) found that the outcomes of grievance cases were significantly influenced by economic and political factors, especially where the facts of a case and alleged contractual violations were unclear. Knight (1987) found that grievants and union officials sometimes file and process grievances lacking merit in order to gain bargaining power in the grievance process more broadly and concluded that such behavior constitutes a violation of the duty of fair representation. Knight's findings are strongly similar to those reported in an earlier study by Kuhn (1961), who concluded that grievance processing is an extension of collective bargaining and who coined the term "fractional bargaining" to represent such use of the grievance process.

All in all, recent literature on grievance processing, settlement, and effectiveness offers some tantalizing empirical findings, especially concerning the speed and level of grievance settlement, the frequency and uses of arbitration, the parties' learning from prior grievance issues and settlements, and the use of grievance processing to influence the larger union-management bargaining relationship. As has been shown, however, attempts to model and measure grievance procedure effectiveness, including those that combine behavioral with attitudinal/perceptual variables, have not led to a consensus definition of or approach to such effectiveness. Perhaps future progress in this regard will come from the development of stronger theoretical foundations of grievance procedure effectiveness that, as Bemmels and Foley (1996) recommend, draw (or draw more) from such concepts and frameworks as expectancy theory, organizational culture theory, commitment escalation theory, decision dilemma theory, and prospect theory.[5]

Further, research into grievance procedure effectiveness might well benefit from consideration of the effectiveness of alternative forms of workplace conflict resolution, such as strikes or lawsuits. For example, given the prominent role assigned to speed of settlement as a criterion of grievance procedure effectiveness, researchers might compare the speed of grievance settlement with the speed of settlement of lawsuits over employment issues. Or researchers might compare the parties' learning through feedback from prior grievance cases on subsequent grievance resolution with the parties' learning through feedback from prior strike settlements on subsequent collective negotiations. If perceived equity of settlement is judged to be an important component of grievance procedure effectiveness, researchers might compare such perceived equity with the perceived equity of strike settlements and lawsuit settlements. The larger point being made here is that grievance procedure research has perhaps focused too narrowly on the grievance procedure and failed adequately to consider the effectiveness of grievance procedures in relation to the effectiveness of other forms of workplace conflict resolution.

Postgrievance Settlement Outcomes

Perhaps the most significant advance in research on unionized grievance procedures is that body of work dealing with postgrievance settlement outcomes. Here, researchers' attention has focused on employee performance following grievance settlement, management reprisal against grievants, and the reinstatement of unfairly dismissed employees. This research is particularly important because it shifts the focus and emphasis of grievance procedure research from grievance activity and grievance settlement to the consequences of grievance involvement for workers and to the behavior of management after grievances are settled. Stated differently, this research addresses the question, What difference does grievance activity/involvement make to the involved parties? In this respect, recent research on postgrievance settlement outcomes can be analogized to recent research on the outcomes of human resource management practices.

Lewin and Peterson (1988) were the first to examine postgrievance settlement outcomes in unionized settings. Using personnel records for samples of employee grievants and nongrievants in four large organizations, Lewin and Peterson (1988) analyzed job performance ratings, work attendance rates, promotion rates, and turnover rates for both employee groups in the year prior to, the year during, and the year following grievance filing and settlement. The researchers found few statistically significant differences between grievants and nongrievants on any of the four measures prior to and during the periods of grievance filing/settlement, and those differences that did exist indicated that the grievants were more upwardly mobile than the nongrievants. In the one-year period following grievance filing/settlement, however, job performance ratings and promotion rates were significantly lower for grievants than for nongrievants. Further, postgrievance settlement turnover rates were significantly higher for grievants than for nongrievants. When the level of grievance settlement was analyzed, Lewin and Peterson (1988) found that grievants whose cases were settled at the first step of the grievance procedure had significantly higher postsettlement performance ratings and promotion rates and significantly lower postsettlement turnover rates than grievants whose cases were settled at higher steps. And, employee losers of grievance cases had significantly higher postsettlement performance ratings and promotion rates and significantly lower postsettlement turnover rates than employee winners of grievance cases.

In the same study, Lewin and Peterson (1988) found similar results when comparing the supervisors of grievants with the supervisors of nongrievants. Specifically, these two groups of supervisors did not differ significantly in terms of job performance ratings, promotion rates, and work attendance rates in the one-year periods prior to and during employee grievance filing and settlement. In the one-year period following grievance filing/settlement, however, the supervisors of grievants had significantly lower performance ratings and promotion rates than the supervisors of nongrievants. Especially notable, the supervisors of grievants had significantly higher turnover rates in the postgrievance filing/settlement period than the supervisors of nongrievants, and this difference was most pronounced for involuntary turnover rates. It thus appears that management exercises reprisal against employees and supervisors who are involved in grievance cases.

There is an alternative explanation for Lewin and Peterson's (1988) findings, which is that grievants and those who supervise them are generally poorer performers than nongrievants and their supervisors. For this explanation to be valid, and because grievants (and their supervisors) and nongrievants (and their supervisors) did not differ significantly on the relevant personnel measures prior to and during the periods of grievance filing/settlement, it must be that the act of grievance filing and the processing of grievances spurs management to pay closer attention to the assessment of employee (and supervisor) job performance. When doing so, according to this reasoning, management discovers (ex post) that grievants (and their supervisors) are indeed poorer performers than nongrievants (and their supervisors). Some support for this alternative explanation of Lewin and Peterson's (1988) findings comes from the "shock theory" of the union's impact on management (Rees 1977). According to this theory, unionization of a firm's workforce shocks management into improving organizational performance such that the costs of unionization (primarily in the form of higher pay and benefits) are offset by productivity improvements—that is, unit labor costs are unchanged.[6] Additional support for this alternative explanation comes from Olson-Buchanan's (1996) laboratory simulation in which grievants had significantly poorer job performance after grievance filing/settlement than nongrievants, who also had access to the grievance system and had similar reasons for filing grievances but chose not to do so. Olson-Buchanan (1996) concludes that because conflict between an employee and his supervisor/manager affects (lowers) the employee's objective job performance, there may be "a real difference between grievance filers' and nonfilers' [job performance] behavior" (p. 62). Still further support for this alternative explanation emanates from court cases involving claims of employment discrimination and wrongful termination in which performance appraisal data introduced by employer-defendants are often found to be upwardly skewed and to not validly distinguish among high, average, and low job performers (Lewin 1997). Stated differently, employers do not give sufficient attention to the validity and reliability of their performance appraisal systems until shocked into doing so by an exogenous event, such as an employment discrimination or wrongful termination lawsuit. Once employers are so shocked, and following the line of reasoning derived from Rees (1977) and Olson-Buchanan (1996), more rigorous use of performance appraisals are likely to show that employees who file discrimination or wrongful termination suits are poorer performers than employees who do not bring such legal actions. By extension, the same explanation applies to grievance filing, settlement, and postsettlement outcomes.

The evidence that employee-grievants suffer management reprisal for filing grievances appears to be growing, however. For example, Klaas and DeNisi (1989) found that employees who file grievances against their supervisors receive significantly lower performance ratings from those supervisors than employees who file grievances over management policies. This effect turned insignificant when the supervisor doing the performance assessment was not the supervisor against whom the grievance was filed, but the effect was even more significant for employees who won their grievance cases compared to employees who lost their cases. In studies of the grievance procedure in a large unionized telecommunications company, Boroff and Lewin (1997) and Lewin and Boroff (1996) found that employee fear of reprisal for filing grievances was significantly inversely related to the probability of an employee filing a grievance—and this finding persisted when employee loyalty to the employer was controlled.

In a major expansion of their original work, Lewin and Peterson (1999) analyzed postgrievance settlement outcomes in four unionized organizations over two separate three-year periods. Once again, they found that grievants and supervisors of grievants had significantly lower job performance ratings and promotion rates and significantly higher turnover rates than nongrievants and their supervisors—differences that either did not exist or favored grievants (and their supervisors) prior to and during the periods of grievance filing/settlement. Taking their turnover analysis a step further than in their original study, Lewin and Peterson (1999) found that grievants were significantly more likely than nongrievants to quit their jobs—turn over voluntarily—following grievance settlement, whereas supervisors of grievants were significantly more likely than supervisors of nongrievants to be involuntarily separated from their jobs following grievance settlement. Both grievants and their supervisors, however, were significantly more likely to be terminated (but not laid off) from work than nongrievants and their supervisors following grievance settlement. Lewin and Peterson (1999) also found that following grievance settlement, the work attendance of grievants who lost their cases was significantly better than grievants who won their cases in three of the four organizations studied. A related study (Klaas, Heneman, and Olson 1991) of employee work attendance and grievance activity over an eight-year period in a public sector organization found a significant positive relationship between the filing of grievances over management policies and subsequent employee absenteeism from their work units but a significant negative relationship between grievance fil- . ing over disciplinary issues and subsequent employee absenteeism.[7]

The weight of the evidence from recent research on postgrievance settlement outcomes appears to support a reprisal explanation of such outcomes. Management does indeed appear to punish employees who file grievances and especially to punish the supervisors of those employees. This finding, in turn, seems to support organizational punishment-industrial discipline theory (Arvey and Jones 1985; O'Reilly and Weitz 1980) over, say, industrial relations due process theory (Staudohar 1977; Peach and Livernash 1974) or exit-voice-loyalty theory (Hirschman 1970; Freeman and Medoff 1984) of the employment relationship. Even if one supports a "performance difference" explanation of the empirical findings about postgrievance settlement outcome differences between grievants (and their supervisors) and nongrievants (and their supervisors), however, the extant research clearly indicates that, on average, grievants and the supervisors of grievants subsequently experience significant deterioration of their employment relationships. Stated differently, the viability of these employees' and supervisors' employment relationships is worsened by their involvement in the grievance process. Therefore, the "deteriorated state" condition advanced by Hirschman (1970) and used by other researchers (Bemmels 1997; Freeman and Medoff 1986) as the starting point for employee exercise of voice appears to result from or be worsened by employee and supervisor involvement in the grievance process.[8]

Recent empirical research on unionized grievance procedures also deals with the reinstatement of dismissed employees, and the vast bulk of these studies examine reinstatement under arbitrator decisions in grievance cases. Most of this research uses United States (Malinowski 1991; Lewin and Peterson 1988; Labig, Helburn, and Rodgers 1985) or Canadian (Barnacle 1991; Ponak 1987; Shantz and Rogow 1984; Adams 1979) data, but a few studies of employee reinstatement following dismissal have also been done using British (Williams and Lewis 1982; Dickens, Hart, Jones, and Weekes 1984) and Italian (Rocella 1989) data.

Research on reinstatement typically begins with the collection of a sample of arbitration awards in dismissal cases and then focuses on the incidence of reinstatement, the factors affecting reinstatement, and the viability of employment relationships following reinstatement. In general, the relevant studies suggest that arbitrator decisions to reinstate dismissed employees are based on assessments of whether the infraction merits the punishment. More specifically, this research indicates that reinstatement occurs in approximately half of the grievance cases, with less severe punishments substituted for dismissal. The proportion of dismissed employees who actually return to work following decisions to reinstate with lesser penalties apparently ranges widely, from 46% in a Canadian study (Malinowski 1981) to 88% in a United States study (Barnacle 1991). Overall, it may be said that employees who are reinstated with lesser penalties than dismissal are reluctant to return to work (Bemmels and Foley 1996). Of particular interest, employees who are fully exonerated by arbitrators seem to have more difficulty following reinstatement than employees who are partially exonerated. For example, in a Canadian study by Adams (1979), quit rates for samples of fully and partially exonerated employees were 31% and 13%, respectively, following arbitrator reinstatement decisions. This finding is consistent with results from Lewin and Peterson's (1988) study, which showed that employees who won their grievance cases (at any step of the grievance procedure) were more likely to quit following grievance settlement decisions than employees who lost their grievance cases. Surprisingly, statistical studies of arbitrator reinstatement decisions have only infrequently been done. In one of these, Ponak (1987) found that women were significantly more likely than men to be reinstated following dismissal. In related research, Lewin and Peterson (1988) found that women were significantly more likely than men to win their grievance cases at higher steps of the grievance procedure, especially arbitration. Both Malinowski (1981) and Barnacle (1991) found that employee seniority was positively associated with return to work following arbitrator reinstatement decisions. With regard to grievance process variables, Ponak (1987) found that time from original incident to arbitrator decision, the arbitrator's experience, and the use of legal counsel to represent the parties had no significant effects on the incidence of reinstatement. When reinstatement is accompanied by full back pay, it occurs because the arbitrator concludes that the employer did not follow proper procedures or did not provide adequate evidence to support employee dismissal. Unfortunately, there is a paucity of research on the determinants of reinstatement with full back pay in relation to other reinstatement decisions, although one study (Brody 1987) found that reinstatement without back pay was significantly negatively associated with postreinstatement job performance.

More broadly, how do reinstated employees perform when they do return to work and what factors influence such performance? A study by Labig, Helburn, and Rodgers (1985) found that employees' prior job performance was positively associated with their postreinstatement job performance. Variables such as employee seniority and reason for discharge were unrelated to postreinstatement job performance, however. Concerning subsequent disciplinary infractions by reinstated employees, these also appear to be significantly associated with prior job performance but not significantly associated with variables such as age, gender, seniority, marital status, or size of the bargaining unit (Adams 1979). Interestingly, the highest rates of postreinstatement disciplinary infractions apparently occur in cases of alcohol-related infractions (Adams 1979). Research on postreinstatement employee turnover is scarce, but studies by Rocella (1989) and Shantz and Rogow (1984) report combined voluntary and involuntary turnover rates of 28% and 58%, respectively, in the two-year period immediately following reinstatement. Unfortunately, these studies did not utilize control groups of nongrievants or grievance cases involving less severe discipline than dismissal so that it is difficult meaningfully to interpret their findings about turnover among reinstated employees. Various other studies (Chaney 1981; Stephens and Chaney 1974), however, suggest that unfair workplace treatment is the main reason why employees choose to quit their jobs after reinstatement.[9]

Much of the contemporary research on reinstatement of dismissed employees features surveys of employer opinions and perceptions of the effectiveness of reinstatement. For example, Shantz and Rogow (1984) found that 53% of the Canadian employers they surveyed believed that employees reinstated to work with lesser penalties than discharge performed satisfactorily in their jobs. Williams and Lewis (1982) report a considerably higher percentage of British employers holding this belief, namely, 85%. Between 50% and 67% of employers believe that employees reinstated to work with lesser penalties than dismissal progress "normally" following reinstatement, according to studies by Ponak (1987) and Barnacle (1991). Taken as a whole, these studies also suggest that employers believe that incidence of postreinstatement disciplinary infractions by reinstated employees do not differ significantly from the incidence of infractions among other employees and that reinstatement does not have detrimental effects on employer authority, supervisory relations, or work group performance. By contrast, between 43% and 55% of surveyed employers said that reinstatement of dismissed employees has negative effects on workforce morale, and between 40% and 55% said that reinstatement has negative effects on relationships between reinstated employees and other employees (Barnacle 1991; Ponak 1987).

Among the limitations of this research are the lack of uniformity of managerial sample selection; the absence of panel or cohort studies of longitudinal changes in managerial perceptions of the effectiveness of reinstatement; and a paucity of data on and analysis of variation by managerial type, level, and function in perceptions of the effectiveness of reinstatement. One might imagine that labor relations/human resource managers who are responsible for and otherwise involved in employee discipline have significantly different perceptions of the effectiveness of reinstatement of dismissed employees than executives, line managers, and managers of other staff functions. Studies that explored such potential intramanagement differences in perceived effectiveness of reinstatement would enhance this particular literature considerably.

Some researchers have examined employee opinions and perceptions of the effectiveness of reinstatement (Rocella 1989; Williams and Lewis 1982), though such studies were more common in earlier periods (for example, Gold, Dennis, and Graham 1978; McDermott and Newhams 1971; Aspin 1971). This research features interviews rather than surveys of reinstated employees and generally concludes that such employees regard reinstatement as an effective remedy for dismissal—largely because the vast bulk of interviewees regard their dismissals as having been unfair. On balance, older, more senior, more skilled employees; employees with relatively good performance records prior to dismissal and reinstatement; and employees reinstated with full back pay appear to have the most positive opinions about the effectiveness of reinstatement as a remedy for dismissal (Rocella 1989; Williams and Lewis 1982; Gold, Dennis, and Graham 1978). Various workplace, grievance process, and arbitration variables, such as size of the work group and bargaining unit, type of offense, length of time from offense to arbitration, and single arbitrators versus arbitration panels apparently are unrelated to employee perceptions of the effectiveness of reinstatement as a remedy for dismissal. The lack of statistical analyses of employee interview data in these studies, however, considerably limits their validity and generalizability. And, as with certain other grievance procedure literature, there is little theoretical modeling of either employee or employer perceptions of the effectiveness of reinstatement as a remedy for dismissal in the research on this specific topic.

In summary, research on postgrievance settlement outcomes suggests that employee-grievants and their supervisors subsequently have significantly less viable employment relationships and significantly higher turnover rates than employees and supervisors who are not involved in grievance activity. This may be primarily due to management reprisal against grievants and their supervisors, although other factors and alternative explanations, including a "true" performance explanation, may be at work in these respects. Similar conclusions emerge from research on the reinstatement of dismissed employees, though here as well factors other than management reprisal influence the viability and continuity of employment following reinstatement. Nevertheless, and taken as a whole, the findings from the studies reviewed in this section provide substantial support for organizational punishment-industrial discipline theory of the grievance procedure and, more broadly, the employment relationship.

Grievance Procedures and Organizational Performance

Another important recent line of research on the grievance procedure examines grievance activity in relation to one or another measure of organizational performance. For example, Katz, Kochan, and Gobeille (1983) included the grievance rate as a measure of industrial relations performance and analyzed such performance in relation to the economic performance of a sample of United States automobile manufacturing plants. The grievance rate was found to be significantly positively associated with labor costs and significantly negatively associated with productivity and product quality in these plants. The researchers concluded that grievance activity has an overall "displacement effect"— time normally devoted to production is instead devoted to grievance filing and settlement—which results in lower plant performance. In a later related study, Katz, Kochan, and Weber (1985) showed that a program to improve the quality of working life could significantly lower grievance rates and thus the displacement effect in automobile manufacturing plants. In a study also set in the United States automobile industry, Norsworthy and Zabala (1985) found the grievance rate to be significantly negatively related to total factor productivity and significantly positively related to unit production costs over a seventeen-year period.

Similar findings have been reported by Ichniowski (1986, 1992) in his studies of grievance activity and plant performance in samples of paper mills. Controlling for other variables, Ichniowski (1986) found a strong negative relationship between grievance rates and monthly tons of paper produced in nine unionized paper mills over a six-year period. Later, and focusing on one of these mills, he showed that a program of labor-management cooperation, introduced because of declining plant performance, significantly reduced the grievance rate and improved the overall labor relations climate in the plant (Ichniowski 1992). The lower grievance rate, in turn, was significantly associated with higher productivity and product quality in this paper mill. Also of note in this regard is a study by Kleiner, Nickelsburg, and Pilarski (1995), which found that the lowest levels of labor costs in plants of a large unionized aerospace company were associated with "moderate" levels of grievance activity.

On the whole, this body of grievance procedure research indicates that conflictual labor-management relations, as reflected in and partially measured by the grievance rate, have significant negative effects on manufacturing plant performance—a conclusion also reached by Belman (1992) in his literature review on this topic. Further, initiatives at labor-management cooperation and improved quality of working life can reduce conflict which, in turn, will lower grievance rates and improve plant performance. Additional support for these findings and conclusions comes from case studies, such as of New United Motor Manufacturing Incorporated (NUMMI), which attribute significant plant performance improvement to reduced grievance rates (Levine 1995). It is important to recognize, however, that these studies focus on actual use of the grievance procedure rather than the availability of the procedure. This distinction is important because another, related line of research strongly suggests that the availability or presence of a grievance procedure in combination with certain other human resource management practices can have a positive effect on organizational performance.

To illustrate, Mitchell, Lewin, and Lawler (1990) constructed an index of the formality of human resource management practices that included the presence of a formal grievance procedure as one component of the index. They then conducted a longitudinal analysis of the relationship between this index and performance measures for a sample of 495 United States companies and found significant positive relationships between the index and return on assets, return on investment, and revenue per employee. Further, interaction analyses of the human resource management index with an index of employee participation in decision making and an index of variable pay found significant positive effects of both interactions on the aforementioned measures of business performance. Following in this vein, Huselid (1995) included the percentage of employees covered by a formal grievance procedure in one of his two main indexes of high-performance work practices. He then conducted a cross-sectional analysis of the relationships between these indexes and employee turnover and productivity in a sample of 855 United States businesses, finding significant positive relationships between the indexes and employee productivity and significant negative relationships between the indexes and employee turnover—results quite similar to those reported by Arthur (1992, 1994) in his studies of steel manufacturing firms. Huselid (1995) then showed that productivity was significantly positively associated and turnover significantly negatively associated with both market and accounting-based measures of company financial performance. In a study set in steel manufacturing, Ichniowski, Shaw, and Prennushi (1997) included the presence of a formal grievance procedure in their measures of innovative "bundles" of human resource management practices and analyzed relationships between such bundles and measures of steel manufacturing plant performance. They found significant positive relationships between bundles of innovative human resource management practices and productivity and product quality in these plants. Similar findings were reported by MacDuffie (1995) in a study of human resource bundles and plant performance in the automobile industry. The findings from these studies are consistent with frameworks advanced by Levine (1995) and Eaton and Voos (1992, 1994) in which they argue that for innovative human resource management practices, especially employee participation in decision making, to have positive effects on organizational performance, such practices must be part of a larger human resource management system that includes guarantees of due process for workers covered by these practices. According to these authors, the main guarantor of due process, especially in unionized firms, is the grievance procedure.

Thus the recent literature on grievance procedures and organizational performance appears at first glance to contain a contradiction or paradox. On the one hand, several studies find significant negative relationships between the use of the grievance procedure, that is, grievance activity, and organizational performance. On the other hand, several studies find significant positive relationships between the presence or availability of a grievance procedure, as part of a large bundle or system of human resource management practices, and organizational performance. This apparent contradiction/paradox is (partially) resolved, however, if we recognize the distinction between availability and use of the grievance procedure. Availability of the grievance procedure signals to employees that a mechanism exists for dealing with workplace conflict and providing a measure of due process in the employment relationship. Such a mechanism, together with other innovative human resource management practices, has positive effects on organizational performance. In contrast, use of the grievance procedure displaces time normally devoted to production and related work activity. Even though workplace conflict is addressed and, in one way or another, resolved through use of the grievance procedure, such use has negative effects on organizational performance.

But the apparent contradiction/paradox between research that finds grievance procedures to be negatively associated with plant performance and research that finds grievance procedures to be positively associated with overall organizational performance is not fully resolved by recognizing the distinction between the use and the availability of grievance procedures. Consider that so-called high-performance workplaces may generally have low grievance procedure usage rates precisely because the grievance procedure is bundled with other human resource management practices, such as work teams and management consultation with workers, in which workplace issues that otherwise might become the subject of grievances are otherwise taken up or addressed. Stated another way, the specific practices included in constructs of human resource management bundles may be highly intercorrelated so that one or more of these practices in effect serves as a proxy for the grievance procedure or, more to the point, for conflict handling and resolution. If this is in fact the case, then formal grievance procedure usage rates will be low in high-involvement workplaces. In this regard, it is notable that extant studies of high-involvement work practices, both at the plant and organizational levels of analysis, typically do not provide controls for conflict in the employment relationship. Also of methodological concern in this regard is that where surveys of managers form part of the database for studies of the effects of high-involvement work practices (including grievance procedures) on business performance, samples of managers may differ considerably as between plant-level and organizational-level studies. Plant-level studies are more likely to sample labor relations managers and plant managers, while organizational-level studies are more likely to sample senior executives of a firm. The former are closer than the latter to workplace conflict and grievance processing, and this may well influence the differences in reported grievance procedure usage rates (and other relevant variables) as between plant-level and organizational-level studies. Still further, and in light of Kleiner, Nickelsburg, and Pilarski's (1995) provocative finding that grievance activity is curvilinearly related to plant performance, it should be noted that extant studies of the effects of high-performance work practices on business performance use linear regression measures of grievance activity and, thus, may be misspecified.

In any case, and whatever one's interpretation of recent research on grievance procedures and organizational performance, it is undeniable that this research takes a larger systems view of the grievance procedure than traditional grievance procedure research. This systems view, however, does not focus on the multiple actors involved in grievance initiation and settlement or more broadly on union-management relations but, instead, focuses even more broadly on the grievance procedure as a mechanism for conflict resolution within a larger package or bundle of human resource management and employment practices that potentially provide competitive advantage to the enterprise. In doing so, this research on grievance procedures and organizational performance has in effect raised the analytical bar for future grievance procedure research. But this research also in effect represents a marked shift away from the dominant focus of traditional grievance procedure research on the protection and enforcement of worker rights in the employment relationship. Recognizing this shift, one may nevertheless ask whether organizational performance by itself is the "correct" measure of the effectiveness of high-involvement work practices (again including the grievance procedure). From both theoretical and empirical perspectives, it may be argued that the extent to which employee rights and workplace democracy are achieved through the grievance procedure constitutes another, equally valid measure of human resource management and/or organizational effectiveness. Recall that Eaton and Voos (1992, 1994) and Levine (1995) contend that by serving as a mechanism for free speech, the enforcement of worker rights, and due process in the employment relationship, the grievance procedure is essential to an effective high-involvement, participative workplace system. This reasoning parallels the argument that unions should not be judged solely (or perhaps even primarily) according to their effects on organizational performance; they should also (and perhaps even primarily) be judged according to their effects on industrial democracy. On this basis, research on high-involvement work practices or human resource management bundles that include grievance procedures should be expanded to analyze their effects on the protection of employee rights as well as their effects on organizational performance.

Overall Assessment and Research Agenda

An overall assessment of recent grievance procedure research can proceed from several different perspectives. From a research perspective, and despite some arguments to the contrary (Labig and Greer

1988), there have in fact been substantial recent advances in empirically grounded knowledge of the grievance procedure. Consider that we know far more now than previously about grievable events; the determinants of grievance initiation; the factors influencing grievance processing and settlement; the variables that affect arbitration decisions in grievance cases; employee, management, and union officials' perceptions of the grievance process; the consequences of grievance involvement for employees and supervisors; the viability of employment relationships for reinstated workers; and the relationship between grievance procedures and organizational performance. Further, this empirical knowledge has increasingly come from studies that (1) use organizations and organizational subunits rather than individuals as the unit of analysis, (2) emphasize environmental and organizational factors influencing grievance activity, (3) incorporate control groups of nongrievants, (4) use longitudinal data and data from several countries rather than only the United States, (5) analyze grievance activity and outcomes for different grievance issues, (6) derive and quantitatively test formal hypotheses, and (7) employ advanced statistical methods of analysis. Indeed, even case-based grievance procedure research increasingly features these characteristics. This empirical record is all the more impressive when one recognizes that researchers must still gain direct access to organizations in order to obtain grievance procedure data—data which are treated as proprietary by most organizations and for which there are no national or otherwise publicly available data sets.

From a theoretical perspective, it no longer seems fair or accurate to characterize grievance procedure research as atheoretical (Bemmels and Foley 1996). True, there is no generally accepted dominant new theory of the grievance process. But this review has shown that systems theory, exit-voice-loyalty theory, procedural-distributive justice theory, compensating differentials theory, efficiency theory, expectancy theory, organizational punishment-industrial discipline theory, and high-involvement work practice/human resource bundles theory have all recently been used to motivate and frame studies of the grievance procedure. That these theoretical perspectives have not been subsumed or integrated into a larger overall theory of the grievance process hardly supports the view that grievance procedure researchers eschew theory. In fact, this lack of theoretical integration and dominant theory of the grievance process may more fundamentally reflect the absence of new theories of workplace, organizational and societal conflict, and conflict resolution.

Where theorizing about grievance procedures and, more basically, workplace conflict does fall short is in what was previously referred to as "preventive conflict resolution." Among the theories reviewed above, only high-involvement work practice/human resource bundles theory appears to provide a conceptual basis for the development of a preventive theory of workplace conflict resolution. This is because this theory (or various versions of the theory) emphasizes broadened employee participation/consultation in decision making as well as broadened employee financial participation in the enterprise. Under such participative arrangements, work-related issues potentially leading to conflict are more likely to be anticipated, surfaced, and resolved through informal consultation and discussion than is the case under traditional work arrangements and grievance procedures. This is so despite the fact that the grievance procedure is also a form of employee participation in decision making. As suggested earlier in this review, informal consultation and discussion between workers and supervisors is virtually always the first "step" in the grievance process and thus may be conceptually and empirically similar to management consultation and discussion with workers under participative, high-involvement work practices. The relatively more "reactive" conflict resolution that takes place when grievances are put in writing and presented for processing, however, makes manifest the deteriorated state of the employment relationship that apparently motivates the initiation of formal grievances—and which may be further deteriorated by grievance handling, settlement, and postsettlement outcomes! With major ongoing changes in the design of work, the configuration of employment relationships, uses of technology, organizational structures, and enterprise leadership, the more traditional form of reactive conflict resolution represented by grievance procedures appears to be giving way to newer, more preventive forms of conflict resolution in the United States and elsewhere. The challenge to researchers, including grievance procedure researchers, is to develop workplace conflict theories that strike a better balance between what have been referred to here as preventive and reactive conflict resolution.

Such a theory might begin with formal and informal management consultation with workers, including as (but not necessarily limited to) components of a high-involvement bundle of human resource management practices as well as informal worker consultation with supervisors/managers to separate and recognize the potentially preventive character of this (otherwise) first grievance processing step. The theory could then proceed to consider formal grievance initiation, processing, and settlement as reactive conflict resolution, using extant empirical research to model the determinants of such grievance activity. Last, the theory should focus on preventive and reactive grievance procedure effectiveness measures, including behavioral and perceptual postgrievance settlement outcomes for workers and supervisors/managers, parties' uses of grievance feedback, effects on total and subunit organizational performance, and protection of employee rights.

The final component or dependent variable in this proposed theoretical framework, protection of employee rights, is especially notable because the grievance procedure was established in negotiated agreements between unions and management primarily to provide workers with a mechanism for resolving workplace disputes arising during the life of such agreements. As was pointed out earlier, while grievance procedures can be assessed along several dimensions, including their effects on organizational performance, it is both historically and contemporaneously important that such procedures be assessed in terms of the extent to which they actually protect employee rights and workplace due process. At present, a favorable assessment in this regard is based on that subset of research which shows that (1) unionized grievance procedures are in fact used; (2) work and therefore employment continue during periods of use; (3) a broad range of issues are taken up in grievance handling; (4) employees win nonnegligible proportions of grievance cases; (5) third-party arbitration is relatively infrequently but nevertheless regularly used to resolve certain grievance cases; (6) both employees and employers generally accept grievance decisions, especially arbitrated decisions; (7) employees found (usually by arbitrators) to have been unfairly dismissed are reinstated in their jobs; and (8) employees can and do rely on union representatives to process their grievances. On the whole, this constitutes impressive evidence of the protection of employee rights and the presence of due process in settling workplace disputes. A more unfavorable assessment in this regard, however, is based on that subset of research which shows that (1) a large majority of employees who believe that they have been unfairly treated at work nevertheless do not file grievances, (2) employees generally fear reprisal for filing grievances, (3) management appears to exercise reprisal against employees and especially supervisors who are involved in grievance activity, (4) employees reinstated in their jobs following dismissal subsequently have relatively high turnover and relatively low internal mobility, and (5) on balance, involvement in grievance activity results in deteriorated employment relationships for employees and their supervisors. This constitutes evidence of an erosion of employee rights and a decline of due process in settling workplace disputes. Additional and potentially more far-reaching evidence supporting this conclusion comes from the aforementioned studies that find the use of the grievance procedure to be negatively associated with organizational performance. This research suggests that workplace conflict resolution sought formally, explicitly, and overtly through the grievance procedure, that is, the traditional reactive exercise of employee rights and due process in the employment relationship, is inimical to organizational performance. If the findings from this research are valid, one would be hard pressed to identify a more compelling threat to longstanding notions about the appropriate mechanism for protecting employee rights and workplace due process.[10]

Research on grievance procedures may also be assessed from the perspective of managers/employers. There is little question that grievance handling through orderly, well understood, and accepted procedures means that production and work time are rarely interrupted by disputes over contractual terms and conditions of employment. Scholars have long commended the grievance procedure as a peaceful means of workplace dispute resolution (Staudohar 1977; Chamberlain and Kuhn 1965) and concluded that managers/employers favor this arrangement primarily because it assures the continuity of business operations (Lewin and Peterson 1988). Recent survey research finds that employers typically have highly favorable opinions and perceptions of grievance procedures, and it is also well known that employers use grievance activity as an information source for the diagnosis and correction of various production, workplace, and labor relations problems. These positive aspects of grievance procedures may also help us better to understand why nonunion employers are increasingly adopting such procedures (Lewin 1998; Delaney and Feuille 1992; Delaney, Lewin, and Ichniowski 1989).

Nevertheless, one may ask why managers/employers are favorably disposed toward grievance procedures when research indicates that the use of such procedures is apparently negatively associated with plant performance and that managers/employers apparently exercise reprisal against those involved in grievance activity. Concerning plant performance, the relevant studies typically analyze grievance activity only among establishments that have grievance procedures in place. They do not examine the incidence or resolution of workplace disputes in establishments with and without grievance procedures, and one might imagine that production and work time are more likely to be interrupted because of workplace disputes in establishments without grievance procedures than in establishments with such procedures. Stated differently, there is something of a restriction of range phenomenon in extant studies of grievance procedure usage and plant performance. Also recall that studies of organizational (as distinct from plant) performance find positive relationships between such performance and the presence of grievance procedures (as part of larger bundles of innovative or high-involvement human resource management practices).

Concerning manager/employer reprisal against those involved in grievance activity, it may be suggested that such reprisal is in part a function of the costs of grievance activity. That is, where grievance activity (overt conflict) is high, managers/employers will be more likely to engage in reprisals against grievants and other involved personnel than where grievance activity is low—a hypothesis that has not been tested in the grievance procedure research reviewed here. Further, in organizations with grievance procedures that are present but not used and in organizations with grievance procedures that have a low usage rate (that is, low costs), manager/employer reprisal against those involved in grievance activity will likely be low and manager/employer opinions of the grievance procedure will likely be high. By contrast, in organizations with grievance procedures that have a high usage rate (that is, costs), manager/employer reprisal against those involved in grievance activity will likely be high and manager/employer opinions of the grievance procedure will likely be low. Note that such reasoning is consistent with efficiency theory of grievance initiation and with the aforementioned evidence of positive relationships between the presence of grievance procedures and organizational performance. In any case, it should be kept in mind that managers/employers typically have relatively favorable opinions of grievance procedures as well as favorable assessments of the overall effectiveness of such procedures.

Turning to an agenda for future grievance procedure research, several expanded as well as new areas can be identified. First, the fact that so many industrial relations researchers have concluded that most grievances are settled informally in consultation and discussions between employees and supervisors but have done so *without any supporting data* suggests that the time has come to inquire more fully into such informal dispute settlement. Of particular interest is whether such informal consultation/discussion is merely the first step along the way to the more formal preparation and processing of written grievances and, thus, reactive conflict resolution or, instead, is qualitatively different behavior that represents relatively more preventive conflict resolution. Laboratory studies of the type recently conducted by Olson-Buchanan (1997) and deep interview and observation-based research designs seem particularly appropriate to such research.

Second, closer examination of the various issues taken through the grievance procedure and the different behaviors associated with these issues seems warranted. Recall, for example, that researchers have found the filing of grievances over management policies to be positively associated with subsequent employee absenteeism from work, while the filing of grievances over discipline issues is negatively associated with subsequent absenteeism (Klaas, Heneman, and Olson 1991). Other researchers have found that senior management is most likely to reverse lower management in grievance cases involving employee training and promotion issues (Lewin and Peterson 1988). Yet, we know very little about why these different behaviors occur. Perhaps management policies involving changes in the design of work, uses of technology, possibly even the strategic direction of the enterprise represent changes and challenges of such magnitude that employee-grievants respond to them and to decisions in their grievance cases primarily by withdrawing from work. Or perhaps senior management regards training and promotion as more central to the achievement of organizational objectives than other areas of human resource management and is thus most likely to overturn the decisions of middle and lower management in these areas (thereby motivating withdrawal behavior on the part of middle and lower level managers/supervisors). It is also possible that grievances involving management policy and discipline have different effects on organizational performance than grievances over training, promotion, pay, and work scheduling. Evidence about these and related propositions about grievance issues and the parties' associated behaviors may be obtained from new, deeper case studies within and across organizations and organizational subunits.

Third, evidence that employers exercise reprisal against employees and supervisors who are involved in grievance activity indicates that the grievance process yields outcomes unanticipated by and presumably contrary to the objectives of those who negotiate, construct, and agree to include grievance procedures in collective bargaining agreements. Here, studies of union and management officials' knowledge of grievance procedure outcomes seem to be in order, as are studies of arbitrators' knowledge of such outcomes. Potentially, such studies can be used to fashion remedies for employer reprisal against those involved in grievance activity and thereby protect employee rights. More fundamentally, such studies can shed light on the proposition that the grievance procedure is a form of reactive conflict resolution and perhaps also be used to identify more preventive forms of conflict resolution unaccompanied by reprisal against grievants and supervisors of grievants.

Fourth, the time appears ripe for comparative studies of union and nonunion grievance procedures. Only one study of this type has been done (Lewin and Boroff 1996), and it used exit-voice-loyalty and procedural-distributive justice theory to analyze grievance procedure data from one large unionized and one large nonunion enterprise. This type of research can be expanded to individual enterprises that have separate grievance procedures for their unionized and nonunion employees, respectively. Here, analysis can concentrate on similarities and differences between the two procedures with respect to grievance initiation, grievance issues, grievance processing and settlement, and postgrievance settlement outcomes. In addition, and because nonunion grievance procedures typically cover a broader range of jobs, skills, and occupations than unionized grievance procedures, it should be possible to determine if grievance initiation, settlement, and outcomes differ significantly between, on the one hand, managerial, professional, and white-collar employees and, on the other hand, skilled, semiskilled, and blue-collar employees.

Finally, it is important for researchers to make further progress in sorting out the effects of grievance procedures on organizational performance. According to this review, grievance procedure usage, measured by grievance rates, has been found to be significantly negatively associated with plant (organizational subunit) performance, whereas the presence of a grievance procedure as part of a package or bundle of high-involvement, participatively oriented human resource management practices has been found to be significantly positively associated with overall organizational performance. What is missing from this research are studies that directly examine grievance procedure presence (availability), usage, and organizational performance. Such studies require samples of organizations and/or organizational subunits with sufficient variation in grievance procedure usage rates to be able to distinguish the presence of grievance procedures from the use of grievance procedures in terms of their effects on organizational performance. Unless and until this is done, the conclusion may well be drawn that from an organizational performance perspective, the "best" grievance procedure is one that exists but is not used!

Acknowledgments

My thanks to Ms. Zeynep Aksehirli and Ms. Kimberly Harris, doctoral degree candidates, for their excellent research assistance in the preparation of this chapter. The helpful comments of the editors of this volume on a previous draft of this paper are gratefully acknowledged.

Endnotes

[1] This review is limited to research on grievance procedures and arbitration involving unionized employees and management who engage in collective bargaining. It is written in part to update a prior review contained in Lewin and Peterson (1988) and consequently focuses largely on research that has appeared since then. For other such reviews, see Peterson and Lewin (forthcoming), Bemmels and Foley (1996), Labig and Greer (1988), and Gordon and Miller (1984). For reviews of research on nonunion dispute resolution see Chachere and Bingham (1999 this volume), Lewin (1997, 1998), Feuille and Delaney (1992), and Peterson (1992).

[2] The terms "reactive" and "preventive" are more or less equivalent to concepts of ex post and ex ante, respectively, as regards the behavior of labor and management. In particular, "reactive" refers to the parties acting after the fact of a workplace dispute or perceived unfair workplace treatment in attempting to resolve the dispute or remedy the unfair treatment. The grievance procedure is posed here as the principal mechanism for resolving ex post workplace disputes/remedying unfair workplace treatment. The term "preventive" refers to the behavior and actions of the parties, such as the introduction of work teams or adoption of labor-management cooperation programs, that appear to anticipate and thus reduce the incidence of workplace disputes/unfair workplace treatment. The term "proactive" can be regarded as a synonym for the term "preventive."

[3] Loyalty is posed by Hirschman as being positively correlated with voice, so that relatively more loyal customers will exercise voice rather than exit the firm.

[4] This figure would likely have to be adjusted downward, say to ten million informal grievance discussions annually, given the significant decline in private sector unionization that has taken place in the last decade or so.

[5] See, for example, Klaas (1989) on expectancy theory, Cooke and Rousseau (1988) on organizational culture theory, Brockner (1992) on commitment escalation theory, Bowen (1987) on decision dilemma theory, and Kahneman and Tversky (1979) on prospect theory. These theories are not included in Table 1 because for the most part they have not (yet) been applied to empirical research on unionized grievance procedures.

[6] The conclusion that unions raise costs and productivity by about the same magnitudes and, hence, leave unit labor costs unchanged has also been reached in studies that apply exit-voice-loyalty theory to union-management relations. See Freeman (1980) and Freeman and Medoff (1984).

[7] In so far as supervisor job performance in the context of grievance involvement is concerned, it may be claimed that grievances filed by employees against supervisors constitute one measure of supervisory job performance. Such grievances represent a "translation" of the labor agreement into day-to-day supervisorial practice and

provide evidence of the supervisor's ability (or lack thereof) to elicit cooperation—and job performance—from workers. According to this reasoning, a grievance essentially is an allegation of mismanagement and, if sustained, should be considered evidence of poor management (supervisor) performance. By extension, if the grievance is not sustained, that is, if the worker's grievance is not upheld and just cause is found to exist for the action challenged by the worker, then no evidence of poor management (supervisor) performance is adduced. One problem with this line of reasoning is that, as noted above, numerous factors influence grievance initiation, including factors unrelated to the merit of a grievance and factors over which supervisors have little or no control. Another problem in this regard is that numerous factors also influence decisions in grievance cases, including factors unrelated to the merit of a grievance. Therefore, it is risky at best to equate grievance filing in general and grievance decisions in favor of employees in particular with "poor" supervisor (manager) job performance.

[8] It is important to note that similar findings and conclusions emerge from recent empirical studies of nonunion grievance procedures. See Lewin (1987, 1992, 1997, 1998), Olson-Buchanan (1996, 1997), Lewin and Boroff (1996), Blancero (1995), Feuille and Delaney (1992), Delaney and Feuille (1992), and Peterson (1992).

[9] These studies also indicate that reinstated employees who decide not to return to work reach such a decision because of fear of employer reprisal.

[10] It should, of course, be recognized that collectively bargained employee rights and workplace due process protections apply to fewer and fewer employees as unionism has declined in the United States and most other nations (Troy 1997).

References

Adams, R. 1979. *Grievance Arbitration of Discharge Cases: A Study of the Concepts of Industrial Discipline and Their Results,* Kingston, ON: Industrial Relations Center.

Allen, R. E., and T. Keaveny. 1985. "Factors Differentiating Grievants and Non-grievants." *Human Relations,* Vol. 38, pp. 519-34.

Arthur, J. B. 1992. "The Link between Business Strategy and Industrial Relations Systems in American Steel Minimills." *Industrial and Labor Relations Review,* Vol. 45, pp. 488-506.

_____. 1994. "Effects of Human Resource Systems on Manufacturing Performance and Turnover." *Academy of Management Journal,* Vol. 37, pp. 670-87.

Arvey, R. D., and A. P. Jones. 1985. "The Uses of Discipline in Organizational Settings." In B. M. Staw and L. L. Cummings, eds., *Research in Organizational Behavior,* Vol. 7. Greenwich, CT: JAI Press, pp. 367-408.

Aspin, L. 1971. "Legal Remedies under the NLRA: Remedies under 8(a)(3)." *Proceedings of the Twenty-Third Annual Meeting* (Detroit, Dec. 28-29). Madison, WI: Industrial Relations Association, pp. 264-72.

Barnacle, P. 1991. *Arbitration of Discharge Grievances in Ontario: Outcomes and Reinstatement Experiences.* Kingston, ON: Industrial Relations Center.

Belman, D. 1992. "Unions, the Quality of Labor Relations, and Firm Performance." In L. Mishel and P. B. Voos, eds. *Union and Economic Competitiveness.* Armonk, NY: Myron E. Sharpe, pp. 41-107.

Bemmels, B. 1991. "Gender Effects in Arbitration." In W. Kaplan, J. Sack, and M. Gunderson, eds., *Labor Arbitration Yearbook*, Vol. 2, Toronto: Butterworths-Lancaster House, pp. 167-80.

_____. 1994. "The Determinants of Grievance Initiation." *Industrial and Labor Relations Review*, Vol. 47, no. 2, pp. 285-301.

_____. 1995. "Shop Stewards' Satisfaction with Grievance Procedures." *Industrial Relations*, Vol. 34, no. 1, pp. 578-92.

_____. 1997. "Exit, Voice, and Loyalty in Employment Relationships." In D. Lewin, D. J. B. Mitchell, and M. A. Zaidi, eds., *The Human Resource Management Handbook*, Part II. Greenwich, CT: JAI Press, pp. 245-59.

Bemmels, B., and J. Foley. 1996. "Grievance Procedure Research: A Review and Theoretical Recommendations." *Journal of Management*, Vol. 22, no. 3, pp. 359-84.

Bemmels, B., Y. Reshef, and K. Stratton-Devine. 1991. "The Roles of Supervisors, Employees, and Stewards in Grievance Initiation." *Industrial and Labor Relations Review*, Vol. 45, no. 1, pp. 15-30.

Blancero, D. 1995. "Nonunion Grievance Systems: System Characteristics and Fairness Perceptions." *Academy of Management Journal*, Best Paper Proceedings, pp. 84-88.

Bohlander, G. 1992. "Public Sector Grievance Arbitration: Structure and Administration." *Journal of Collective Negotiations*, Vol. 21, no. 4, pp. 271-86.

Boroff, K. E., and D. Lewin. 1997. "Loyalty, Voice, and Intent to Exit a Union Firm: A Conceptual and Empirical Analysis." *Industrial and Labor Relations Review*, Vol. 51, no. 1, pp. 50-63.

Bowen, M. G. 1987. "The Escalation Phenomenon Reconsidered: Decision Dilemmas or Decision Errors?" *Academy of Management Review*, Vol. 12, pp. 52-66.

Brockner, J. 1992. "The Escalation of Commitment to a Failing Course of Action." *Academy of Management Review*, Vol. 17, no. 1, pp. 39-61.

Brody, B. 1987. "Reinstatement of Unjust Dismissals: New Evidence from Quebec." Paper presented to the annual meeting of the Canadian Industrial Relations Association, Hamilton, Ontario.

Cappelli, P., and K. Chauvin. 1991. "A Test of an Efficiency Model of Grievance Activity." *Industrial and Labor Relations Review*, Vol. 45, no. 1, pp. 3-14.

Chachere, D. R., and L. B. Bingham. 1999. "Nonunion Alternative Dispute Resolution and a Close Look at Employment Arbitration." In J. Keefe and A. E. Eaton, eds., *Employment Dispute Resolution in the Changing Workplace*. Madison, WI: Industrial Relations Research Association.

Chamberlain, N. W., and J. W. Kuhn. 1965. *Collective Bargaining*, 2d ed. New York: McGraw-Hill.

Chaney, W. 1981. "The Reinstatement Remedy Revisited," *Labor Law Journal*, Vol. 32, pp. 357-65.

Chayowski, R., G. Stotsve, and J. Butler. 1992. "A Simultaneous Analysis of Grievance Activity and Outcome Decisions." *Industrial and Labor Relations Review*, Vol. 45, pp. 724-37.

Clark, P. F., and D. G. Gallagher. 1988. "Membership Perceptions of the Value and Effect of Grievance Procedures." *Proceedings of the Fortieth Annual Meeting* (Chicago, Dec. 28-30). Madison, WI: Industrial Relations Research Association, pp. 406-15.

Clark, P. F., D. G. Gallagher, and T. J. Pavlak. 1990. "Member Commitment in an American Union: The Role of the Grievance Procedure." *Labor Studies Journal*, Vol. 21, pp. 147-57.

Cooke, R. A., and D. R. Rousseau. 1988. "Behavioral Norms and Expectations: A Quantitative Approach to the Assessment of Organizational Culture." *Group and Organization Studies*, Vol. 13, no. 3, pp. 245-73.

Dalton, D. R., and W. D. Tudor. 1982. "Antecedents of Grievance Filing Behavior: Attitude/Behavior Consistency and the Union Steward." *Academy of Management Journal*, Vol. 25, no. 1, pp. 158-69.

Dalton, D. R., W. D. Tudor, and C. L. Owen. 1987. "Sex Effects in Workplace Justice Outcomes: Two Field Assessments." *Journal of Applied Psychology*, Vol. 72, pp. 156-69.

Dastmalchian, A., and I. Ng. 1990. "Industrial Relations Climate and Grievance Outcomes." *Industrial Relations*, Vol. 45, no. 2, pp. 311-24.

Davy, J. A., G. Stewart, and J. Anderson. 1992. "Formalization of Grievance Procedures: A Multifirm and Industry Study." *Journal of Labor Research*, Vol. 13, no. 3, pp. 307-15.

Delaney, J. T., and P. Feuille. 1992. "The Determinants of Nonunion Grievance and Arbitration Procedures." *Proceedings of the Forty-Fourth Annual Meeting* (New Orleans, Jan. 3-5). Madison, WI: Industrial Relations Research Association, pp. 529-38.

Delaney, J. T., D. Lewin, and C. Ichniowski. 1989. *Human Resource Policies and Practices in American Firms.* Washington, DC: U.S. Department of Labor, BLMR #137.

Dickens, L., M. Hart, M. Jones, and B. Weeks. 1984. "The British Experience under a Statute Prohibiting Unfair Dismissal." *Industrial and Labor Relations Review*, Vol. 37, no. 4, pp. 497-514.

Duane, M. 1991. "To Grieve or Not to Grieve: Why Reduce It to Writing?" *Public Personnel Management*, Vol. 20. pp. 83-90.

Eaton, A. E., M. Gordon, and J. Keefe. 1992. "The Impact of Quality of Work Life Programs and Grievance System Effectiveness on Union Commitment." *Industrial and Labor Relations Review*, Vol. 45, pp. 591-604.

Eaton, A. E., and P. B. Voos. 1992. "Unions and Contemporary Innovations in Work Organization, Compensation, and Employee Participation." In L. Mishel and P. B. Voos, eds., *Unions and Economic Competitiveness.* Armonk, NY: Myron E. Sharpe, pp. 173-215.

_____. 1994. "Productivity-enhancing Innovations in Work Organization, Compensation, and Employee Participation in the Union Versus the Nonunion Sectors." In D. Lewin and D. Sockell, eds., *Advances in Industrial and Labor Relations*, 6. Greenwich, CT: JAI Press, pp. 63-109.

Feuille, P., and J. T. Delaney. 1992. "The Individual Pursuit of Organizational Justice: Grievance Procedures in Nonunion Workplaces." In G. R. Ferris and K. M. Rowland, eds., *Research in Personnel and Human Resource Management*, 10: pp. 187-232.

Fleishman, E. A. 1957. "A Leader Behavior Description." In R. M. Stodgill and A. E. Coons, eds., *Leader Behavior: Its Description and Measurement.* Columbus, OH: Ohio State University.

Freeman, R. B. 1980. "The Exit-Voice Tradeoff in the Labor Market: Unionism, Job Tenure, Quits, and Separations." *Quarterly Journal of Economics,* Vol. 94, no. 3, pp. 643-73.

Freeman, R. B., and J. L. Medoff. 1984. *What Do Unions Do?* New York: Basic Books.

Fryxell, G. E. 1992. "Perceptions of Justice Afforded by Formal Grievance Systems as Predictors of a Belief in a Just Workplace." *Journal of Business Ethics,* Vol. 11, pp. 635-47.

Fryxell, G. E., and M. E. Gordon. 1989. "Workplace Justice and Job Satisfaction as Predictors of Satisfaction with Union and Management." *Academy of Management Journal,* Vol. 32, no. 4, pp. 851-66.

Gold, C., R. Dennis, and J. Graham. 1978. "Reinstatement after Termination: Public Teachers." *Industrial and Labor Relations Review,* Vol. 31, pp. 310-21.

Gordon, M. E. 1988. "Grievance Systems and Workplace Justice: Tests of Behavioral Propositions about Procedural and Distributive Justice." *Proceedings of the Fortieth Annual Meeting* (Chicago, Dec. 28-30). Madison, WI: Industrial Relations Research Association, pp. 390-97.

Gordon, M. E., and R. C. Bowlby. 1988. "Propositions about Grievance Settlements: Finally, Consultation with Grievants." *Personnel Psychology,* Vol. 41, pp. 107-23.

_____. 1989. "Reactance and Intentionality Attributions as Determinants of the Intent to File a Grievance." *Personnel Psychology,* Vol. 42, no. 2, pp. 309-29.

Gordon, M. E., and G. E. Fryxell. 1993. "The Role of Interpersonal Justice in Organizational Grievance Systems." In R. Cropanzano, ed., *Justice in the Workplace: Approaching Fairness in Human Resource Management.* Hillsdale, NJ: Lawrence Erlbaum, pp. 231-55.

Gordon, M. E., and S. Miller. 1984. "Grievances: A Review of Research and Practice." *Personnel Psychology,* Vol. 37, no. 2, pp. 117-46.

Greenberg, J. 1990. "Looking Fair and Being Fair: Managing Impressions of Organizational Justice." In B. M. Shaw and L. L. Cummings, eds., *Research in Organizational Behavior,* Vol. 12, pp. 111-57.

Hirschman, A. O. 1970. *Exit, Voice and Loyalty.* Cambridge, MA: Harvard University Press.

Huselid, M. A. 1995. "The Impact of Human Resource Management Practices on Turnover, Productivity, and Corporate Financial Performance." *Academy of Management Journal,* Vol. 38. no. 3, pp. 635-72.

Ichniowski, C. 1986. "The Effects of Grievance Activity on Productivity. *Industrial and Labor Relations Review,* Vol. 40, no. 1, pp. 75-89.

_____. 1992. "Human Resource Practices and Productive Labor-Management Relations." In D. Lewin, O. S. Mitchell, and P. D. Sherer, eds., *Research Frontiers in Industrial and Human Relations,* Madison, WI: Industrial Relations Research Association, pp. 239-71.

Ichniowski, C., and D. Lewin. 1987. "Grievance Procedures and Firm Performance." In M. M. Kleiner, R. N. Block, M. Roomkin, and S. Salsburg, eds., *Human Resources and the Performance of the Firm,* Industrial Relations Research Association, Washington, DC: Bureau of National Affairs, pp. 159-93.

Ichniowski, C., K. Shaw, and G. Prennushi. 1997. "The Effects of Human Resource Management Practices on Productivity: A Study of Steel Finishing Lines." *American Economic Review,* Vol. 87, no. 2, pp. 291-313.

Kaminski, M. 1999. "Impact of Teams on the Grievance Procedure: Issues of Voice and Union Commitment." In J. J. Keefe and A. E. Eaton, eds., *Employment Dispute Resolution in the Changing Workplace*, Madison, WI: Industrial Relations Research Association.

Katz, H. C., T. A. Kochan, and K. R. Gobeille. 1983. "Industrial Relations Performance, Economic Performance, and QWL Program: An Interplant Analysis." *Industrial and Labor Relations Review*, Vol. 37, pp. 3-17.

Katz, H. C., T. A. Kochan, and M. R. Weber. 1985. "Assessing the Effects of Industrial Relations and Quality of Work Life Efforts on Organizational Effectiveness." *Academy of Management Journal*, Vol. 28, no. 3, pp. 509-27.

Kahneman, D., and A. Taversky. 1979. "Prospect Theory: An Analysis of Decision under Risk." *Econometrica*, Vol. 47, pp. 263-91.

Klaas, B. 1989. "Determinants of Grievance Activity and the Grievance System's Impact on Employer Behavior: An Integrative Perspective." *Academy of Management Review*, Vol. 14, no. 3, pp. 445-58.

Klaas, B., and A. DeNisi. 1989. "Managerial Reactions to Employee Dissent: The Impact of Grievance Activity on Performance Ratings." *Academy of Management Journal*, Vol. 32, no. 4, pp. 705-18.

Klaas, B., H. G. Heneman, and C. Olson. 1991. "Effects of Grievance Activity on Absenteeism." *Journal of Applied Psychology*, Vol. 76, no. 6, pp. 818-24.

Kleiner, M. M. 1992. "Employee Voice: An Economic Perspective." Paper presented to the Forty-Fourth Annual Meeting of the Industrial Relations Research Association, New Orleans, LA, January.

Kleiner, M. M., G. Nickelsburg, and A. Pilarski. 1995. "Monitoring, Grievances, and Plant Performance." *Industrial Relations*, Vol. 34, no. 2, pp. 169-89.

Knight, T. R. 1986. "Feedback and Grievance Resolution." *Industrial and Labor Relations Review*, Vol. 39, no. 4, pp. 585-98.

_____. 1987. "The Tactical Use of the Union's Duty of Fair Representation: An Empirical Analysis." *Industrial and Labor Relations Review*, Vol. 40, pp. 180-94.

Kuhn, J. W. 1961. *Bargaining in Grievance Settlement: The Power of Industrial Work Groups*. New York: Columbia University Press.

Labig, C. E., Jr., and C. R. Greer. 1988. "Grievance Initiation: A Literature Survey and Suggestions for Future Research." *Journal of Labor Research*, Vol. 9, no. 1, pp. 1-27.

Labig, C. E., Jr., and I. Helburn. 1986. "Union and Management Policy Influences on Grievance Initiation." *Journal of Labor Research*, Vol. 7, pp. 269-84.

Labig, C. E., Jr., I. Helburn, and R. Rodgers. 1985. "Discipline History, Seniority, and Reason for Discharge as Predictors of Postreinstatement of Job Performance." *The Arbitration Journal*, Vol. 40, pp. 44-52.

Lawler, E. E., III. 1986. *High-Involvement Management*. San Francisco, CA: Jossey-Bass.

Levine, D. I. 1995. *Reinventing the Workplace*. Washington, DC: Brookings.

Lewin, D. 1983. "Theoretical Perspectives on the Modern Grievance Procedure." In J. D. Reid, Jr., ed., *New Approaches to Labor Unions: Research in Labor Economics*, Supplement 2. Greenwich, CT: JAI Press, pp. 127-47.

_____. 1984. "Empirical Measures of Grievance Procedure Effectiveness." *Labor Law Journal*, Vol. 35, no. 8, pp. 491-99.

_____. 1987. "Dispute Resolution in the Nonunion Firm: A Theoretical and Empirical Analysis." *Journal of Conflict Resolution*, Vol. 31, no. 3, pp. 465-502.

_____. 1992. "Grievance Procedures in Nonunion Workplaces: An Empirical Analysis of Usage, Dynamics, and Outcomes." *Chicago-Kent Law Review*, Vol. 66, no. 3, pp. 823-44.

_____. 1997. "Workplace Dispute Resolution." In D. Lewin, D. J.B. Mitchell, and M. A. Zaidi, eds., *The Human Resource Management Handbook, Part II*. Greenwich, CT: JAI Press, pp. 197-218.

_____. 1998. "Nonunion Dispute Resolution: What Have We Learned and What More Do We Need to Know?" Paper presented to the Sixth Bargaining Group Conference Institute of Labor and Industrial Relations, University of Illinois, May.

Lewin, D., and K. E. Boroff. 1996. "The Role of Loyalty in Exit and Voice: A Conceptual and Empirical Analysis." In D. Lewin, B. E. Kaufman, and D. Sockell, eds., *Advances in Industrial and Labor Relations*, Vol. 7, pp. 69-96.

Lewin, D., and R. B. Peterson. 1988. *The Modern Grievance Procedure in the United States*. New York: Quorum.

_____. 1998. "Lessons from Research on Unionized Grievance Procedures: A Critical Review and Appraisal." *Human Resources Management*, Vol. 38.

_____. Forthcoming. "Behavioral Outcomes of Grievance Activity." *Industrial Relations*, Vol. 38, no. 4, in press.

Lind, E. A., and E. R. Tyler. 1988. *The Social Psychology of Procedural Justice*. New York: Plenum.

MacDuffie, J. P. 1995. "Human Resource Bundles and Manufacturing Performance: Organizational Logic and Flexible Production Systems in the World Auto Industry." *Industrial and Labor Relations Review*, Vol. 48, no. 2, pp. 197-221.

Malinowski, A. 1981. "An Empirical Analysis of Discharge Cases and the Work History of Employees Reinstated by Labor Arbitration." *The Arbitration Journal*, Vol. 36, pp. 31-46.

McDermott, T., and T. Newhams. 1971. "Discharge Reinstatement: What Happens Thereafter?" *Industrial and Labor Relations Review*, Vol. 42, pp. 526-40.

Mesch, D., and D. Dalton. 1992. "Unexpected Consequences of Improving Workplace Justice: A Six-Year Time Series Assessment." *Academy of Management Journal*, Vol. 35, pp. 1099-114.

Meyer, D. 1994. "The Political Effects of Grievance Handling by Stewards in a Local Union." *Journal of Labor Research*, Vol. 15, no. 1, pp. 33-51.

Meyer, D., and D. Cooke. 1988. "Economic and Political Factors in Formal Grievance Resolution." *Industrial Relations*, Vol. 27, no. 3, pp. 318-35.

Mitchell, D. J.B., D. Lewin, and E. E. Lawler, III. 1990. "Alternative Pay Systems, Firm Performance, and Productivity." In A. S. Blinder, ed., *Paying for Productivity*, Washington, DC: Brookings, pp. 15-94.

Morishima, M. 1996. "The Evolution of White-Collar Human Resource Management in Japan." In D. Lewin, B. E. Kaufman, and D. Sockell, eds., *Advances in Industrial and Labor Relations*, Vol. 7, pp. 145-76.

Nelson, N. E. 1979. "Grievance Rates and Technology," *Academy of Management Journal*, Vol. 22, no. 4, pp. 810-15.

Ng, I., and A. Dastmalchian. 1989. "Determinants of Grievance Outcomes: A Case Study." *Industrial and Labor Relations Review*, Vol. 42, no. 3, pp. 393-403.

Norsworthy, J. R., and C. A. Zabala. 1985. "Worker Attitudes, Worker Behavior, and Productivity in the U.S. Automobile Industry, 1959-76." *Industrial and Labor Relations Review,* Vol. 38, no. 4, pp. 544-57.

Olson-Buchanan, J. 1996. "Voicing Discontent: What Happens to the Grievance Filer after the Grievance?" *Journal of Applied Psychology,* Vol. 81, no. 1, pp. 52-63.

_____. 1997. "To Grieve or Not to Grieve: Factors Relating to Voicing Discontent in an Organizational Simulation." *International Journal of Conflict Management,* Vol. 8, no. 2, pp. 132-47.

O'Reilly, C. A., and B. A. Weitz. 1980. "Managing Marginal Employees: The Use of Warnings and Dismissals." *Administrative Science Quarterly,* Vol. 25, no. 2, pp. 467-84.

Peach, D., and E. R. Livernash. 1974. *Grievance Initiation and Resolution: A Study in Basic Steel.* Boston, MA: Harvard Graduate School of Business Administration.

Peterson, R. B. 1988. "A Multiple-Measure Test of Grievance Procedure Effectiveness." *Proceedings of the Fortieth Annual Meeting* (Chicago, Dec. 28-30). Madison, WI: Industrial Relations Research Association, pp. 398-405.

_____. 1992. "The Union and Nonunion Grievance System." In D. Lewin, O. S. Mitchell, and P. D. Sherer, eds., *Research Frontiers in Industrial Relations and Human Resources,* Madison, WI: Industrial Relations Research Association, pp. 131-62.

Peterson, R. B., and D. Lewin. 1982. "A Model for Research and Analysis of the Grievance Process." *Proceedings of the Thirty-Fourth Annual Meeting* (Washington, DC, Dec. 28-30). Madison, WI: Industrial Relations Research Association, pp. 304-12.

Pfeffer, J. 1994. *Competitive Advantage through People.* Boston, MA: Harvard Business School.

Pil, F. K., and J. P. MacDuffie. 1996. "The Adoption of High-Involvement Work Practices." *Industrial Relations,* Vol. 35, no. 3, pp. 423-55.

Ponak, A. 1987. "Discharge Arbitration and Reinstatement in the Province of Alberta." *The Arbitration Journal,* Vol. 42, pp. 39-46.

Ponak, A., and C. Olson. 1992. "Time Delays in Grievance Arbitration." *Industrial Relations,* Vol. 47, pp. 690-705.

Rees, A. 1977. *The Economics of Trade Unions,* 2d. ed. Chicago: University of Chicago Press.

Rees, D. I. 1991. "Grievance Procedure Strength and Teacher Quits." *Industrial and Labor Relations Review,* Vol. 45, no. 1, pp. 31-43.

Rocella, M. 1989. "The Reinstatement of Dismissed Employees in Italy: An Empirical Analysis." *Comparative Labor Law Journal,* Vol. 10, pp. 166-95.

Sayles, L. R. 1958. *Behavior of Industrial Work Groups.* New York: McGraw-Hill.

Shantz, E., and R. Rogow. 1984. "Post-reinstatement Experience: A British Columbia Study." Paper presented at the annual meeting of the Canadian Industrial Relations Association, Guelph.

Sheppard, B. H., R. J. Lewicki, and J. W. Minton. 1992. *Organizational Justice,* New York: Lexington.

Slichter, S. H., J. J. Healy, and E. R. Livernash. 1960. *The Impact of Collective Bargaining on Management,* Washington, DC: Brookings.

Staudohar, P. D. 1977. "Exhaustion of Remedies in Private Industry Grievance Procedures." *Employee Relations Law Journal,* Vol. 7, no. 3, pp. 454-64.

Stephens, E., and W. Chaney. 1974. "A Study of the Reinstatement Remedy under the National Labor Relations Act." *Labor Law Journal,* Vol. 25, pp. 31-41.

Stewart, G. L., and J. A. Davy. 1992. "An Empirical Examination of Grievance Resolution and Filing Rates in the Public and Private Sector." *Journal of Collective Negotiations,* Vol. 21, no. 4, pp. 323-35.

Thomson, A. W. J., and V. F. Murray. 1976. *Grievance Procedures.* Westmead, England: Saxon House.

Troy, L. 1997. "The Twilight of Old Unionism." In D. Lewin, D. J.B. Mitchell, and M. A. Zaidi, eds., *The Human Resource Management Handbook, Part II.* Greenwich, CT: JAI Press, pp. 137-55.

Walton, R. E. 1985. "From Control to Commitment in the Workplace." *Harvard Business Review,* Vol. 63, no. 2, pp. 57-74.

Williams, K., and D. Lewis. 1982. "Legislating for Job Security: The British Experience of Reinstatement and Reengagement." *Employee Relations Law Journal,* Vol. 8, pp. 482-504.

CHAPTER 6

Grievance Mediation

PETER FEUILLE
University of Illinois

Consider these two grievance resolution scenarios:

On the date of the *grievance arbitration* hearing, which is eight months after the grievance was filed, the hearing participants drift into the hearing room. These participants include the arbitrator, the court reporter, the union team (attorney, staff representative, grievant, local union officers, and witnesses the union will call), and the company's team (attorney, human resources director, line supervisor involved in the grievance, and witnesses the company will ask to testify). During the hearing, witnesses are sworn, examined, and cross-examined, and documents are offered as exhibits. Both attorneys offer frequent objections, which are usually denied. After the four-to-six hour hearing is concluded, the court reporter will take two weeks to prepare a transcript; the two attorneys will take a month after that to prepare and submit posthearing briefs, and then the arbitrator will prepare and issue his/her award in another month. The parties will receive the award about ten months after the grievance was filed, and the combined out-of-pocket cost of the arbitration proceeding will be in the $7,000-$10,000 range (about $2,800 will cover the arbitrator's fee and expenses, about $500 will go to pay for the court reporter and the transcript, and the rest will go to cover the combined attorneys' fees and expenses; the costs of the company and union participants are not included in this estimate).

On the day of the *grievance mediation* conference, which is being held about three months after the grievance was filed, the conference room fills up with the mediator and the representatives of the union and the employer. There are no attorneys or court reporters. Each side presents a narrative description to the mediator that summarizes its view of the facts of the grievance and the arguments supporting its position. After the narratives and any resulting discussion are completed, the two groups of representatives go into separate rooms. The mediator visits each group in turn and discusses with them the strengths and weaknesses of their position in the mediation. Each side is keenly interested in the mediator's prediction of which side would prevail if the grievance went to arbitration. In less than three hours the parties agree on how the grievance should be resolved. After a break for lunch, the mediator meets with many of the same representatives to discuss another grievance. Following a similar joint meeting and then separate meetings process, this grievance also is resolved. The mediator is not required to write any postconference awards. On the out-of-pocket dollar cost dimension, the parties paid about $1,000 for the mediator's fee and travel expenses, which means that each of the two grievances was resolved for about $500 (as with the arbitration example, this calculation ignores the costs of the other participants' compensation).

The available research evidence indicates (1) the relative costs of grievance mediation and grievance arbitration in these two examples are accurate; (2) almost all collective bargaining agreements contain grievance procedures culminating in arbitration; (3) only about 3% contain a mediation step in the grievance procedure; and (4) the number of grievance arbitration cases each year dwarfs the number of mediated grievances.

In this chapter I will review the evidence about the extent of grievance mediation's use, examine how the process works, show that its efficiency benefits are quite substantial, and suggest reasons why mediation's use as a grievance resolution method has remained limited. In addition, I will examine the use of mediation in nonunion workplaces, although the primary focus will be on unionized employment relationships. After offering some research suggestions, I conclude by considering how mediation's role in the grievance resolution process might be enhanced, particularly in workplaces with "transformed" union-management relationships.

Development and Use of Mediation

Development

The mediation of grievances under collective bargaining agreements is not new, for it has been practiced at least since the 1930s (Nolan and Abrams 1983a, 1983b; Goldberg 1982). In particular, during the 1940s one school of arbitral thought advocated a version of arbitration that relied much more upon mediation than upon adjudication to resolve the grievances that unions and employers could not resolve in direct negotiations.

By the 1950s, however, the adjudication form of grievance arbitration, which asks the arbitrator to adopt the role of an arms-length judge and issue a formal interpretation of the contractual provision in dispute, clearly had eclipsed the mediation form as the final step in almost all union-management grievance procedures (Mittenthal 1991). In 1960 the U.S. Supreme Court solidified the ascendancy of the adjudication type of arbitration with its rulings favoring arbitration in three landmark cases known as the Steelworkers Trilogy.[1] Grievance mediation did not disappear (Cole 1963; Handsaker 1966; Simkin 1971), but this informal method of resolving grievances took a distant back seat to the much more formal method of contractual arbitration. Accordingly, when unions and employers cannot resolve grievances and arbitration occurs, the usual result has been to engage in semiformal adversarial hearings in which union and employer advocates vigorously press for their preferred grievance outcome and do their best to discredit the other side's preferred outcome. Similarly, the arbitrator's written award usually adopts one side's preferred outcome to the exclusion of the other (evidence indicates that arbitrators fully sustain or fully deny grievances in more than 80% of their awards [American Arbitration Association 1993]).

Ever since the adjudication form of arbitration became established, unions and employers alike have complained of the dollar cost, time delays, and legalistic trappings (lawyers, court reporters and transcripts, written briefs, subpoenas, motions and objections, etc.) associated with the process (Goldberg 1982).[2] A suggested alternative was the mediation of grievances in order to avoid arbitration altogether (Bowers 1980; Bowers, Seeber, and Stallworth 1982; O'Grady 1976; Weiler 1978; Zack 1978).

By far the biggest boost in grievance mediation's visibility occurred due to the efforts of Northwestern University Professors Stephen Goldberg and Jeanne Brett to improve the grievance resolution track record in the unionized portion of the coal mining industry. During the 1970s, this industry was the scene of thousands of wildcat strikes, in large part due to miner disgruntlement with the industry's grievance arbitration process (Brett and Goldberg 1979). The union (the United Mine Workers), the miners, and many of the coal companies were unhappy with their grievance resolution system and were willing to try something new.

During 1980-82, with support from the U.S. Department of Labor, Goldberg and Brett experimented with grievance mediation as a new and voluntary step in the union-management grievance procedure immediately preceding the arbitration step. In four coalfield areas the union and coal companies agreed to participate, and the new procedure was implemented. Its two central features were (1) selected grievances still unresolved after the third step of the grievance procedure would be discussed informally with a mediator (at a mediation "conference" rather than a "hearing"); and (2) if the discussions did not produce an agreement, the mediator, who in each instance was a highly experienced arbitrator, would issue an advisory oral opinion on the spot predicting how the grievance would be decided if it was arbitrated. The parties could pursue additional settlement discussions after they heard the advisory opinion. Any grievances unresolved after mediation could be arbitrated.

By now, the results of this experiment are quite well known: 89% of the 153 mediated grievances were settled without arbitration; the time necessary for a mediated resolution was a small fraction of the time necessary to obtain an arbitration award; the dollar cost of resolving a grievance in mediation was reduced by more than two-thirds compared with the cost of arbitration; and the disputants were much more satisfied with mediation than with arbitration. Interestingly, grievants were less satisfied than the union and company representatives, though these mediating grievants were more satisfied with mediation than a control group of other arbitrating grievants were with arbitration (Brett and Goldberg 1983). This experiment was carefully designed, implemented, and researched, and its results were widely publicized (Brett and Goldberg 1983; Goldberg 1982, 1984, 1989; Goldberg and Brett 1983, 1990; Goldberg and Hobgood 1987; Ury, Brett, and Goldberg 1988).

The successful outcomes in the coal mediation experiment served, at least in part, as the impetus for additional experiments with grievance mediation in the public and private sectors (see, e.g., Block, Beck, and Olson 1996; Bureau of National Affairs 1987, 1990; Quinn, Rosenbaum, and McPherson 1990; Reed 1990; Roberts, Wolters, Holley, and Feild 1990; Silberman 1989; Skratek 1987, 1990; Ury, Brett, and Goldberg 1988). In 1983 Goldberg and Brett founded the Mediation Research and Education Project (MREP), a nonprofit organization designed to help parties implement grievance mediation.

Use

The precise extent of grievance mediation's use cannot be determined, for there is no central mediation data collection agency. The available evidence suggests that the MREP and the Federal Mediation and Conciliation Service are the two largest providers of grievance mediation services. As seen in Table 1, the MREP reported that almost 2,900 grievances had been mediated under its auspices during the 1980-97 period, and it has handled more cases per year during the 1990s than during the

TABLE 1

MREP Grievance Mediation Results

Mediation Results:	1980-89	1990-97	Total
To mediation	1,483	1,409	2,892
Resolved at mediation	1,189 (80.2%)	1,255 (89.1%)	2,444 (84.5%)
Arbitrated			
(incl. "pending")	294	10	304
Pending	—	144	144

Mediation results By issue (1990-97 only):	Discharge	Other Discipline	Contract Interpretation	Total
Total	160	280	848	1,288
Resolved at mediation	132 (82.5%)	268 (95.7%)	759 (89.5%)	1,159 (90.0%)
Arbitration	5 (3.1%)	0	5 (0.6%)	10 (0.8%)
Pending	23 (14.4%)	12 (4.3%)	84 (9.9%)	119 (9.2%)

Type of settlement (for grievances resolved at *mediation conference*)	1990-97 only
Total	1,084
Compromise	861 (79.4%)
Noncompromise	223 (20.6%)
Employer grants	65 (6.0%)
Union withdraws	158 (10.2%)

Costs of mediation and arbitration (1997 only)	Mediation (MREP calendar 1997 data)	Arbitration (FMCS fiscal 1997 data)
Third-party fee	$383	$2,421
Third-party expenses	118	253
Total	500	2,674

Data supplied by the Mediation Research and Education Project, Inc.

1980s. The MREP's data indicate that 85% of the mediated grievances were resolved without arbitration and at a small fraction of the cost of arbitrating each one of these grievances.

During the 1990s the Federal Mediation and Conciliation Service has devoted increased resources to the resolution of grievances. The FMCS maintains regional offices around the country, and the mediators assigned to these offices serve as mediators in grievance disputes as well as interest disputes. The data in Table 2 indicate that during the past few years the FMCS may have become the country's largest provider of grievance mediation services. Not only do FMCS mediators work to resolve already existing grievance disputes (the "dispute grievance cases" in Table 2), they also provide training to unions and employers in how to

TABLE 2

FMCS Grievance Mediation Activity

Fiscal Year	1992	1993	1994	1995	1996	1997	1998
Dispute grievance mediation cases closed	72	91	100	90	116	361	545
Dispute grievance cases with agreement	43 (59.7%)	68 (74.7%)	78 (78%)	65 (72.2%)	82 (70.7%)	293 (81.2%)	435 (79.8%)
Industries:							
Private sector	35	32	35	24	37	246	364
Federal govt.	37	56	65	66	78	75	101
State/local govt.	0	3	0	0	1	36	55
Preventive grievance mediation cases closed	0	0	0	0	189	403	314

Data supplied by the Federal Mediation and Conciliation Service.
"Dispute" grievance mediation cases are those involving already existing grievances.
"Preventive" grievance mediation cases are those involving efforts by FMCS staff to train unions and employers in how to handle and resolve grievances without third-party intervention.
In some years the total number of industry-specific cases may not sum to the total number of dispute cases closed in that year.

handle and resolve grievances without third-party intervention (the "grievance preventive mediation cases" in Table 2). These preventive mediation training programs provide unions, employees, and managers with the problem-solving skills that will enable the parties to resolve more grievances themselves.

In addition to the grievance mediation activity reported by the MREP and the FMCS, other ADR service agencies, such as the American Arbitration Association, supply grievance mediators to disputants upon request. Further, unions and employers can select mediators directly to resolve grievances. In addition, more nonunion employers are adopting using mediation for their ADR programs (Lipsky and Seeber 1998). Although there is no accurate way to determine the total extent of grievance mediation activity, the information reported in Tables 1 and 2 and elsewhere in this chapter indicate that grievance mediation has become more widely used in recent years.

Types of Mediation

There are two primary ways that grievance mediation can be practiced in unionized workplaces. One way is for the grievance arbitrator to use the informal techniques of mediation to explore settlement possibilities on an ad hoc basis with the parties, usually at the arbitration hearing (Nelson and Uddin 1995). This is often called mediation-arbitration ("med-arb") because the same person serves as the mediator and the arbitrator. This is the kind of arbitration which was largely eclipsed during the postwar years by the adjudication method of arbitration (Mittenthal 1991). For instance, in his study of labor arbitrator caseloads during 1986, Coleman (1992:92) estimated from his survey results that arbitrators handled about 2,900 med-arb cases that year from among a total of 80,000 dispute resolution cases.

In contrast, the type of grievance mediation featured here functions in a different manner. In this version, the parties usually incorporate mediation in their grievance procedure via the following processes:

- They insert mediation into the grievance as an optional step immediately prior to the arbitration step.

- They retain the arbitration step, which can still be used for grievances not resolved at mediation and for those grievances not referred to mediation.

- They strictly separate the mediator and arbitrator roles and procedures by prohibiting the same person from mediating and arbitrating a grievance and by prohibiting the parties from using at arbitration what was said or done in mediation.

- They use experienced arbitrators as mediators.

- They use official or unofficial prediction by the mediator of how an arbitrator would decide the dispute (if it goes to arbitration) as a settlement technique (see Brett and Goldberg [1983:69] for the operational rules used in the coal mediation experiment).

In other words, mediation is an explicit and separate step in the grievance procedure and is designed not to replace the arbitration step but to reduce its use.

Mediation's Advantages

The popularity of grievance mediation can be traced to the tangible benefits it provides. In addition to the MREP results reported in Table 1, several published reports of mediation's benefits are summarized in Table 3. Together, these reports indicate that the vast majority of mediated grievances are resolved short of arbitration. In addition, the few studies that have collected processing data indicate that the average dollar cost of

TABLE 3

Reported Grievance Mediation Results

Study (Sample)	Grievances Mediated[a]	Percent Resolved w/o Arb[a]	Average Cost of Mediator[b]	Average Cost of Arbitrator[b]	Average Speed of Mediation[c]	Average Speed of Arbitration[c]
McPherson (1956) (14 private firms)	293	80%	NR[d]	NR	NR	NR
O'Grady (1976) (8 state mediation agencies)	Private: 669 Public: 335	83%	58%	NR	NR	NR
Gregory & Rooney (1980) (one office of state med agency)	60	77%	NR	NR	NR	NR
Bowers, Seeber, & Stallworth (1982) (survey of state and federal mediators)		State: 87% Fed.: 25%	NR	NR	NR	NR
Brett & Goldberg (1982) (coal industry 1980-82)[e]	153	89%	$295	$1,034	15 days	109 days
Butt (1988) (Ontario arb cases)	6,130	67.5%	NR	NR	NR	NR
Ury, Brett, & Goldberg (1988) (coal industry 1980-88; other industries 1983-88)[e]	Coal: 827 Others: 276	80% 81%	$330 $435	$1,692 (est.) NR	24 days 26 days	NR
Skratek (1990) (Wash. public educ. 1985-88)[e]	32	94%	$330	$1,577 (union-only costs)	NR	NR
Reed (1990) (20 mediation conference participants)[e]	838	93%	$304	$1,856	30 days	174 days
Roberts, Wolters, Holley, & Field (1990) (BellSouth managers)	64	69%	NR	NR	NR	NR
Block, Beck, & Olson (1996) (Midwest mfr. co. 1991-93)	22	91%	NR	NR	NR	NR

Notes:

[a] These two columns specify the reported number of mediated grievances and the percentage resolved without arbitration.

[b] These two columns specify the reported average costs, in nominal collars, for mediator and arbitrator fees and expenses except for the Skratek study, which reports the union's average costs for its mediation and arbitration expenses.

[c] These two columns specify the reported average amount of time from mediation request to a mediated conclusion and from an arbitration request to the issuance of an award.

[d] NR = not reported

[e] The cases reported in these studies overlap.

mediating a grievance is a small fraction of the average cost of arbitrating a grievance and also that grievances are resolved much faster in mediation than in arbitration. In addition, many of the participants in four of these studies expressed considerable satisfaction with mediation, particularly the way in which its informal character permitted them to engage in problem-solving efforts instead of clinging to and defending previously staked-out win/lose positions as usually occurs in arbitration (Brett and Goldberg 1983; Reed 1990; Skratek 1990; Ury, Brett, and Goldberg 1988). In other words, mediation is a much more efficient way to resolve grievances than arbitration, and it is associated with the use of more cooperative DR efforts.

Mediation's Key Features

The information about mediation indicates that there are two key features of the process that deserve special attention. The first is the role played by the mediator, and the second is the motivation of the parties who have adopted it.

Mediator's Role

The available evidence, particularly from the coal mediation experiment, indicates that the crucial feature of the mediator's role is his/her ability, as an experienced arbitrator, to inform the parties of the contractual strength or weakness of their grievance position. This information can be provided in two ways. The first is the private ("sidebar" or "caucus") discussions with each party where the mediator may point out the contractual weak points of each party's position. If these informal discussions do not result in a resolution, the mediator is either permitted or required to issue an oral advisory opinion on the spot, which provides the mediator's arbitration outcome prediction.

As a result, the driving force in this type of grievance mediation is "peek-a-boo arbitration." This arrangement provides the parties with a low-cost, expert prediction about the likely arbitration outcome, either unofficially in private discussions with the mediator or officially via the advisory opinion. In the coal mediation project, the mediators issued unofficial outcome predictions 79% of the time and they issued official advisory opinions 22% of the time (Brett and Goldberg 1983).

The use of mediator prediction in grievance mediation is particularly feasible due to the relatively precise nature of the dispute (i.e., an allegation of a violation of a specific part of the collective bargaining agreement) and to the precise form and limited range of an arbitrated resolution (the arbitrator will either sustain or deny the grievance). Accordingly, this type of outcome prediction can be credibly and, hence, persuasively offered by mediators who are experienced arbitrators.

At the same time, the feasibility of the peek-a-boo arbitration feature of grievance mediation should not obscure the fact that it is a more intrusive form of third-party intervention than the negotiation facilitation form of interest mediation that is regularly used in private sector union-management contract negotiations (Carnevale 1986; Carnevale and Pegnetter 1985; Kolb 1983; Kressel 1972). The grievance mediator's prediction of the arbitral outcome is designed to create substantial settlement pressure by making the parties, particularly the party with the weaker position, eager to avoid the costs of losing in arbitration. With this intrusive form of third-party intervention, it is not surprising that most mediated grievances are resolved without arbitration.

This peek-a-boo arbitration feature appears to be the same kind of process that has been called "early neutral evaluation" in the context of civil litigation (Brazil et al. 1986). In the litigation context, McEwen (1991) differentiates between "predictive settlement" procedures, such as nonbinding arbitration and summary jury trials, designed to provide litigants with early and hence low-cost predictions of the adjudicated outcome of their lawsuit, if it proceeds to trial, and "problem-solving settlement" procedures, such as mediation, designed to discover a mutually acceptable outcome based on the interests of the parties.

Grievance mediation certainly allows the parties more opportunity to search for a mutually acceptable outcome than does grievance arbitration. For instance, the Mediation Research and Education Project (1998—see Table 1) reports that among 1,084 mediated grievances resolved at mediation conferences during 1990-97 period, 79% of the resolutions were "compromise" settlements and the other 21% were "noncompromise" resolutions (either the employer granted the grievance or the union withdrew it). In comparison with labor arbitration awards, which result in grievances being fully sustained or completely denied more than 80% of the time (American Arbitration Association 1993), this large proportion of compromise outcomes suggests that grievance mediation allows and even encourages more cooperative problem-solving behavior than occurs during or after the arbitration hearing.

At the same time, it is important to keep in mind that mediation's driving force is the "early neutral evaluation" or the "predictive settlement" provided by the mediator. In turn, it stretches credulity to believe that mediator predictions by themselves cause unions and employers to adopt more cooperative attitudes and behaviors in their grievance processing. It seems more likely that these predictions force the parties, particularly the weaker party, to undergo a more critical scrutiny of the costs and benefits of taking the dispute to arbitration and then to work harder at avoiding the downside risk of arbitration by exploring settlement possibilities. Thus the grievance resolution cooperation reported by the users of grievance mediation may or may not reflect any intrinsic features of the mediation process. Instead, as will be discussed next, this improved cooperation may have preceded rather than followed the adoption of this procedure.

Motivation of the Parties

The second key feature that appears to contribute heavily to mediation's success is the motivation of the parties who have adopted it. The available research indicates that it has been adopted by a limited number of self-selected parties who are sufficiently motivated to try and improve their grievance self-resolution track record. To the extent that these mediation adopters are able to resolve grievances via mediation and thereby avoid arbitration, it is likely that they will give mediation most of the credit for their grievance resolution success. However, a large portion of that success should be attributed to the parties' preferences for resolving their own grievances in lieu of arbitral adjudication (Goldberg 1982; Quinn, Rosenbaum, and McPherson 1990). Accordingly, it may be more accurate to view mediation as a proxy for the positive grievance resolution attitudes held by its adopters than as a procedure which possesses some intrinsic ability to resolve grievances in a more cooperative manner than arbitration.

Why Isn't Mediation More Widespread?

The evidence indicates that mediation has been written into contractual grievance procedures in only about 3% of surveyed union contracts (Bureau of National Affairs 1989). The annual number of mediated grievances is not known, but it is much less than the estimated 20,000-plus grievance arbitration awards that are issued each year (Coleman 1992).

Given the substantial grievance resolution benefits that have been thoroughly reported for this process, why hasn't mediation been more widely adopted and used? The process has received widespread and very favorable publicity, so its limited use cannot be attributed to bad press. Similarly, the answer cannot be found in mediation's efficiency benefits, for if the decision to adopt and use mediation were made exclusively on that basis, presumably all unions and employers would have adopted it long ago. In this section we explore several reasons why the demand for grievance mediation has been relatively modest and is likely to remain so. These reasons, which overlap, include the fact that most grievances are resolved anyway without using arbitration, the fragility of mediation, managerial reluctance, and the lack of an influential mediation constituency.

Grievances Are Resolved without Using Arbitration

The available evidence about grievance resolution in conventional grievance procedures (those without mediation) indicates that the vast majority of grievances are resolved without the use of arbitration. For instance, eight studies that examine grievance processing data from more than 250 bargaining units indicate that only a small fraction of all filed grievances (usually less than 20% and often as low as 2%) are taken to arbitration in conventional grievance procedures.[3] In addition, several years of arbitration data from the American Arbitration Association and the Federal Mediation and Conciliation Service (the two largest arbitrator referral agencies) indicate that awards are issued in less than half of the combined arbitration cases handled by these two agencies.[4]

As we have seen, the rationale for mediation rests heavily upon the efficiency benefits of avoiding arbitration. However, the evidence indicates that in conventional grievance procedures the vast majority of grievances are not taken to arbitration, and a majority of the grievances that are referred to arbitration are not arbitrated but instead are resolved without an award. In other words, the evidence suggests that most unions and employers do not need to reduce their reliance upon arbitration for the simple reason that they already use arbitration rather sparingly. In turn, to the extent that mediation's primary benefit is as an efficiency-enhancing arbitration avoidance technique, most parties will have inadequate motivation to change their grievance resolution practices to incorporate mediation.

Mediation Is Fragile

Union and employer perceptions of the need for mediation may be influenced by the fact that standing alone, mediation may not appear to be a particularly hardy or durable grievance resolution technique. This assessment flows from the following mediation procedural characteristics: mediation's inability to resolve difficult disputes, the prescreened nature of mediated grievances, and mediation's dependence upon arbitration for its success.

First, mediation cannot guarantee resolved grievances. In particular, mediation cannot withstand either party's desire for a "win" over the other via an adjudicated grievance decision. Mediation requires voluntary agreement to be successful, and it cannot be successful whenever either party insists upon a voluntary agreement in such self-favorable terms that agreement is prevented and adjudication is required. In other words, mediation is an uncertain process when compared with the certain resolution available in arbitration.

Second, mediation's limited ability to resolve thorny disputes is confirmed by the fact that most grievances referred to mediation are carefully screened, either by prior agreement that only particular subject matters will be referred to mediation or by making the mediation step optional (which requires mutual consent to take a grievance to mediation) (Block, Beck, and Olson 1996; Brett and Goldberg 1983; House 1992; Roberts et al. 1990; Skratek 1990; Valtin 1993). With this kind of screening it is not surprising that the vast majority (80%-90%) of mediated grievances are resolved without arbitration. However, this focus on the mediation success rate ignores the fact that mediation is not even attempted for many other grievances. This kind of premediation screening and subsequent selective use of the process suggest that mediation's adopters perceive the process as too limited to serve as an all-purpose grievance resolution method in the same manner as arbitration.[5]

Third, mediation's success as a settlement technique depends very strongly upon the continued existence of arbitration as the next step in the grievance procedure. As discussed above, the centerpiece of mediation as a technique is the mediator's prediction of how the grievance will be resolved if the dispute is taken to arbitration ("peekaboo arbitration"). Because most mediators are experienced arbitrators, these predictions are taken seriously by the disputing parties. In fact, ethnographic reports of mediation conferences indicate that the parties are quite eager to discover the mediator's prediction (Kolb 1989; Warren 1985). These predictions also play a key role in the high settlement rate that mediation enjoys, in that these predictions cause the parties, and particularly the party with the weaker contractual position, to reevaluate the desirability of taking the dispute to arbitration.

Why does the continued presence of arbitration inhibit the adoption and use of mediation? For one thing, arbitration's prominent role in the mediation discussion process reinforces the image of mediation as a process that cannot do much on its own. For another, arbitration's cheek-by-jowl presence with mediation may weaken the parties' incentives to make mediation work, since arbitration is always present to pick up the grievance resolution pieces if the parties decide to abandon mediation. This means that arbitration enables reluctant parties to refuse to adopt mediation or to reject its continued use, with these refusals/rejections amounting to little more than a blip on the union-management relationship (i.e., grievances will still be resolved by arbitration). In short, arbitration makes it easy to say no to mediation.

In sum, these mediation characteristics may cause most potential adopters to conclude that mediation is too fragile or limited a process to justify its implementation. Moreover, mediation's advocates tend to reinforce this conclusion by their claim that mediation is not needed in all union-management relationships and instead is best suited for "troubled" relationships (Valtin 1993). To the extent that parties in troubled relationships have come to rely upon arbitration as a weapon to "get" each other, mediation indeed can perform an extremely useful service by demonstrating the benefits of voluntary grievance resolution and thereby reducing the parties' reliance upon arbitration. However, if most union-management pairs do not see themselves in troubled relationships or at least do not see their grievance resolution practices as troubled, they will be unlikely to adopt mediation.

At the same time, it is important to keep in mind that the most successful use of third-party mediators to resolve grievances should eventually result in the disputing parties acquiring the DR skills displayed by the mediators and then using those skills to resolve subsequent grievances on their own, thereby reducing or even eliminating their need for external mediators. In these workplaces, mediation has been so successful that it has put itself out of business. This self-resolution of grievances is the goal of the "preventive mediation" training programs offered by the FMCS, and Table 2 indicates that these programs have become much more widespread in the past few years.

Managerial Reluctance

The parties' incentives to embrace mediation may not be symmetrical. Consider that almost all grievances are union-initiated challenges to the contractual correctness of the employer's behavior, with the grievance typically framed as a claim that the employer has violated the contract and should cease or reverse the offending decision. As a result, in the grievance process the union usually is the change-seeking party, and the employer is the advocate of continuing the status quo. To the extent that mediated grievance resolutions involve anything more than the union's withdrawal of the grievance, mediation requires the employer to agree to some modification in the direction sought by the union in order to achieve a resolution. In particular, the compromise grievance resolutions championed by mediation's advocates require the employer to agree to enough of the change sought by the union that the union is willing to forego its right to take the dispute to arbitration. In turn, employers may perceive mediation as a process designed primarily to persuade management to give something to the union that the union could not obtain in arbitration.

It is important to keep in mind that the adjudication type of arbitration tends to serve employer interests more than union interests (Nolan and Abrams 1983b). For more than forty years grievance arbitration in most workplaces has been confined to a quasi-judicial determination of contract violations. In this process, the union plays a reactive role, and the union's influence is channeled into an administrative proceeding, where it must prove its case with legalistic evidence rather than rely upon economic power or some abstract notion of justice. Nolan and Abrams (1983b) persuasively argue that this judicial conception of arbitration helped persuade employers to accept this method of grievance resolution because it limited the extent to which unions could use the grievance process to intrude upon managerial prerogatives.

In practice, then, the dynamics of the grievance mediation process may allow it to function as one more opportunity for the union to "get something" from the employer in return for resolving the grievance and avoiding arbitration and its attendant costs, since it is usually the union that makes the decision that the grievance will be kept alive and appealed to mediation. If each mediated grievance would have been arbitrated in the absence of mediation, this "absorption" process should be minimal or nonexistent. However, if mediation "absorbs" or keeps alive grievances that the union has no intention of taking to arbitration, employers will perceive mediation as detrimental to their interests. In such a situation, the union is using mediation in a last effort to barter some sort of employee-favorable outcome in exchange for avoiding the arbitration of grievances that would not be arbitrated anyway.

Further, union efforts to use mediation in this manner may be facilitated by mediation's low cost, for the expense of mediating a grievance is a fraction of the expense of arbitrating that same grievance. This low cost may make mediation more accessible than arbitration, which in turn may increase the incentive to mediate.[6] If mediation functions in this manner, such a result would be consistent with Labig and Greer's (1988) proposition that procedures that lead to the quick and economical resolution of grievances may provide increased incentive to use such procedures. To the extent this absorption process occurs, managerial incentives to establish or continue the process also are reduced.

There are reports that some employers have developed these perceptions about mediation. For instance, most users of mediation report that they like it. However, in the coal mediation experiment, company labor relations representatives were the least enthusiastic group about the process (Brett and Goldberg 1983). Brett and Goldberg (1983) also report that in one of the four coalfield areas where mediation was used, the grievance resolution rate in the lower steps declined. Further, in the years since this experiment was completed, some coal companies have ended their participation in the process (Ury, Brett, and Goldberg 1988). Also, the spread of mediation from the four coalfield areas that were the site of the original experiment to the remainder of the coal industry has been modest (Ury, Brett, and Goldberg 1988). Given mediation's substantial and widely reported benefits in the portions of coal industry that experimented with it, it is instructive that most other coal companies (and the other administrative districts in the miners' union) apparently remain unconvinced that mediation is worth adopting.

Similarly, a study of BellSouth managers who had experience with both the mediation and arbitration of grievances found that these managers were no more satisfied with mediation than with arbitration and that they were slightly less satisfied with mediation settlements than with arbitrated awards (Roberts et al. 1990). This BellSouth study also reported a slight decline in the grievance resolution rate in the lower steps after mediation was introduced (Roberts et al. 1990). In addition, a report on the use of mediation by AT&T and the Communications Workers of America indicated that the process generally worked quite well but that for awhile it suffered (in management's view) from one union representative's propensity to take to mediation too many weak grievances (House 1992).

A report on the use of grievance mediation in Ontario found that the majority of users were satisfied with the process (Butt 1988). However, this study also reported that 91% of the union respondents were satisfied, compared with 64% of the employer respondents. Similarly, 75% of union respondents reported that mediation led to an improvement in the union-management relationship, but only 38% of the employer respondents held this view. In a case study in a Midwest manufacturing facility, the researchers reported that both parties benefited from mediation but that the employer still preferred arbitration and its attendant costs as a way of forcing the union (with its limited treasury) to drop marginal grievances (Block, Beck, and Olson 1996).

Lack of Trust

As expressed above, grievance mediation cannot long survive either party's desire to score victories over the other. Instead, mediation will be successful only to the extent that each party is willing to be accommodating to the other party in those grievances where the available information indicates that such accommodation is justified. This can include acceding to the other party's grievance position if the evidence is one-sided in the other party's favor (i.e., the union can withdraw the grievance, or the employer can grant the grievance), or it can include some sort of compromise that partly addresses each side's interests if there is meritorious evidence supporting each party's position. The key to the emergence of these kinds of grievance resolutions is union and employer beliefs that the "quality" of the grievance outcomes is enhanced when they are mutually agreed to by the parties rather than being imposed by an outsider.

Resisting the urge to press for a "win" over the other party requires a spirit of cooperation or trust that may not be present in many union-management relationships. The paradigm collective bargaining relationship in this country involves an arms-length relationship between a union determined to wrest employee-favorable terms from a reluctant employer determined to protect its control of the workplace. In this adversarial context, the union's ability to attain its objectives is based upon its ability to threaten or use various sorts of concerted activities to create economic pressure upon the employer, and the employer's ability to attain its objectives is based upon its ability to resist the pressures created by these threatened or actual concerted activities. In short, U.S. unions and employers have been and continue to be more accurately characterized as workplace antagonists than partners (Bakke 1966; Kochan and Katz 1988; Wheeler 1985).

In the grievance resolution context, the threatened or actual use of arbitration is the pertinent concerted activity, for it is arbitration that creates the possibility of a union-favorable outcome over the employer's objection. In this context, the union's acceptance of mediated accommodations with management may undermine union representatives' support among rank-and-file members on the grounds that the representatives did not press hard enough for the members' interests. On the management side, the acceptance of mediated accommodations with the union similarly may make employer representatives vulnerable to claims that they were insufficiently vigilant in protecting managerial prerogatives. To the extent these constituency pressures exist or are perceived by union or employer representatives, they make mediation a less tenable grievance resolution method.

As this implies, the adoption and use of grievance mediation may require a mutual commitment to greater cooperation in grievance handling and a mutual ability to withstand constituent pressures than it is possible for many unions and employers to achieve given their customary adversarial roles and the concomitant expectations from their constituents. Employer and union representatives accustomed to pressing for procedural and substantive advantages over each other may not be able or willing to shed their learned attitudes and behaviors sufficiently to adopt the more cooperative approach that effective grievance mediation seems to require.

As noted above, one of the key reasons for mediation's success is the motivation or attitudes of the parties who have adopted it. These adopters are a self-selected group of unions and employers who are trying to improve their grievance self-resolution track record. This motivation to resolve grievances by mutual agreement may explain why mediation's users are willing and able to agree to the outcomes necessary to resolve most grievances via mediation. What is left unexplained is why the parties developed this motivation in the first place and how these cooperative attitudes can be maintained.

Lack of a Natural Constituency

Mediation is not in the self-interest of arbitration advocates and arbitrators. To the extent that mediation resolves grievances that would have been arbitrated, it infringes upon the livelihoods of everybody who earns part or all of their professional income and status by arbitrating grievances. As an example, this threatened self-interest emerged in a study of grievance mediation and arbitration in Washington public education, where the management attorneys who represented the school districts in arbitration and mediation expressed dissatisfaction with mediation (Skratek 1987). This lack of support for a process designed to reduce the use and attendant cost of arbitration is hardly surprising considering that the vast bulk of the cost of arbitration is income to the arbitration professionals, and this income is lost if grievances are successfully mediated and not arbitrated. The members of the arbitration community may not actively express opposition to mediation, and a few may be avid supporters of the process. However, it is unrealistic to expect most of the people whose professional livelihoods are based partly or fully upon the continued use of arbitration to be the zealous disciples of the mediation gospel. As a result, the DR constituency that carries the torch for mediation apparently has been modest. However, the FMCS, the MREP, and other mediation providers have strong incentives to play this role, and mediation's constituency may be increasing.

In sum, the substantial and widely reported benefits of grievance mediation have not yet persuaded large numbers of union and management decision makers that mediation needs to be officially adopted in their grievance procedures. In other words, by their actions union and management practitioners apparently have substantially discounted mediation's benefits. Given this track record and the possible reasons for it, mediation seems destined to play a limited supporting role rather than be the star on the grievance resolution stage in unionized workplaces.

Mediation in Nonunion Workplaces

During the 1980s and 1990s many employers created formal grievance procedures for their nonunion employees (Conti 1985; Ewing 1989; Feuille and Chachere 1995; Lipsky and Seeber 1998; Rowe 1991; U.S. Government Accounting Office 1995, 1997). There have been at least three factors which have contributed to this phenomenon: (1) The increased willingness of disgruntled employees to file lawsuits and administrative agency complaints alleging discriminatory treatment or wrongful discharge and the correspondingly increased desire of employers to avoid the costs of resolving disputes in external forums; (2) the passage of the 1991 Civil Rights Act, which for the first time allowed successful plaintiffs in discrimination lawsuits to collect punitive damages from employers; and (3) the May 1991 decision by the U.S. Supreme Court in *Gilmer v. Interstate/Johnson Lane Corp.* (500 U.S. 20) that required an employee with a statutory-based age discrimination lawsuit to instead use an arbitration process unilaterally imposed upon him and other employees to address employment disputes. Among other things, many employers have responded by imposing mandatory arbitration procedures on their nonunion employees (this subject is examined in the Stone, Bingham/Chachere and Zack chapters).

This growth of formal nonunion grievance procedures has included the increased adoption and use of mediation to resolve grievances. A

1997 survey of 606 general counsel offices in large corporations found that company use of ADR was quite widespread and that firms are willing to use ADR methods in many dispute arenas (this survey was not limited to employment disputes). Specifically, 87% of these firms reported using mediation within the prior three years (with 80% having used arbitration); that mediation is used most often on an ad hoc, voluntary basis in contrast to arbitration's use being triggered most often because it is contractually required; that mediation and arbitration are used most frequently in employment and commercial disputes; and that respondents strongly preferred mediation over arbitration, particularly in employment disputes (Lipsky and Seeber 1998). Looking at how employers handle employment discrimination complaints from nonunion employees, a 1994-95 survey of 1,500 firms by the U.S. Government Accounting Office found that 38% reported using internal mediation and 9% reported using external mediation (U.S. GAO 1995; 10% reported using arbitration).

A more recent study by the Government Accounting Office examined the internal operations of the grievance procedures in five large private firms: Brown & Root, Inc., Hughes Electronics Corp., Polaroid Corp., Rockwell International Corp., and TRW, Inc. (U.S. GAO 1997). All five companies reported that they have adopted arbitration as the final dispute resolution step for some or all of their nonunion employees. In addition, all five firms also provide a variety of prearbitration DR techniques, including an ombuds office, management review boards, peer review boards, and/or mediation. Three companies (Brown & Root, Polaroid, TRW) reported the use of internal and/or external mediation to resolve grievances to reduce the use of arbitration. Brown & Root reported that in the first three and one-half years of its ADR program most of the 1,600 employment disputes had been resolved by informal methods (including internal mediation by company employees trained in mediation methods) without "formal mediation or arbitration," that 155 disputes had been formally mediated (apparently with an external mediator), and that 90% of these mediated grievances were resolved. Polaroid reported that its use of internal mediators has been successful but did not provide data. TRW reported that external mediation is required for grievances in which arbitration has been requested. Of 40 cases in which arbitration had been requested at the time of this study, 27 had been mediated, and 16 of these 27 were resolved. The GAO study did not report how these mediation procedures operated, and the amount of information provided varied across firms. In other words, the reported information does not allow us to compare the mediation processes used in these firms with the Brett-Goldberg mediation process described in detail above. However, it was clear that the firms using mediation with their nonunion employees were doing so in an effort to resolve grievances before they proceeded to an internal (arbitration) or external (litigation) adjudication forum, and thus the motivation for mediation's use appears quite similar across the two sectors.

During 1999 the U.S. Equal Opportunity Employment Commission launched a national ADR initiative that uses internal and external mediators to resolve employment discrimination charges filed by employees, most of whom are nonunion, against their employers (Bureau of National Affairs 1999). This use of mediation is designed to occur early in the charge-handling process (prior to a formal "investigation" and the decision to issue or not issue a formal complaint against the charged party) and thereby enable the agency to obtain faster resolution of many of these charges. This national mediation effort follows several EEOC pilot programs that resulted in a settlement rate above 50% among the mediated charges. If we consider these discrimination charges as a particular category of grievances filed in an external forum, the EEOC's increased use of mediation is consistent with the trend toward increased reliance on mediation in nonunion workplaces.

The use of third-party intervention to resolve employment disputes in nonunion workplaces is much less widespread than it is in unionized establishments. At the same time, employers increasingly are providing nonunion grievants with access to mediators and arbitrators in an attempt to resolve more disputes internally and thereby have fewer disputes processed and resolved in external forums.

Research Needs

The new conventional wisdom that has emerged about grievance mediation is quite positive and may contain more uncritical admiration than is warranted by mediation's limited track record. There has been only one careful research study of mediation's operational features and its costs and benefits, which means that a disproportionate amount of our knowledge about grievance mediation in practice comes from the coal mediation experiment (Brett and Goldberg 1983). At the time of that research, the coal industry was plagued by wildcat strikes, considerable dissatisfaction with arbitration, and an abundance of union-management hostility. As a result, that industry's experience with mediation may or may not offer a useful guide to mediation's value in other places.

In short, we need additional research that is of the same quality as the Brett and Goldberg analysis.

This future research should profitably address several mediation dimensions. First, assessments of mediation should carefully establish the arbitration benchmarks to use in determining how well or poorly mediation performs. As noted earlier, the fact that most nonmediated grievances are resolved without arbitration suggests that it is unrealistic to assume that every successfully mediated grievance would have been arbitrated if mediation had not been used.

Second, grievance mediation's peek-a-boo arbitration feature should be more fully recognized as the central feature of the process. This advisory prediction feature gives grievance mediators a powerful hammer with which to work, but there is little systematic information about exactly how much these mediator predictions contribute to grievance resolutions. Accordingly, future research could usefully measure the impact of the peek-a-boo arbitration feature by examining how likely unions are to withdraw grievances, employers are to grant grievances, or both sides are to agree to compromise outcomes, before and after the mediator's arbitration predictions are first delivered. Although it is difficult to gather this kind of process information, the results of this research could determine if grievance mediation is a genuine problem-solving procedure that fosters increased cooperation, or if it is simply a specific type of "early neutral evaluation" vehicle designed to give the disputants a low-cost prediction of the arbitrated outcome.

Third, there has been very little careful research on the contributions of different mediator attitudes and behaviors to mediation's effectiveness. Brett and Goldberg's (1983) research indicated that the coal mediators were a carefully selected group of highly experienced arbitrators who were specifically trained in grievance mediation techniques. Kolb's (1989) study of one mediator in action portrayed him as being strongly committed to cooperative union-management problem solving, and his motivation clearly played a role in producing nonarbitrated grievance resolutions. However, human differences mean that mediators are not perfect substitutes for each other. Accordingly, there is a need for systematic research on how mediator motivation, attributes, and tactics contribute to the success or failure of grievance mediation. How much variation occurs across mediator success rates, and what factors are associated with these variations? Do some mediators see their role as "problem solvers" while others see themselves as "predictors," and do their behaviors differ accordingly? To what extent are mediators able to obtain settlements without delivering arbitral predictions? How forcefully do mediators deliver their arbitral predictions? How do they differentiate their messages to the parties with the stronger and weaker positions? How vigorously do they press for settlements? These are difficult questions to investigate, in large part because answers require the kind of ethnographic research for which access is hard to obtain, time-consuming to conduct, and likely to produce qualitative results that are difficult to publish in prestigious academic journals.

Fourth, mediation seems to work partly because the parties who adopt it are motivated to resolve grievances in a less adversarial manner than formerly. Our understanding of grievance mediation would be greatly improved by research that isolates the influence of the parties' grievance resolution attitudes from the settlement pressures created by the mediator's arbitration predictions. Part of this research also might profitably focus on the extent to which dissatisfaction with arbitration contributes to the adoption and continued use of mediation (i.e., are there significant differences between adopters and nonadopters on this and other dimensions?).

In sum, dispute resolution professionals are saying nice things about grievance mediation because it has compiled an impressive track record. Any procedure that can help unions and employers resolve grievances faster, more cheaply, and more cooperatively deserves strong praise and wide use. At the same time, the grievance mediation process deserves more careful scrutiny than it has received. In particular, it should be more thoroughly researched in a wide variety of settings so that the roles of the various components of the procedure will be better understood. In addition, this research should be careful to document failures as well as successes. Any process that shows this much promise for helping the parties negotiate their own resolutions to grievances deserves the increased attention.

Conclusions

Almost fifty years ago the results of a very successful grievance mediation experiment were published (though not under that name; Prasow 1950), and this study was cited in a subsequent study published a few years later which reported additional evidence of grievance mediation's success (McPherson 1956). In the 1960s other studies touted mediation as a useful mechanism for rehabilitating "distressed" grievance procedures (McKersie and Shropshire 1962; Simkin 1964). Accordingly, grievance mediation is not a new process, but in the past two decades it has been newly rediscovered. This rediscovery has generated favorable attention from academic observers. This favorable attention, however, should not cloud our realistic assessment of mediation's future role in the workplace.

Grievance mediation has not attracted a stampede of adherents in spite of its reported successes and benefits. Mediation's toughest obstacle to widespread use in unionized workplaces is that it has come into the grievance resolution process on the coattails of one of the longest-running and most successful features of the American industrial relations system. Arbitration was almost universally adopted as the terminal step in the American grievance procedure because employers, unions, employees, and public policymakers saw it as highly preferable to relying on strikes and slowdowns to resolve grievances (Nolan and Abrams 1983a, 1983b). Arbitration's three-fold ability to (1) guarantee the dispute will be resolved (2) while preventing workflow disruption (3) at an affordable level of transaction costs makes it an extremely attractive grievance resolution process. The strongest evidence of this attractiveness is that arbitration has had no serious contenders for grievance procedure terminal step supremacy for more than forty years. Further, the process of grievance arbitration is one of the most stable and enduring features of U.S. union-management relationships, and the arbitrator in 1959 who took a forty-year career detour would have little or no difficulty resuming the trade in 1999.

In contrast, grievance mediation is not offered to replace an unpalatable dispute resolution method. There have been no serious claims by mediation's advocates that arbitration is inherently flawed as a dispute resolution procedure and must be discarded. Instead, the complaints about arbitration are only that some unions and employers use it too often, that it is more formalistic and adversarial than is desirable in a continuing relationship, and that it is more expensive and time-consuming than its users prefer. As a result, mediation may appear to be a modest and hence optional refinement of third-party involvement in the grievance resolution process rather than as an altogether different way to resolve grievances.

How could mediation play a larger role in the grievance resolution process? Many unionized workplaces have experienced a transformation effort designed to improve workplace productivity and the quality of the employer-employee relationship (Appelbaum and Batt 1994; Kochan, Katz, and McKersie 1986; Osterman 1994). The most observable characteristic of these transformation efforts is a higher level of employee involvement and participation in workplace decisions than previously existed. One of the more visible participation methods is self-managed work teams. The main impetus for these efforts is the market-driven need for improved productivity on both the quantitative and qualitative dimensions. To the extent these efforts are successful, employers receive improved productivity, and employees obtain enhanced job security and increased satisfaction.

One of the obstacles to a transformed employment relationship is contentious labor-management relations, and one indicator of such contention is a high level of formal grievance activity. Research evidence shows that high rates of grievance filing are associated with reduced levels of productivity (Cutcher-Gershenfeld 1991; Ichniowksi 1986; Katz, Kochan, and Gobeille 1983; Katz, Kochan, and Weber 1985; Norsworthy and Zabala 1985). However, in "transformed" workplaces where grievances need to be resolved more quickly to meet changing production processes, mediation could play a prominent role in the dispute resolution process. Grievance mediation could be used as a process that not only resolves grievances more quickly after they are filed but also as a process that allows the parties to construct resolutions that go beyond the immediate dispute and provide for agreed-upon ways to handle similar situations that arise in the future (Block, Beck, and Olson 1996). Mediation could contribute to this transformation by (1) providing a forum where disputes and their underlying causes can be addressed, and (2) providing workplace participants with the experience and skills to approach problems in a problem-solving rather than adjudicative manner (these two contributions parallel the FMCS's "dispute" and "preventive" grievance mediation efforts described earlier).

In sum, mediation will continue to be adopted and used in those unionized workplaces where unions and employers are trying to improve their ability to resolve grievances by agreement instead of by adjudication. Similarly, it will be adopted and used by an increasing number of nonunion employers for the same reason, though the mediation process in nonunion workplaces may differ from the Brett-Goldberg process featured here. The available data suggest that mediation is becoming more widely used as a grievance resolution method. However, grievance mediation does not yet appear to be a prominent feature in either stable or transformed workplaces. As a result, for the foreseeable future, mediation likely will continue to exist at the margin of union-management relationships rather than as a central tendency. Given the substantial efficiency and effectiveness benefits that mediation has generated, many

American unions and employers are letting an excellent opportunity for dispute resolution improvement pass them by.

Acknowledgment

I am indebted to Adrienne Eaton and Jeff Keefe for their helpful comments. I am particularly grateful to Steve Goldberg at the Mediation and Education Research Project and Vickie Carlisle and Eileen Hoffman at the Federal Mediation and Conciliation Service for their valuable data-gathering assistance.

Endnotes

[1] *United Steelworkers of America v. American Manufacturing Co.*, 363 U.S. 564 (1960); *United Steelworkers of America v. Warrior and Gulf Navigation Co.*, 363 U.S. 574 (1960); and *United Steelworkers of America v. Enterprise Wheel and Car Corp.*, 363 U.S. 593 (1960). As Schmedemann (1987) notes, the law provides strong enforcement of contractual promises to arbitrate grievances and of the awards issued by grievance arbitrators. However, the law supporting grievance mediation is not nearly as well-developed.

[2] According to the Federal Mediation and Conciliation Service's statistics for the arbitration cases it processed during fiscal 1997, arbitrator fees and expenses averaged $2,674 (at recent rates of increase this figure should reach $2,800 in fiscal 2000); the average amount of time from filing a grievance to the issuance of the arbitration award was 302 days; transcripts were taken in about 29% of the cases; and briefs were filed in about 78% of the cases (Federal Mediation and Conciliation Service 1998). According to data compiled by the American Arbitration Association regarding arbitration cases it processed in 1992-93, employers were represented by attorneys 82% of the time and unions were represented by attorneys 56% of the time (AAA 1993).

[3] These studies show that (1) less than 2% of several thousand grievances were arbitrated in several Canadian companies (Gandz 1982); (2) 2% of 194 grievances were arbitrated in a Pacific Northwest pulp and paper mill (Gideon and Peterson 1979);(3) an average of 7% of several thousand grievances were arbitrated across eight bargaining units in the airline, basic steel, chemical, and utility industries (Knight 1986);(4) across several thousand grievances filed with a total of 79 employers in the retail trade, hospital, school, and steel industries, arbitration rates averaged 9%, 12%, 12%, and 16%, respectively (Lewin 1984); (5) 2% of 1,174 grievances were arbitrated in a Canadian federal government department (Ng and Dastmalchian 1989); 10% of 957 grievances were arbitrated in a utility (Todor and Owen 1991); (6) 1% of 4,130 grievances were arbitrated in two utilities (Mesch and Dalton 1992); and 6% of many thousands of grievances went to arbitration in 73 private firms while 22% of many thousands of grievances went to arbitration in 87 public sector organizations (Stewart and Davy 1992).

[4] During the 1981-85 calendar years the American Arbitration Association reported that 86,951 labor arbitration cases were filed with the AAA and that only

30,682 (35%) were closed with an award (Lewin and Peterson 1988: 10). Similarly, during the 1990-97 fiscal years, the Federal Mediation and Conciliation Service appointed arbitrators in 93,616 cases and closed only 39,803 of these cases (43%) with an award (Federal Mediation and Conciliation Service 1998). Further, arbitrators were appointed in only about 35% of the arbitration panel requests unions and employers referred to the FMCS. These AAA and FMCS data are confirmed by the thousands of scheduled arbitration hearings that are canceled each year because the parties settled the grievance (Coleman 1992).

[5] Interestingly, the MREP (1998) data in Table 1 indicate that mediation is used for discharge, lesser discipline, and contract interpretation grievances and that settlement rates for all three categories of mediated grievances exceed 80%. Considering the all-or-nothing nature of discharge cases (the grievant either remains terminated or is reinstated), the discharge grievance settlement rate is quite impressive. Also, the 34% of these mediated grievances that involved discipline and discharge compare with 31% of arbitration awards that involved discipline and discharge issues among 2,228 arbitration cases handled by the American Arbitration Association in 1992-93 (AAA 1993). The similar proportion of discipline and contract interpretation cases in these two samples suggests that mediation can be used for the entire range of grieved issues that are taken to arbitration.

[6] The relatively high cost of arbitration very likely keeps down the number of grievances that unions arbitrate, and thus this cost barrier serves employer interests. In addition, the high cost of arbitration also provides union representatives with a convenient and nonthreatening explanation to offer to grievants with weak grievances as to why the union cannot take their grievance to arbitration. Because mediation is so much cheaper than arbitration, it may be correspondingly more difficult for unions to resist member desires to resolve grievances without mediation.

References

American Arbitration Association. 1993. *Study Time* (a newsletter for labor arbitrators), No. 4.

Appelbaum, Eileen, and Rosemary Batt. 1994. *The New American Workplace: Transforming Work Systems in the United States*. Ithaca, NY: ILR Press.

Bakke, E. Wight. 1966. *Mutual Survival: The Goal of Unions and Management*. 2d ed. Hamden, CT: Archon Books.

Block, Richard N., John Beck, and A. Robin Olson. 1996. "Low Profile/High Potential: A Look at Grievance Mediation." *Dispute Resolution Journal*, Vol. 51 (October), pp. 54-61.

Bowers, Mollie H. 1980. "Grievance Mediation: Another Route to Resolution." *Personnel Journal*, Vol. 59, pp. 132-36.

Bowers, Mollie H., Ronald L. Seeber, and Lamont E. Stallworth. 1982. "Grievance Mediation: A Route to Resolution for the Cost-Conscious 1980s." *Labor Law Journal*, Vol. 33, pp. 459-66.

Brazil, W. D., M. A. Kahn, J. P. Newman, and J. Z. Gold. 1986. "Early Neutral Evaluation: An Experimental Effort to Expedite Dispute Resolution." *Judicature*, Vol. 69, pp. 279-85.

Brett, Jeanne M., and Stephen B. Goldberg. 1979. "Wildcat Strikes in Bituminous Coal Mining." *Industrial and Labor Relations Review*, Vol. 32, pp. 467-83.

_____. 1983. "Grievance Mediation in the Coal Industry: A Field Experiment." *Industrial and Labor Relations Review,* Vol. 37 (October), pp. 49-69.

Bureau of National Affairs. 1979. *Collective Bargaining Negotiations and Contracts: Basic Patterns.* Washington, DC: GPO.

_____. 1987. "Grievance Mediation Said Gaining as Useful Alternative to Arbitration." *Daily Labor Report* (May 15), No. 193, pp. C1-C3.

_____. 1989. *Collective Bargaining Negotiations and Contracts: Basic Patterns.* Washington, DC: GPO

_____. 1990. "Grievance Mediation Cheaper, Quicker than Arbitration, Seminar Speakers Agree." Daily Labor Report (June 5), No. 108, pp. A11-A12.

_____. 1999. "EEOC's New Nationwide Mediation Plan Offers Option of Informal Settlements." *Employment Discrimination Report,* Vol. 12, no. 7 (Feb. 17), pp. 217-18, 244-45.

Butt, Elizabeth Rae. 1988. "Grievance Mediation: The Ontario Experience." Research Essay Series No. 14. Kingston, ON: Queen's University at Kingston, School of Industrial Relations.

Carnevale, Peter. 1986. "Strategic Choice in Mediation." *Negotiation Journal,* Vol. 2, pp. 41-56.

Carnevale, Peter, and Richard Pegnetter. 1985. "The Selection of Mediator Tactics in Public-Sector Disputes: A Contingency Analysis." *Journal of Social Issues,* Vol. 41, pp. 65-82.

Cole, David L. 1963. *The Quest for Industrial Peace.* New York: McGraw Hill.

Coleman, Charles J. 1992. "The Arbitrator's Cases: Number, Sources, Issues, and Implications." In Mario J. Bognanno and Charles J. Coleman, eds., *Labor Arbitration in America: The Profession and the Practice.* New York: Praeger, pp. 85-106.

Cooke, William N. 1990. *Labor-Management Cooperation: New Partnerships or Going in Circles?* Kalamazoo, MI: W.E. Upjohn Institute for Employment Research.

Conti, A. J. 1985. "Mediation of Workplace Disputes: A Prescription for Organizational Health." *Employee Relations Law Journal,* Vol. 11, pp. 291-310.

Cutcher-Gershenfeld, Joel. 1991. "The Impact on Economic Performance of a Transformation in Workplace Relations." *Industrial and Labor Relations Review,* Vol. 44, pp. 241-60.

Ewing, David W. 1989. *Justice on the Job: Resolving Grievances in the Nonunion Workplace.* Boston: Harvard Business School Press.

Federal Mediation and Conciliation Service. 1998. "Arbitration Statistics Fiscal Year 1997." Unpublished data distributed to arbitrators.

Feuille, Peter, and Denise Chachere. 1995. "Looking Fair or Being Fair: Remedial Voice Procedures in Nonunion Workplaces." *Journal of Management,* Vol. 21 (January), pp. 27-42.

Gandz, Jeffrey. 1982. "Grievances and Their Resolution." In John Anderson and Morley Gunderson, eds., *Union-Management Relations in Canada.* Don Mills, ON: Addison-Wesley, pp. 289-315.

Gideon, Thomas F., and Richard B. Peterson. 1979. "A Comparison of Alternate Grievance Procedures." *Employee Relations Law Journal,* Vol. 5, pp. 222-33.

Goldberg, Stephen B. 1982. "The Mediation of Grievances under a Collective Bargaining Contract: An Alternative to Arbitration." *Northwestern University Law Review,* Vol. 77, pp. 270-315.

_____. 1984. "Grievance Mediation: The Coal Industry Experiment." In James L. Stern and Barbara D. Dennis, eds., *Arbitration–Promise and Performance, Proceedings of the 36th Annual Meeting of the National Academy of Arbitrators.* Washington, DC: Bureau of National Affairs, pp. 128-36.

_____. 1989. "Grievance Mediation: A Successful Alternative to Labor Arbitration." *Negotiation Journal*, Vol. 5, pp. 9-15.

Goldberg, Stephen B., and Jeanne M. Brett. 1983. "An Experiment in the Mediation of Grievances." *Monthly Labor Review* (March), No. 106: 23-30, pp. 23-30.

_____. 1990. "Disputants' Perspectives on the Differences between Mediation and Arbitration." *Negotiation Journal*, Vol. 6, pp. 249-55.

Goldberg, Stephen B., and William Hobgood. 1987. *Mediating Grievances: A Cooperative Solution.* Washington, DC: U.S. Department of Labor.

Gregory, Gordon A., and Robert E. Rooney, Jr. 1980. "Grievance Mediation: A Trend in the Cost-Conscious Eighties." *Labor Law Journal*, Vol. 31 (August), pp. 502-08.

Handsaker, Morrison. 1966. "Grievance Arbitration and Mediated Settlements." *Labor Law Journal*, Vol. 17, pp. 579-83.

Heckscher, Charles C. 1988. *The New Unionism.* New York: Basic Books.

House, Nancy C. 1992. "Grievance Mediation: AT&T's Experience." *Labor Law Journal*, Vol. 43 (August), pp. 491-95.

Ichniowski, Casey. 1986. "The Effects of Grievance Activity on Productivity." *Industrial and Labor Relations Review*, Vol. 40 (October), pp. 75-89.

Knight, Thomas R. 1986. "Feedback and Grievance Resolution." *Industrial and Labor Relations Review*, Vol. 39, pp. 585-98.

Katz, Harry C., Thomas A. Kochan, and Kenneth R. Gobeille. 1983. "Industrial Relations Performance, Economic Performance, and the Effects of Quality of Working Life Efforts: An Interplant Analysis." *Industrial and Labor Relations Review*, Vol. 37 (October), pp. 3-17.

Katz, Harry C., Thomas A. Kochan, and Mark. R. Weber. 1985. "Assessing the Effects of Industrial Relations and Quality of Working Life Efforts on Organizational Effectiveness." *Academy of Management Journal*, Vol. 28 (September), pp. 509-27.

Kochan, Thomas A., Harry C. Katz, and Robert B. McKersie. 1986. *The Transformation of American Industrial Relations.* New York: Basic Books.

Kochan, Thomas A., and Harry C. Katz. 1988. *Collective Bargaining and Industrial Relations,* 2d ed. Homewood, IL: Irwin.

Kolb, Deborah M. 1983. *The Mediators.* Cambridge, MA: MIT Press.

_____. 1989. "How Existing Procedures Shape Alternatives: The Case of Grievance Mediation." *Journal of Dispute Resolution*, Vol. 1989, pp. 59-87.

_____. 1994. "Conditioning Parties to Settle Labor Grievances: A Profile of William B. Hobgood." In Deborah M. Kolb, ed., *When Talk Works: Profiles of Mediators.* San Francisco: Jossey-Bass.

Kressel, Kenneth. 1972. *Labor Mediation: An Exploratory Survey.* New York: Association of Labor Mediation Agencies.

Labig, Chalmer E., and Charles E. Greer. 1988. "Grievance Initiation: A Literature Survey and Suggestions for Future Research." *Journal of Labor Research*, Vol. 9, pp. 1-27.

Lewin, David. 1984. "Empirical Measures of Grievance Procedure Effectiveness." *Labor Law Journal*, Vol. 35 (August), pp. 491-99.

Lewin, David, and Richard B. Peterson. 1988. *The Modern Grievance Procedure in the United States*. New York: Quorum Books.

Lipsky, David B., and Ronald L. Seeber. 1998. *The Appropriate Resolution of Corporate Disputes: A Report on the Growing Use of ADR by U.S. Corporations*. Ithaca, NY: Cornell University, PERC Institute on Conflict Resolution.

McEwen, C. A. 1991. "Pursuing Problem-solving or Predictive Settlement." *Florida State University Law Review*, Vol. 19, pp. 77-88.

McKersie, Robert B., and William W. Shropshire, Jr. 1962. "Avoiding Written Grievances." *Journal of Business*, Vol. 35 (April), pp. 135-52.

McPherson, William H. 1956. "Grievance Mediation under Collective Bargaining." *Industrial and Labor Relations Review*, Vol. 9, pp. 200-12.

Mediation Research and Education Project, Inc. 1998. "MREP Grievance Mediation Report – June 1998." Unpublished report on grievances mediated under MREP's auspices, Northwestern University Law School.

Mesch, Debra J., and Dan R. Dalton. 1992. "Unexpected Consequences of Improving Workplace Justice: A Six-Year Time Series Assessment." *Academy of Management Journal*, Vol. 35, pp. 1099-1114.

Mittenthal, Richard. 1991. "Whither Arbitration? Major Changes in the Last Half Century." *Arbitration Journal*, Vol. 46 (December), pp. 24-32.

Nelson, Nels E., and A. N. M. Meshquat Uddin. 1995. "Arbitrators as Mediators." *Labor Law Journal*, Vol. 46 (April), pp. 205-13.

Ng, Ignace, and Ali Dastmalchian. 1989. "Determinants of Grievance Outcomes: A Case Study." *Industrial and Labor Relations Review*, Vol. 42, pp. 393-403.

Nolan, Dennis R., and Roger I. Abrams. 1983a. "American Labor Arbitration: The Early Years." *University of Florida Law Review*, Vol. 35, pp. 373-421.

_____. 1983b. "American Labor Arbitration: The Maturing Years." *University of Florida Law Review*, Vol. 35, pp. 557-632.

Norsworthy, J. R., and Craig A. Zabala. 1985. "Worker Attitudes, Worker Behavior, and Productivity in the U.S. Automobile Industry, 1959-1976." *Industrial and Labor Relations Review*, Vol. 38 (July), pp. 544-57.

O'Grady, J. P., Jr. 1976. "Grievance Mediation Activities by State Agencies." *Arbitration Journal*, Vol. 31, pp. 125-30.

_____. 1990. "Grievance Mediation: Does It Really Work?" *Negotiation Journal*, Vol. 6, pp. 269-80.

Osterman, Paul. 1994. "How Common Is Workplace Transformation and Who Adopts It?" *Industrial and Labor Relations Review*, Vol. 47 (January), pp. 173-88.

Prasow, Paul. 1950. "Preventive Mediation: A Technique to Improve Industrial Relations." *Labor Law Journal*, Vol. 1, pp. 866-68.

Quinn, Thomas J., Mark Rosenbaum, and Donald S. McPherson. 1990. "Grievance Mediation and Grievance Negotiation Skills: Collaborative Relationships." *Labor Law Journal*, Vol. 41, pp. 762-72.

Reed, Bessie B. 1990. "An Analysis of Mediation as an Alternative to Arbitration in the Resolution of Rights Disputes." Unpublished paper, Institute of Labor and Industrial Relations, University of Illinois.

Roberts, Matthew T., Roger S. Wolters, William H. Holley, and Hubert S. Feild. 1990. "Grievance Mediation: A Management Perspective." *Arbitration Journal*, Vol. 45 (September), pp. 15-23.

Rowe, Mary P. 1991. "The Ombudsman's Role in a Dispute Resolution System." *Negotiation Journal*, Vol. 7, pp. 353-62.

Schmedemann, Deborah A. 1987. "Reconciling Differences: The Theory and Law of Mediating Labor Grievances." *Industrial Relations Law Journal*, Vol. 9, pp. 523-95.

Silberman, Allan D. 1989. "Breaking the Mold of Grievance Resolution: A Pilot Program in Mediation." *Arbitration Journal*, Vol. 44 (December), pp. 40-5.

Simkin, William E. 1964. "Positive Approaches to Labor Peace." *Industrial Relations*, Vol. 4 (October), pp. 37-44.

_____. 1971. *Mediation and the Dynamics of Collective Bargaining*. Washington, DC: Bureau of National Affairs.

Skratek, Sylvia P. 1987. "Grievance Mediation of Contractual Disputes in Public Education." *Missouri Journal of Dispute Resolution*, Vol. 1987, pp. 44-75.

_____. 1990. p. 8.

Stewart, Greg L., and Jeanette A. Davy. 1992. "An Empirical Examination of Grievance Resolution and Filing Rates in the Public and Private Sectors." *Journal of Collective Negotiations in the Public Sector*, Vol. 21, pp. 323-336.

Todor, William D., and Crystal L. Owen. 1991. "Deriving Benefits from Conflict Resolution: A Macrojustice Assessment." *Employee Responsibilities and Rights Journal*, Vol. 4, pp. 37-49.

Ury, William L., Jeanne M. Brett, and Stephen B. Goldberg. 1988. *Getting Disputes Resolved: Designing Systems to Cut the Costs of Conflict*. San Francisco: Jossey-Bass.

U.S. Government Accounting Office. 1995. *Employment Discrimination: Most Private-Sector Employers Use Alternative Dispute Resolution*. Report GAO/HEHS-95-150 (July).

_____. 1997. *Alternative Dispute Resolution: Employers' Experiences with ADR in the Workplace*. Report GAO/GGD-97-157 (August).

Valtin, Rolf. 1993. "The Real and Substantial Benefits of Grievance Mediation." *Negotiation Journal*, Vol. 9 (April), pp. 179-83.

Warren, James. 1985. "Mediation Cools Off the Coalfields." *Chicago Tribune*. October 8: Section 3, p. 1.

Weiler, Paul C. 1978. "The Role of the Labor Board as an Alternative to Arbitration." In Barbara D. Dennis and Gerald G. Somers, eds., *Arbitration—1977, Proceedings of the 30th Annual Meeting of the National Academy of Arbitrators*. Washington, DC: Bureau of National Affairs.

_____. 1990. *Governing the Workplace: The Future of Labor and Employment Law*. Cambridge, MA: Harvard University Press.

Wheeler, Hoyt N. 1985. *Industrial Conflict: An Integrative Theory*. Columbia, SC: University of South Carolina Press.

Zack, Arnold M. 1978. "Suggested New Approaches to Grievance Arbitration." In Barbara D. Dennis and Gerald G. Somers, eds., *Arbitration—1977, Proceedings of the 30th Annual Meeting of the National Academy of Arbitrators*. Washington, DC: Bureau of National Affairs.

Chapter 7

New Forms of Work Organization and Their Impact on the Grievance Procedure

Michelle Kaminski
University of Illinois

Grievance handling is a core function in most local unions. Lewin and Peterson's (1988) model of the grievance procedure suggests that labor-management relations is one factor that determines the functioning and outcomes of the grievance procedure. Since the early 1980s, new forms of work organization have dramatically altered the labor-management relationship in many workplaces. Has the implementation of these new forms changed grievance procedure as well, and if so, how?

There are established bodies of literature on both grievance handling and on new forms of work organization. But there is little that examines the intersection of the two, except to report a change in the number of grievances as teams or other workplace changes are implemented. On the one hand, union representatives and workers have more input into decision making with new forms of work organization than they have had in the past. On the other hand, as union-management relationships become more cooperative, some representatives are backing away from their traditional roles as "prosecuting attorney" and "defense lawyer" in resolving grievances. In this context, what happens to workers' rights? Do workers still receive due process?

This paper examines these issues by focusing on the issue of worker voice. First, different forms of worker voice are described. This is followed by a discussion of new forms of work organization at both the workforce level and the institutional level and how they affect worker voice. Because relatively little is known about how the grievance procedure itself changes, each of these sections is followed by some propositions for future research. Finally, some comments on methodology are included.

Worker Voice

Both grievances and many of the new forms of work organization (e.g., self-managed work teams) can be seen as forms of worker voice.

219

The "exit-voice" tradeoff holds that workers who have a voice are seen as less likely to exit, or quit, the organization. Organizations that provide voice mechanisms may benefit from reduced turnover as a result. But there are a variety of types of voice. The grievance procedure is primarily a *reactive* form of voice. A formal grievance is essentially a complaint that a worker's contractual rights and/or the organization's past practices have been violated. Thus a grievance is a *reaction* to a managerial action. (Grievances are not entirely reactive in that the threat of a grievance can lead to more proactive influence, and skilled union leaders can use the grievance procedure in more creative ways, but the majority of grievances are individual reactions to managerial behavior.)

Reactive voice is only one kind of voice found in the workplace (see Lewin and Mitchell 1992; McCabe and Lewin 1992). Another kind of voice is having a genuine opportunity to influence decisions over a broad range of issues *before* action is taken. Issues might include deciding who runs which machine today, how best to protect workers' health and safety, or even what products to sell. Workers can influence some of these issues reactively via the grievance procedure (e.g., a work assignment that violates the job classification system), and union leaders with constructive relations with management are able to exert influence informally as well. But in traditional workplaces, some important issues are either minimally covered or not included in the contract. For example, it is very rare in U.S. industry for a union to influence what products or services a firm sells, even though those decisions have a major impact on the job security of the membership.

Indeed, in traditional unionized workplaces, the management's rights clause severely limits the proactive form of worker voice by proclaiming that management can unilaterally decide any issue not explicitly covered by the union contract. While union leaders can often find ways to address some issues that are not covered in the contract, they are still working within a system that does not recognize their role in decision making on many topics. In contrast, some of the new forms of work organization significantly limit—often in writing—the scope of the management's rights clause. They provide a more proactive form of employee voice because teams and union representatives have legitimately recognized decision making authority over a number of issues that were formerly in management's domain.

The kinds of voice available to citizens in a democracy provide a useful analogy to voice in the workplace. In the U.S., citizens have a certain set of rights as defined in the constitution. If any of their rights are violated—such as the right to vote or the right to equal treatment under the law—citizens can use the judicial system to seek remedy for the violation. But citizens are also interested in having the opportunity to voice their concerns and preferences about a wide array of government policies, such as social welfare, economic policies, environmental regulation, and the U.S. role in world affairs. The opportunity to redress complaints provided by the judicial system generally does not provide this kind of policy voice. Similarly, in the workplace, the grievance procedure provides a process to follow when one's contractual rights are violated, while teams can provide a more proactive voice that give workers decision-making authority over how work is done.

Both proactive and reactive voice are essential. Without reactive voice, one has no recourse when a policy is violated; there is no enforcement. Without proactive voice, one has no possibility of influencing policy decisions in the preferred direction. Unions have given workers a strong reactive voice through the grievance procedure and a proactive voice over selected issues in the collective bargaining process. But some new forms of work organization also offer workers a proactive voice over an expanded range of issues—such as scheduling of work, job rotation, vendor selection, choice of new technology, and input into the organization's strategic direction (see Table 1).

TABLE 1

Forms of Employee Voice

| | Type of Voice | |
	Proactive Voice	Reactive Voice
Collective	Worker-centered teams Collective bargaining Works councils	Union grievance procedure, including mediation and arbitration
Individual	Supervisor-centered teams Committees appointed by management Favoritism	Nonunion grievance procedures: • managerial review • ombudsman • arbitration • peer review

Voice mechanisms can be individual or collective in nature. While most grievances are indeed based on a complaint from a particular individual, in unionized settings they are part of a collectively negotiated process—the grievance procedure. Thus even though the complaint is expressed by an individual, the voice and weight of the collective body stands behind each individual in that process. Further, the collective provides the individual with an advocate to support his or her case. Thus most grievances can be seen as a form of collective reactive voice.

Forms of individual voice are more typically found in nonunion settings or in some cases in union settings in which the parties do not negotiate a particular mechanism of collective voice. For example, many workplaces, both union and nonunion, have problem-solving teams whose members are selected by management. Workers on those types of teams cannot be seen as representing the collective interests of the workers, because they are not selected by the workers and because they typically do not have the authority to set an agenda that reflects workers' concerns. Many workplaces also have teams only in certain departments and further have no formal agreement about what the responsibilities of the team are (e.g., does the team determine who does what job each day or does the supervisor?). There is likely to be considerable variation from team to team within such a workplace. In these settings, any authority the team has is essentially granted by individual managers and can just as easily be removed when the manager leaves or has a change of heart. Like employment at will in a nonunion setting, these teams are a form of individual voice at the discretion of management. There is no collective agreement in place to enforce workers' voice.

The same is true of nonunion grievance procedures. They provide individuals with an opportunity to appeal a wrongful act, but the appeal process itself is defined by management and can be changed unilaterally by management. Individuals have some limited reactive voice within such a system, and a significant percentage do indeed win their cases (e.g., Briggs and Gundry 1994), but the individual is not backed by the collective will of the employees and does not have equal standing with management.

Writers on workplace democracy also recognize the importance of both proactive and reactive voice and often emphasize collective voice. For example, Schurman and Eaton (1996) identify six components of democratic workplaces. Two of these—shared sovereignty and participation—are forms of collective proactive voice, and another three are inputs to or outcomes of proactive voice—access to information and education, minimum standards, and the right to a fair share of value for contributions. The sixth component, respect for individual dignity and guaranteed individual rights, is similar to collective reactive voice. Guaranteed individual rights protect workers from the arbitrary use of power—whether by management or a dominant group of workers.

Although the rights are guaranteed *to* the individual, they can only be guaranteed *by* the collective. Just as in a political democracy, individual rights are guaranteed through legislation; in the workplace they are guaranteed through a collectively negotiated agreement and thus can be seen as a form of collective voice. However, while the collective agreement is essential to guarantee individual rights, grievances are often seen as strictly individual issues and not of concern to the workforce as a whole. This has not always been the case. Earlier this century, many unions staged work stoppages and slowdowns over unresolved grievances because they were seen as a threat to the collective welfare (see, for example, Kuhn 1961.) But in today's workplace, winning a grievance is often seen as a victory only for the individual worker, whereas losing grievances—and especially losing a number of grievances in a short time span—is sometimes seen as a collective failure on the part of the union.

Some of the ongoing tensions in workplaces with teams or other innovations are framed as a conflict between individual and collective rights. Grievances are typically filed by an individual, whereas many other decisions are made by the group. But on further examination, the tension can be seen as a tradeoff between two forms of collective voice: proactive and reactive. Workers have more collective proactive voice to influence both organizational policies and how work is done. But in some cases, they also feel that they have less access to the collectively bargained grievance procedure and a reduced ability to exercise reactive voice. It is a tradeoff between the upper right- and the upper left-hand cells in Table 1. How common is this tradeoff? Can teams and other new forms of work organization significantly increase proactive voice while maintaining high levels of reactive voice? The next section describes some new forms of work organization and their potential effects on worker voice.

New Forms of Work Organization

The number and variety of workplace innovations that have occurred since the early 1980s has been dramatic. Examples include quality of work life, quality circles, employee involvement, labor-management committees, total quality management (TQM), lean production, high-performance work organizations, human resource bundles, and learning organizations. Even within each model there is considerable variation. A useful way to organize these workplace changes into categories for further discussion is the matrix used by Rubinstein, Bennett, and Kochan (1993) shown in Table 2. Although the model was originally developed to describe the various forms of joint union-management decision making at Saturn, it is also useful as a typology of joint union-management decision making.

TABLE 2

Forms of Joint Union-Management Decision Making

From Rubinstein, Bennett, and Kochan (1993)

	Union (Institutional)	Work Force
Off-line	Labor-Management Committees	Problem-solving Teams
On-line	Comanagement	Self-directed Work Teams

Briefly, off-line groups are those that are separate from the regular work operations of the organization. They typically bring together volunteers from a variety of departments into one group. At the workforce level, they are generally assigned to solve specifically identified problems. Examples of this type of group are quality circles (QCs), employee involvement (EI) groups, and quality-of-work-life (QWL) groups. Institutional-level off-line groups include plant steering committees, labor-management committees, and union representation on boards of directors. Typically, members are assigned to these committees because of their leadership positions in either management or the union.

On-line groups at the workforce level are those that are part of regular operations. Everyone who works in a particular department or area belongs to the group, which meets regularly to handle issues such as scheduling of equipment, staff, and leave time. They may also deal with quality problems and production targets. On-line groups include self-directed work teams and worker-centered teams (Babson 1997).

At the institutional level, on-line groups are quite rare. Indeed, the only example in U.S. industry may be comanagement at Saturn, in which a represented (i.e., union) and nonrepresented (i.e., manager) module advisor pair up to handle middle management responsibilities for a particular work area. The module advisors are equals. They jointly approve payroll, overtime, and purchase orders. However, they do not have authority to hire or fire or to file grievances (Rubinstein et al. 1993; Rubinstein 1998).

Each of these forms of joint decision making has the potential to impact the grievance procedure and/or how disputes are settled outside the formal grievance process. They present both threats to and opportunities for different forms of worker voice.

Joint Decision Making at the Workforce Level

An ironic feature of joint decision making at the workforce level is that it can be described as both widespread and scattered in U.S. firms. The practices are widespread because most firms report having some mechanisms in place. But they are also scattered, because within those firms the practices often cover only a small percentage of workers. Applebaum and Batt (1994) reach this conclusion after reviewing several national surveys and extensive case literature. A recent survey of participative practices in Fortune 1000 companies by Lawler, Mohrman, and Ledford (1995) shows that employee participation groups (EI) are the most widespread, with 91% of firms having at least some and 35% having relatively extensive ones (see Table 3). On-line teams are reported to exist in 68% of firms, but only 5% of firms have a sizable portion of employees working in teams. Most of these results are based on surveys of managers. In a survey of union leaders, Eaton (1990) found that 42% of local unions in the Midwest reported having some participative program at their work site. Only 9% reported having teams.

TABLE 3
Frequency of Joint Decision Making in Fortune 1000 Firms
Adapted from Lawler, Mohrman, and Ledford (1995) 1993 Data

Form of Joint Decision Making	Percent of Firms with Any Employees Involved	Percent of Firms with More Than 40% of Employees Involved	More Common in Manufacturing or Service Sector?
Union-management QWL committees	35	8	Manufacturing
Quality circles	65	15	No difference in 1993; More common in manufacturing in 1987 and 1990
Employee participation groups	91	35	Manufacturing
Teams	68	5	Manufacturing

Osterman (1994) found a much higher percentage of self-directed work teams, perhaps due to a somewhat different definition.[1] He found that just over half of establishments had teams, and 40% reported that half or more of their employees worked in teams. Other practices that were common among his sample were quality circles (41%), rotation (43%), and TQM (33%). For each of these practices, about one-quarter of establishments reported that 50% or more of their employees were involved.

Lawler et al. also report that all four of these practices are more common in firms facing heavy foreign competition or extreme performance pressure. Two practices, teams and QWL, are also more common in rapidly growing markets. All four practices are (or have been) more common in the manufacturing sector than the service sector. There have been some notable exceptions in the service sector, particularly in telecommunications. AT&T and the CWA and IBEW have experimented with different forms of joint decision making over a number of years. Hospitals are beginning to implement some of these practices. Preuss (1998) conducted a survey of over 6,000 health care employees and found that 50% of registered nurses report direct (on-line) participation in decision making and 62% belong to a quality circle or other off-line team. Reports of joint activities in the public sector have only recently been published (e.g., Kriesky in this volume; AFGE 1996).

A recent nationally representative survey (Gittleman, Horrigan, and Joyce 1998) of close to 6,000 establishments reports the frequency by industry of six flexible work practices: worker teams, TQM, quality circles, peer review of employee performance, worker involvement in decisions to purchase new technology and equipment, and job rotation. Across all industries, 42% of establishments had at least one of the practices.[2] Larger establishments and those in manufacturing and wholesale trade were more likely to follow these practices (see Table 4 for a comparison by industries).

TABLE 4
Flexible Work Practices[3] by Industry[*]
Adapted from Gittleman, Horrigan, & Joyce, 1998

Industry	Percent with any one practice	Average number of practices
All industries	42	0.80
Mining	43	0.78
Construction	40	0.76
Manufacturing	56	1.17
Transportation, Communications, Public Utilities	46	0.97
Wholesale Trade	55	1.14
Retail Trade	36	0.70
Finance, Insurance, Real Estate	41	0.71
Services	41	0.73

[*] Practice include worker teams, TQM, quality circles, peer review of employee performance, worker involvement in decisions to purchase new technology and equipment, and job rotation.

On-line Teams

The implementation of teams is generally said to decrease the number of grievances in a workplace (e.g., Katz, Kochan, and Weber 1985; Cooke 1990; Cutcher-Gershenfeld 1991; Ichniowski 1992; Applebaum and Batt 1994; Kaminski, Bertelli, Moye, and Yudken 1996). However, it is unclear how to evaluate this change. Is it constructive, signifying either that there are fewer problems or that the problems that do exist are solved quickly and to all parties' satisfaction? Or does it mask other issues, such as peer pressure to conform to managerial goals and decreased union commitment?

One study of a different form of cooperation had some unexpected results that highlight the difficulty of equating a low number of grievances with success. Mesch and Dalton (1992) report on a natural field experiment in which management and union leadership agreed to implement a fact-finding procedure with the goal of resolving grievances more quickly and at a lower step in the grievance procedure. The procedure achieved these goals, but it was discontinued after two years. Mesch and Dalton found that the grievance rate was significantly *higher* during the time the fact finding was in effect than it was either before or after the experiment. In fact, it almost doubled. Grievance rates in a nonequivalent control group remained steady during the same period. One interpretation of these results are that workers who had legitimate complaints found the traditional grievance system unapproachable. Only when a new, more open, less confrontational system became available did they feel comfortable filing their complaints. This view is supported by Lewin's (in this volume) conclusion that a majority of workers who feel they have been treated unfairly do not currently file grievances.

In spite of this result, the general trend still holds that on-line teams are associated with lower grievance rates. Saturn is among the best-known workplaces with teams and it has had a very low level of grievances since its inception. Initially, only five elected UAW officials at Saturn—the president and four vice presidents—could file formal grievances, far less than the approximately 30 grievance committeemen who would be available in other comparably sized General Motors plants (Rubinstein, 1996). Those who designed the system believed that the majority of disputes would be solved by teams or other mechanisms, and there would be fewer formal grievances as a result (Shaiken, Lopez, and Makita 1997). While there are indeed fewer grievances than in traditional plants, there has been a rise in the grievance load over time. In a bargaining unit of approximately 7,300 members, there was a total of 205 grievances from 1988 to 1994 (Rubinstein 1998). However, over time, workers reported frustration with the inability to file grievances and have voted to increase the number of union officers who are allowed to file grievances. There has been a corresponding increase in grievances over time at Saturn, with 279 grievances in 1995, 245 in 1996, and 127 through the first ten months of 1997 (Rubinstein 1998). One issue of particular concern is that attendance problems are handled differently from team to team. Another is that workers who go through the consultation process (i.e., an advisory process for poor performers) do not have traditional union representation to protect them.

Because Saturn has all four forms of joint decision making described in Table 2, it is difficult to attribute either the low grievance rate or its recent increase to any one form of joint decision making. Therefore, it is useful to examine other workplaces with teams to see if similar patterns emerge.

At NUMMI, a joint GM-Toyota auto assembly plant with on-line teams, the issue of reactive voice became increasingly important over time (Adler, Goldoftas, and Levine 1997). Workers were involved in redesigning jobs, and quality and productivity were high (Adler 1995). The number of grievances was relatively low.

However, problems arose at NUMMI on a number of fronts. Reports circulated about team members pressuring each other to work when injured and sometimes questioning the authenticity of their injuries. In 1993 California OSHA cited NUMMI for extensive ergonomics problems. Workers also report charges of favoritism in selecting people for preferred positions. Parker and Slaughter (1994) state that some issues that are covered in a traditional union contract (such as specific selection criteria) are not included in the NUMMI–UAW contract, and so the same problem may no longer be grievable. They also suggest that the union discourages workers from filing grievances. Both proponents and critics of the team system at NUMMI seem to agree that it resulted in a split in the local union. The Administration Caucus emphasized collective proactive voice by actively contributing to policy. But they were criticized for not exercising collective reactive voice strongly enough (i.e., not advocating members' grievances as aggressively as traditional UAW leadership). The Administration Caucus prevailed for a number of years but was later defeated by the People's Caucus, which campaigned in part on the issue of stronger representation in the grievance procedure. Although the level of joint decision making at NUMMI is not quite as high as at Saturn, the pattern over time for union leadership is strikingly similar. For a number of years, members are very supportive of the new work organization in spite of its flaws and are very satisfied with the increase in proactive voice. But after some time, they become dissatisfied with the loss of reactive voice and begin to demand more aggressive representation in the grievance procedure. At Saturn first the membership voted for an increase in the number of union officers who could file grievances. Then after thirteen years, they voted out of office the union officials most closely associated with the partnership in favor of ones who promised more traditional reactive voice (Bradsher 1999).

Union leadership at another auto plant with teams, Ford Wayne Stamping, has not faced the same challenges over the grievance procedure as at Saturn and NUMMI (Kaminski 1998). At Wayne the union bargaining committee actively promotes both proactive and reactive voice for workers. On-line teams at Wayne give workers substantial control over scheduling, job rotation, job assignment, and quality. In addition, there is joint decision making at the institutional level on some issues. The union leadership meets weekly with top management to review problems and upcoming issues. The union also sends a representative to management's weekly cost meetings, participates in job interviews for some managerial positions, and participates in joint strategic planning meetings. The union appointed representatives to a committee on the most recent model changeover that made decisions on how jobs would be set up and what equipment would be purchased.

Hourly employees at Wayne rated the team concept very positively overall. Specific items addressed the role of the union and the grievance system. For example, 64% agreed and 17% disagreed that "the local union represents my needs well" (N = 64). Further, 50% disagreed and 24% agreed with the statement "the team concept weakens the position of the union in processing grievances" (N = 58). For other items that rated the union's performance, see Table 5.

The number of grievances at Wayne did decline after the implementation of teams. However, the union and management both identified a reduction specifically in overtime grievances as a goal, and they negotiated a change in their contract to help make that happen. They created the position of union overtime coordinator, whose job it is to keep and monitor weekly records of who is available for and who received offers of overtime work. The coordinator reviews this information with area supervisors. The goal is to prevent violations rather than simply grieving them after the fact. But managers—not the union—still distribute overtime,

TABLE 5

Ford Wayne Integrated Stamping and Assembly/
UAW Local 900
Survey Items Related to Union Performance

Item	Agree or Strongly Agree	Neither Agree Nor Disagree	Disagree or Strongly Disagree	Valid N
The local union represents my needs well	64.1%	18.8%	17.2%	64
The team concept strengthens the bargaining power of the union in contract negotiations	72.2%	22.2%	5.6%	54
The team concept gives management more control over the union	32.8%	25.9%	41.4%	58
The team concept weakens the position of the local union in processing a grievance	24.1%	25.9%	50.0%	58
The team concept threatens the very existence of the union	10.2%	22.0%	67.8%	59

and workers who believe they have been unfairly passed over are still able to use the traditional grievance procedure to seek redress. Since the overtime coordinator positions have been put in place, overtime grievances have declined.

While the three plants discussed above have on-line teams for the entire location, this is not always—perhaps not even typically—the case across U.S. industry. Many workplaces have a more modest implementation of teams, one in which certain departments have on-line teams and others do not. The teams' responsibility and authority may not be clearly defined, or employees may not have been trained in the skills they need to be effective in the new system. Unions at these workplaces often face the worst of both worlds: workers have less power than in team workplaces, and the union cannot derive as much power as in a traditional workplace from uniformity and standardization of work practices.

The interview data below are from one such in-between workplace.[4] At this location, an equipment repair facility, management has proposed and the union has agreed to implement a high-performance work organization (HPWO) that includes on-line teams. But at the time of data collection, the implementation was far from complete. Some areas had teams, some did not. Most teams had an identified leader, but they were selected differently (i.e., appointed vs. elected) in different departments. The role of the team leader was not standardized across teams.

Both management and union leadership reported a decline in the number of grievances since the move towards HPWO and felt that issues were resolved in a more constructive manner. The quotes below refer to that and also describe a new role for the union that at least in one case brought better results for the worker.

> *Team leader A:* One of the biggest successes that we have had [is that] a lot of the disciplinary actions have been avoided . . . because the company in many cases is attempting to work with the union, to solve problems before they become bigger problems, to resolve potential problems.

> *Supervisor A:* Some [workers have] personal problems, absenteeism. . . . You get to the point where you push company rules to the max.

> I had one incident where it was the last step. And the union got in, and we talked about it. As a matter of fact, I was a hothead. And the union convinced me [not to take the last step] after probably two weeks of working back and forth. And I think it was very good work on the part of the union. . . . This individual was going to get terminated for one more absence. That absence came. And the rules are the rules. And they were able to convince us, say "Hey, you have to give this guy a chance. It's a legitimate absence."

> And at least I opened my mind to see the facts, and I think it was . . . a good approach. As a matter of fact, this individual now has changed 180 degrees completely from what he was doing.

While some unions could achieve similar results within a traditional union-management relationship, both union and management at this location say that this particular case was a significant step forward for them.

On the other hand, the interviews also revealed problems with the grievance procedure. Below, one team leader describes a counseling approach, and another team leader responds by identifying problems with it:

> *Team leader B:* As a team leader, when something's not working as far as the disciplinary actions, instead of getting management involved, we normally try to get the union . . . and try to counsel this person before it goes any further.

Team leader C: I don't like that situation at all. That's very touchy. Because a lot of people here look at you as one of them. And they're going to say, "Who the hell are you to come to me to tell me, hey, I'm not doing a good job? . . . It's something I'd rather not even deal with, because you make a lot of enemies for something that's not really your call.

Union members were divided in how they felt about the union's new role. Some supported their efforts, even while recognizing problems in the transition to a new system. Others were opposed to it. One was quite articulate about what the union's role should be:

Worker A: The [union was] organized for the purpose of negotiating contracts and for defending employees when wrongfully challenged by the company. And they collect union dues . . . in order to function. They were never intended to run the company. . . .

It's a conflict of interest when you're collecting union dues from John Doe and then telling him that you're going to get on him because he's not producing. It's just a conflict of interest. So . . . you don't do that.

The union leaders themselves are quite aware of this viewpoint. However, they feel that they are accomplishing more for their members by using a more cooperative approach before resorting to traditional adversarial techniques. They still use adversarial techniques when they feel it is necessary.

This example raises the issue of peer evaluation and peer discipline in teams. International unions typically advise locals that members should never be involved in disciplining other members (Parker and Slaughter 1992). But because teams evaluate their own work, and because poor performance can lead to discipline, teams create a mechanism for peer evaluation and discipline that typically does not exist in traditional workplaces.

There is relatively little data about how common peer evaluation and peer discipline are. The studies that exist suggest that it applies to a small but significant minority of workplaces. Gittleman et al. (1998) report that 11% of establishments have some form of peer review of employee performance, although this figure rises to 18% in establishments with more than 50 employees. Unpublished data by Luria (1997) reports that in 89% of small manufacturing firms, individual employees have no say at all in evaluating the performance of other employees. But workplaces with teams say that 35% of teams do have a say—although generally a very small say—in evaluating performance. Among the entire sample, in 97% of cases, workers have no say in disciplining other workers and 84% of teams have no say in discipline. Thus it appears that peer review and peer discipline is somewhat limited in scope, but there are significant inroads from many unions' position of complete noninvolvement in evaluation and discipline of peers.

There is at least one historical example of a union taking a quite different approach. Cobble (1991) reports that a union-driven model of peer review among waitresses was successful in contributing to high quality standards for employers and did not diminish union commitment among workers. Performance standards were developed by the union without management involvement. Violations of those standards were seen as issues to be dealt with by the union alone and not by management or via collective bargaining. Union officers held trials of workers accused of poor performance and/or behavior not befitting a union member. Members could be fined if the accusations were substantiated. In addition to setting and maintaining performance standards, the union also provided a hiring hall, took care of sick members, negotiated minimum wage standards, distributed work evenly during downturns (in lieu of layoffs), and was involved in providing training and apprenticeships. This experience suggests that under certain circumstances, union involvement in peer review and even discipline need not be detrimental to member loyalty to the union.

The occupational model of unionism described by Cobble is similar to the way many unions operate in the building trades today. Jobs are short-term and workers move from one employer to another, so the union is the force for setting and maintaining standards. But the occupational model is quite different from the industrial unionism found in many of the manufacturing sites where teams are found. In industrial unionism, standards and rules are negotiated between union and management or set by management alone.

But even within traditional industrial unions, workers do evaluate each other's performance. Putting pressure on workers to end rate-busting or goldbricking are common examples. But these efforts are informal, and workers do not communicate their views of other workers' performance with management. Indeed, workers typically use different standards to evaluate other workers than management does. In contrast, teams might be asked by management to write formal evaluations of their peers that become part of the human resources management system. Unions are likely to protest these requests—although they may make an exception when workers' positive evaluations lead to higher wages for other workers via a pay-for-knowledge system.

On-line teams can also be implemented in nonunion settings, although there they are more likely to be dominated by supervisors. Supervisors grant some workers more voice at their discretion. In this sense, they represent a form of individual proactive voice rather than collective proactive voice that is guaranteed to all workers. In nonunion settings, peer pressure and peer discipline are perhaps even more of an issue than at unionized sites. Graham (1995) describes workers in a Japanese transplant increasing pressure on other workers to meet performance standards, even when injured. She reports that self-discipline and peer pressure were two of the primary means of inducing compliance with the system.

A similar effect is reported by Barker (1993) in the transition to teams at a telecommunications equipment manufacturer. Workers at this site accepted a management-defined set of values and used those values to develop norms and, later, rules to regulate behavior. They felt very committed to the firm and responsible for its performance. They also had a great deal of control and discretion, including the ability to determine if overtime was needed on their team. As these teams evolved, workers began to enforce the rules, which they themselves had created, in a stricter manner than many traditional supervisors would. This led Barker to observe that "the team members had become their own masters and their own slaves" (p. 433).

Off-line Teams

If the data reported by Lawler, Mohrman, and Ledford (1995) and Eaton (1990) above are correct, many more managers and union leaders deal with off-line teams like QWL, QCs, and EI than with on-line teams. In the evolution of joint labor-management decision making, these groups tended to come earlier and were approached much more cautiously. For example, Eaton (1990) reports that about 75% of the local unions in her sample had a policy that under no circumstances are groups permitted to discuss grievances. For 56% that policy is enforced. Kriesky and Brown (1992) report that 57% of UPIU (United Paperworker International Union) locals had some experience with employee involvement programs. Those locals that experienced a significant decline in grievance rates were significantly more supportive of the EI program.

A study by Eaton, Gordon, and Keefe (1992) highlights the importance of the grievance system in new work organization: workers' perceptions of grievance system effectiveness accounts for significant amounts of variance in attitudes toward QWL, union loyalty, responsibility to the union, and satisfaction with the union. Fryxell and Gordon (1989) also find that workers' perceptions of procedural justice in grievance handling is significantly related to satisfaction with the union.

These surveys are useful in assessing the extent of off-line teams, but case studies can be more instructive in understanding the dynamics related to grievances and worker voice. One case study of a failed QWL program identifies a specific problem with grievance handling and the way QWL was implemented (Ellinger and Nissen 1987). That is, union grievers did not have enough time to monitor QWL meetings and be available on the floor to handle grievances. There was a considerable range of opinions among union leaders at this workplace about whether or not QWL interfered with the grievance procedure.

Overall, both on-line teams and off-line teams are quite common in today's workplace. They are often associated with more proactive voice for workers and union leadership, but in some cases workers also suffer a loss of reactive voice. Reactive voice in the form of the grievance procedure is very important in how members evaluate their local union in settings with teams, and its decline can be a threat to incumbent union leadership and perhaps to the union as an institution. Teams can usher in other kinds of problems as well, especially in nonunion settings such as peer pressure and extreme self-discipline.

Impact of Workforce-Level Changes on the Grievance Procedure: Research Directions

Lewin and Peterson's (1988) systems model of the grievance procedure holds that characteristics of the labor-management relationship have an effect on the grievance procedure. Teams significantly modify the relationship, making it less adversarial. Therefore, the model predicts that teams will alter the grievance procedure and its outcomes. The general trend is for grievances to decline with the implementation of on-line or off-line teams. But there is still much to learn about how the process is affected and what impact it has on workers, unions, and management.

One issue is determining what becomes a formal grievance. In a traditional (i.e., nonteam) workplace, the first step in the grievance procedure usually involves a worker taking a complaint to a supervisor and discussing it. A union steward might or might not be present. If the worker is dissatisfied with the outcome, the worker then asks the union to file a written grievance. Because teams have much of the authority that supervisors have in traditional workplaces, a worker who has a complaint in a team setting will first raise that complaint with the team. Teams also have the problem-solving skills to resolve many of the disputes, and they have the opportunity to do so in regular meetings. Cutcher-Gershenfeld (1991) reports that there is more informal resolution of grievances in transformational than in traditional workplaces. Thus it is quite possible that workers in teams and traditional workplaces have approximately the same number of complaints, but that with teams, fewer complaints become written grievances, and so the grievance rate is lower.

Proposition 1: In team settings, worker complaints are more likely to be resolved within the team before they become written grievances.

But inevitably, some disputes will become written grievances. In a team workplace, union leaders and managers receive considerable training in problem-solving skills, which could be applied to settling grievances. In addition, team work organizations typically place a premium on resolving problems quickly and at lower levels of the hierarchy.

Proposition 2: The grievance system will be more effective in workplaces with teams.

Measures of effectiveness might include speed of resolution, resolution at earlier steps in the process, and taking fewer cases to arbitration. The effect will likely be greater for on-line teams than for off-line teams.

Another question is what constitutes a legitimate grievance. This becomes an issue in workplaces with extensive on-line teams. As workers gain decision-making authority over more aspects of their work, they are less likely to be satisfied with decisions made by managerial fiat. As the scope of the management's rights clause shrinks, the area of potential grievances expands. However, this expansion can be counteracted by changes in the union contract associated with on-line teams. For example, contracts that incorporate teams often reduce the number of job classifications to one, virtually eliminating the possibility of any grievance alleging the assignment of work outside of one's classification.

Proposition 3: The grievance system will address different kinds of issues. Some old types of grievances will be eliminated, and some new ones will be added.

A major concern workers have about the grievance procedure under team systems is access to it. Workers at some sites report pressure not to file grievances—either from other workers or from union leaders themselves. Access to an aggressive form of reactive voice (i.e., having a strong advocate in the grievance process) appears to be a major factor in the outcome of union elections; in cases where workers report that there is not enough reactive voice (i.e., NUMMI and Saturn), new leaders were elected. In at least one case in which workers are satisfied with grievance handling (i.e., Wayne), the incumbent leadership was unopposed in three consecutive elections.

Proposition 4: Union leaders who actively enforce both proactive and reactive voice will receive substantial long-term support from the membership. Union leaders who emphasize proactive voice at the expense of reactive voice will ultimately lose support.

There are at least two other potential effects of teams on the grievance procedure that are of special concern to unions. One is an issue more with on-line teams and the other with off-line teams. In workplaces in which all workers belong to on-line teams, one of the union's traditional sources of power—the application of standards and rules equally to all members—may be diminished. Because teams have authority over some decisions that were formerly managerial, and because each team has the latitude to make its own decisions, a variety of practices may evolve within any given workplace. For example, some teams might rotate jobs every day, others every two hours, and still others every week. And so, the outcome of an identical complaint about a job assignment might be different from team to team. Rubinstein (1996) also reports that penalties for absenteeism varied from team to team at Saturn.

Proposition 5: There will be less uniformity in the outcome of disputes in a team setting than in a nonteam setting.

Juravich (1996) suggests that when worker complaints are settled outside the formal grievance procedure, the union loses the ability to use the decisions as precedents, contributing further to a decrease in uniformity. If predicted decline in uniformity does occur, there are potential legal consequences to consider. Workers in the same workplace might be receiving disparate treatment. Each team adopts the practice that works best for the majority of its members, even if the practice differs from other teams. But the question still remains: What recourse is available to the person who holds a minority view and feels harmed by that practice?

Finally, off-line teams (or alternately, workplaces in which only some employees belong to on-line teams) face a special challenge. Employees who participate in teams may obtain special treatment that deviates from the contract. This is similar to the problem described by Kuhn (1961) as fractional bargaining. Work groups that are relatively powerful, perhaps because of the key position they hold in the production process, are able to extract greater benefits than the union can for the membership as a whole. Unless the benefits are ultimately spread to the rest of the membership, this practice can lead to divisions within the local union.

Proposition 6: Fractional bargaining can result when only selected employees participate in on-line or off-line teams, reducing the overall effectiveness of the grievance procedure.

Joint Decision Making at the Institutional Level

Joint decision making at the institutional level includes off-line labor-management committees and the on-line comanagement system found at Saturn. Off-line committees are usually comprised of top management and union leadership, either at the workplace or corporate level. They cover a very broad range of purposes, including general information sharing, overseeing training programs, improving health and safety, planning and implementing organizational change, and planning the strategic direction of the organization. Cohen-Rosenthal and Burton (1993) claim that these committees are the most common form of labor-management cooperation. Cooke (1990) reports that 48% of a sample of manufacturing firms in Michigan had joint health and safety committees and 15% had other kinds of labor-management committees. In his study of 16 hospitals in Minneapolis-St. Paul, Preuss (1998) reports that every hospital that had a union had at least one labor-management committee. Most of those committees were formed in the 1990s.

Many workplaces with on-line or off-line teams at the workforce level also have an institutional level committee to oversee them. For example, Xerox and UNITE (formerly ACTWU) and Corning and AFGWU (American Flint Glass Workers Union) have had a number of labor-management committees since the early 1980s that have guided a relatively long-term process of cooperation (Kochan, Katz, and McKersie 1986; Applebaum and Batt 1994).

Union leaders involved in labor-management committees typically have access to much more business information than they had in the past (Cohen-Rosenthal and Burton 1993). Some union activists fear that by being exposed to the same information as management, union leaders will begin to adopt management's positions. One study of a joint health and safety committee (Kaminski, Graubarth, and Mock 1995) suggests that by having a union-only health and safety committee in addition to the joint committee, the union was able to achieve more of its goals. This approach can also be valuable for the union members of joint steering committees that are guiding the process of designing and implementing new forms of work organization. By taking time to identify union-only goals and meeting regularly to evaluate progress towards those goals, union representatives can ensure that the ensuing plan is one that meets the needs of workers as well as management.

Having union representatives on corporate boards of directors is also a way for the union as an institution to have input into decisions that have traditionally been strictly managerial. But Hunter (1998) concludes that in most cases, these are not joint forms of decision making; they are the primary mechanism for stockholders to monitor managerial performance.

Like workforce-level cooperation, institutional-level cooperation creates opportunities to solve problems in a constructive manner, sometimes before they become written grievances. But unlike workforce level teams, joint committees tend to deal with problems that affect large numbers of workers rather than individual complaints. Thus they may be less likely to deal with grievances concerning discipline and individual overtime complaints and more likely to deal with issues like patterns of work assignments.

Proposition 7: Labor-management committees will contribute to increased effectiveness in resolving certain kinds of worker complaints (i.e., those involving work processes and assignments and those that affect large numbers of workers).

Proposition 8: Labor-management committees will have no significant impact on resolving complaints that are individual in nature (e.g., individual instances of absenteeism or overtime distribution, favoritism, abusive supervision).

A different approach to grievances has begun as a result of a recently formed labor-management partnership between Kaiser Permanente and an AFL-CIO coalition of eight international unions. They have created a voluntary collaborative issue resolution process to handle both contractual and noncontractual issues. The process follows the principles of interest-based bargaining. Workers can choose to use either the traditional grievance procedure or the new collaborative process (Schmidt

1999). This process is quite new, and it is not yet possible to evaluate its effectiveness.

Criticism of existing labor management committees arises when union members of the committee seek to preserve harmony at the joint institutional level at the expense of individual grievances. They might discourage individual workers from filing grievances because it would harm the collaborative relationship between union and management. This is another way in which reactive voice is sometimes sacrificed for more proactive voice. When this occurs, it can result in decreased effectiveness of the grievance procedure and a perception of diminished organizational justice and democracy.

Other issues related to joint decision making at the institutional level and its impact on the grievance procedure can be best illustrated by the experience at Saturn. Saturn has off-line committees that are perhaps more extensive than any others in U.S. industry. It includes the Strategic Action Committee and the Manufacturing Action Council, where decisions are made by consensus regarding long-term planning and ongoing operations, respectively (Rubinstein, Bennett, and Kochan 1993). The union has had an important influence on the strategic direction of the company through these mechanisms (Parker and Slaughter 1994).

But it is the day-to-day management system at Saturn, in which a represented (i.e., union worker) and nonrepresented (i.e., manager) jointly comanage the workplace that is unique. While this dramatically improves the level of collective proactive voice, the design of the Saturn governance system also limits individual workers' access to forms of reactive voice (Rubinstein 1996). Workers sometimes confused the responsibilities of the represented comanager with the role of grievance committeeman and were frustrated when the comanager took a problem-solving approach to individual complaints. Instead, they expected the comanager to take on the traditional union role of worker advocate.

Another feature of the Saturn governance system is that workers cannot file grievances over decisions that the union is party to (Rubinstein 1996). Because so many decisions are made by consensus between union and management, this takes away a very substantial amount of reactive voice for workers. As with other cases in which access to the grievance procedure is limited, this has created some dissatisfaction with the union.

Proposition 9: Forms of joint decision making at the institutional level that limit workers' access to the grievance procedure necessarily decrease the effectiveness of the grievance system.

Proposition 10: Forms of joint decision making at the institutional level that limit workers' access to the grievance procedure will decrease members' commitment to the union.

Some Thoughts on Methodology

Research into the effect of new forms of work organization on the grievance procedure involves some challenges. One of the most fundamental issues to address is to determine what is a grievable event. As noted above, in some forms of joint problem solving, oral disputes that would otherwise become grievances are instead settled via the joint structure. Thus in order to compare traditional with joint problem solving, a necessary first step is to identify disputes that might or might not become formal written grievances. Even among traditional workplaces, there might be considerable variation in the percentage of disputes that become formal grievances.

In general, there will be a far more incomplete record for disputes that do not become grievances than for those that do. Grievances are documented as they wind their way through the various steps. But disputes that are solved orally might or might not become part of a written policy; they might or might not be recorded in the minutes of a team meeting. And so, some method other than examining written records is needed.

The first step might well be a qualitative one, involving interviews with workers, union representatives, and managers about the kinds of disputes or complaints that exist in their workplace and how they are resolved. If such data are obtained from a wide enough variety of workplaces, it could then be used to create quantitative measures about disputes and complaints that can be used to gather data from a larger number of workplaces.

After establishing a clear understanding of potential grievable events, surveys of large samples of workplaces would be very useful in comparing how grievable events are handled in traditional and new workplaces. While this chapter focuses on the problems and successes with grievance handling under cooperative labor-management relations, grievance handling in the traditional workplace has its own set of strengths and weaknesses (e.g., trading of grievances). These should be included for comparative purposes.

One key element of survey work must be the careful definition of the forms of joint decision making that exist in the workplace. Using overly broad definitions or combining terms in indeterminate ways only serves to make the results difficult to interpret. Another important element is to collect surveys from multiple respondents per site. In most organizations, no one individual has enough information to accurately generalize about the dispute resolution process overall. And because of the obvious potential for management, union leadership, and workers to have different views, it is important to get the perspective of all three.

It seems particularly challenging to be able to assess the predicted lack of uniformity in grievance outcomes across teams and the reduced availability of resolutions to serve as precedent. Qualitative work would be especially helpful in this area. One approach would be to select a number of standard grievable events (e.g., absenteeism, work assignment) and follow the event from its initial airing to its final resolution. It would be necessary to collect information about similar grievable events across a number of teams within one workplace, as well as collecting comparable data about grievable events in a traditional workplace.

As with research on many other issues, both qualitative and quantitative data are required to develop a full understanding of the impact of new forms of work organization on the grievance procedure. Qualitative data are required to understand the process but lack the generalizability of quantitative data.

Summary

New forms of work organization have the potential to provide workers with substantially more influence over how work is done and, in some cases, the future direction of their workplace. By creating more collaborative work environments, these new workplaces are also likely to improve the dispute resolution process by solving more problems before they become formal grievances and then by solving grievances more promptly.

However, initial evidence also suggests that workers become dissatisfied when these new forms of proactive voice come at the expense of reactive voice. New limits on access to the grievance system—either through informal pressure from peers or union leaders or by formal mechanisms that disallow grievance against decisions that the union was party to—are sometimes found in workplaces with advanced forms of proactive voice. Further research can explore in a more systematic way how often this tradeoff occurs, how workers respond to it, and what mechanisms can be used to ensure that workers in these new forms of work organization continue to have a strong form of reactive voice. Both proactive voice and reactive voice are essential for maintaining democracy—whether in the political realm or in the workplace.

Endnotes

[1] Osterman's (1994) definition of a self-directed work team is "employees supervise their own work, they make their own decisions about pace and flow and occasionally the best way to get work done" (p. 187). This definition focuses on responsibility but does not make any mention of a group. A respondent could conceivably believe that workers who have this type of responsibility for their own individual work and who necessarily are assigned to a department are therefore a self-directed team, even if there is no team structure in place. Contrast this with Lawler et al.'s (1995) definition: "The work group (in some cases, acting without a supervisor) is responsible for a whole product or service and makes decisions about task assignments and work methods. The team may be responsible for its own support services (such as maintenance, purchasing, and quality control) and may perform certain personnel functions (such as hiring and firing team members and determining pay increase)" (p. 173). Gittleman et al. (1998) define worker teams as "small, intact groups of workers whose members have the authority to handle internal processes as they see fit in order to generate a specific group product, service, or decision" (p. 114).

[2] Some of the discrepancies between these data and the Lawler et al. (1995) data can be explained by the level of analysis. Lawler's group collected information at the corporate level, while Gittleman et al. (1998) focused on the establishment. Large variation is possible within a single corporation, and so the percent of firms using a practice at all is likely a significant overstatement of the extent of the workforce affected. Also, the specific workplace practices included in the two studies differ to some extent.

[3] Some of these practices, especially TQM and QCs, promote standardization rather than the variation that is implied in the term "flexible work practices." According to Gittleman et al. (1998), "flexible work practices" exist when "there is a movement away from a traditional, hierarchical structure in which employees have rigid, narrowly defined roles" (p. 100).

[4] This site was one of several that participated in a study designed to understand how the implementation process is related to the success of HPWO. It was selected by the research staff because implementation was incomplete at the time, and the ultimate level of success was not yet known. About 250 employees work at this company, all in one facility. The majority of hourly employees are represented by one local union. Thirty-five interviews were conducted at this location, all by the author. Some interviews were conducted individually, but most were focus groups of people with the same rank. Participants included 14 hourly employees, 10 team leaders (also hourly), 3 union officers, 5 supervisors, and 3 managers. Hourly employees were specifically selected to reflect the diversity of opinions about HPWO and to include people from a variety of departments. All remaining interviewees were selected on the basis of their position with the company or the union.

References

Adler, Paul S. 1995. "'Democratic Taylorism': The Toyota Production System at NUMMI." In Steve Babson, *Lean Work: Empowerment and Exploitation in the Global Auto Industry*. Detroit, MI: Wayne State University Press.

Adler, Paul S., Barbara Goldoftas, and David I. Levine. 1995. "Voice in Union and Nonunion High-Performance Workplaces: Two Toyota Transplants Compared." Paper presented at IRRA Annual Meeting, Washington, DC.

_____. 1997. "Ergonomics, Employee Involvement, and the Toyota Production System: A Case Study of NUMMI's 1993 Model Introduction." *Industrial and Labor Relations Review*, Vol. 50, no. 3, pp. 416-37.

American Federation of Government Employees (AFGE). 1996. *Government That Works: AFGE Labor-Management Partnerships Making the Difference*. Washington, DC.

Applebaum, Eileen, and Rosemary Batt. 1994. *The New American Workplace: Transforming Work Systems in the United States*. Ithaca, NY: ILR Press.

Barker, James R. 1993. "Tightening the Iron Cage: Concertive Control in Self-Managing Teams." *Administrative Science Quarterly*, Vol. 38, no. 3, pp. 408-37.

Babson, Steve. 1997. "When 'Empowerment' Means 'Exploitation': Negotiating the Terms of Lean Production." *Working USA* (May/June), pp. 69-76.

Bradsher, Keith. 1999. "Saturn Plant's Union Leaders Are Voted Out." *New York Times*, February 26.

Briggs, Steven, and Lisa Gundry. 1994. "The Human Dimensions of Grievance Peer Review." *Journal of Collective Negotiations*, Vol. 23, no. 2, pp. 97-113.

Cobble, Dorothy Sue. 1991. "Organizing the Postindustrial Workforce: Lessons from the History of Waitress Unionism." *Industrial and Labor Relations Review*, Vol. 44, no. 3, pp. 419-36.

Cohen-Rosenthal, Edward, and Cynthia E. Burton. 1993. *Mutual Gains: A Guide to Union-Management Cooperation*. 2d ed. Ithaca, NY: ILR Press.

Cooke, William N. 1990. *Labor-Management Cooperation: New Partnerships or Going in Circles?* Kalamazoo, MI: W.E. Upjohn Institute for Employment Research.

Cutcher-Gershenfeld, Joel. 1991. "The Impact on Economic Performance of a Transformation in Workplace Relations." *Industrial and Labor Relations Review*, Vol. 44, no. 2, pp. 241-60.

Eaton, Adrienne E. 1990. "The Role of the Local Union in a Participative Program." *Labor Studies Journal*, Vol. 15, no. 1, pp. 33-53.

Eaton, Adrienne E., Michael E. Gordon, and Jeffrey H. Keefe. 1992. "The Impact of Quality of Work Life Programs and Grievance System Effectiveness on Union Commitment." *Industrial and Labor Relations Review*, Vol. 45, no. 3, pp. 591-604.

Ellinger, Charles, and Bruce Nissen. 1987. "A Case Study of a Failed QWL Program: Implications for Labor Education." *Labor Studies Journal*, Vol. 11, no. 3, pp. 195-219.

Fryxell, Gerald E., and Michael E. Gordon. 1989. "Workplace Justice and Job Satisfaction as Predictors of Satisfaction with Union and Management." *Academy of Management Journal*, Vol. 32, no. 4, pp. 851-66.

Gittleman, Maury, Michael Horrigan, and Mary Joyce. 1998. "'Flexible' Workplace Practices: Evidence from a Nationally Representative Survey." *Industrial and Labor Relations Review*, Vol. 52, no. 1, pp. 99-115.

Graham, Laurie. 1995. *On the Line at Subaru-Isuzu: The Japanese Model and the American Worker*. Ithaca, NY: ILR Press.

Hunter, Larry W. 1998. "Can Strategic Participation Be Institutionalized? Union Representation on American Corporate Boards." *Industrial and Labor Relations Review*, Vol. 51, no. 4, pp. 557-78.

Ichniowski, Casey. 1992. "Human Resource Practices and Productive Labor-Management Relations." In David Lewin, Olivia S. Mitchell, and Peter D. Sherer, eds., *Research Frontiers in Industrial Relations and Human Resources*. Madison, WI: Industrial Relations Research Association.

Juravich, Tom. 1996. "Empirical Research on Employee Involvement: A Critical Review for Labor." *Labor Studies Journal*, Vol. 21, no. 2, pp. 51-69.

Kaminski, Michelle. 1998. "The Union Role in the Team Concept: A Case Study." In Huberto Juarez Nunez and Steve Babson, eds., *Confronting Change: Auto Workers and Lean Production in North America*. Detroit, MI: Wayne State University Press.

Kaminski, Michelle, Domenick Bertelli, Melissa Moye, and Joel Yudken. 1996. *Making Change Happen: Six Cases of Unions and Companies Transforming Their Workplaces*. Washington, DC: Work & Technology Institute.

Kaminski, Michelle, Robin Graubarth, and Amy Mock. 1995. "Using Grant-based Training as a Vehicle for Lasting Change: Strengthening the Role of Local Health and Safety Activists." *New Solutions* (Winter), pp. 6-14.

Katz, Harry C., Thomas A. Kochan, and Mark R. Weber. 1985. "Assessing the Effects of Industrial Relations Systems and Efforts to Improve the Quality of Working Life on Organizational Effectiveness." *Academy of Management Journal*, Vol. 28, no. 3, pp. 509-26.

Kochan, Thomas A., Harry C. Katz, and Robert B. McKersie. 1986. *The Transformation of American Industrial Relations*. New York: Basic Books.

Kriesky, Jill, and Edwin L. Brown. 1992. "Implementing Employee Involvement: How Paper Companies Gain Local Support." *Employee Responsibilities and Rights Journal*, Vol. 5, no. 2, pp. 117-30.

Kuhn, James W. 1961. *Bargaining in the Grievance Settlement: The Power of Industrial Work Groups*. New York: Columbia University Press.

Lawler, Edward E. III. 1986. *High-Involvement Management: Participative Strategies for Improving Organizational Performance*. San Francisco: Jossey-Bass.

Lawler, Edward E. III, Susan Albers Mohrman, and Gerald E. Ledford, Jr. 1995. *Creating High Performance Organizations: Practices and Results of Employee Involvement and Total Quality Management in Fortune 1000 Companies*. San Francisco: Jossey-Bass.

Lewin, David, and Daniel J.B. Mitchell. 1992. "Systems of Employee Voice: Theoretical and Empirical Perspectives." *California Management Review*, Vol. 34, no. 3, pp. 95-111.

Lewin, David, and Richard B. Peterson. 1988. *The Modern Grievance Procedure in the United States*. New York: Quorum Books.

Luria, Dan. 1997. Performance Benchmarking Service. Ann Arbor, MI. Industrial Technology Institute.

McCabe, Douglas M., and David Lewin. 1992. "Employee Voice: A Human Resource Management Perspective." *California Management Review*, Vol. 34, no. 3, pp. 112-23.

Mesch, Debra J., and Dan R. Dalton. 1992. "Unexpected Consequences of Improving Workplace Justice: A Six-Year Time Series Assessment." *Academy of Management Journal*, Vol. 35, no. 5, pp. 1099-114.

Osterman, Paul. 1994. "How Common Is Workplace Transformation and Who Adopts It?" *Industrial and Labor Relations Review*, Vol. 47, no. 2, pp. 173-88.

Parker, Mike, and Jane Slaughter. 1994. *Working Smart: A Union Guide to Participation Programs and Reengineering*. Detroit, MI: Labor Notes.

_____. 1992. *A Union Strategy Guide for Labor-Management Participation Programs*. Detroit, MI: Labor Notes.

Preuss, Gil. 1998. *Committing to Care: Labor-Management Cooperation and Hospital Restructuring*. Washington, DC: Economic Policy Institute.

Rubinstein, Saul. 1996. Saturn, the GM/UAW Partnership: The Impact of Comanagement and Joint Governance on Firm and Local Union Performance. Unpublished doctoral dissertation, MIT.

_____. 1998. "A Different Kind of Union: Balancing Comanagement and Representation, A Model of the New Local." Working paper.

Rubinstein, Saul, Michael Bennett, and Thomas Kochan. 1993. "The Saturn Partnership: Comanagement and the Reinvention of the Local Union." In Bruce Kaufman and Morris Kleiner, eds., *Employee Representation: Alternatives and Future Directions*. Madison: Industrial Relations Research Association.

Schmidt, Kathy. 1999. "Update on Kaiser-Permanente Joint Labor-Management Partnership." Presentation at annual Union Representatives in the Health Care Industry Conference. Chicago.

Schurman, Susan J., and Adrienne E. Eaton. 1996. "Labor and Workplace Democracy: Past, Present and Future. Introduction to the Special Issue." *Labor Studies Journal*, Vol. 21, no. 2, pp. 3-26

Shaiken, Harley, Steven Lopez, and Isaac Mankita. 1997. "Two Routes to Team Production: Saturn and Chrysler Compared." *Industrial Relations*, Vol. 36, no.1, pp. 17-45.

CHAPTER 8

Trends in Dispute Resolution in the Public Sector

JILL KRIESKY

West Virginia University

If the availability of a contractually mandated grievance procedure represents a guarantee of access to dispute resolution in the workplace, public sector workers enjoy greater protection than their private sector counterparts in the United States. Nearly 44% of federal, state, and local government employees, or about 7 million individuals, work under collective bargaining agreements, virtually all of which include grievance procedures (Brock 1997: 29). Further, most union and nonunion public sector workers can employ a complex array of alternative resolution procedures depending upon the nature of the dispute.

Although the experience varies between federal, state, and local levels, a fair generalization is that the processes available to government employees have evolved substantially over time. At the advent of federal and state public sector bargaining laws, marked approximately by President Kennedy's 1962 Executive Order 10988 granting organizational and bargaining rights to federal employees, large amounts of federal, state, and local organizing occurred. With newly established bargaining relationships, a period of negotiations under new laws and dispute resolution procedures emerged.[1] By 1967, 21 states provided for public sector bargaining (Schneider 1988: 198); by 1988, the number was 38; and by 1996, it was 39 (Lund and Maranto 1996: 23, 48). This slow expansion of public sector bargaining since the 1980s leads Hebdon to conclude that "[m]ost public sector dispute resolution mechanisms were designed over twenty years ago" (Hebdon 1996: 85). He also notes that today public sector dispute resolution procedures are "adapting to meet the more extreme economic, political, and financial environment of the 1990s" (Hebdon 1996: 86). Although his subsequent analysis focuses on changes in strikes and other manifestations of disputes around contract negotiations, the same is true for other forms of dispute resolution as well.

247

Thus the central questions of this chapter are as follows: What is the state to which dispute resolution for public employees at the federal, state, and local levels has evolved? Do the current procedures succeed in upholding the rights of the affected workers, governmental entities, and public? What are the legitimate forces in society pressuring for further change in dispute resolution processes? Are the newly emerging systems likely to respond to the changing environment while holding constant or improving the ability of dispute resolution procedures to protect or restore the rights of involved parties? After a brief overview of the dimensions of the dispute resolution issue, this chapter will address each of these questions in turn.

What Is "Public Sector Employee Dispute Resolution?"

Generally speaking, employment dispute resolution procedures must encompass processes that address both unitwide and individual employment issues. Thus the term refers to avenues such as collective bargaining, union and nonunion grievance procedures, labor-management problem-solving committees, and a myriad of informal processes used in the workplace. This is particularly noteworthy in the case of the public sector in part because federal and state laws mandate a variety of procedures to resolve collective bargaining disputes. While these factfinding, mediation, interest arbitration, and other contract settlement methods legitimately fall within the definition of "employment dispute resolution," an impressive body of scholarly research exists elsewhere, and this chapter will not revisit it.[2]

In addition, civil service reforms through history have produced multiple channels for pursuing violations of rights relating to merit pay, hours of work, pensions, vacations, and insurance and other issues (Craver 1988). Thus government employees frequently face more options for resolving a particular problem than do private sector workers. Given that the options vary between federal, state, and local levels; and between federal agencies; each state; and localities within states; this chapter only attempts to provide the general overview of types of "rights disputes" procedures at each level necessary to summarize their efficacy and proposed changes.

Finally, it is important to note that this chapter focuses most specifically on the influences government bureaucracy and the larger public responsibilities have on the structure and function of dispute resolution procedures. There are other factors which undoubtedly influence public sector dispute resolution which, although acknowledged here, are not fully discussed in the chapter. For example, although public sector union members represent about 40% of the union movement, almost all unionized managers, administrators, and professionals work in the public sector. In some cases, the union-represented managers are the subject of union grievances and arbitration cases filed by member subordinates. The supervisory employees' need for representation and their loyalties to employer and union undoubtedly influence how traditional dispute resolution processes function. Managerial and professional employees may also be more familiar and/or comfortable with peer review procedures and thus may view emerging alternative dispute resolution procedures differently than blue-collar workers. To date, however, there is little to no research on this topic, and it will not be reviewed here.

Existing Avenues for Dispute Resolution at the Federal, State, and Local Levels

The Federal Level—Traditional Dispute Resolution

Unionization and union coverage in the federal sector stand at approximately 31% and 39% respectively (Freeman 1996: 61). Federal workers enjoy use of the grievance procedure to enforce both their collective bargaining agreements and the laws covering employment in the federal government. As is the case with private sector workers, the grievance procedures negotiated in the contract typically provide several steps at which the grievance is discussed and ultimately decided. At successive steps, agents at higher levels of both the management and union structure participate. The final step of most grievance procedures here, as elsewhere, provides for a neutral arbitrator or panel to render a binding decision. Unions can appeal such decisions to the Federal Labor Relations Authority (FLRA) for review on specified grounds relating to the "compelling need" for rules or regulations and exceptions to arbitration awards (Elkouri and Elkouri 1997: 75).

Unlike most private sector workplaces, federal sector collective bargaining agreements do not address many significant workplace issues. Most importantly, wages—paid from departmental budgets set by congressional action—fall outside of contractual negotiations. But many other issues do as well. For example, according to Title VII of the Civil Service Reform Act (CSRA) which governs union-agency bargaining, the following are not mandatory subjects:

> (1) the numbers, types, and grades of employees or positions assigned to any organizational subdivision, work project, or

tour of duty or on the technology, methods, and means of per-
forming work; (2) procedures which management officials of
the agency will observe in exercising any authority under this
section; or (3) appropriate arrangements for employees adversely affected by the exercise of any authority under this
section by such management officials. (Carver 1988: 393)

The Civil Service Reform Act, Section 7106(a)(12) requires that "management rights" subjects such as an agency's mission, budget, number of
employees, and so forth, fall outside of the collective bargaining realm.
Thus many disputes arising over specific issues as well as those regarding the exercise of management rights are not immediately admissible to
the grievance procedure.

Regarding other types of workers' rights, however, federal sector laws
provide multiple avenues for redress. For example, when grievances arise
regarding some suspensions, reduction in grade, or removal for unacceptable performance, the Merit Systems Protection Board (MSPB) can adjudicate the case. Further, because there are also certain disallowed personnel
practices under the Civil Service Reform Act (CSRA) of 1978, an employee
disciplined or allegedly treated unfairly in some circumstances may ask the
MSPB to review agency rules and regulations. If the directive in question
violates the act, the worker can get relief through the subsequent rule
change (Elkouri and Elkouri 1997: 75). However, if the employee chooses,
he/she may instead use the grievance procedure. In either case, the decisions of these bodies may be reviewed by the U.S. Court of Appeals for the
Federal Circuit (see Elkouri and Elkouri 1997: 77-8).

When their claims involve discriminatory employment practices
based on race, color, religion, national origin, sex, age and handicap discrimination and equal pay, federal sector workers have access to the dispute resolution procedures of the Equal Employment Opportunity
Commission (EEOC) after complaining to their agency. But they may
alternatively choose to first use the grievance procedure before going
before the EEOC. Again, under some circumstance, review in District
Court is available. There are also cases in which a worker proceeds
directly to the U.S. District Court after complaining to her/his agency
(see Elkouri & Elkouri 1997 for details). If the worker's dispute involves
both discrimination and other issues, it is referred to as a "mixed" case.
Depending on the grievant's choice, the case could actually receive a
hearing (on various grounds) in the grievance procedure before the
FLRA, MSPB, EEOC and U.S. District Court; or it might proceed
through the agency to the MSPB, to the EEOC, and/or District Court.

Finally, the Comptroller General who oversees the General Accounting Office (GAO) can audit and review laws, rules, and regulations to determine the soundness of federal personnel management. Indeed, because the GAO must analyze on an annual basis whether the Office of Personnel Management (which administers recruitment, hiring, and promotion) complies with the CSRA, a limited opportunity exists to seek redress in this review. In particular, the GAO's review authority extends over any condition of employment which involves the use of appropriated monies. However, as a practical matter, the Comptroller General only responds to joint requests from management and a union for interpretation or application of laws to avoid being "disruptive of the grievance arbitration process" (Elkouri and Elkouri 1997: 97).

Alternative Dispute Resolution (ADR)

Relatively new to the mix of dispute resolution procedures available to federal workers are those labeled alternative dispute resolution procedures (ADRs). ADR procedures usually entail participation by a neutral third party to assist in resolving disputes. The most commonly used procedures, according to a 1997 General Accounting Office report on the subject, are:

- an ombudsman or advisor who as a third party, counsels disputants, researches their situation, and tries to reconcile opposing sides in a dispute;
- mediation, in which a trained neutral aids in the negotiation of a mutually acceptable agreement by suggesting (but without power to implement) an expanded range of options to consider;
- peer review, whereby a trained panel of designated coworkers (employees or employees and managers) hear disputants' positions, then offers a binding or nonbinding decision;
- management review or dispute resolution boards, which provide for disputants' hearing before a panel of managers and, like peer review, issue either a binding or nonbinding decision; and
- arbitration, a voluntary or mandatory process in which a neutral third party conducts a hearing and renders a binding decision (GAO 1997: 12).[3]

The Administrative Dispute Resolution Act of 1990 and its extension in 1996 mandated the voluntary availability of these procedures in federal agencies laboring under multiple and overburdened dispute resolution procedures. Although these new methods would seem to add to the overall number of procedures available, their goal was to reduce the use of the more formal and adversarial fora described above. In 1992 the EEOC similarly encouraged ADR use to resolve cases in the federal discrimination complaint process (GAO 1997: 10). EEOC surveys in subsequent years revealed that to the extent federal agencies used ADR, their focus was almost singularly on the method of mediation. As the limited data described more fully below indicate, mediation appears to be more effective than the traditional discrimination complaint process for resolving this type of grievance thus far (GAO 1997: 16-17).

The State and Local Levels—Traditional Dispute Resolution

At least 35 states under 76 separate laws allow collective bargaining for some or all of the public sector workers in their jurisdictions. Two others provide bargaining rights by the governors' executive orders (Bilik and Dahl 1997: 36).[4] As in the federal and private sectors, the approximately 6.2 million workers covered by agreements typically have access to contractual dispute resolution procedures. Indeed, by the late 1980s, most of the state laws specifically authorized binding grievance arbitration and two states mandated it (Schneider 1988: 233).

To date, no comprehensive database of grievance processes under these laws exist. But again, as in the federal sector, some of the workplace issues typically governed in the private sector by the collective bargaining procedure (and, therefore, the grievance process) are instead governed by law and government adjudication systems. Interestingly, Elkouri and Elkouri (1997) report that "often statutory provisions for collective bargaining and arbitration in public employment are silent regarding the relationship between contractual grievance procedures and statutory procedures such as those under civil service laws." Where the relationships are identified, grievants often have the choice of procedures, though occasionally the collective bargaining procedure prevails. Some of these laws also allow employees to handle grievances without the participation of the union as long as the settlement is consistent with the contract (pp. 123-24).

Again similar to the federal sector, the right to bargain and, therefore, dispute treatment with respect to specific issues is limited at the state and local levels. One analysis of these issues finds that many of the most commonly circumscribed topics relate to school teachers including the right to grieve a tenure decision on anything but procedural grounds; the right to inspect teacher personnel files; the right to bargain class size, curriculum, and school calendars; and other personnel-related matters (Elkouri and Elkouri 1997: 120-22).[5] In a few states, most notably Hawaii and Wisconsin, significant "management rights" issues are removed from dispute resolution (Elkouri and Elkouri 1997: 118).

State and Local ADR

There appear to be no comprehensive data on the use of ADR procedures in the public sector or even on trends for its adoption into state laws and/or local ordinances. However, in 1992, based on a compilation of participants' observations on mediations completed by the State and Local Government Labor-Management Committee and the Federal Mediation and Conciliation Service, Bonner concluded that mediation was much more widespread in the public sector than in the private (Bonner 1992: 7). The Task Force on Excellence in State and Local Government through Labor-Management Cooperation sought information on ADR and workplace collaboration efforts through surveys, contact with international and independent unions representing public sector workers, state and local government professional management associations, the Federal Mediation and Conciliation Service regional offices, and others. The goal of its study was not to determine precisely how widespread the adaption of ADRs to resolve grievances is. However, the project's executive director, Jon Brock, characterizes the proportion of workplaces using these methods as "large, but not a majority, and greater than the proportion involved in cooperative relations around service delivery issues" (Brock 1999).[6]

Interestingly, Brock also notes that unionized teachers stand out as an occupational group which has pursued innovations around ADRs (see, for example, Task Force 1996: 159). The task force's efforts to solicit similar examples from other unionized professional employee and blue-collar occupational groups produced little evidence of ADR use by the former group but considerable use by the latter.[7] While the study did not analyze adoption of ADRs by occupation or offer reasons for these results, one explanation may be that professionals (other than teachers) organize infrequently, only when working conditions are extraordinarily unfavorable. In these situations, the labor relations climate may be too hostile for acceptance of ADR methods.

Overall, it appears that there is a wide variety of dispute resolution procedures in the public sector. In part, this is a result of the continuation of civil service and other administrative procedures developed prior to collective bargaining, coupled with negotiated grievance procedures. But according to the task force report, "the public workplace might be more receptive to . . . [ADRs since] one of the stumbling blocks to wide acceptance of such systems in the private sector was the insistence . . . that use of a company ADR system be a precondition of employment, precluding access to courts" (Task Force 1996: 81). Public sector employers appear more willing to allow continued access to both court processes and grievance procedures.

Efficacy of the Current Dispute Resolution Procedures

Evaluating public sector dispute resolution procedures' efficacy requires consideration of both the extent to which the processes are used and if they are processes yielding equitable outcomes. Researchers have not systematically compiled comprehensive data on either factor across all governmental agencies whether at the federal, state, or local levels, or even completely within a government agency over time. However, their limited examination of data on both questions, as described below, indicate that governmental workers' rights receive relatively good protection.

Before reviewing this collective bargaining-based grievance procedure research, it is important to acknowledge the state of affairs in the nonunion portion of the public sector. It appears that there is little published data analysis on the operation of state civil service or other dispute resolution procedures used in the nonunion public sector. These are procedures presumably used by a significant number of workers, considering that approximately 4.6 million state and local government workers are not affected by a state collective bargaining law (Brock 1997: 36).[8] Further, in some states without laws, cities may provide for collective bargaining by their employees (Elkouri and Elkouri 1997: 103), as is the case in Phoenix, Arizona, and Clarksburg, West Virginia. In instances such as these, grievance procedures may be in place, but we know little about how they work.

The Breadth of Issues Addressed

Katz and LaVan (1991) examined 1300 public sector arbitration cases to identify the types of employees who used the procedure and the central issues of the cases. Suggestive of the wide range of workers' rights issues handled in contractual grievance procedures, they found that unions carried to arbitration cases on wages and benefits, performance evaluation, work assignments, discipline, seniority, unit determination, and hiring (pp. 297, 299). The latter three topics made up more than half of the sample. The subjects mirror those arbitrated in the private sector, although some such as arbitrability, management rights, and union security occur more frequently in the public sector.

A similar study completed in 1996 by Mesch and Shamayeva reports that about half of the 994 public employee arbitration cases studied focused on discipline, wage and benefit issues, with working conditions and assignments, arbitrability, job bidding, union activity, and leave of absence representing another 20% of the cases (p. 123). It is also relevant to this discussion that Mesch and Shamayeva found significantly fewer arbitration cases on termination in the public sector than in the private sector (18% versus 30.4%). One reasonable explanation for the difference is the heavy use of civil service, federal EEO, and other procedures available for solving specific types of grievances.[9] The slightly different explanations Mesch and Shamayeva cite for this phenomenon—that alternative dispute resolution procedures resolve the procedure at earlier stages of the grievance procedure or that the equal employment opportunity laws, public statutes, or civil service systems may temper management's inclination to discharge workers—also speak to the strong safeguards for workers' rights in the public sector (Mesch and Shamayeva 1996: 131).

An analysis of labor-management relations where grievance resolution is disallowed similarly points out the protections provided by grievance resolution mechanisms. Public sector bargaining is banned by law in North Carolina. Through a series of interviews with public managers and a review of discussions between public workers and supervisors under city "meet and confer" policies, Brown and Rhodes found that "the rights of both managers and employees are afforded less protection than would be guaranteed under a formal system governed by standards of 'fair labor practices'" and that the suppressed conflict hurt pursuit of organizational goals. Because women and minorities are more heavily represented in the public sector, they are particularly disadvantaged in these situations (Brown and Rhodes 1991: 27-8).

Actual and Perceived Procedural and Substantive Equity

Evidence of grievance procedures' equity emerges from several measures. One approach to evaluating equity examines whether one party prevails far more frequently than the other in the final resolution of cases. While prevailing on a majority of cases might indicate the superior ability of one side in choosing and presenting arbitration cases, one assumes that over time the losing side would adjust its behavior in these dimensions and that the "win rates" would even out. If the same side still prevails by a significant margin, it may well be true that some aspect of the procedure does not allow for substantive equity. Whether or not there is actual substantive equity, the *perception* by those on the losing side will be that there is not.

In the Katz and LaVan study mentioned above, neither management nor labor appears to prevail more frequently in the procedure. The employer win rate for the sample was 42.6%; for the employee, 43.2%; and 14.1% of cases ended in split decisions (Katz and LaVan 1991: 298). The 1996 Mesch and Shamayeva analysis found management's "win rate" to be slightly higher than the union's (44% versus 37.8%) and a higher percentage split decisions (18.2%). Interestingly, this study also found that when analyzed by category of grievance, management prevailed in two-thirds of the issue areas. Unions prevail more frequently on issues related to an employee's right to appropriate representation in or use of the grievance procedure and discrimination. Cases in the termination, suspension, discrimination, and subcontracting categories ended in split decisions approximately one-third of the time (Mesch and Shamayeva 1996: 125). These figures suggest something of a balance between the parties. If they have about an even chance of overturning all or part of a management decision through grievance arbitration, unions should (and apparently do) feel the procedure is worth using.[10]

Another yardstick of grievance procedure equity appears in studies that review directly the perceived fairness of the process and its outcomes. Two such examinations are given by Mesch (1995) and Zirkel and Winebrake (1994). Reporting on previous studies, Mesch states that a sex bias is present insofar as "a series of studies has described more lenient treatment of female arbitrants (Mesch 1995: 209). However, her statistical analysis of a sample of 271 public sector arbitration cases over five years finds that women lose more cases than men (although the difference is not statistically significant) and receive significantly fewer split decisions even when one controls for the severity of the case (Mesch 1995: 214). While Mesch offers several possible reasons for this outcome—women pursuing grievances less aggressively, receiving less support from male union leaders in arbitration, receiving favorable treatment in earlier stages based on gender, or being allowed to proceed to arbitration by their union even if their case is weak—each suggests shortcomings by the players, but not the actual procedure.

Zirkel and Winebrake undertook a review of case law to determine where the boundaries of "acceptable connections and conduct of labor arbitrators" lie. In short, they attempted to determine whether arbitrators are compromising the procedural or substantive equity of arbitration. They conclude that "reported court decisions setting aside labor awards based on arbitral bias are rare, and those based on misconduct are almost nonexistent" (Zirkel and Winebrake 1994: 166).

Such studies provide only limited evidence of the equity offered by public sector grievance procedures. Given the absence of such data, available information on stewards and grievants' attitudes toward the procedural and substantive outcomes of their grievances at least identifies how well the system is perceived to work. Duane (1991) sought to determine the factors which compelled public sector stewards to use their grievance procedures. The perception of management's willingness to accommodate, a lack of competitive attitude toward management, and access to informal dispute resolution are factors which reduce the likelihood that a public sector steward will file a grievance (pp. 86-7). Private sector grievance handlers on both sides of the table will recognize these as familiar determinants of grievance filing, again inferring that the decision to use the procedure parallels that found in private industry.

The Public Sector Worker Survey of approximately 1,000 public employees, conducted in 1995 for the Secretary of Labor's Task Force on Excellence in State and Local Government through Labor-Management Cooperation, offers some insights into this subject. For example, the survey found that similar to private sector union members, 50% of public employees in unions preferred collective action (in the form of assistance of coworkers) to deal with a workplace problem, and 43% of nonunion workers wanted such help (Freeman 1996: 73).

These figures certainly do not indicate overwhelming support for formal grievance resolution procedures, whether traditional or ADR. But other questions provide stronger evidence of government workers' support for their dispute settlement processes. In particular, 90% of publicly employed union members selected settlement by an outside arbitrator as the preferred method of settling conflict. Of their nonunion counterparts 67% made the same choice. Further, in administering labor-management relations, almost two-thirds of government union members wanted their organizations to rely on independent budgets and staff rather than their employers, and 40% of the public employees agreed. Both numbers are substantially higher than the results for private sector workers (Freeman 1996: 77). Freeman attributes the public workers' confidence in "independence and power vis-à-vis management," in part, to various constraints on their management by civil service regulations and other laws. He found that of the 40% of employees covered by civil service regulations, 71% think that the regulations afford them the fair treatment (Freeman 1996: 74).

Based on these examinations of both the extent to which public sector workers use grievance procedures and the outcomes of grievance cases, public sector workers appear to have reasonable procedural and substantive fairness in the handling of workplace disputes. However, there is a need for additional research to determine whether other administrative avenues for dispute resolution used by union and nonunion grievants provide results similar to those described here. Moreover, the effectiveness of dispute resolution processes described above will not be judged in isolation from the questionable efficiency of the system examined above. It is this concern which produces the pressures for change in relatively well-functioning procedures and which is addressed next.

Pressures for Change in Dispute Resolution

Strong pressures for change in federal, state, and local governments' multiple systems of dispute resolution procedures have emerged over the last decade. These demands for transformation have not gone unheeded. Both government agencies and specially appointed panels have documented the social, economic, and political conditions contributing to the need for new systems; they have recommended alternative procedures; and legislation and/or pilot projects have moved governments at all levels to resolve workplace rights issues in different ways.

At the federal level, two forces—the recognition of the inefficiencies stemming from the multiplicity of the employee grievance fora and the growing demands for more efficient delivery of services in general—have encouraged significant workplace dispute resolution process adjustments. Reflective of longstanding concerns about the existing process, a 1997 General Accounting Office report states, "the redress system—especially insofar as it affects workplace disputes involving claims of discrimination—has been criticized by federal managers, as well as by employee representatives, as adversarial, inefficient, time consuming, and costly" (GAO 1997: 4).[11] Further, largely as a result of the passage of the Americans with Disabilities Act of 1990, the Civil Rights Act of 1991, and downsizing, federal workers' discrimination complaints increased from 17,696 to 27,472—a 55% rise—from 1991 to 1995 (GAO 1997: 9). As a result of these conditions, Congress first passed the Administrative Dispute Resolution Act of 1990, directing federal agencies to develop ADR policies and establishing an office to assist with the task and to compile information on ADR use in the federal sector. Then, after its expiration in 1995 under a sunset provision, Congress permanently reauthorized the act in 1996.

In addition, growing out of the Reagan-inspired demands to "get government off the people's backs" by reducing taxes and the activities they supported, successive administrations have struggled with how to provide higher quality services with fewer resources.[12] In 1993 the Clinton administration produced the most recent solution in its pledge to "reinvent" government with the National Performance Review led by Vice President Al Gore. The subsequent Executive Order 12871 directed federal agencies to evaluate their customer bases and service delivery using labor-management partnerships. The executive order promises "labor-management partnerships will champion change in federal government agencies to transform them into organizations capable of delivering the highest quality services to the American people" (Verma and Cutcher-Gershenfeld 1996: 228). According to one source, because the executive order explicitly enumerates permissive bargaining subjects as mandatory subjects for partnership forum discussions, it provides unions an opportunity to expand their representation of members in a "lasting infrastructure of local-, agency-, and national-level councils" (p. 229). Moreover, the joint problem-solving methods appropriate for restructuring work processes to create services more efficiently may also be applied to solving the workplace disputes in place of more formal grievance procedures.

Some similar and other even stronger pressures have acted on state and local governments during this time period. In May 1996 the U.S. Secretary of Labor's Task Force on Excellence in State and Local Government through Labor-Management Cooperation issued its report documenting these influences.[13] As its title suggests, the task force served as an advocate for change at the state and local levels through efforts similar to those outlined in Executive Order 12871. It argued that the labor-management relations systems set up in most states are twenty or more years old, and the context of labor-management interactions was different then. It asserted that the conflictual collective bargaining relations (including grievance procedures) which are still in place today make it hard to work on the long-term solutions to service improvement and better efficiency.

The task force report lists some of the newly emerging forces. For example, as part of its call for collaboration between labor and management, it argues that government's "customers" have evolving expectations about the services delivered. The task force noted that, as is the case in their private sector purchases, citizens demand better quality output from government. The public is aware of the positive impact of the quality improvement movement in major U.S. industries and wants similar improvements from their tax investments in government services. At the same time, the public has long viewed government leaders and bureaucracy with skepticism and, thus, views its operation (whether with traditional or new methods) with suspicion. The move to improve government efficiency by turning over some of its functions to the private sector is perhaps the most dramatic evidence of this mistrust.[14]

Other factors exert pressure for change too. With increasing longevity of, diversity of, and handicap accommodation for citizens, governments handle an increasing range of problems. Because many federal programs have devolved to the state and local levels, the load is further expanded. Government's roles in other areas are central but not yet clearly defined, as evidenced by the conflict over economic development and environmental protections with which many state and local governments are struggling.

Each of these factors, in turn, affects the attitudes of government workers toward their jobs and the public. Fewer resources and expanded workloads have forced many public workers to "do more with less" and/or abandon more innovative programs. Further, as the task force noted, "Generalized antigovernment sentiment is wearing away at employees' pride, job satisfaction, and productivity" (Task Force 1996: 31). The threat of privatization makes public sector jobs less secure and therefore even less attractive. Indeed, the one positive influence on employees' jobs identified by the task force is the collaborative work relationship developing in workplaces seeking total quality improvement through joint labor-management committee work.

Will the New Forms of Dispute Resolution "Work" for the Parties?

At both the federal and state/local levels, leadership appears convinced that despite the multiplicity of forces pressuring for changes in how government works, the adjustments needed in the public sector will simultaneously improve the quality and efficiency of public service production and allow for quicker and more equitable solutions of workers' grievances. The assumption at the foundation of this conclusion is that alternative dispute resolution procedures are a necessary concomitant to labor-management collaboration on service delivery. Barry Shapiro, administrator in the Office of Personnel Management, makes the following connection:

What do we have to do to make [labor-management coopera-tion] the norm? We need to focus our attention away from our differences on various issues and toward areas of common interest, away from prosecuting legal positions and toward finding solutions to problems.

We need to train the entire workforce, but especially supervi-sors and managers in how to avoid and solve problems rather than just adjudicate disputes. (Shapiro 1992: 511)

Based on the testimony from multiple state and local governments, the Secretary of Labor's Task Force, which included both top labor and management leadership, concludes that "[w]here practiced in a less conflictual and formalistic manner, and more in a way that focuses on workplace participation, collective bargaining relationships demonstrate particular value in supporting better service results" (Task Force 1996: 33). Task Force Executive Director Brock observes more specifically that in most instances of labor-management partnerships, the parties are experimenting with or have instituted ADRs. He notes that in several task force case studies, the first issue around which labor and manage-ment sought to work collaboratively was grievance caseload manage-ment. Generally, when the union and management want to build better relations, they seek to find ways to handle the two areas of traditional conflict—grievances and contract negotiations (Brock 1999).[15]

The supporters of collaboration and ADR offer significant, if not sys-tematic, evidence in support of its effectiveness. At the federal level, the best documented results describe the experiences within the United States Postal Service (USPS). Beginning in 1986,[16] the USPS established pilot EEO complaint mediation projects. In 1994 the agency launched the REDRESS (Resolve Employment Disputes, Reach Equitable Solutions Swiftly) program both to comply with the ADR Act of 1990 and to capital-ize on the federal employee EEO regulations which encourage ADR. Under REDRESS, grievants can request mediation instead of counseling at the informal stage of the procedure. If approved, a mediation session is scheduled within two weeks. If the parties to the mediation reach an agreement, they sign a settlement statement. Both EEO counselors and neutrals external to the process have heard cases in various locations.

Two studies of REDRESS in different locations produce impressive statistics about the effectiveness of the program. A GAO report found that 90% of mediation users believed the process was fair compared to 41% who characterized the traditional process that way. Where only

40% of traditional process users were satisfied with their outcomes, 72% reported satisfaction with their results (GAO 1997: 67). Survey results published by Anderson and Bingham report similar levels of satisfaction. They also found that a majority of respondents acknowledged the perspective of their codisputants, and 70% of both supervisors and employees felt empowered by the mediation (Anderson and Bingham 1997: 609-10).

Under the contractually mandated labor and management partnerships (LAMPs) program, the USPS and the American Postal Workers Union (APWU) undertook collaborative efforts to resolve a grievance overload created and exacerbated by contentious relations between the parties. Starting in 1990, union and management leaders at the Lansing Mail Sorting Center experimented with a combination of joint investigation and screening of grievances, research on frequently filed grievances, peer mediation, and joint task forces on contract interpretation. The efforts produced a reduction in unresolved and new grievances and support for the training of labor and management to continue the use of mediation (Verma and Cutcher-Gershenfeld 1996: 230-32).

Other anecdotal success stories have emerged from federal organizations operating under the Administrative Dispute Resolution Act including the U.S. Air Force, U.S. Department of State, Walter Reed Army Medical Center, and a consortium of federal agencies in the Seattle area (see, for example, GAO 1997). Although it acknowledged the limited amount of data on which it based its conclusions, the GAO found that "ADR processes, especially mediation, resolved a high proportion of disputes, thereby helping [the parties] avoid formal redress processes and litigation" and that "almost all [the employers studied] had positive perceptions of the results of their ADR programs" (GAO 1997: 15, 25). One brief review of the National Partnership Council and various agency partnership councils in the Department of Agriculture, Food, and Consumer Services, and various military installations does not address specifically how these partnerships affect dispute resolution at the agency level. However, it does emphasize that because Executive Order 12871 makes previously permissive subjects of bargaining appropriate topics for partnership discussions, unions have "a unique avenue to expand their capability to represent their members" (Verma and Cutcher-Gershenfeld 1996: 229).

At the state and local levels, the most comprehensive study to date was conducted by the aforementioned Task Force on Excellence in State and Local Government through Labor-Management Cooperation.

After a close study of 47 examples of service-oriented cooperation, the Task Force's Executive Director Jonathan Brock reports dramatic impacts on dispute resolution:

> It was not unusual to see a 75% or greater reduction in filed grievances or a 90% decline in time to settlement. Contracts were often revised to be more flexible and reflective of the need to use problem-solving methods that resolved workplace issues in the context of mutual service obligations. All parties described a quantum jump in trust and informal problem solving. (Brock 1997: 30)

Specifics described in many of the task force case studies are similarly impressive. In Oregon, American Federation of State, County, and Municipal Employees (AFSCME) Council 75, the Oregon Nurses Association, and management of the Oregon Health Sciences University have both reduced the number of steps in their grievance procedure and instituted a grievance adjustment board resulting in a 40% drop in grievances and less reliance on arbitration. While making these changes in their dispute resolution procedures, the parties have also moved forward with labor-management teams. Their work in streamlining and improving the efficiency of the university procurement procedures is predicted to yield substantial savings over time (Task Force 1996: 143). In Phoenix, Arizona, leadership of the International Association of Fire Fighters (IAFF) Local 493 and Phoenix Fire Department management began ten years ago to hold annual planning retreats. Improvements in their relations have resulted in more efficient problem solving. No grievances have required arbitration in ten years (Task Force 1996: 22). In a similar labor-management relationship between a regulated utility and its union in Boston, the problem-solving approach reduced costs of grievance handling significantly.[17, 18] Mediation cases cost $200 on average to complete, where arbitrators' fees alone had averaged $3000 (Task Force 1996: 145).[19]

But other students of labor-management collaboration experiments both at the federal and state/local levels express serious reservations about both the likelihood that collaboration (and the accompanying ADR methods) can work in the public sector and about the usefulness of specific legislation designed to implement it. Dilts summarizes a frequently acknowledged observation that the federal and state laws, regulations, and constitutions limit the scope of issues on which workers, their unions, and management can collaborate (Dilts 1993: 308-9). Likewise, the National Performance Review and joint labor-management teams it created, cited above as a potential source of expanded federal employees rights, faces strong criticisms from observers. One analysis asserts that because it sought to "[graft] greater employee voice onto a merit model that was grounded in management prerogative, the NPR model did not resolve the inherent contradictions between management prerogative and employee voice" (Doeringer et al. 1996: 184). While the GAO's 1997 report on the ADR Act of 1990 presents evidence supportive of the role ADR can play in expediting and improving disputants' satisfaction with resolution procedures, it reports on only one case in which ADR applied to a variety of issues. "The others generally reported confining the use of mediation to discrimination and to a point very early in the discrimination complaint process" (GAO 1997: 23).

Even those who extol collaboration and ADR as virtually essential to the survival of the public sector appear to harbor reservations about their wide applicability. In a chapter entitled "Food for Thought," the Secretary's Task Force outlines extensive topics requiring future research in order to succeed in joint labor-management activities. These include further study on how to "gain and gauge leadership commitment" from both union and management leaders, "how to reconcile different levels of interest among elected and administrative officials" to ensure the consistency necessary for cooperative programs, how to make the "connection between collective bargaining and quality efforts," how best to address "bargainable issues" in problem solving, and how to provide skills needed at all levels to effective participation in cooperation (pp. 110-14).

It is, perhaps, most telling that this committee even suggests that there is not sufficient evidence of "the effect of improved dispute resolution practices on other parts of the service improvement process and other dimensions of the workplace relationship" (Task Force 1996: 114). For example, the GAO study of the U.S. Department of Agriculture use of dispute resolution boards (staffed by the agency's EEO counselors) concludes that there may not be cost savings compared to traditional procedures when one considers the more costly settlements rendered by this process (GAO 1996: 20). This raises the question of whether ADR necessarily contributes to efficiency either in dispute resolution or, given the cost impact on the agency, in the production of services.

In addition, even among the "best practice" studies, there are ample examples of ADR programs curbed or possibly terminated as a result of cost-cutting measures. For example, as already mentioned, training for labor and management mediation representatives is an essential part of preparing for a successful program. But when the comprehensive training program undertaken by the Oregon Employment Relations Board was curtailed in budget cuts, the more than 60 jurisdictions assisted by the board (and others which had not yet started the process) could no longer depend on this expert resource (Brock 1997: 33). The aforementioned, successful LAMPs program at the USPS Lansing Sorting Center reduced grievances and the number of cases taken to arbitration. "The sustainability of the initiative was tested, however, by agencywide layoffs and other cost-based actions" (Verma and Cutcher-Gershenfeld 1996: 323). In short, if the urgency to cut costs overwhelms the necessary start-up cost and time required to establish ADR procedures, they cannot contribute to the effective operation of government agencies.

Finally, the positions of the various stakeholders in government deserve consideration in assessing the potential for change in how public sector services are delivered and the system that resolves workers' grievances in the process. At least one author suggests that the public's generally suspicious attitudes toward both unions and public sector employers "has the potential of geometrically increasing the electorate's suspicion of the public sector . . . [and thus, give] rise to potential difficulties in establishing labor-management cooperation programs" (Dilts 1993: 307).

While Dilts offers no examples of such public resistance to labor-management collaboration, his conclusion raises the need to examine reservations that the central players—labor and management—may have about both joint labor-management programs and ADR. Here, again, research is limited. The task force and the cochairs of the State and Local Government Labor-Management Committee believe that "if public managers and workers fail to seize the initiative . . . sweeping changes may be foisted upon them by . . . citizenry frustrated by government's perceived lack of responsiveness and effectiveness" (Bilik and Dahl 1997: 38). But public employees may view the situation differently according to the Public Sector Worker Survey conducted by Rogers and Freeman (1996). When compared to their private sector counterparts, both unionized and nonunion public sector employees are more likely to have participated in employee involvement programs and are less likely to rank them as effective (and more likely to rank them as ineffective) (Freeman 1996: 75). Moreover, the public sector workers (again, both union and nonunion) are both more likely than private sector workers to believe that employee organizations can be effective even if management does not cooperate with them and to prefer a powerful organization that the employer opposes (Freeman 1996: 77). In sum, the survey results suggest that public workers may not view joint labor-management efforts as an ultimate solution and are more supportive of unions which take a conflictual stand toward management.

There is little hard evidence beyond a limited number of surveys indicating participants' satisfaction with the processes and decisions rendered through ADRs to assess how workers and their public sector unions view such changes in their grievance procedures. Based on their case studies, the task force concludes that "it appeared that the public workplace might be more receptive to such alternative systems, particularly to setting them up in a manner that protected the fact and appearance of neutrality and independence and providing employees access to courts if they felt their case was meritorious or did not choose to use the ADR system" (Task Force 1996: 81). However, even in the approximately half of all federal agencies where ADRs were available in 1996, GAO found that their use was not widespread (GAO 1997: 14-5). Insofar as ADR's use is not similarly advocated by law in state and local jurisdictions, the likelihood of a speedy, extensive implementation of the process is unlikely.

Conclusions

When the first two facets of public sector dispute resolution examined in this chapter—its structures and their effectiveness—are evaluated, they appear to fill important workers' needs reasonably well. While the multiple structures found at various levels of government may not seem appropriately streamlined or efficient, they *do* appear to ensure that public workers' rights disputes will receive fair hearings. That conclusion is reinforced by studies indicating that the procedures succeed in resolving problems on a broad range of issues without inordinately favoring either management or union in the decisions and with an impressive degree of support from the workers who are eligible to use them.

Despite these results, there are calls to streamline and even replace those procedures with ADR. Increasingly, these alternatives are tied to demands that government, whether at the federal or state and local levels, become more efficient in their delivery of services to the public. This is clearly a push for change initiated by taxpayers and their representatives—stakeholders outside of the labor-management relationship. As such, it is unlikely that their primary concern is the protection of dispute resolution procedures that offer strong protection for workers rights. Indeed, a frequently discussed solution to lagging government productivity is the privatization of public sector work—a move that promises to reduce workers' access to dispute resolution procedures, at least until the workers reorganize into a private sector union.

Of course, unionized workers and public managers, recognizing the need to respond to the efficiency demands, have participated in developing and using ADR systems in an increasing number of locations. They have often found that mediation and other processes appear to satisfy grievants and save time and other scarce union and management resources. Top leadership of AFL-CIO public sector unions and state and local governments have endorsed collaborative approaches to problem solving.

But the current examples of ADR use are far from a wholesale adoption of these methods. They are most frequently alternatives in the sense that the formal, traditional union grievance procedures and many civil service processes are still options for grievants, and most government employees do not have access to the ADRs. Neither are today's ADRs fully understood and embraced where they exist. That will take time and training for the parties to accept and to understand the new system. And given the urgency with which some legislators, interest groups, and public managers seek to change the quality and methods of service delivery and to reduce operating costs, neither the time nor money needed will be available. Even then, unions may be loathe to abandon the contractually mandated, neutral-administered, precedent-setting grievance arbitration processes. These were won when the unions exercised considerable power vis-à-vis inexperienced management bargainers in contract negotiations. The security they represent will surely not be surrendered lightly.

For federal, state, and local governments, their employees and their unions, and public stakeholders to make informed choices regarding the changes needed in dispute resolution procedure, considerably more research is needed. All parties need a better understanding of which of the existing contractual and administrative procedures available to public sector workers provides the most efficient and equitable outcomes at each level of government. In addition, they need a systematic and comprehensive view of the variety of ADRs available in federal, state, and local governments. Further, before embracing ADRs, a necessary ingredient to the success of labor-management collaboration efforts, there should be an evaluation of their efficacy. Finally, examining the effectiveness of traditional and alternative dispute resolution systems by occupational group may suggest that dispute resolution is not a "one size fits all" proposition. The procedure appropriate for teachers and other professionals familiar with peer evaluations may not be the same that will resolve conflicts for blue-collar occupational groups with a tradition of union representation or for protective service officers who more frequently than other types of workers are targets of internal administrative reviews that ultimately end in criminal investigations. While this represents an ambitious research agenda, the analysis it would provide could certainly lead to dispute resolution choices that benefit the broadest range of stakeholders.

Whether public employee unions have the power to maintain the current system or at least manage changes in it to preserve the elements essential to them is unclear. Undoubtedly, the approximately 60% of government employees who do not have either collective bargaining rights or representation can expect to face an increasing array of ADRs in conjunction with or maybe even replacing legal and administrative procedures now available. Indeed, there is a desperate need for research which describes and analyzes practice in that portion of the public sector. For the remaining 40% of the workforce, the public sector unions might appear to have considerable strength facing management. But because bargaining is decentralized across federal, state, and local agencies where diverse legislation governs collective bargaining, the public sector labor unions face decentralized negotiations over the issues of workplace collaboration and the changes in dispute resolution they may spawn. A coordinated effort to manage (or even resist) changes in dispute resolution is therefore unlikely. In the federal government, states, and localities where public sector unionism is high, workers may be able to withstand changes they consider threatening. But even in these situations, the demands of the public and elected policymakers and management and union leaders anxious to assuage them may produce significant changes in public sector dispute resolution procedures in the future.

Endnotes

[1] For a discussion of the causality between these public policies and organizing, see Burton and Thomason (1988).

[2] As Jonathan Brock recently noted, more than 100 books have been published on public employee bargaining rights since 1965 (Brock 1997: 29). For thorough treatment of the topic, see Aaron, Najita, Stern (1988); Belman, Gunderson, and Hyatt (1996); and Horowitz (1994).

[3] The GAO report addresses both federal public and some private sector cases. As some of the private sector case studies described nonunionized firms, arbitration appears as an ADR. However, in the federal public sector this form of dispute resolution operates under the collective bargaining agreement.

[4] Scholars have counted the number of states with collective bargaining legislation differently. Thus Bilik and Dahl's (1997) count varies from the 39 states with enabling legislation for at least one sector reported by Lund and Maranto (1996) one year earlier.

[5] The number and location of states under which each of the practices named here have been ruled nonbargainable varies. Interestingly, even though teachers are the largest occupational group represented by unions in this country, they do not appear to have pursued standardization of professional rights across states.

[6] Because there is no formal requirement for reporting state and local government collective bargaining agreements, it is unlikely that comprehensive data on this subject are available even for a single state. Where they operate, state employment relations boards and the FMCS regional offices have the limited existing data.

[7] The committee also found a few examples of collaborative efforts where no union exists, but they represent a small portion of the case studies (see U.S. Secretary of Labor's Task Force 1996: pp. 149-52). None appeared to include ADR processes for resolving workplace disputes.

[8] The states without any public sector bargaining laws are Alabama, Arizona, Arkansas, Colorado, Louisiana, Mississippi, and West Virginia (Elkouri and Elkouri 1996: 103).

[9] Recall that the overburdening of these procedures prompted the passage of the Administrative Dispute Resolution Acts of 1990 and 1996.

[10] According to this line of reasoning, public sector workers might be more likely to use their grievance procedures than those in the private sector, since the union "win rate" for private sector arbitrations is lower (37.8% for public sector versus 30.4% for private sector) (Mesch and Shamayeva 1996: 125). The authors of the study reporting these figures note that the scope of bargaining and therefore arbitration is more limited in the public sector. They postulate that the categories of public sector grievances settled by arbitrators are those which unions are more likely to win (Mesch and Shamayeva 1996: 130).

[11] GAO characterized the labor-management relationship similarly in 1991 (see citation). Feder (1989), writing from experience in (though not on behalf of the Office of the General Counsel of the Federal Labor Relations Authority), also spotlights the duplicative and inefficient nature of the available procedures.

[12] For a brief overview of recent attempts at total quality management in the federal sector, see Doeringer, Watson, Kaboolian, and Watkins (1996: 182-4).

[13] The following description relies heavily on Chapter 2, pp. 29-40, *Working Together for Public Service*, the report of the U.S. Secretary of Labor's Task Force on Excellence in State and Local Government through Labor-Management Cooperation, May 1996. Hereafter, the body is referred to as the task force.

[14] The Secretary's Task Force found significant discussion around this issue, but concluded that "[d]espite the increased level of discussion and debate on privatization or contracting out, especially in non-traditional areas, the extent of any increase in it is far less clear, and may be overstated in the current conventional wisdom" (Task Force 1996: 47). Further, the committee found that when public sector workers were given

opportunities to bid against private companies for delivery of services, their output and quality exceeded the private competitors (Task Force 1996: 32). However, whether increasing at a slow or significant rate, public sector workers whose jobs are privatized will at least in the short run lose access to the dispute resolution procedures available to them in the union or even nonunion public sector.

[15] This is not to say that the parties are immediately dismantling traditional dispute resolution procedures. Typically, they use ADRs as "pilot programs" which either operate alongside contractual grievance procedures or replace the traditional language only after they have proven their effectiveness as described below.

[16] The U.S. Postal Service actually began experimenting with one form of ADR, expedited arbitration, in 1974. Grievances on most suspensions of 30 or less days were eligible for a hearing within 10 days of the request; hearings lasted no longer than 1 day; and the arbitrator rendered a decision at the conclusion of the case or within 48 hours. In 1975 this became a permanent part of the contract dispute resolution procedure (Kriesky 1994: 244).

[17] Although the employer was privately owned, the Task Force included it in its study since as a regulated utility its operation was similar to a public sector agency (Task Force 1996: 145).

[18] It is typically assumed that such savings accrue, particularly to mediation processes which reduce the need for more expensive arbitration proceedings (see GAO 1997: 3). To the extent that unions are able to process more grievances through the mediation step than through arbitration because of the lower cost, one can argue that this form of ADR expands workers' rights by providing wider availability to advanced steps of grievance resolution.

[19] See Bonner (1992), Skratek (1987), and Silberman (1989) for additional discussion of positive results.

References

Aaron, Benjamin, Joyce M. Najita, and James L. Stern. 1988. *Public Sector Bargaining.* 2d ed. Washington, DC: Bureau of National Affairs.

Anderson, J. F., and L. B. Bingham. 1997. "Upstream Effects from Mediation of Workplace Disputes: Some Preliminary Evidence from the USPS." *Labor Law Journal,* Vol. 48, pp. 601-15.

Belman, Dale, Morley Gunderson, and Douglas Hyatt. 1996. "Public Sector Employment in Transition." In Dale Belman, Morley Gunderson, and Douglas Hyatt, eds., *Public Sector Employment in a Time of Transition.* Madison, WI: Industrial Relations Research Association.

Bilik, Al, and Roger Dahl. 1997. "State and Local Government Labor Relations: Past, Present and Future." *Perspectives on Work,* Vol. 1, no. 3 (December), pp. 35-8.

Bonner, J. 1992. *Grievance Mediation in State and Local Government.* Washington, DC: State and Local Government Labor-Management Committee.

Brock, Jonathan. 1997. "Labor Relations in Public Employment, Three Decades Later: The Prospects in State and Local Government." *Perspectives on Work,* Vol. 1, no. 3 (December), pp. 28-34.

_____. 1999. Telephone interview with author, March.

Brown, Roger G., and Terrel L. Rhodes. 1991. "Public Employee Bargaining under Prohibitive Legislation: Some Unanticipated Consequences." *Journal of Collective Negotiations*, Vol. 20, no. 1, pp. 23-30.

Burton, John F., Jr., and Terry Thomason. 1988. "The Extent of Collective Bargaining in the Public Sector." In Benjamin Aaron et al., eds., *Public Sector Bargaining*. 2d ed. Washington, DC: Bureau of National Affairs.

Craver, Charles B. 1988. "The Regulation of Federal Sector Labor Relations: Overlapping Administrative Responsibilities." *Labor Law Journal*, Vol. 39, no. 7, pp. 387-400.

Dilts, David. 1993. "Labor-Management Cooperation in the Public Sector." *Journal of Collective Negotiations*, Vol. 22, no. 4, pp. 305-11.

Doeringer, Peter B., and Linda Kaboolian, Michael Watkins, and Audrey Watson. 1996. "Beyond the Merit Model: New Directions at the Federal Workplace?" In Dale Belman et al., eds., *Public Sector Employment in a Time of Transition*. Madison, WI: Industrial Relations Research Association.

Duane, Michael J. 1991. "To Grieve or Not to Grieve: Why 'Reduce It to Writing'?" *Public Personnel Management*, Vol. 20, no. 1 (Spring), pp. 83-90.

Elkouri, Frank, Edna Elkouri, and Marlin M. Volz and Edward P. Goggin, co-editors. 1997. *How Arbitration Works*. 5th ed. Washington, DC: Bureau of National Affairs.

Feder, D. L. 1989. "Pick a Forum—Any Forum: A Proposal for a Federal Dispute Resolution Board." *Labor Law Journal*, Vol. 40, no. 5 (May), pp. 268-80.

Freeman, Richard B. 1996. "Through Public Sector Eyes: Employee Attitudes toward Public Sector Labor Relations in the U.S." In Dale Belman et al., eds., *Public Sector Employment in a Time of Transition*. Madison, WI: Industrial Relations Research Association.

Hebdon, Robert. 1996. "Public Sector Dispute Resolution in Transition." In Dale Belman et al., eds., *Public Sector Employment in a Time of Transition*. Madison, WI: Industrial Relations Research Association.

Horowitz, Morris A. 1994. *Collective Bargaining in the Public Sector*. New York: Lexington Books.

Katz, Marsha, and Helen LaVan. 1991. "Arbitrated Public Sector Employees Grievances: Analysis and Implications," *Journal of Collective Negotiations*, Vol. 20, no. 4, pp. 293-305.

Kriesky, Jill. 1994. "Workers' Rights and Contract Grievance Dispute Resolution." In Jack Rabin, Thomas Vocino, W. Bartley Hildreth, and Gerald J. Miller, eds., *Handbook of Public Sector Labor Relations*. New York: Marcel Dekker, Inc.

Lund, John, and Cheryl Maranto. 1996. "Public Sector Law: An Update." In Dale Belman et al., eds., *Public Sector Employment in a Time of Transition*. Madison, WI: Industrial Relations Research Association.

Mesch, Debra J. 1995. "Arbitration and Gender: An Analysis of Cases Taken to Arbitration in the Public Sector." *Journal of Collective Negotiations*, Vol. 24, no. 3, pp. 207-18.

Mesch, Debra J., and Olga Shamayeva. 1996. "Arbitration in Practice: A Profile of Public Sector Arbitration Cases." *Public Personnel Management*, Vol. 25, no. 1 (Spring 1996), pp. 119-32.

Schneider, B. V. H. 1988. "Public-Sector Labor Legislation—An Evolutionary Analysis." In Benjamin Aaron et al., eds., *Public Sector Bargaining*. 2d ed. Washington, DC: Bureau of National Affairs.

Shapiro, Barry. 1992. "The Future of Labor Relations in the Federal Sector." *Labor Law Journal*, Vol. 43, no 8 (August), pp. 508-13.

Silberman, A. D. 1989. "Breaking the Mold of Grievance Resolution: A Pilot Program in Mediation." *The Arbitration Journal*, Vol. 44, no. 4, pp. 40-5.

Skratek, S. P. 1987. "Grievance Mediation of Contractual Disputes in Washington State Public Education." *Labor Law Journal*, Vol. 38, no. 6, pp. 370-76.

U.S. General Accounting Office. 1997. *Alternative Dispute Resolution Employers' Experiences with ADR in the Workplace*. Report GAO/GGD-97-157 (August).

U.S. Secretary of Labor's Task Force on Excellence in State and Local Government through Labor Management Cooperation. 1996. *Working Together for Public Service*. Washington, DC: Government Printing Office.

Verma, Anil, and Joel Cutcher-Gershenfeld. 1996. "Workplace Innovations and Systems Change." In Dale Belman et al., eds., *Public Sector Employment in a Time of Transition*. Madison, WI: Industrial Relations Research Association.

Zirkel, Perry A., and Peter D. Winebrake. 1994. "'Ain't Misbehavin'? The Legal Boundaries of Bias and Misconduct of Labor Arbitrators." *Journal of Collective Negotiations*, Vol. 23, no. 2, pp. 163-69.

CHAPTER 9

Dispute Resolution in the Building and Construction Trades

HEATHER GROB
The Center to Protect Workers' Rights

> No single major feature of collective bargaining in this industry,
> such as the geographical scope of bargaining and areawide agree-
> ments or jurisdiction or hiring arrangements can be understood
> apart from the industrial relations system as a whole. (Dunlop
> 1984)

Declining employer attachments and increasing firm mobility have
meant that long-term careers with one employer are no longer the
norm. For many, significant tenure or seniority is not a normal expectation. Workers in alternative work arrangements have found themselves
unable to achieve statutory rights, since those governing working conditions were written with traditional employment relationships in mind.
Simultaneously, workers want greater voice on a wide range of issues on
the structuring of work and benefits, challenging traditional union
strategies under uncertain employment conditions. Given these trends,
industrial and service unions and their observers in academe might consider learning from the construction unions' representational model,
including various self-organizational and multiemployer systems for
determining professional rules of entry, qualifications, and job referrals.

Construction unions typically play a key role in training, skill qualification, job referrals, maintenance of craft lines and craft discipline.
These reduce the occasion for grievance arbitration arising from the
exercise of employer authority. In the unionized portion of the construction industry, authority is frequently exercised by the union (or joint
labor-management committees in which unions are often the moving
party) rather than the employer. Because of these major differences,
union tribunals play a greater role in settling workplace disputes than
they do in industrial settings. Thus rules are often enforced through
arbitration or internally by the union.

273

Research on the adaptability of the craft union through perilous economic conditions could provide important lessons for industrial and service sector unions facing the same conditions that have always characterized construction: highly competitive bidding processes, institutionalized outsourcing and subcontracting, constant introduction of new technology and new work organizations. A comprehensive review of forms of self-organization would also provide direction on issues of great moment to construction workers, including questions about how these organizations are self-directed and peer reviewed.

The major objective of this chapter is to outline the important role of dispute resolution systems in construction and to provide background for further research. I first outline major differences in dispute resolution between the industrial and craft bargaining system. Second, I review types of disputes that are most common and point to some gaps in the literature. Finally, because there is not much known about how dispute resolution systems function in practice and because there is a great deal of variation by agreement, I outline some research questions.

How Construction Is Different: Defining and Preserving Craft Jurisdiction

Employment relationships in construction differ in important respects from those in other industries, and those differences carry important implications for dispute resolution. For the industrial worker, job attachment precedes union attachment such that industrial union disputes center around one large employer. For the craft worker, union attachment often precedes attainment of employment (with a certain occupational status) such that union activities are centered around labor-management agreements, jurisdiction, and professional standards. The union typically assists the individual in obtaining employment with signatory contractors through a formal hiring hall or other type of referral system. This means that craft union membership is not contingent on employment with any particular employer but on upholding certain standards, work rules, and codes of conduct.

Further, the nature of the construction industry, where long-term employment is rare, virtually eliminates grievance arbitration over layoffs and terminations. The pattern is rather to return to the hiring hall and seek employment elsewhere through the union. (Important exceptions occur on large industrial and heavy construction projects where long-term employment provides an appropriate setting for grieving layoffs and discharges.) The absence of seniority provisions in construction employment further reduces the motive to grieve layoffs and terminations.

The crucial roles unions play in determining skill qualification, access to apprenticeship and training programs, and access to referral systems all lead to the exercise of authority by the union in employment matters. This increases the occasion for conflict between union executive authority and individual workers. Thus union tribunals at both the local and national levels play critical roles in adjusting employment disputes that in other industrial settings are resolved through grievance arbitration. Interestingly, the preeminence of internal union dispute settlement has not reduced collective bargaining provisions for grievance arbitration in construction. In 96% of agreements on file at the Construction Labor Research Council, familiar and standard grievance arbitration clauses are present. However, interviews with both management and union representatives indicate that those provisions are mainly used on long-term projects.

Doeringer and Piore (1971) provide a useful comparison between craft and other labor markets. Unions that are organized with a single establishment are typically passive regarding wage structures and administration but seek to affect internal allocation of jobs. Craft labor unions are actively involved in determining the wage structure and administration and seek to control entry to the occupations. They note, "Occupational internal labor markets predominate where the employment relationship is casual" (1971: 3). The craft internal labor market is defined by the local union's geographical and occupational jurisdiction. In craft unions, entrance rules are more selective than those often found in blue-collar manufacturing, where workers are assumed to be of roughly equal skill and rank. Also germane to the discussion of dispute resolution is the particular craft identification achieved, skills acquisition, assignment of risk, uncertainty and litigation, and income instability that typify building and construction work.

Because of this multiemployer system of organization, union construction workers tend to identify with a particular and fairly well defined craft, such as "electrician" or "laborer," rather than as employees of a construction firm. There are fifteen international craft unions affiliated with the Building and Construction Trades Department of the American Federation of Labor and Congress of Industrial Organizations (AFL-CIO).[1] Each one is organized by a major trade, or group of trades, represented in building, construction, and many maintenance activities. A single employer may have agreements with several local or international unions, depending on the type of work done.

Craft loyalty is built through a system of apprenticeship and training that will allow an individual to obtain "journeyman" qualifications.[2] Journeyman qualifications are typically obtained through two to five years of

apprenticeship consisting of classroom instruction and on-the-job training and conferred through an examination board. This system of skills
attainment differs from the industrial union model where the employer
is expected to hire trained workers or to invest in the training of individual workers. Union responsibility for this system of review and development of apprentices into journeymen establishes the union's commitment to professionalism and quality rather than merely to seniority in
employment decisions. Several sociological studies, most notably Applebaum (1991) and Reimer (1980), have detailed the role of the apprenticeship process in building craft identity, loyalty, and pride.

The union sector's interest in training is clearly shown in its bargaining activities and inclusion of cents-per-hour contributions to joint
apprenticeship and training programs. This interest appeals not simply
to a specific establishment's obligation to its employees but to general
workforce quality, craft loyalty, and pride. A contractor is clearly responsible for quality of the end construction product or service, but the craft
union also takes responsibility, often assigning the first-hired journeyman as the foreman. The craft union employee is entrusted with significant autonomy on the job. This differs from an industrial union model,
where it is traditionally assumed that the company-assigned foreman is
responsible for quality control. The standard, code, or work rules of the
craft are taught through apprenticeship and are upheld through member oath and enforcement of the union's constitution. Together these
elements form a system of self-regulation governed by legal requirements, selection of members, and peer review.

In addition to the fundamental employment relationship, there are
unique economic factors affecting building and construction disputes.
Except for prefabrication shops, the production site is the same as the
end product, placing workers in close proximity with the owner and further strengthening the level of professionalism required by the union. In
fact, construction workers may file mechanics' liens, which legally enti-
tle workers to claim some interest in the improved value of the property
itself, much as a basketball team or symphony orchestra may claim some
ownership of profits in the event of dispute over pay. In addition, specialized products require specialized skills. There must be agreement
that certain tasks will require a certain set of skills. Unions and employers try to agree on a general journeyman to apprentice ratio that will
provide on-the-job training to a sufficient number of new employees.

The construction industry is dominated by small employers. While
union employers tend to be larger than average, 82% of the industry's

employers have fewer than ten employees (U.S. Department of Commerce 1997). This organizational structure—with a few project coordinators and general managers and several subcontractors—persists because it is a means of spreading risk over uncertain financing, bidding, and production processes. The product owner or general manager of the project will coordinate activities among many employers. In the industrial sector, this type of industrial organization is generally the exception to the rule and is met with a great degree of resistance from industrial unions.

Perhaps most importantly, construction activities are characterized by a great degree of uncertainty and litigation. The business is particularly vulnerable to changes in the weather and financial and economic crises. Project financing or budgetary allotments may fall through or delays may occur, constituting breach of contract. There is a higher degree of business failure during economic downturns than for other industries (Center to Protect Workers Rights 1998). The *Engineering News Record* described the "awful litigious nature of the industry" that has developed from "unabashed risk shifting" in highly competitive bidding for construction contracts. Several actors—owners, developers, engineers, professional societies, general and specialty contractors, architects, designers, and insurers—all invested in a single construction project may be involved in business disputes. Disputes between contractors are common. The Construction Industry Dispute Avoidance and Resolution Task Force (discussed briefly in Dunlop and Zack 1997) is designed to reduce litigation and promote alternative dispute resolution methods among employers.

Workers are greatly affected by such large degree of uncertainty and assignment of risk. One contractor association representative described the phenomenon as "pushing risk to the lowest common denominator."[3] Many craftspeople work from day to day, with little guarantee of a paycheck at the end of a work period. Income instability is also a common effect of frequent bouts of unemployment with sporadic job tenure patterns. Skilled workers may work 60 to 70 hours a week during peak seasons and may draw unemployment insurance or work a few indoor jobs during the winter. Additionally, although they may know others on their work crew, workers will not generally know others employed on the project, particularly if those workers come from a nonunion employer or temporary agency. An environment that establishes few qualifications for construction employment will lend itself to little trust and makes it difficult to coordinate team-building activities.

Labor laws have recognized the unique character of the industry in its allowance of prehire and "restrictive subcontracting" agreements (Hardin

1992: 1350-62). This recognition enables building and construction trade unions and their employers to engage in a number of preproject agreements. Dispute resolution is a key component of most of these agreements.

Types of Disputes and Mechanisms for Resolution

In the construction sector, timely resolution of disputes has long been an objective of bargaining agreements and has been addressed in a number of ways. Dispute resolution activities are not limited to arbitration but range from judicial processes to mediation of disputes by union representatives, joint labor-management boards, or neutral arbitrators. On larger, long-term construction or maintenance jobs, the ongoing employment relationship lends itself to standard arbitration clauses in collective bargaining agreements. Both the employment relationship and dispute resolution more closely resemble industrial-style arbitration. The short-term relationships that are more typical in the industry are fertile ground for the development of a multiemployer system of employment security and justice that would otherwise be difficult for itinerant workers to achieve.

Disputes over Terms of Collective Agreement

Disputes may arise over the interpretation of the meaning and application of a collective bargaining agreement (grievance arbitration) or through negotiations on the terms and conditions to be incorporated in agreements (interest arbitration) (Dunlop and Zack 1997: 4). Grievances filed by a union against an employer are less likely to arise in construction than they are in other industrial settings, unless in response to a mass layoff on a long-term job. When disputes arise, they are more likely to be issues of unresolved negotiations than grievances, but most construction agreements contain grievance procedures as part of the collective bargaining agreement.

As mentioned above, grievance procedures are almost universal. They are found in 1,026 of 1,070 (or 96%) of construction's collective bargaining agreements in effect in 1994.[4] Most of these procedures contain no strike/no lockout clauses and provide for arbitration through a list supplied by the Federal Mediation and Conciliation Service or the American Arbitration Association. Several provide for arbitration through a national labor-management group operating in their industry segment. Parties are generally fairly comfortable with these agreements. The Federal Mediation and Conciliation Service reported only 21 work stoppages in construction in 1998, representing less than 1% of all notices to mediation agencies of bargaining impasse.[5] Unfortunately, no further information was available on whether these disputes were over rights or interests.

Some of the national labor-management groups deal with both rights and interest disputes. In 1920 the International Brotherhood of Electrical Workers and the National Electrical Contractors Association established the Council on Industrial Relations for the Electrical Contracting Industry, providing a "medium for coming together, carrying on frank discussion and effecting an understanding." The objective in establishing a national joint labor-management council was to resolve labor disputes in a just and equitable fashion, rather than to succumb to turmoil and strife characterizing the time period following World War I. The council is one of the longest-standing and best examples of successful resolution of disputes. John H. Fanning, former chairman, National Labor Relations Board, remarked on June 29, 1987:

> After virtually a lifetime of observing Labor and Management trying to devise successful mechanisms for the fair and peaceful resolution of their disagreements, I have seen none better than the Council on Industrial Relations for the Electrical Contracting Industry. (Council on Industrial Relations 1995: 22)

According to both IBEW and NECA, the joint resolution of disputes through the council has been met with considerable success. Through December 1998, the council heard and adjudicated 6,909 cases, resolving every case before it through voluntary cooperation and unanimous decision of its joint labor-management board (Council on Industrial Relations 1995). From 1988-98 a total of 1,479 decisions were rendered by the council; 928 (63%) were unresolved interest negotiation issues and 551 (27%) were grievances over rights (Council on Industrial Relations 1999). According to the council, many more thousands of cases were amiably resolved at the local level without resort to higher-level procedures or strikes. In 1974 the IBEW Convention briefly altered the system by passing a resolution for "modified language" that did not require compulsory arbitration. This change resulted in several strikes and impasses in negotiations. A few of those strikes resulted in cancellation of agreements by some employers. Since then, a majority of local unions returned to the "standard language" in their contracts that binds parties to honor decisions by the council. The council has saved the industry many millions of dollars while providing stable employment and income for IBEW's members (IBEW 1991).

Other union-contractor association agreements will provide for national, regional, or local joint labor-management boards to resolve disputes. For instance, the bricklayers constitution states:

> The formulation of a collective bargaining agreement shall be the work of the Negotiating Committee which, when meeting with like representatives of employers, shall, together with the employer representatives, constitute a Joint Arbitration Board which shall consider all matters of mutual interest to employers and employees as may be referred to it. The decisions and findings of the Joint Arbitration Board shall be conclusive and binding upon all parties concerned. All questions to be settled by the Joint Arbitration Board must be referred to it without being acted upon independently by any party to the agreement. Such other matters as the Local Union may direct, or that have a tendency to cause controversy between the Local and the employers, shall be referred to the Negotiating Committee and to the Joint Arbitration Board, subject to any provisions for an alternative method of settlement in the collective agreement between the Local and the employers. The Negotiating Committee shall consist of at least three (3) members, one of whom shall be the Business Manager of the Local Union (or other officer primarily responsible for the day-to-day affairs of the Local), who shall serve as the committee's chairperson. The remaining members of the committee shall either be separately elected to the committee at the Local's general election of officers, or shall be elected officers of the Local designated by Local's Constitution and By-Laws to serve on the committee by virtue of office. (International Union of Bricklayers and Allied Craftworkers 1995: 31-32)

It is assumed, as is often the case, that disputes with employers will be settled by informal resolution through negotiating boards before they require resolution through a higher and more formal structure. The decision to use certain forms of arbitration is highly decentralized: local unions may have the option to use arbitrators from FMCS, AAA, or institute other modern forms of dispute resolution as long as they are in conformity with the respective International Union's constitution.

Disputes over Union Membership and Referral to Employment

Member-to-union disputes often center around employment referral issues. Some unions have exclusive hiring halls where all employment is determined through local union referral procedures under its agreements with signatory contractors. Disagreement between the union and the employer may arise as to the qualifications of particular individuals for the job. In that case, especially where there is no formal hiring hall, unions will sometimes replace an individual in order to satisfy the employer's demands for a certain set of skills. If the employer's assessment is contrary to the terms of the agreement, to the principles of the union constitution, or to local or national employment laws, the union official is expected to remind the employer of his or her obligation. The official, often called the "business agent" or "business representative," is often given the responsibility of enforcing the employment contract but may choose how to conduct the business of the union. The level of formality ranges from phone calls or meetings with employers to filing charges with joint labor-management boards or the National Labor Relations Board.

The "hiring hall" or referral system may work on a local, regional, national, or international level. Most bricklayer locals no longer operate local hiring halls but have merged to "mega-locals" which operate referral systems on a broader regional basis. Rules on hiring hall operation are usually set forth in local collective bargaining agreements, with guidelines on fairness to members set and enforced by the international union. Local unions and employers are given a great deal of flexibility in determining hiring decisions. The unions' relative level of sophistication in anticipating demand for employment and matching craftsmen and craftswomen to employers also varies greatly from computer generated lists, to manual lists, to a business agents' mental list of projects planned and individuals out of work. The technology may depend on contractual requirements set forth in collective bargaining agreements, national union policies, size of the local union, and its economic position. In a craft union, the principle of "first in, first out" often is used to allocate job opportunities to those with longest periods of unemployment but may be modified by considering total days worked, pay, skill, or personal factors (Doeringer and Piore 1971: 5).

Most building and construction trades agreements will attempt to uphold the requirements set forth in the constitutions of the international unions, all of which contain tribunal systems that help to regulate their own membership and union activities. The constitutions typically lay out the offenses for which a member may be charged and prescribe the method by which cases will be investigated by the union's business agent, business representative, or international representative. The constitutions also specify avenues for appeal by a member found guilty or a party dissatisfied with the dispute adjustment. Any action "unbecoming a member," "bringing disrepute," or otherwise damaging the labor-management agreement is generally considered a serious offense. For example, the International Brotherhood of Electrical Workers (IBEW) constitution includes the types of charges commonly specified in building and construction trade constitutions (see Appendix). Any member convicted of any one or more of the named offenses may be assessed fines or suspended or both or expelled. (An officer convicted may be removed from office.)

Two rules in particular are typical of building trade union constitutions. First, offense (f) forbids an IBEW member from working for or on behalf of any organization whose position is adverse or detrimental to the union. Many constitutions specifically forbid "independent contracting," or "lumping" (working for a lump sum) and view those work arrangements as detrimental to sound union principles. Second, section (o) makes poor quality of work an offense. Maintenance of quality and safety standards is of great importance to all building trade unions and is enforced through peer review and management.

In the building and construction trade unions, charge and trial systems typically operate through an executive board or trial committee of the local union, unless the charge is brought against officers and representatives of the local union. Charges are normally presented in writing, signed by the charging party, referencing the codes or rules allegedly violated. Relevant dates and places and sometimes witnesses are also required. According to the IBEW constitution, the accused must allow an active IBEW member in good standing to represent him and must be granted a fair and impartial trial. The findings must be reported to the next local union meeting. The IBEW constitution also contains language setting limits on the time periods for which charges can be filed (60 days), and the trial board shall proceed with the case (45 days). Not all trade union constitutions contain such time provisions.

Charges against officers of a local union must be presented in writing; signed by the charging party; and specify section(s) of the constitution, bylaws, rules, or working agreements violated. These charges are typically filed with an officer of the international union or regional council with jurisdiction over that district, who will render a decision that can be appealed to the national union's executive committee or board. The tribunals also range in degree of formality and types of charge that will be handled through its system. For instance, some union constitutions contain very specific rules on methods for handling "barred conduct," racketeering charges, or other charges of an official for mishandling pension, health, and welfare funds.

The constitutions also authorize the general president to appoint international representatives, to police contracts and to interpret the constitution. The position of international representative is sometimes an elected position and serves as a mediator between the local and the international union. Local decisions and decisions by the general president are generally appealable through the General Executive Board and then to the General Convention which may also render decisions interpreting the rules and regulations of the union regarding constitutional and labor-management relations policy. Many of the 15 international constitutions contain statements discouraging litigation without first exhausting the tribunal or promising no payment of legal defenses if they bypass the unions' procedure.

When disputes arise through the union's "charge and trial" systems, they are most often between a member or officer and a union, or at the regional or national level, between a union and another union in the same craft. Statistics are not usually collected or printed on the cause and nature of the dispute, making generalizations difficult to quantify. General counsel of building trade unions are, however, often responsible for reporting the disposition of higher-level internal tribunal cases to national conventions.

It is well established that union constitutions are contracts under both state and federal law. Decisions of union tribunals, including determination of rights and fines, are enforceable and collectable. Enforceability extends to agreements between union and union, local and national union, and member to union. Union constitutions, however, do not cut off statutory rights under civil rights law and the National Labor Relations Act. Accordingly, decisions of union tribunals are subject to relitigation under Title VII of the Civil Rights Act of 1964. Unfairness in the administration of union hiring halls will be subject to the jurisdiction of the NLRA, notwithstanding any prior decisions of any union tribunals. On the other hand, fines for violating internal union rules are collectable so long as the discipline does not violate statutory rights. An exception exists in the case of members who resign from the union, thereby avoiding the disciplinary authority of the union tribunal.

In addition to legal questions, there are questions about how effective charge and trial systems are in distinguishing between economic factors and other issues affecting fairness of outcomes. For instance, during various recessions occurring in the years 1969-71, 1974-75, 1980, and 1982-83, the number of unfair labor practices filed against construction unions (including cases where the employer was also charged) appear to have increased (see Figure 1). One explanation would be that tensions around union referral practices rise when labor markets are slack. The most recent recession (1990-91), however, did not conform with this trend. It should be noted that in all of these time periods, the number of unfair labor practices filed against employers increased. And in the last decade, cases filed against employers comprise a much larger portion of all unfair labor practice cases. This phenomenon may reflect the growth in antiunion behavior by some construction employers and the simultaneous growth of workforce organizing by construction unions in response to deunionization drives by some construction users and employer associations.

The NLRB data displayed in Figure 1 also points to the importance of construction unions in employment matters. The number of unfair labor practices filed against unions has declined over the past few decades, while the number of cases filed against employers in violation of Section 8a(1-5) have increased. In 1997 there were 5,000 total construction cases received by the NLRB. Comparing unfair labor practices in construction to manufacturing (with 10,837 cases), a higher proportion of charges were filed against a labor organization, but construction unions had a greater proportion of cases filed under Section 8(b)(4)(i) and/or (A)(B) or (c) (or any combination thereof) and were less likely to have cases under Section 8(b)(1),(2),(3),(5),(6) of the National Labor Relations Act (NLRB, 1997: 114).[6] There were also proportionally fewer charges against employers for violating sections 8a(1)-(5), but this may be due to classification of many jurisdictional disputes under Section 8(b)(4)(i) or (ii)D, which comprised 2.5% of all unfair labor practices charges. (Other charges against unions for violating sections 8(b)(7)(A,B,C), 8(e), and 8(g) totaled less than 1% in both manufacturing and construction sectors.) The composition of cases differs significantly from previous years, where charges against labor organization were more common (NLRB, 1960-1997, Table 5).

More detailed research is needed to determine whether or not these caseload increases are statistically significant as well as the meaning of the variations over the business cycle. An in-depth analysis of the subject matter of these complaints would be a good starting point. Case histories might also tell us something about the prior use of internal dispute resolution procedures to handle these complaints and the fairness and consistency of those dispute resolution systems.

FIGURE 1

NLRB Cases Received
Construction, FY 1960-1997

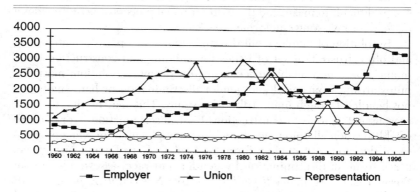

Other Industries, FY 1960-97

Note: The numbers for the "union" category in both graphs include a handful of cases where either the labor organization or the employer, or both jointly were charged under a violation of section 8(e) or a 10(k) filing.

Employment Discrimination

As a result of the sometimes informal peer-determined hiring rules, craft markets were noted by Doeringer and Piore (1971) as being particularly susceptible to exclusion of some groups of workers. However, unilateral employer decisions on employment present the same kind of opportunities for arbitrary and discriminatory process with few opportunities for review. From this standpoint, Doeringer and Piore's observation is gratuitous. Certainly, the important role of construction unions in employment decisions as referral unions and in providing peer review was cited by the U.S. Commission on Civil Rights (1974). Every employment decision is difficult to make, and the union tribunal process at least provides a method for reviewing employment decisions.

Resolution of employment discrimination cases poses an interesting and often frustrating set of issues for building and construction trade unions. Despite available mechanisms for dispute resolution, most disputes arising from racial and gender discrimination or harassment are not handled through union tribunal systems. This may be due to a few reasons not unique to construction. First, discrimination is difficult to establish when all union members face unemployment or when employment decisions are made informally. Cycles of layoffs and hirings can serve to mask discrimination by gender and race, asserts electrician Susan Eisenberg in *We'll Call You If We Need You: Experiences of Working Women in Construction* (1998: 5). Further, a growing body of law surrounding hiring halls (and discussed by Hardin 1992: 1533-47) may have reduced the willingness of unions to operate *formal* referral systems. Second, there is a question about whether or not such decisions would be enforceable in court as a result of the *Alexander v. Gardner-Denver* case (415 US 36, 1974). The Supreme Court held in that case that the EEOC could independently pursue an EEO matter in court, notwithstanding any outcome in arbitration from collective agreement. Third, aggrieved women and minorities protected by Title VII and their legal counsel are likely to believe they can secure review by an administrative agency committed specifically to vindicating Title VII rights and in fact will not be referred back to an internal process. In 1998 there were 2,961 cases filed (both union and nonunion) in construction with the EEOC and state reporting agencies; 76.2% of those were Title VII cases (the remainder distributed between Equal Pay Act and Age Discrimination in Employment Act).

Important opportunities exist for local unions to develop creative and effective mechanisms for prevention of employment discrimination. A variety of construction union strategies (changing apprenticeship and referral policies, introducing antidiscrimination or affirmative action clauses, preapprenticeship programs, sensitivity training) have been tried but received little evaluation in the literature. At least one case study by O'Farrell and Moore (1993) concludes that tradeswomen and tradesmen can use the grievance process and other union activities (such as victim assistance, affirmative action, and training) to address inequality in wages and working conditions. This area remains ripe for additional research.

Employment Benefits and Alternative Dispute Resolution

Other member-to-union disputes can occur on some union-provided, employment-based benefits. Most employees work for a certain number of hours on union jobs. After obtaining a certain number of hours, the individual is offered benefits (death benefits, retirement club benefits), provided the individual remains in "good standing" (paying dues, retaining continuous membership except in allowable cases, and not being found guilty of failing to uphold the union's constitution). Dispute resolution over multiemployer benefit systems are often handled through the union's tribunal system. Thus the union not only has some control over employment conditions but also over some benefits. However, the union cannot legally make negotiated benefits contingent on good standing.

One area in which construction unions have made recent progress in alternative dispute resolution mechanisms has been in collective bargaining agreements on workers' compensation. Nine states adopted legislation to allow unions to bargain with employers to "carve out" their own private adjudicatory procedures and medical provider from the states' administration of payments to injured workers. These types of bargained systems can be successful in reducing the number of injuries and claims as evidenced by a case study of the Pioneer Valley Agreement with the Massachusetts Building and Construction Trades (Dunlop and Zack 1997). However, controversies have arisen over rights to an attorney, due process, and restraint of physician choice (Markowitz and Van Bourg 1995). In California ten of eleven reported carve-out programs had ADR systems. All provide for an "ombudsperson," a third-party neutral who is available to all parties, who resolves disputes at an early stage, or even before disputes arise. After some specified time period, failure to resolve the dispute will escalate the dispute to formal mediation by an outside neutral or through joint labor-management committees, followed by arbitration. In California two-thirds of all 661 construction claims filed in 1997 were resolved through ombudspeople or other resolution of dispute issues before mediation; only four claims were taken to mediation (Young 1998).

An independent evaluation of California's carve-out programs has provided preliminary results which indicate that such arrangements result in substantial savings on both medical and indemnity costs, precipitous drops in litigation, and possible marked improvements in safety. However, these conclusions were drawn from limited data and mirror similar declines in medical and indemnity costs for non-carve-out employers. It was suggested that ADR processes and medical/legal provisions are still evolving; improvements are expected to provide expected savings (California Commission on Health and Safety and Workers' Compensation 1998).

More research is needed to determine the effectiveness, fairness, and feasibility of expanding these types of programs. This type of revision to the workers' compensation system is relatively recent but gaining in popularity in several industries. The building and construction trades have led legislative reform to allow this type of collective bargaining over the administration of workers' compensation.

Jurisdictional Disputes

Historically, the construction industry has developed dispute resolution machinery to contend with jurisdictional disputes and resulting work stoppages which have declined in number in recent years. It is quite natural that in an industry of this nature, with multiple craft unions and subcontracting relationships, questions of jurisdiction may arise. The causes of jurisdictional disputes were discussed by Dunlop long ago (1953). The introduction of new technologies (materials and processes), union mergers, or change in employee benefit structures can pose questions of jurisdiction. Work assignment, the degree of specialization, and locality of deployment are important factors in jurisdictional disputes. Increasingly, unions use travelers (individuals who, for a variety of personal and professional reasons, may work in one jurisdiction but retain membership in another local), and this presents its own set of jurisdictional and skills development problems for which unions employ a variety of strategies. Jurisdictional statements are prominent and quite detailed in the constitutions of the international unions.

Today, jurisdictional disputes are less likely to disrupt work, in part due to a series of settlements between international unions and a dispute resolution plan agreed upon and periodically updated by the fifteen international unions affiliated with the Building and Construction Trades Department, AFL-CIO. In addition, disputes between local unions of the same craft are handled by the international union, often by request of the local unions, through internal procedures described in the international's union constitution.

For disputes arising between unions, the Building and Construction Trades Department, AFL-CIO, has a set of procedural rules and regulations to follow in order to reach a binding agreement, the important history of which is covered in Dunlop (1984). The *Plan for the Settlement and Procedures for Resolution of Jurisdictional Disputes*, in addition to listing a series of historic settlements reached between unions, outlines the responsibilities of the parties to respect contractor jurisdiction and to ensure continuation of work (no strike, no work stoppage). The employer notifies the administrator of the plan of a breach of contract, who then notifies the international presidents of the violation. The presidents may instruct the local union to cease violation of the jurisdictional agreement or may work out an agreement. If they are unable to resolve the dispute within five days, they may request arbitration. The administrator sends a list of impartial arbitrators who are selected by alternate elimination. The arbitrator holds a hearing within seven days of selection and renders a decision, with expenses to be borne by the losing party to the dispute.

Jurisdiction remains an important concept for unions *and employers*. As Dunlop (1984) noted, jurisdiction is "intertwined with a myriad of other industrial relations and bargaining issues" in construction. I echo Dunlop's surprise that with the exception of Hardin (1992: 1395-98), the literature continues to view jurisdictional disputes solely as conflicts among unions, not recognizing involvement of contractors that contribute to such disputes.[7] Violations of the National Labor Relations Act provisions on jurisdiction have occurred through employer attempts to deal with one union and to assign work in violation of well-established practice. That predictably causes an aggrieved union and its members to protest and sometimes to violate Section 8(b)4(D) of the National Labor Relations Act. Once a Section 8(b)4(D) complaint is issued, the jurisdictional dispute is resolved by the NLRB in a Section 10(k) hearing and the board's decision will almost invariably favor the employer's assignment. For those 107 cases filed in 1998, most were settled informally or were withdrawn prior to opening of a hearing. Roughly 20% were dismissed outright (National Labor Relations Board 1997: 125).

Today construction unions continue to be actively engaged in resolving jurisdictional disputes with each other, but the National Joint Board no longer operates. Under 1984 revisions to the plan, the administrator of the plan is authorized to form a panel of arbitrators knowledgeable in construction with agreement of unions involved in the disputes. Most cases are resolved before arbitration due to the "loser pays" clause in the plan. The administrator is not allowed to proceed to formal arbitration without agreement by contractors to be stipulated to the plan. While employers are entitled to participate, they often play no direct role in arbitration, and they continue to have significant power to either comply with arbitral decisions or not to do so.

Other Types of Disputes

Table 1 categorizes dispute resolution processes by the parties to and issues provoking the dispute. It summarizes and adds to the types of disputes and the resolution processes described above. The first category listed in the table is the member-to-member dispute. Formal charges by one member against another member appear to be relatively rare in construction. They can arise when one member feels another member has violated any of the chargeable offenses stated in their union's constitution and discussed above. Member-to-member disputes can also arise when an individual makes defamatory statements, threatens, or otherwise harasses another union member. In this case the wronged member has the option to file a charge with the union since, as stated in a few constitutions, slander or libel of a fellow member is a chargeable offense.

Peer management of the tribunals is extremely important, but little information on the functioning of these systems is presently available. I cannot estimate how often charges are filed or whether or not guilty verdicts—for instance, those based on alcohol or drug abuse—are followed by expulsion. Informal discussions with local union officials indicate that expulsion of full-fledged members seldom happens, since apprenticeship and training programs are designed to "weed out the troublemakers." Screening appears to happen according to the values of the local union, and the conditions for screening may be based on a variety of motives. Cobble (1991) discussed a number of instances in prewar, multiemployer waitress unions where supervisory members filed charges against other members for poor work. Since apprenticeship and peer review boards screen members, these types of charges appear to be rare in the building trades but are an area for future research.

There may be other reasons member-to-member charges are less frequent. Some constitutions make unwarranted charges or charges based on political motives grounds for fine or expulsion from the union. Additionally, some local union procedures may require charges to be read aloud at local union meetings, which may serve as a deterrent. Potential for peer review may affect the number and type of cases received.

Discussion and Suggestions for Future Research

Evolution of Dispute Resolution in the Building Trades

Many dispute resolution practices have evolved throughout the building trades' history of collective bargaining, and they are closely related to

TABLE 1

A Summary of Dispute Resolution in the Building and Construction Trades

Claimant/Defendant Relationship	Typical Dispute	Compare to Industrial Setting	Typical Avenues of Appeal, Internal Union Procedure for the Building Trades	Role of Peer Review among Building Trades
Member to member	working in violation of work rules, standards, "lumping" (working for lump sum)	crossing picket lines	claim filed with local union, can be appealed	apprenticeship and other programs to build solidarity and respect among members
Member to union	discrimination, assignment of work, violation of Constitution or bylaws	duty of fair representation	appeals board with the international union	views of qualifications of individuals for work, social norms, diversity training
Member to employer	(rare, but sometimes in response to mass layoff)	violation of work rules or contract; layoff or discrimination	file complaint with employer or file unfair labor practice charge	workmanship, qualifications established by joint labor-management committee
Union to employer	pay and contribution to multiemployer benefit funds, contractual obligations	pay, benefits, contractual obligations to employees, good faith bargaining	informal reminder, arbitration if ADR exists, litigation	labor-management trust relationship and views of industry standards
Union to member	violation of work rules, lumping (working for lump sum)	crossing picket lines	Fine or forfeiture of union rights and privileges, member can appeal	apprenticeship and training building respect for work rules

TABLE 1 (*Continued*)

A Summary of Dispute Resolution in the Building and Construction Trades

Claimant/Defendant Relationship	Typical Dispute	Compare to Industrial Setting	Typical Avenues of Appeal, Internal Union Procedure for the Building Trades	Role of Peer Review among Building Trades
Union to union	jurisdiction	jurisdiction	appeal to international, Building and Construction Trades Department, following the Plan and Procedures for Settlement of Jurisdictional Disputes	agreement or understanding between parties
Local Union to International	receivership or election procedures	receivership or election procedures	file unfair labor practice with NLRB or complaint to U.S. Department of Labor	great degree of autonomy provided to local union as long as rules of International are followed
International to Local Union	discriminatory hiring practices, failure to abide by constitution	failure to abide by constitution	informal and formal procedures, constitutional rules, place in receivership	appointment of representative to police boundaries, rules, serve as liaison to national office

collective bargaining and economic conditions. Those dispute resolution systems are key to mitigating unstable conditions as unions and employers continually shape new strategies to deal with organizational, work assignment, and bargaining issues. In each of the processes discussed, peer management plays a large role in union procedures (determination of chargeable offenses, trial procedures, determination of damages, jurisdictional agreements) and issues affecting the employment relationship (transfer, travel, journeymen qualifications) as well as decisions concerning the ability of an individual to do certain types of work. Many of the tribunal structures are similar in nature: most unions stress the importance of good labor-management relations, and international unions set a pattern for local unions to follow.

Although the evolution of the building trades structure is discussed by a few authors, the literature has given short shrift to the craft bargaining system and its historical emphasis on dispute resolution as a means for solving several problems that can arise in the production process and employment rationalization. More research is needed on the evolution of the building and construction trade system of dispute resolution, especially as it relates to the varied union organizations, training, and referral practices. In particular, a better understanding of how these systems function in practice is needed.

Contemporary textbooks often and unfortunately only mention building and construction trade unionism as an anachronism, simply cite problems of minority inclusion, or generally fail to represent its occupational unionism in the context of short-term and uncertain employment relations (Sloane and Witney 1997; Fossum 1992; Kochan and Katz 1988; Kleiner, McLean, and Dreher 1988). Although Sloane and Witney (1997) survey the historical, legal, and structural environments shaping contractual content, they provide little reference for understanding current developments in building and construction trade unionism. While Fossum (1992) discusses employer discipline, he does not turn attention inward to the union's own membership and the role it can play in resolving employment disputes. These oversights are disappointing given an important body of research discussing various aspects of those topics. Especially important to consider are the *scope* and *applicability* of the arrangements in the context of the industrial relations systems at work in construction, as argued in John T. Dunlop's revised *Industrial Relations Systems* (1998).

The literature explores the evolution of a craft-based system in contrast to the industrial system of organizing (Dunlop 1998; Montgomery

1980, 1989). Mills (1982) also argues that in construction, the present system developed from complex, locally directed bargaining patterns. Stinchcombe (1959) discussed the role of the craft institution in administering work to its members. Cobble's (1991) discussion of occupational unionism among waitresses provides a model for further discussion on craft unionism and the role of dispute resolution. While the evolution of the craft-based system of employment and employment disputes reflects the special nature of the industries involved, there has been no detailed analysis of the historical role of dispute resolution in this system. Also needing further attention in any discussion of evolutionary differences between occupational and industrial unionism is the role of legal institutions in recognizing and reinforcing the building and construction trade union employment system. For instance, property laws play a unique role in building and construction trades employment and organizing and may have served to legitimize the workers' claim to control certain aspects of the work. Labor law has also recognized the unique nature of the industry and multiemployer arrangements in construction.

John T. Dunlop, whose unique insights are derived from having personally mediated many of the most important construction agreements of this century, provides the most significant framework for conceptualizing particular features of construction industrial relations and dispute resolution systems, and he describes the history of dispute resolution mechanisms as they shape many modern institutions. Dunlop's (1998) discussion of the rules governing the building trades understandably covers only a small fraction of the larger universe of rules governing relations among workers (their organizations), employers (their organizations), and the government in the construction industry. Those rules deal with technological factors, variability of site location, weather, apprenticeship, small scale operations, hiring, provision of tools, and area wage rates. In comparing construction with other industries in several countries, Dunlop notes, "Building rules everywhere recognize the need for greater flexibility in layoffs than in industry generally" (1988: 208).

Dunlop (1984) argues that the principle features of dispute resolution (areawide determinations, jurisdiction, area pools of labor, apprenticeship and training, diversity and uniformity among branches) can be understood in the context of industrial relations features (technical conditions, status of relationships among contractors, labor organizations, government, markets, commonly shared ideas, beliefs, values within the industry). In construction, he convincingly argues, the central problems concern hiring, jurisdictional disputes falling outside of the 1984 machinery, and issues surrounding secondary boycotts. He also discusses a number of nation-wide agreements between craft unions and their respective contractor organizations. Despite a widening geographical scope, persistent local differences remain. Dunlop and Zack (1997) provide several important examples from the building and construction trades unions and employers, but their discussion focuses on the nonunion sector's experience in mediation and arbitration of employment disputes.

Explaining Heterogeneity in Methods of Dispute Resolution

A great deal of variation exists among building and construction trade unions (even among local unions of the same trade) in the methods of resolving disputes. The experience of building trades with peer discipline and participation in personnel decisions tells us that fair representation and timely resolution of disputes may be contingent upon the personal convictions of its members and leadership as much as any structure imposed through the union's policies and contract negotiations. Local unions have a great deal of autonomy, and while national unions may have an interest in pursuing certain policies, they rely to a great extent on voluntary action of the locals and signatory contractors to pursue those aims. Future research should focus on how these systems evolved, how they work in practice, and how they act in relation to the varied referral systems in practice today.

In order to conduct dispute resolution research, more information is needed to illuminate the various methods building and construction trade unions have employed to preserve craft jurisdiction in response to challenges by outside contractors, double-breasting (a union company's operation of a separate nonunion operation), temporary and leasing employment services, and deregulation of prevailing wage laws. What models work well and for whom? How does a union make headway in organizing unorganized workers and preserve craft jurisdiction and unity? How does a craft union respond to employers' pressure for "flexibility" without damaging employment security? How much should a union attempt to do, given its size and potential influence in a given market? Certainly, the building and construction trade unions do not, nor perhaps should they, behave in a homogenous way.

More information is also needed on specific types of disputes and available methods for their resolution. While most collective bargaining agreements use AAA or FMCS arbitrators, who presumably follow the guidelines of their respective organizations ensuring due process, little data are available on the specific types of disputes that occur in the building and construction trades. Disputes not covered under a collective bargaining agreement may be required to go through the union's procedure. Only a few of the international union constitutions impose time limits on the various steps involved in the tribunal system, a potentially troubling procedural problem. Problems in obtaining highly qualified arbitrators relative to more expensive but perhaps better informed litigators should be examined in greater detail. Such problems, when combined with management involvement in employment benefits, will make extension of dispute resolution into other labor cost items such as workers' compensation more difficult. A review of existing labor-management boards and their ability to settle disputes is also in order. The example of the Electrical Industry Council suggest that joint dispute resolutions can clearly benefit both the employer and the member, and in so doing, the union. Yet, no in-depth study evaluating the council's structure and scope has been performed, and it has received little attention from academe.

Describing Change in Self-organizing Systems

The problems facing self-organizing work teams, construction unions, and employers basically fall into two sometimes incongruous categories: matching of skills and organizational issues. Skills-matching issues arise from decisions regarding who has or who is allowed to learn the skills that can be matched to specific employers with specific requests. The problem of skills development may depend on local labor market conditions: unemployment presents placement problems and reduces on-the-job training, while skills shortages place downward pressure on job entry requirements.

A local union also has a host of organizational issues to contend with that are interrelated with skills-matching issues and that can sometimes result in disputes. Often new technologies or procedures are introduced to the work site and may not be addressed under concurrent jurisdictional agreements. Respect for work rules, jurisdiction, or inclusion of new workers in the organization may become lax when unemployment is high. The apprenticeship and training system, including the review committee, is the future of the union and of individual members but has been threatened with decline in union membership preceding 1995. Skills-matching and organizational issues have been raised by other authors including Kaminsky (1999), Weil (1994), Cobble (1991), Dunlop (1990; 1984), Kazin (1987), Mills (1972) and Betram (1966).

The role of contemporary forms of arbitration in resolving disputes needs to be reviewed with the goals of the building trades unions and their employers in mind. What changes in existing labor-management structures, practices, and rules are necessary to resolve disputes quickly and fairly? Specifically, research should evaluate the successful prevention of disputes associated with entry requirements, referral systems, and strategies to increase workforce quality. The role of peer discipline remains important and does not lend itself well to quantitative research methods. One area of inquiry would be the degree of management satisfaction with peer management in the construction industry.

Research is needed on the best ways to ensure that women and minorities gain a real foothold in the best paid blue-collar occupations, thereby reducing potential disputes. Given my discussion of internal labor markets' importance in controlling entry as well as allocation of jobs, an important research project would be to examine how well dispute resolution systems work for women and minorities, comparing union and nonunion approaches in different industries.

One major area for research is to determine why it is that professionals—from nurses, lawyers, physicians, faculty, teachers—choose to develop their own internal disciplinary procedures. What special claims to legitimacy do they have? Who has a right to "government by the governed" as opposed to external and often uninformed regulation by the state or unilateral exercise of employer power? Is alternative dispute resolution, in effect, a form or outgrowth of self-government and for that reason a special claim to legitimacy?

The Challenge Ahead

In this chapter I have attempted to define the special characteristics of the construction industry pertaining to its employment dispute resolution systems. A variety of dispute resolution species exist, and they have a long evolutionary history that is not fully understood. I highlight some common elements of these dispute systems but suggest a great deal of variety exists in the specific structure, operation, and effectiveness of these systems which are grouped by trade.

Despite its treatment in many labor relations textbooks, occupational unionism is not only relevant but is becoming increasingly important to workers as they are denied long-term employment in modern labor markets. I have suggested some important areas of research in property law, workforce quality, and collective bargaining as they relate to organizing and well-functioning union referral and dispute resolution systems.

This research could be extremely important, not only from the standpoint of understanding dispute resolution in the context of short-term and contingent employment but also to improve understanding between unions and employers as to the historical role of building and construction trade unions in maintaining high labor standards and workforce productivity. I recognize that peer discipline is an important element to any union activity, including dispute resolution mechanisms.

Stability and productivity in the building and construction sector is extremely important to the nation's economy and well-being. From an economic standpoint, a well-functioning dispute resolution mechanism provides economic stability and has been a century-long commitment between unions and signatory employers. For decades the unionized segment of the building and construction industry has upheld principles of quick resolution to disputes through their collective bargaining activities. Those dispute resolution mechanisms seem to be working well in the unionized sector of building and construction, but no systematic research has investigated them in relation to varied entry requirements and referral practices in construction. The unions' ability to play its representative role effectively will depend on the building and construction trade unions' ability to quickly organize, assimilate, train, and place new workers, while in addition providing strong foundations of quality and professionalism. Dispute resolution is an important element to that success.

Acknowledgments

I am grateful to Xiuwen Dong and Lee Sayrs for their research assistance. I am also grateful to several members of the building and construction trades unions and contractor associations who shared their views with me. All statements and opinions are my own and are not to be construed as representing the policies or views of any organization or association with which the author may be affiliated.

APPENDIX

Excerpt from International Brotherhood of Electrical Workers Constitution

Sec. 1. Any member may be penalized for committing any one or more of the following offenses:

(a) Violation of any provision of this Constitution and the rules herein, or the bylaws, working agreements, or rules of a L.U. [Local Union].

(b) Having knowledge of the violation of any provision of this Constitution, or the bylaws or rules of a L.U., yet failing to file charges against the offender or to notify the proper officers of the L.U.

(c) Obtaining membership through fraudulent means or by misrepresentation, either on the part of the member himself or others interested.

(d) Engaging in activities designed to bring about a withdrawal or secession from the I.B.E.W. of any L.U. or of any member or group of members, or to cause dual unionism or schism within the I.B.E.W.

(e) Engaging in any act or acts which are contrary to the member's responsibility toward the I.B.E.W., or any of its L.U.'s, as an institution, or which interfere with the performance by the I.B.E.W. or a L.U. with its legal or contractual obligations.

(f) Working for, or on behalf of, any employer, employer-supported organization, or other union, or the representative of any of the foregoing, whose position is adverse or detrimental to the I.B.E.W.

(g) Wronging a member of the I.B.E.W. by any act or acts (other than the expression of views or opinions) causing him physical or economic harm.

(h) Entering or being present at any meeting of a L.U., or its Executive Board, or any committee meeting while intoxicated, or drinking intoxicants in or near any such meeting, or carrying intoxicants into such meeting.

(i) Disturbing the peace or harmony of any L.U. meeting or meeting of its Executive Board, using abusive language, creating or participating in any disturbance, drinking intoxicants, or being intoxicated, in or around the office or headquarters of a L.U.

(j) Making known the business of a L.U., directly or indirectly, to any employer, employer-supported organization, or other union, or to the representatives of any of the foregoing.

(k) Fraudulently receiving or misappropriating any moneys of a L.U. or the I.B.E.W.

(l) causing or engaging in unauthorized work stoppages or strikes or other violation of the laws and rules of the I.B.E.W. or its L.U.'s.

(m) wilfully committing fraud in connection with voting for candidates for L.U. office, or for delegates to conventions . . .

(o) Failure to install or do his work in a safe, workmanlike manner, or leaving work in a condition that may endanger the lives or property of others, or proving unable or unfit mentally, to learn properly his trade.

(p) causing a stoppage of work because of any alleged grievance or dispute without having consent of the L.U. or its proper officers.

(q) working for any individual or company declared in difficulty with a L.U. or the I.B.E.W., in accordance with this Constitution.

(r) wilfully committing fraud in connection with obtaining or furnishing credentials for delegates to the I.C. [International Convention] or being connected with any fraud in voting during the I.C.

(s) allowing another person to use, or altering in any manner, his membership card, receipt, or other evidence of membership in the I.B.E.W. (IBEW 1998)

Endnotes

[1] Affiliates of the Building and Construction Trades Department, AFL-CIO, as of January 1, 1999, are International Association of Heat and Frost Insulators and Asbestos Workers; International Union of Boilermakers; Iron Ship Builders, Blacksmiths, Forgers and Helpers; International Union of Bricklayers and Allied Brotherhood of Carpenters and Joiners of America; International Brotherhood of Electrical Workers; International Union of Elevator Constructors; International Association of Bridge, Structural, Ornamental and Reinforcing Ironworkers; Laborers' International Union of North America; International Union of Operating Engineers; Operative Plasterers' and Cement Masons' International Association of the United States and Canada; International Brotherhood of Painters and Allied Trades; United Union of Roofers, Waterproofers and Allied Workers; Sheet Metal Workers' International Association; International Brotherhood of Teamsters; United Association of Journeymen and Apprentices of the Plumbing and Pipe Fitting Industry of the United States and Canada.

[2] "Journeyman" is defined as an experienced and reliable worker who has learned a trade and works for another person usually by day. While I refer to both women and men who have achieved this status, and while "journey-level-workers" and "journey-person" are sometimes used to reduce gender bias in common parlance, "journeyman" is most often used in the trades.

[3] Comments of Nicholas Fiore, president, National Constructors Association, to the Economics Research Network conference, The Center to Protect Workers' Rights, Washington, DC, October 21, 1997.

[4] Personal communication with Robert Gasperow, director, Construction Labor Research Council, Washington, DC, December 1998.

[5] Personal communication with Federal Mediation and Conciliation Service, United States Government, Washington, DC (Lynn Garity, deputy general counsel), January 15, 1999.

[6] Section (8)(b)4 of the LMRA is extremely complex. Subsection (A) prohibits unions from forcing employers (or a self-employed person) to join a labor or employer organization or to enter into agreements prohibited by Section 8(e) ("hot cargo" agreements). Subsection (B) deals with secondary activities. Subsection (C) prohibits a union from forcing an employer to deal with it when another union is the certified bargaining agent.

[7] The importance of joint decision making through jurisdictional dispute resolution is further illustrated through Dunlop's description of his involvement with the National Joint Board from 1948-57, when he served as active mediator for a number of agreements under 6 national decisions by the machinery provided for in the plan and 33 new national agreements negotiated between national unions and (in a number of cases) affected national contractors. He wrote, "I almost never cast a deciding vote as chairman. Contending unions and contractors are more likely, in my experience, to comply with 'decisions' and settle future disputes of a similar nature if they have consensual role in the process and in the result, even if the 'decision' is adverse" (Dunlop 1984: 200).

References

Applebaum, Herbert A. 1981. *Royal Blue: The Culture of Construction Workers*. New York: Holt, Rinehart, and Winston.

Betram, Gordon W. 1966. *Consolidated Bargaining in California Construction: An Appraisal of Twenty-Five Years' Experience*. Los Angeles, CA: University of California Institute of Industrial Relations.

Building and Construction Trades Department, AFL-CIO. 1993. *Plan for the Settlement of Jurisdictional Disputes in the Construction Industry Including Procedural Rules and Regulations: Agreements and Decisions Affecting the Building Industry Covering the U.S. and Canada. Approved by the Building and Construction Trades Department, AFL-CIO. June 1984 as amended through March 1993*. Washington, DC: Building and Construction Trades Department, American Federation of Labor and Congress of Industrial Organizations.

Bureau of the Census, U.S. Department of Commerce. 1997. *County Business Patterns, 1995*. Washington, DC: U.S. Printing Office.

Bureau of Labor Statistics, U.S. Department of Labor. 1997. *1997 Current Population Survey Earnings Files*. Washington, DC: U.S. Government Printing Office.

California Commission on Health and Safety and Workers' Compensation. 1998. "'Carve-Outs' Study of Alternative Dispute Resolution Systems." *The California Commission on Health and Safety and Workers' Compensation: 1997-98 Annual Report*. San Fransisco: State of California Department of Industrial Relations.

Center to Protect Workers' Rights, The. 1998. *The Construction Chart Book: The U.S. Construction Industry and Its Workers*. 2d ed. Washington, DC: The Center to Protect Workers' Rights.

Cobble, Dorothy Sue. 1991. *Dishing It Out: Waitresses and Their Unions in the Twentieth Century*. Chicago: University of Illinois Press.

Council on Industrial Relations for the Electrical Contracting Industry. 1995. *Council on Industrial Relations for the Electrical Contracting Industry*. 18th ed. (Contact: Secretary, Council on Industrial Relations, 1125 15th St., Washington, DC 20005.)

_____. 1999. Unpublished tabulations on case rates, Bethesda, MD.

Doeringer, Peter B., and Michael J. Piore. 1971. *Internal Labor Markets and Manpower Analysis*. Armonk, NY: M.E. Sharpe, Inc.

Dunlop, John T. 1953. *Jurisdictional Disputes: 10 Types*. The Constructor (journal of the Associated General Contractors) (July) 165.

_____. 1990. *The Management of Labor Unions: Decision Making with Historical Constraints*. Lexington, MA: Lexington Books.

_____. 1994. *Dispute Resolution: Negotiation and Consensus Building*. Dover, MA: Auburn House.

_____. 1998. *Industrial Relations Systems*. 3d ed. Cambridge, MA: Harvard University Press.

Dunlop, John T., and Arnold Zack. 1997. *Mediation and Arbitration of Employment Disputes*. San Francisco: Jossey-Bass Publishers.

Eisenberg, Susan. 1998. *We'll Call You If We Need You: Experiences of Working Women in Construction*. Ithaca, NY: Cornell University Press/Industrial Relations Press.

Engineering News Record, Special Advertising Section, Oct. 19, 1992, pp. 8, 10.

Fossum, John A. 1992. *Labor Relations: Development, Structure, Process.* Homewood, IL: Richard Irwin, Inc.

Hardin, Patrick, editor-in-chief. 1992. *The Developing Labor Law: The Board, the Courts, and the National Labor Relations Act.* 3d ed., Vol. II. Washington, DC: Bureau of National Affairs.

International Brotherhood of Electrical Workers. 1991. *Proceedings of the Thirty-Fourth Convention: President's Report.* Washington, DC: International Brotherhood of Electrical Workers.

_____. 1998. *Constitution and Rules for Local Unions and Councils under Its Jurisdiction, as Amended at the 35th IBEW Convention, Philadelphia, Pennsylvania, September 1996 and Further Amended by Referendum Vote March 1998.* Washington, DC: International Brotherhood of Electrical Workers.

International Union of Bricklayers and Allied Craftsworkers. 1995. *Constitution, Rules of Order and Codes as Amended at the 1995 Convention.* Washington, DC: International Union of Bricklayers and Allied Craftsworkers.

Kaminski, Michelle. 1999. "New Forms of Work Organization and Their Impact on the Grievance Procedure." In A. Eaton and J. Keefe, eds., *Employment Dispute Resolution and Work Rights in the Changing Workplace.* Madison, WI: Industrial Relations Research Association.

Kazin, Michael. 1987. *Barons of Labor: The San Francisco Building Trades and Union Power in the Progressive Era.* Urbana, IL: University of Illinois Press.

Kleiner, Morris, Robert A. McLean, and George Dreher. 1988. *Labor Markets and Human Resource Management.* Glenview, IL: Scott, Foresman and Company.

Kochan, Thomas A., and Harry C. Katz. 1988. *Collective Bargaining and Industrial Relations.* 2d ed. Homewood, IL: Irwin Publishers.

Markowitz, E., and Victor Van Bourg. 1995. "Carve-Outs and the Privatization of Workers' Compensation in Collective Bargaining Agreements." *Syracuse Law Review,* Vol. 46, no. 1, pp. 1-60.

Mills, D. Quinn. 1972. *Industrial Relations and Manpower in Construction.* Cambridge, MA: M.I.T. Press.

Montgomery, David. 1980. *Workers Control in America.* New York: Cambridge University Press.

_____. 1989. *The Fall of the House of Labor. The Workplace, the State, and American Labor Activism: 1865-1925.* New York: Cambridge University Press.

National Labor Relations Board (NLRB). 1960-1997. "Table 5: Industrial Distribution of Cases Received, Fiscal Year." *Annual Report of the National Labor Relations Board.* Washington, DC: U.S. General Printing Office.

_____. 1997. *Sixty-Second Annual Report of the National Labor Relations Board for the Fiscal Year Ended September 30, 1997.* Washington, DC: U.S. General Printing Office.

O'Farrell, Brigid, and Suzanne Moore. 1993. "Unions, Hard Hats, and Women Workers." In Dorothy Sue Cobble, ed., *Women and Unions.* Ithaca, NY: ILR Press.

Reimer, Jeffrey. 1980. *Hard Hats: The Work World of Construction Workers.* London: Sage Publications, Inc.

Sloane, Arthur A., and Fred Witney. 1997. *Labor Relations.* 9th ed. Princeton, NJ: Prentice Hall.

Stallworth, Lamont E. 1997. "Government Regulation of Workplace Disputes and Alternative Dispute Resolution." In Bruce Kaufman, ed., *Government Regulation of the Employment Relationship*. Madison, WI: Industrial Relations Research Association, pp. 369-401.

Stinchcombe, Arthur L. 1959. "Bureaucratic and Craft Administration of Production: A Comparative Study." *Administrative Science Quarterly*, Vol. 5, pp. 168-87.

U.S. Commission on Civil Rights. 1974. *The Challenge Ahead: Equal Opportunity in Referral Unions*. Washington, DC: U.S. Commission on Civil Rights.

Weil, David. 1994. *Turning the Tide: Strategic Planning for Labor Unions*. New York: Lexington Books.

Young, Casey, 1998. *The Construction Carve-Out Program: A Report of Activities in Calendar Year 1997*. San Francisco: California Division of Workers' Compensation.